The

Private Journal

of

Judge-Advocate Larpent,

Attached to the Head-quarters of Lord Wellington during the Peninsular War, from 1812 to its close

The

Private Journal

of

Judge-Advocate Larpent,

Attached to the Head-quarters of Lord Wellington during the Peninsular War, from 1812 to its close

by

Francis Seymour Larpent

The Spellmount Library of Military History

SPELLMOUNT
Staplehurst

British Library Cataloguing in Publication Data:
A catalogue record for this book is available
from the British Library

Copyright © Spellmount 2000
Introduction © Ian C Robertson 2000

ISBN 1-86227-100-3

Third edition published in 1854
This edition first published in the UK in 2000
in
The Spellmount Library of Military History
by
Spellmount Limited
The Old Rectory
Staplehurst
Kent TN12 0AZ
United Kingdom

Tel: 01580 893730
Fax: 01580 893731
E-mail: enquiries@spellmount.com
Website: www.spellmount.com

1 3 5 7 9 8 6 4 2

Printed in Great Britain by
T.J. International Ltd
Padstow, Cornwall

AN INTRODUCTION
By Ian C. Robertson

It was in September 1812 that thirty-six-year old Francis Larpent set sail for Lisbon to take up the exacting position of Judge-Advocate-General, with the responsiblity of reforming and simplifying the disciplinary machinery of courts-martial throughout Wellington's army in the Peninsula, where no form of overall professional regulation, which was long overdue, had yet been instituted. While the Provost Marshal attached to head-quarters had charge of prisoners to be tried by general court-martial, deserters, and prisoners of war, he had powers of jurisdiction only over offenders caught red-handed. As defined in *General Orders* (Freneida, 1 November 1811), 'Whatever may be the crime of which a soldier is guilty, the Provost Marshal has not the power of inflicting summary punishment for it, unless he should see him in the act of committing it.' Those arrested on evidence only, had to be tried by courts-martial. It was largely for the more expeditious management of these, and to ensure that they were conducted with proper forms and due appreciation of the validity of evidence, in which Wellington considered that they had often failed, that the commander-in-chief added a Judge-Advocate-General to his staff to take this legal weight off his own shoulders.

This Introduction replaces the Preface to the first and second editions provided for this book by Sir George Larpent (1786–1855), a politician created a baronet in 1841, who was the author's half-brother and sole executor. In his preface, Sir George confirmed that with the exception of some matters exclusively private and connected with family affairs, the letters, addressed to the author's step-mother, were 'published as they were written, without a word being added'. Their publication had been delayed until after the Duke of Wellington's death from motives of delicacy, abounding as they did in so many personal anecdotes and opinions. It was these – 'not always discreet' – and for the 'hard facts' that it contained, that make Larpent's *Private Journal* one of the more appealing contemporary accounts of the latter stages of the Peninsular War; and the fact that it is free of any military rhetoric makes it no less valuable.

In his 26-page article in the *Edinburgh Review* (July, 1853), Richard Ford, the foremost authority on Spain since his *Hand-Book* to that country was published in 1845, stated that he had picked it out from the many works on the war under which his table groaned, as having 'the singular attraction, that it was composed in the full tide of affairs . . . at head-quarters, and by one living among the most intelligent and best informed', and as what he wrote was 'really private', composed 'with no attempt at book-making or fine writing', 'second only to his graphic sketches of the Duke', it revealed a charming self-portrait, and abounded also in 'many incidents of the highest interest to a home circle, but which public history passes as beneath her notice', which gave it both an idiosyncratic quality and a particular value. Ford also reminds us that the Duke had referred to Larpent in a *Dispatch* dated 16 March 1813 as being a 'most valuable addition to the staff of the army', even if at times he regarded the decisions of Larpent's courts-martial as being too lenient; but, as Wellington once protested: 'How can you expect a Court to find an officer guilty of neglect of duty, when it is composed of members who are all more or less guilty of the same?'

S. G. P. Ward, in his *Wellington's Headquarters* (1957), regarded the *Journal* as 'a source of first-class importance', even if 'indifferently edited'. While acknowledging that it retains a number of infelicities – one pointed out by Antony Brett-James is that *Adonde vayas, Marmont* (Wellington's favourite Spanish song) is incorrectly entitled *Ah Marmont, onde va Marmont?* – it was Sir George Larpent's intention not to stray from the text of the original manuscript. Although several errors will be noticed, few require any explanatory footnote. While the first edition was issued in three volumes, it has been decided to reproduce in facsimile the main text of the more convenient third edition, warts and all, and without providing superfluous annotations.

Some errors in topographical names and surnames will be noted – Niga rather than Niza, and Dr McGregor instead of McGrigor, for example – easily enough made on hearing them pronounced, or by the printer in deciphering the author's manuscript. Some are less easy to recognise, such as Flagenan for Hagetmau, unless following the army's movements with a large-scale map to hand. Less excusable is the repression of too many surnames, replacing them by a dash – a reprehensible habit perhaps caught from Colonel Gurwood's editing of the Duke's *Dispatches*. Was it Larpent or his half-brother, surely not for motives of delicacy, who was responsible for this foible in what is otherwise a most stimulating and vivid first-hand record of everyday events in the Peninsula as described from what was a privileged position in the close proximity of Wellington himself?

For detailed information concerning discipline and punishment, readers are referred to chapters 14 and 7 respectively of Oman's *Wellington's Army* and Richard Glover's *Peninsular Preparation*. Wellington's men, notably in the wake of a storming, were too frequently incited by the criminal element, the deliquents, bruisers, and unruly spirits; those described by Glover as drunken toughs 'with a ruggedness unknown and scarcely conceivable in the decorous modern England of today'. These brutes could only be brought to heel by flogging, the commonest form of punishment, which was some deterrent to other than the incorrigible and thick-skinned; and while 'nothing is easier than to denounce so barbarous a punishment as this, yet it baffled the wit of the authorities to devise a milder punishment that could control the appalling thugs of whom the rank and file of the British Army was largely composed'.

However, by and large, flogging was reasonably effective 'in maintaining an adequate degree of subordination'. In general it was not necessary when the men were serving in their own units; but when separated from them, they had too sporting a chance to get away with robbery and murder. Under the eyes of their own officers and NCOs, detection was too certain and punishment too severe for the same temptation to exist. One can well sympathise with Sergeant Joseph Donaldson of the 94th Foot, when describing the illiterate louts with whom he found himself, for in such society 'it was a hard matter for a man of any superior education to keep his ground, for he had no one to converse with . . .'; one was forced down to the level of those with whom one had to associate, 'and everything conspired to sink them to that point where they became best fitted for *tractable beasts of burden*. Blackguardism held sway, and gave tone to the whole. Even the youngest were led to scenes of drunkedness and debauchery by men advanced in years. All, therefore, with few exceptions were drawn into this overwhelming vortex of abject slavishness and dissipation'.

Francis Seymour Larpent was the eldest son of John Larpent (1741-1824) of East Sheen, Surrey, by his first wife, Frances, daughter of Maximilian Western of Cokethorpe Park, Oxfordshire. In 1763 John Larpent was Secretary to the Duke of Bedford at the Peace of Paris, and subsequently Secretary to the first Marquess of Hertford, when Lord-Lieutenant of Ireland, who, when Lord Chamberlain in 1778, appointed him Examiner of Theatrical Entertainments. For forty-three years he was employed in the Foreign Office, the last twenty-five as chief clerk.

Francis was born on 15 September 1776; his mother died in the November of the following year. In April 1782 his father married Anna Margaretta (1758–1832), daughter of Sir James Porter, a distinguished diplomat (Ambassador to Constantinople, (1746–62). She was a fond step-mother and later the recipient of Larpent's letters from the Peninsula. He was educated at Cheam School under the Rev. William Gilpin (also the author of several biographies) before entering St John's College, Cambridge, where he took his degree as Fifth Wrangler in 1799 and was elected Fellow. He was later called to the Bar and went on the Western Circuit. Here Larpent formed friendships with such eminent men as Robert, First Baron Gifford, Francis Horner, and Charles Manners-Sutton, who as Judge-Advocate-General since 1809, was to tempt him to accept the position of Deputy Judge-Advocate-General in the Peninsula.

Larpent is referred to in several contemporary narratives, among them the *Letters* of Colonel Sir Augustus Simon Frazer, who, writing from Pasajes on 3 September 1813, noted that all was quiet and there had been no losses for a day or two 'except that of Mr Larpent . . . who having (as I hope) a clearer knowledge of law than of military positions, wandered into the enemy's lines on the 31st, having mistaken them for ours. He timed his mistake well: law is silent here'.

It was his civilian title that was to cause a problem when he and Commissary Jesse, intent on seeing some action at closer quarters, incautiously approached too near, and fell into the hands of a company of Voltigeurs creeping up on them. According to Captain Thomas Henry Browne, on being escorted to the banks of the Bidasoa, marking the frontier, they were 'made to mount the carriage of a gun, & were passed thro' on it. As we gave the French a good beating, they retired, & Mr. Larpent, & the Commissary were made to march all night in the rain, until they reached Bayonne'. Browne, later sent to negotiate an exchange of prisoners, found that it had been assumed by the enemy that they held a high-ranking officer, and it was not until after proper representations had been made and the misunderstanding explained, that it was agreed to exchange the 'General' for a French Commissary, and he was freed. Browne recorded that 'It appeared that he had been terribly frightened when taken, & his health must have suffered very much, for he was miserably meagre when I received him from the French'.

Once released and back at Allied Headquarters, he found his experiences behind enemy lines to be a focus of interest. Frazer commented that although the Judge-Advocate had noticed 6,000 troops at work on the defences of Bayonne, 'not knowing any thing of fortifications', he was unable to give any useful account of them. Larpent had also told him that Marshal Soult, in his hearing, had remarked that 'were he Lord Wellington, after having acquired such a name in Europe, he would go home. "Your English generals", and added he, "may retire when they please: we cannot".'

At the close of war, Larpent sailed for home, returning to his father's house at East Sheen on 8 August 1814 after an absence of two years less a fortnight. Not long after, he was commissioned to set up the courts-martial at Winchester of General Sir John Murray. In June 1813 Murray, in attempting to raise the siege of Tarragona, had neglected making proper preparations and shown indecision, and then had hastily re-embarked his forces, leaving his guns and stores behind. Nevertheless, in the event the court, under the presidency of Sir Alured Clarke, had largely acquitted him after a fifteen-day trial.

Larpent was later given the confidential assignment of enquiring into the allegations of improper conduct on the part of the Princess of Wales, an appointment he accepted on condition that his duties should in no way consist as acting as a spy upon her actions, but merely in 'examining and sifting the facts of the case, as stated and discovered by others'. After interviews with Lords Liverpool, Castlereagh, and Bathurst, Larpent was sent to consult with Count Münster at Vienna on behalf of the British Government, a delicate mission which he conducted with prudence and discretion.

He then proceeded to Gibraltar to take up the post of Judge-Advocate under the governorship of Sir George Don, a position he retained until 1820. In the following year Lord Liverpool appointed Larpent to be one of the Commissioners of the Board of Audit of the Public Accounts, and in 1826 he became Chairman of the Audit Board, where he remained until his retirement due to ill health in March 1843.

His first wife, whom he married in 1815, not long after his return from the Peninsula, was Catherine, daughter of Frederick Reeves, in the East India Company's Civil Service; she died in 1822. In 1829 he married Charlotte, daughter of George Arnold of Halsted Park, Kent, who long survived him, but they were no children of either marriage. Larpent only briefly enjoyed his release from a long and active life of public service, dying at Holmwood, near Dorking, on 21 May 1845.

As his step-brother remarked, 'The Journal carries the reader, as it were, behind the scenes in the great drama of War. The sufferings of individuals, the hardships endured in a campaign, are scarcely ever recorded by the historian – they are lost in the blaze of glory which surrounds such narratives. In this Journal not only will be seen the miseries which are endured in the attainment of military glory by the soldier, but the still greater miseries of the unfortunate people whose country is the scene of military operations'.

The first letter in Larpent's *Private Journal* is dated 14 September 1812, written while approaching the Portuguese coast and three days before disembarking at Lisbon. Here he was entertained by General Sir Marmaduke Warren Peacock, the Commandant, who, according to Commissary Schaumann, had been chosen by Wellington for this position as he was 'incapable of taking command in the field'. He had a reputation also as having an eccentric and harsh character, a person who made the life of English officers extending their leave by skulking in Lisbon as difficult and unhappy as possible. Wellington himself was intolerant of those requesting leave from the front to visit the capital, and it is recorded that on one occasion when a certain officer had insisted on going, he had told him that he might 'stay there forty-eight hours, which is as long as any reasonable man can wish to stay in bed with the same woman'.

Larpent's time in Lisbon was spent purchasing mounts, both for himself and his servants, and to transport his baggage, and in 'bargaining for travelling necessaries'. Peacock provided him with a route to the front, which would also procure him bread and forage at intervening depôts. Travelling, via Abrantes, Castelo Branco, Sabugal, and Salamanca, was slow, and his party did not reach the front until early in November. On the 5th, his first interview with Wellington took place at Rueda, not far south of Tordesillas. His arrival at that temporary Headquarters coincided with a nadir in operations against the French. After the great victory over Marmont's army at Salamanca on 22 July, and Wellington's triumphal entry into Madrid three weeks later, a proportion of the Allied forces was marched north towards Burgos. The castle there, invested on 19 September, had stubbornly resisted all attempts to take it. It was all very frustrating. Wellington had not expected such strong opposition, and had no proper siege train at hand, nor adequately trained sappers and miners. Southam's troops were menacing, and were expected to be receiving reinforcements, while the armies of both King Joseph and Soult were converging on the capital and likely to threaten Wellington's vital lines of communication with Portugal. After several ineffectual and costly assaults in the face of determined sorties on the part of General Dubreton's well-provisioned garrison, Wellington reluctantly decided to raise the siege and retreat south-west. It was at this point that Larpent's narrative commences.

Ian C. Robertson
Arles
2000

THE

PRIVATE JOURNAL

OF

JUDGE-ADVOCATE LARPENT,

ATTACHED TO THE HEAD-QUARTERS OF

LORD WELLINGTON DURING THE PENINSULAR WAR,

FROM 1812 TO ITS CLOSE.

EDITED

By SIR GEORGE LARPENT, BART.

THIRD EDITION.

LONDON:

RICHARD BENTLEY, NEW BURLINGTON STREET,

Publisher in Ordinary to Her Majesty.

MDCCCLIV.

CONTENTS.

PAGE

CHAPTER I.

Departure from England—Exercises on Ship-board—Off the Coast—
Arrival at Lisbon—Residence there—Journey to head-quarters commenced—Abrantes—General features of the march—Salamanca   .   1

CHAPTER II.

Arrival at head-quarters—Ciudad Rodrigo—The Retreat—Its disasters
—Capture of General Paget—Personal Anecdotes—Scarcity of Provi-
sions—Courts-martial in the army—Business of a Judge-Advocate—
Wellington   21

CHAPTER III.

Arrival of the Gazette—More Courts-martial—The Mad Commissary—
Intentions of Lord Wellington—Social Amusements—Sporting—Wel-
lington's fox-hounds—His stud—A dinner at the Commander-in-Chief's
—Number of Courts-martial—Anecdotes of Wellington   .   .   .   37

CHAPTER IV.

More Courts-martial—Bal Masqué—Anecdotes of Wellington—Songs in
his praise—Spanish banditti—Excesses of the Army—Carnival—More
Anecdotes of the Duke—The staff—Grand entertainment at head-
quarters—Wellington's opinion of affairs at home—Murder of an officer
—General Craufurd   54

PAGE

CHAPTER V.

News of the French—Castilian costume—Equipment of the army—
Melancholy Court-martial case—Wellington in the battle of Fuentes
d'Onore—The chances of war—Anecdotes of Wellington—His opinions
of the war—The new Mutiny Act—Wellington on " Vetus"—General
Murray—Advance of the French . . . ' . . . 87

CHAPTER VI.

Newspaper complaints—Wellington's comments—Review of the Portuguese—Gatherings at head-quarters—Reviews—Recommencement of
the march—The route 106

CHAPTER VII.

The march commenced—Scenes on the road—Villa Dalla—Toro—Castro
Monte—Palencia—Prospects of a general action—Skirmishing—Massa 121

CHAPTER VIII.

March continued—Quintana—Anecdote of Wellington—Morillas—Vittoria—The battle—Its results—Plunder—Kindness to the enemy—
Madame de Gazan—The hospital—Sufferings of the wounded—Estimated loss 150

CHAPTER IX.

Pamplona—Pursuit of Clausel—Wellington on the march—Prospects of
more Fighting—Effects of the war—The French position turned—
Anecdote of Wellington—Ernani—St. Sebastian—Wellington's movements 166

CHAPTER X.

Movements of the army—Wellington on the Portuguese—His personal
habits—St. Sebastian—The siege—Miseries of war—Wounded officers
—The Prince of Orange—Vestiges of the retreat—English papers—
False accounts of the campaign—Incidents of the war . . . 195

PAGE

CHAPTER XI.

Rejoicings for the victory—Sufferings of Cole's division—Complaints of the French—Statements of a French prisoner—Decay of Spain—Characteristics of Wellington—His opinion of Bonaparte—Prospects of a renewal of the attack—Exchange of Prisoners—Wellington's Spanish estate—His opinion of Picton—Disposition of the army . . . 220

CHAPTER XII.

Reported renewal of operations against St. Sebastian—Effects of the war on Spain and Portugal—Wellington's account of recent proceedings—Courts-martial—Prisoners shot—Discussions on war between Wellington and a French deserter—The siege resumed—Work of the heavy batteries—Trial of General O'Halloran—Volunteers for the storming parties 238

CHAPTER XIII.

The Author taken prisoner—Kind treatment by the French General—Life of a prisoner—Release—Details of the Author's captivity—Curious scene at General Pakenham's—A Basque squire . . . 250

CHAPTER XIV.

Picturesque quarters—Spanish reverses—A strange adventure—Spanish jealousy—Distribution of the army—A pleasant companion—News from the North—Morale of the French army—The artillery . . 276

CHAPTER XV.

Fall of Pamplona—Deterioration of the army—Duke of York's orders—Orders of merit—Church service—Capture of Franch redoubts—March of the army—Incidents of foreign service—Frequency of desertion—Wellington and the lawyers . . . . , 289

CHAPTER XVI.

News from France—Lord Fitzroy Somerset—Departure of the Prince of Orange—Exchange of prisoners—Proximity of the two armies—Wellington's cooks—Warlike movements—French attack—The Guards—Deserters—More fighting 308

b

PAGE

CHAPTER XVII.

French attack—Plan of desertion—Excesses of the French—A Basque witness—Sir John Hope—Movements of the army—Sale of effects—Wellington's simplicity of character—A French emigré—Return of Soult to Bayonne 323

CHAPTER XVIII.

Reports from France—More desertion—Anecdote of General Stewart—Wellington and his casualty returns—The courtesies of war—Scarcity of transports—Wellington and the trial-papers—Sir G. Collier . . 339

CHAPTER XIX.

Rumours of war—The rival dinner tables—" Slender Billy"—Bonaparte's trickery—Spanish violence—Wellington with the hounds—French and English aspects—The outsides of the nations . . . 352

CHAPTER XX.

State of feeling in France—Rocket practice—The Prince Regent's hobby—The Mayor's ball—The flag-of-truce 362

CHAPTER XXI.

Army supplies—Offending villages—Symptoms of work—Arrival of the Duke d'Angoulême—The bridge across the Adour—Wellington and his Chief Engineer—His activity 377

CHAPTER XXII.

Movements of the army—Narrow escape of Wellington—Anecdote of Wellington at Rodrigo—Novel scaling ladders—Sir Alexander Dickson—Wellington's vanity—Operations resumed—Spanish officers—The passage of the Adour—The road to Bayonne—Death of Captain Pitts 401

PAGE

CHAPTER XXIII.

Passage of the river—Start for Orthes—Effect of the battle—Feelings of the French—Wellington wounded—St. Sever—Church and School—Aire—Wellington on the conduct of the Allies—Indurating effects of War 417

CHAPTER XXIV.

Reports from the seat of war—The Duke d'Angoulême—The German cavalry—Misconduct of the Spaniards—Attacks on our grazing parties—Movement of head-quarters—Death of Colonel Sturgeon—Visit to the hospital—New quarters—Skirmishes—Wellington and the mayor 436

CHAPTER XXV.

Difficulties of the march—Failure of the bridge of boats—The Garonne—Excesses of Murillo's corps—Bad news—Exchange of prisoners—Arrival before Toulouse—A prisoner of war—Anecdote of Wellington . 452

CHAPTER XXVI.

Uncertain intelligence—Capture of Toulouse—Wellington at the theatre—The " Liberator "—Ball at the Prefecture—The feelings of the French—Soult and Suchet—Ball at the Capitole 478

CHAPTER XXVII.

Toulouse—Its churches—Protestant service—Libraries—Reception of the Duke d'Angoulême—The French Generals—Popularity of Wellington 501

CHAPTER XXVIII.

Toulouse—Mr. Macarthy's Library—The Marquess of Buckingham—General Hope—Wellington's dukedom — The theatre—A romantic story—Feeling towards the English—The Duke on the Russian cavalry 523

CHAPTER XXIX.

Preparations for departure—Bordeaux—Imposition on the English—
Greetings from the Women—Mausoleum of Louis XVI. . . . 541

CHAPTER XXX.

The opera-house—The cathedral—The synagogue—A Jewish wedding—
Strange show-house—Wellington and King Ferdinand . . . 553

CHAPTER XXXI.

Country Fêtes—Brawls with the French—The Duke d'Angoulême—
Mademoiselle Georges—The Actress and the Emperor—French acting
and French audiences—Presentation of a sword to Lord Dalhousie—
Georges' benefit—Departure 566

APPENDIX 579

PRIVATE JOURNAL,

&c. &c.

CHAPTER I.

Departure from England—Exercises on Ship-board — Off the Coast—
Arrival at Lisbon—Residence there—Journey to Head-quarters commenced—Abrantes—General features of the March—Salamanca.

H. M. S. *Vautour*, off Mondego Bay,
Sept. 14, 1812. Monday.

MY DEAR M———,

It was very fortunate that I kept to my post at
the George Inn, at Portsmouth; for at seven in the
morning of Saturday the 5th I was called from my bed
by the Admiral, who told me that, in consequence of
the news from Madrid, he had received orders to send
a ship of war after the *Pylades*, to endeavour to prevent
her landing the money she had carried out to Oporto,
and to direct her captain to take it on to Lisbon. He
told me that, if I could get ready and on board immediately, I might accompany him. Accordingly, soon
after nine o'clock I was on board His Majesty's ship
the *Vauteur*, or *Vautour*, or *Vulture*, a fast-sailing brig
of sixteen guns — fourteen carronades, twenty-four
pounders, and two long nines; the only remaining trophy
in our Navy of the glorious expedition to the Scheldt!
The Captain, a most open-hearted, friendly man, by name

B

Lawless, is a native of the south of Ireland. The vessel
is an excellent sailer, and the whole in good order, with
a fine crew of a hundred and five men; but the accommodations are very small, as all is made for use, and
nothing for convenience or ornament. The Captain's
cabin, about ten feet by twelve, he shared with me.
One of us hung up a cot on each side at night, and
we lived there when these cots were removed in the daytime; there was no opening but the hatches at top, no
windows at all. I had, however, what was most material,
a most friendly, kind reception, and shared every comfort
the Captain was possessed of. This consisted of a joint
daily, generally fresh, good wine and brandy, vegetables,
and, up to this day, good bread, great attention, and a
thorough welcome.

Friday the 11*th.*—At eleven o'clock precisely, as our
timepieces and observations had indicated, we sighted
Spain; and had the additional amusement of good charts,
and maps, and telescopes, to examine the coasts, besides
assisting in the observations on deck, and watching all
that was going on. The scene was one of constant
activity during the voyage, not a moment's idleness; the
sails were mended; the masts were repaired; the deck
was caulked, and made water-tight for the winter; the
winter rigging was made ready; the sides of the ship
painted. All this, besides the usual routine duty of the
ship, was done whenever there was smooth water. One
fine calm evening the Captain amused me with a sham-
fight, and put the men through their exercises; first at
one set of the guns, then at the other; marines and all
were at work. He showed me also the effect of a long
shot and a grape shot from the carronades in the water.
These occupations, with a little reading and writing,
preparatory to my land journey, filled up the days until
dark, when we took to our cots. We first made the land
off Cape Adrian, half way between Cape Ortegal and

Cape Finisterre, and got in close to the Sisarga Island, about one o'clock on Friday the 11th. We then coasted close in shore all the way to Cape Finisterre, which we reached at dark: the shore is very bold and fine, but with a barren aspect, and the appearance of an inhospitable and almost uninhabited land. The high tracts towards Corunna, and perhaps about Ferrol, were only just visible at first; but from Sisarga to Finisterre we saw them about as plainly as we should have done on shore.

Saturday 12th.—This morning we found ourselves close off Cape Saliers, having passed Vigo Bay in the night. Thence we slowly crept along shore all that day in sight of the country, buildings, &c., until we arrived at dark within about twelve miles of Oporto, off Villa de Condé. The country is very beautiful and picturesque, nearly as bold as the former, but very much built over, dotted with many villages and detached houses, and verdant with much wood; all externally very loveable and delightful. Monte Santa Tecla, at the entrance of Minho, is an imposing object, and the whole coast interesting, especially from Viana to Oporto, and most of all about Villa de Condé and Oporto. Condé is a handsome-looking town, well situated, with several large good-looking houses, and an aqueduct, reaching nearly three miles I should think, parallel to the shore, through two villages to the hills. The hills were well wooded, and many houses, villas, &c., covered their sides: whether the aqueduct was still in use we could not discover; but I saw no breaks in it as I viewed it through the glass. We made signals to the pilots to come out from Oporto on Saturday evening, but were too far off to be observed; and from the fear of an accident, though within ten miles, were obliged to stand off all night, and try to keep our place.

Sunday the 13th.—Still abreast of Condé, and having

no wind, the whole day getting near to Oporto. Several fishermen came on board from the boats around. They all agreed that the *Pylades* had not been at Oporto—tidings which delighted the Captain; but upon the Consul's boat coming off at a signal, when we got near the bar in the evening, we found that the *Pylades* had been off the bar three nights before, just the time she sailed before us at Portsmouth, and had landed General Oswald, the medical men, and the money at nine o'clock at night, and had gone on; and that the money was on its way to the army. We, therefore, put right about again, and got about ten miles from the bar of Oporto, which we had heard roaring many miles off, before dark. Last night we were again becalmed, and at twelve to-day (the 14th) we were only in Mondego Bay, near the spot where the *Apollo*, and forty of her convoy, were lost in 1804. Here we met a wind right ahead, and have been beating out ever since. At three it shifted a little, and we are now returning, and hope to clear Mondego Point and get in sight of the Burlingas before dark to-night. From about ten miles below Oporto, near Aveiro, to the Mondego highlands, the coast is flat, and we have only seen in Mondego Bay sand-hills and a few huts, and have only heard the surf roaring at a distance of nearly ten miles. We are now about fifty miles from the Burlingas and about ninety from Lisbon, and hope to be there to-morrow.

Our officers are, the Captain, Lawless; first lieutenant, Soper; the second lieutenant, a fine, stout Irishman, who has amused me much, by recounting the escapes of his past life.

Tuesday 15*th*, 12 *o'clock.*—Still about twenty miles from Mondego Point. Marshal Beresford, who is lying at Oporto badly wounded, sent out to ask for a passage to Lisbon on board our vessel; and it was arranged that we were to fire two guns if we could accommodate him :

but the Captain was not able to do so in his small cabin, even if we had both given up our berths, which we would cheerfully have done. It was fortunate, however, he did not come on board, as he would have passed three miserable nights if he had made trial of our scanty accommodation.

Lisbon, September 17*th.*—Two more nights out becalmed—one, off Mondego Bay; and another, off the rock of Lisbon. We got in here this morning at seven o'clock, and have been all the morning running about the town. The view at the entrance into the harbour is very beautiful. We anchored at dusk off Cascaes Fort last night. The General, Peacock, has given me quarters at the Marquis d'Abrantes', and to-day I dine with the General. It is said that there is a great mortality in the army; the officers sickly, and a great want of money.

Lisbon, September 20*th,* 1812.—I have now been three days in this town, which resembles the description of certain ladies whom I have a right to suppose to be within your knowledge, for I think they are described in the Bible, and in other good books which you study—all outside show, except in the state apartments of a few individuals, which are certainly very magnificent. Streets very offensive, palaces by the side of ruins, and sometimes even the palaces in a state of partial decay, though in other parts stately and magnificent in their architectural proportions. Everywhere there is an aspect of extreme poverty side by side with some showy indications of wealth; and it is evident that among the lower classes impostors are as plentiful as mosquitos. The heat is extreme—worse than I found it at Paris in August 1802. The evenings, however, are cool, and near the water the breezes are refreshing. They congratulate me, indeed, on the comparative mildness of the season, which is favourable for my journey to headquarters, which are at Dulmas, in advance of Valladolid.

On landing, I proceeded immediately to General Peacock, the commanding officer, who received me with great civility, and I dined with him that day. As to forwarding me to the army, it appears all that he can do is to give me a route, which will procure me at different stations (though at times two or three days distant from each other), rations for bread and forage, as there are depôts at intervals of from one to three days' journey all the way. I shall have to purchase two mules and two horses. The price of horses is high; on an average, two hundred and twenty dollars each. Captain C——, of the staff here, has offered to go to the fair with me on Tuesday to buy cattle and all other necessaries for my journey. There is no route except by Ciudad Rodrigo, and, therefore, though it is said that head-quarters may be at Madrid before my arrival, I shall be compelled to go that way. Baron Quintilla was not in town. The Envoy asked me to dinner immediately to his country-house at Benefica, and was extremely civil to me, remarking that mine was not a common letter of introduction. He asked me again yesterday, but being unwell, I declined the flattering invitation. He also offered to carry me in his suite to a bull-fight, twelve miles off; but as this would detain me from Sunday to Tuesday, and interfere with my whole plan, I am obliged reluctantly to forego the amusement. I am not here for my pleasure. When I arrived at the Envoy's he was absent, and I had a *tête-à-tête* with General Abadia, who is here on his way to Cadiz, where he is to take a high official position. He appeared a clever man, but I understand his loyalty to Ferdinand is doubtful, for a letter addressed to him by his wife, who is with the French, inquiring when he would fulfil his promise of joining their party, has been intercepted.

This may be all a trick, but there is something suspicious about it. He blamed us very much, charging us

with having made two great blunders, in not seizing
Santona, by troops from England, and securing that river
communication and post to land all our men in, instead
of Lisbon; and also in not allowing the Sicilian expedition to seize Tortosa, and maintain a post on that river,
the most important and most annoying to Soult. He
spoke in high terms of Lord Wellington, but seemed to
think that the fate of Europe depends upon the conduct
of Russia in this conjuncture.

The idea seems now to be, that Soult, Suchet, and
Joseph have formed a junction. They have above sixty
thousand effective men; and it is added, that the French
now have their old position on the Ebro always in their
power. General Carrier was brought in here a prisoner
on Thursday, from Salamanca: he had five wounds,
which are nearly healed, but he thought he should lose a
finger. He came in to the General whilst I dined there.
He seemed to be out of spirits, but said that Marmont
was nearly well, and would resume his command. The
French, I hear, are intrenched near Burgos.

I have obtained quarters at the *casa* of the Marquesa
d'Abrantes, a good situation, and a lieutenant-colonel's
quarters. Her husband is a prisoner in France. I have
a separate door, which leads away to four small rooms
to the street; bare walls, painted with military trophies,
and the whole kept as quarters. In these I have two
tables, a dozen chairs, a bedstead, a mattress, a worked
flounced quilt, some fine sheets, but, of course, no blankets.
At first we had nothing else; but I have now got a silver
basin and ewer, some knives and forks, and a supply of
water. These apartments might easily be made very
comfortable. The state rooms of this house, looking
over about an acre of garden (which is open to the
public), are very handsome. As the marquesa lost her
mother last week, about twenty cabriolets a-day have
brought visitors to pay respects, &c., and about a hundred

and fifty beggars to receive their alms. By the way, the English have caused everything here to become very dear. The churches are gaudy, and in some respects not a little ridiculous, but still, to my mind, nothing like so trumpery, absurd, and indeed indecorous in every respect as those in Flanders, and in some parts of Switzerland and Piedmont. The Roman Catholics here certainly have the appearance of devotion, and seem more in earnest, much more so than in France, and more so than in any country I have seen.

Lisbon, September 23rd, 1812.—I was at the fair, in the heat of the sun, all yesterday, and have bought two small mules, one small horse, and have agreed for another, a small pony, to carry me. The fair has knocked me up as well as my man Henry. I have been all this day with Captain C——, almost my only friend here, at market, bargaining for travelling necessaries. Commissary P—— will lend me one public mule ; so now I hope I am equipped as far as that goes. The General offers to send me with the next treasure, which goes nobody knows when; but refuses me two soldiers to go with me, though it is said that it is really dangerous to go without them.

Lisbon, September 26th, 1812, *Saturday.*—Though in a constant fever from fleas and mosquitos, we should have started yesterday with some treasure, but my servant Henry could not stir, and my Portuguese servant took himself off at eight in the morning. I have now got a German deserter as servant instead of the Portuguese; and trust he will not carry on the old game, and desert with my baggage. He is said to speak a little English and Portuguese, and know the country well.

Sunday.—For one day more I have postponed my journey, intending to start with some treasure and two officers on Tuesday. The Opera-house here is a dull, heavy building, about the size of the Haymarket Opera-house; but the dancing more like Sadler's Wells than the Opera in England: great activity and force in the buffo style like comic masks—this appears to be the favourite style here. Macbeth was turned into a pantomine; the death and dagger scene very fine, but the whole effect marred by the mummery of fantastic dancing and skipping witches. I have not had time to see any thing except Lisbon, and the aqueduct: the latter work certainly fine, but not of an attractive shape. Round arches would have had a better effect, and the piers want evenness and regularity; nevertheless it is a work worthy of the Romans. I contrived to-day to go to Belem church, a very fine specimen of arabesque, the best thing I have seen here; in style it is between the Saxon and Antique, with a little Gothic intermixed, the ornaments beautiful and in high preservation.

Abrantes, October 6th, 1812.—A day's halt here enables me to write to you. I left Lisbon on the 30th September, by two o'clock, with my sick party, and thence eight miles to Saccavem in about three hours. The road to Saccavem and nearly to Villa Franca is fine; and, except that there are no trees besides olive-trees, which appear like apple-trees at a distance, and no verdure, the river and country are picturesque.

On the second night we reached Villa Franca, sixteen miles; the third night, Agembiga twelve; the fourth, Santarem sixteen. The positions and accounts in our gazettes made this route interesting, but the road itself is dull and sandy. Suppose a few olive-trees and firs on Bagshot Heath, and you have the scene. Saccavem and Santarem are both fine positions for appearance, and the latter for defence. All the towns are half in ruins, as well as almost all the single houses on the road to this place. On the fifth day we reached Galegao, sixteen miles; on the sixth, Punhete, twelve miles; on the seventh, Abrantes, eight miles. I am now eighty-eight

miles from Lisbon. From Galegao to Abrantes the road
runs near the river, the verdure increases, there are a few
chestnut, oranges, and larger firs, and in the spring the
scenery must be very picturesque. Abrantes, on a commanding eminence, is in a very fine situation, and looks
over much fine country. Finding my sick men unequal
to the fatigue, I applied to the officer of the treasure, and
got a soldier, a fine active Tyrolese, who does more work
in an hour than my poor creatures in a day. He cleans
down the animals, waters them, loads, &c., and as I carry
his baggage for him, and give him rather better fare, he
seems to be very well pleased with the post. He leads a
mule on the road, walking at his ease: by this means I
now get off about six o'clock every morning.

The treasure-party, finding the heat made the men ill,
now start at five o'clock; still I am much better than I
was when I started, and when on the march I go quicker
than the treasure, as I have easy loads. Henry leads the
first mule on horseback, the soldier walking by the side
to keep everything right, whilst I bring up the rear
myself, always on the watch, and thus have but few
accidents. One of my mules is a nice fat round fellow,
who eats so much they cannot keep the baggage from
rolling off him without holding it on ; another mule had
a troublesome propensity of lying down with the baggage.
My Tyrolese only speaks German, French, and a little
Portuguese.

So many of the men of another treasure-party were ill,
that they halted, and then went on with us; this
crowded the road and made it more uncomfortable.
Here at Abrantes we separate—they go to General Hill.
On arriving at a place, the first thing is to hunt for the
Juge de Fores, to procure quarters, but if there is an
English commandant, he must first be beaten up for an
order, then the quarters are to be found ; sometimes those
allotted are full ; then another billet must be obtained :

sometimes the stables are full of kicking mules, and other stables must be found elsewhere. At length we unload, all in one room with four walls, a table, and a chair. Then at every third place we have to go to the Commissary to draw rations, straw, and barley for the animals to eat—spirits, meat, and bread for ourselves, and wood for firing. These must sometimes be fetched from half a mile to a mile and a half off, and be procured from roguish Portuguese under-commissaries. Sometimes great pieces of green wood are allotted to us, which will not burn, and we have nothing to cut it with. This, which we often leave as not worth carriage, costs Government a large sum: a third of the quantity, if good, would serve better. As the wood and straw we cannot manage to take with us, we carry on barley, and buy a little straw, or Sadran corn straw, which is the best when fresh. At first the Portuguese were very civil at quarters, but we are now too numerous, and many behave ill from disgust and weariness. They are now very backward to supply anything, even when they have it, which often is not the case. They provide a room, a lamp, water, a basin, a towel by night, a table, a chair, and something to lie upon; some furnish very decent beds.

Two days ago the scene changed, and it has since rained almost incessantly. We got wet yesterday, halted to-day, and to morrow I probably shall start, to be soaked to the very bones. My mode of living may interest you. I rise, then, at half-past four, take some bread, spirits and water, and. a raw egg when I can get one, or sometimes a few grapes. When we stop to water, I eat some bread and cheese, a dear luxury on the road, a very little country wine and water, and now and then coffee or chocolate. In the evening, a stew (when we can get it) comes as a treat, and then we lie down on the floor at eight o'clock in hope of sleep—a hope more frequently fulfilled than it was at Lisbon. Stores are all

now at double price, and will soon not be procurable at
any cost.

The Commissary says we shall have six hours' walk
in the rain instead of the sun now; and after two or
three days we shall find only deserted ruins where the
French came, and we after them, last year. I hope
this is exaggeration. Windows in this great town are
not to be seen even in Colonels' quarters, or in the best
shops. This is an active, busy place—thoroughly
military. The vintage was going on as we proceeded on
the road, and we had abundance of grapes. The poor
soldiers, having three days' rations served out at
once, consume all the drink on the first day, sell the
meat to save carriage and the trouble of cooking it,
and live upon bread and grapes and water, till their next
supply comes to hand. At Santarem and here, hospitals
are established as well as at Lisbon; many fine-looking
fellows, reduced to skeletons, are in them. I have a new
route to-morrow round about: first day, Garvao; second,
Nisa; third, Villa Velha; fourth, Cernados; fifth, Castello Branco: sixteen miles, twenty miles, twelve miles,
eight, and eighty.

Sunday, Castello Branco, October 11th, 1812.—Here
am I thus far safe on my pilgrimage, and tolerably well
considering all things, for I seldom get above two or
three hours' sleep, and many nights none at all, from
noises, fleas, gnats, mosquitos, bad accommodation, and
anxiety. From Abrantes I got safely to Garvao, which
is finely situated, and the walk to it wildly beautiful.
The next day I warned my people to rise by half-past
four; we loaded in the dark, but started by daylight,
and got in before the treasure to Niga. A good mattress
and clean sheets, &c., on the floor, without fleas, are
genuine luxuries. For the first time in Portugal I got
six hours' sleep. In the same manner I started again
from Niga by five o'clock, and got through two treasure

days' journey in one to Cernados. Understanding that
at Villa Velha there were only desolate ruins, scarcely
supplying a dry cover, by starting again early yesterday
from Cernados (which consists only of one house, half of
it a ruin, with a nest of ruined cottages round it), I
reached this place by ten yesterday, and thus had all the
remainder of the day to rest, and this in addition (Sunday), for the treasure arrived only to-day.

I have thus avoided the common piggery of being all
in one house at Cernados, and a bad night at Villa Velha.
By calculating distances and time also, I have kept my
men and myself dry. As the rains generally come on
hitherto after twelve in the day, and in the night, we
have only been caught in two English showers. It
rained all the time we were at Abrantes, from twelve on
the day we arrived, entirely through the following day,
to about an hour before we started. All the rest of the
day was fine, rain again all the evening—the same at
Niga, and the same here also. And such rain! it would
saturate anything in ten minutes. As it is now cooler, I
walk half the way, which also saves my pony. I have
here assigned to me the quarters of the Generals who
pass through. These consist of the ruin of a fine house
for quarters, and a large room with four great windows
without glass, and four doors in it; gold frames around
without their looking-glasses in them, fine chairs without
bottoms, &c., &c. The house belongs to the *Illustrissimo
Signor Barao.* I have a mattress on the floor with fleas
innumerable. I have my route, and here it is: first
day, Eschalas de Cimo; second, San Miguel; third,
Menoa; fourth, Sabugal; fifth, perhaps a halt; sixth,
Aldea da Ponte; seventh, Sturno; eighth, Ciudad Rodrigo. We are to carry provisions for four days with us,
then provide for three, and start to-morrow or next day
as the treasure mules are able; then go on to Fuentes de
Castelegos, Forgadilla, Calçade de Don Diego, Salamanca.

Few of these places are in Faden's map. Nothing can
be had on the road, it is said, not even dry stabling or a
dry room; and much wet is expected. The place is
finely situated on the east side of a hill which is crowned
by an old Moorish castle and walls, and a modern monas-
tery in ruins! It is one of the best towns we have seen,
and there are the ruins of some good houses; provisions
and necessaries are to be bought here, but at a high price.
There is part of the fine episcopal palace (where a Portuguese General is quartered), with a garden in tolerable
order, a good church, and several picturesque-looking
ruined monasteries, with crosses at every step. I have
taken a few sketches where we stop on the road, though
too much occupied with business to think much of the
picturesque. Niga is also picturesque.

My adventures are all much alike. The only variety
is an arrival wet through to the skin. No one can say
where we shall go to at last. I suppose I must now proceed to Salamanca, and then something must be determined upon. Things do not go on well at Burgos, I
fear; there is much delay, more than was expected.
Lord Wellington is, it is said, not satisfied. At Cernados
a cobbler was the *Juge de Fores*, and gave us our billets.
On the walls was an excellent likeness in chalk of Lord
George Lennox, done by the shadow, I suppose from the
lamp which is allowed us. I hear of sickness everywhere; much at head-quarters. The general orders have
many more on the list of absent from sickness, than on
that of arrivals at the army. Soult is very strong.
General Hill, I believe, is still at Toledo.

Near the mountains on the other side of the Tagus is
an old castle or two, and some pleasant glimpses of fine
valleys, and the deep banks of the river which is hidden
from the view. The sandy commons like Bagshot,
over which the road passes, are more bold, the hills
higher, and covered almost entirely with the gum cistus,

which has a sweet scent, but, being out of bloom in that state, is not so pleasing as our heaths with their various colours. There is a little heath like the Devonshire heath, and some parts of the road rather like Dartmoor. Near Niga are seen the mountains about Elvas, and in the line to Badajoz, and the Spanish mountains of Estramadura. The country proved to me the merit of some of Rubens' Spanish views, which are, like his Flemish pictures, most correct in the character of the scenery. From Niga, after proceeding a league, you wind down a wild Devonshire or Welsh sort of road; first cross a small river, then the Tagus again, almost down steps—not so bad as some wild parts of Ireland, to be sure, though very bad for the loaded mules. Here is very little oak, underwood, some fir, but chiefly and perpetually the gum cistus, which grows to about four feet high. Villa Velha is a village in ruins, finely situated on the side of a hill looking over the river. It is now nearly deserted. The soldiers with baggage pitched a tent below the office in the cellar. From the hills above the river, before we crossed the Tagus, we saw Castello Branco standing high on the hill, and the Moorish ruins. Cernados is like a Welsh village of the worst sort : rocks for streets, ruined stone houses inhabited in part, and used for quarters. Their few architectural large buildings alone constitute the difference between these and the worst Welsh or Irish villages. From Cernados to this place we again crossed a country like a large Bagshot Heath, but by a very tolerable good road; adieu.

P.S.—The Captain has just sent me word we must start to-morrow instead of the day after; he says that the treasure is not safe without the serjeants. Our detachments are all foreigners; many are drunk, and have quarrelled with the inhabitants !

Salamanca, October, 1812.—The first day after leaving Castello Branco, we reached Eschalo de Cimo, a pretty,

and once a thriving village, with a good church, not so
much destroyed as damaged; one handsome large house
in the vicinity belonging to the Squiress, Donna Joanna,
the best rooms in which were gutted and used as quarters,
the rest inhabited by two or three families of the better
kind, with some smart misses among them. The other
houses mostly in ruins, but still some of them occupied.
In this place bread was not to be bought, nor even an
onion! but we fared well, in good rooms, with good fires.
On our road thither we kept Castello Branco in sight
nearly all the way; we also saw the distant mountains
in Spain and Portugal. The road was over a sort of
Dartmoor, stones, rock, sand, with fern oak a foot high,
and abundance of apples. The second day we reached
San Miguel de Cima. The same sort of village as Eschalo
de Cimo, one good house for quarters, the rest small, and
generally, like the church, in ruins; but the inhabitants
were fast returning to it. Here we obtained bread,
onions, and some hay. The appearance on entering the
village, with the trees about it, very pleasant. The
third day's route was to Memoa, five long leagues. At
first a good road and picturesque country, with a very
fine view of Monsanto, with its town and castle on the
right, and of the other hills grouped with it in the
distance. Pennamacor, which is almost destroyed, we
left on our right, about a mile, with its castle, standing
boldly on the side of a hill, with rock and wood around
it, and a rich-looking valley below. This is a fine situation, backed, as we left it, by Monsanto. We also passed
Pedrigoa, a large village, nearly destroyed and deserted,
and at last, after passing over a hill by a horrible road,
through an oak copse, where we had nearly lost our way,
we arrived at the heap of ruins called Memoa. This was
the worst place we had stopped at all the way. There
was only one room in the town, that only water-tight,
and there were no stables. I took the driest corner

in a large common room, because there was a stable under it.

I could see and hear everything in the stables, for the floor was still less tight than the roof. The leg of a chair or a table, in spite of all possible care, went two or three times through it. I got a little hay, and slept behind a great chest, in my blanket. Three of the natives were in the room at night. The fourth day we had three leagues of fine road, though bad travelling, through a hilly wood of arbutuses in bearing, and Portugal laurels in flower, heath in bloom, a plant like the lignum vitæ, and broom. This day's route brought us to Sabugal, where there is generally a halt, but this our captain declined. Sabugal stands on a hill, very finely situated, but commanded by other hills; the way is over a bridge and river, and with a winding road up to it. The situation is not unlike that of Ludlow; the town very inferior in size and beauty, but picturesque. The castle itself, with its square Moorish towers, more so than Ludlow. The town is all in ruins; not even a weather-tight room in it. I got a large sort of barn, open in the roof in several places, with no doors, and two large windows, without even shutters, and four others half closed. On our road thither from Memoa we found half the body of a man, nearly a skeleton, but with flesh and nails on the toes. It was lying on the road, as if to scare travellers.

The market-place at Sabugal is, I think, very pretty, and everything in it very cheap: this, indeed, was the cheapest place through which we had passed. The fifth day we reached Aldea da Ponte, the last Portuguese village. The road was interesting, as we passed near Fuente Guinaldos, so long head-quarters, and Alfayetes, also head-quarters. We passed just under Alfayetes, and saw Lord Wellington's house on the side of the hill, with the old castle. This place is now in ruins, like the rest. We then passed over the plain where our cavalry dis-

tinguished themselves in a sharp affair with the French.
Aldea da Ponte is much cleaner than the other villages.

Here we saw more pots, pans, basins, &c., than usual ;
these the people desired us to make use of instead of
hiding them from us, as was generally done in Portugal.
On the sixth day, we came, after a short league, to a small
village on the side of a hill, the first in Spain, then on to
two or three more, and in less than six leagues we reached
Ciudad Rodrigo. This town stands on a rise, in an undulating sort of rough Salisbury Plain. It is two-thirds
in ruins, but the public buildings appear to have suffered
comparatively little, and might, most of them, be restored.
The entrance to the town is striking. We got an indifferent quarter in the suburbs, immediately opposite the
place where the light battalions entered. The main
breach was round the corner of our abode. The Spaniards
had nearly restored these two breaches, but from ill luck
or neglect both had entirely given way, and there must
still be some months' work before they can undo and
clear enough away to begin to rebuild again. Everything
was scarce in the town, and the people imposing and
uncivil. On the seventh day we proceeded to Brondillo,
where we were obliged to stop, as there were only two
houses in Castel Legos, to which the route sent us. This
was by far our worst day's journey ; the distance was
seven leagues, that is, twenty-eight miles. It took us to
accomplish this from six in the morning to past three,
of which time it rained eight hours and a half, nearly
all that time like a bad English thunder-shower of ten
minutes' duration. No coats could keep out the wet,
and it was accompanied by a strong, cold November wind,
for the weather for the last week has been as cold as an
English November. We all suffered, and I have been
chilly and aguish ever since. We then, for the first time,
entered a Spanish cabin ; and oh ! how superior to those
of Portugal ! of Ireland ! of Scotland ! and if I did not

consider these cottages as farms and not as cottages, I
should say of England too! All neat and clean; with
pots, dishes, boilers in abundance.

The people are proud, but if treated with civility,
courteous and kind, though they are turned away from
their own firesides by us and the Portuguese three or
four nights in the seven. They made us a great fire, and
did all they could for us. The women seem chatty and
merry—the men, the handsomest and best-grown, with
the finest countenances I ever saw, except perhaps in
Switzerland. We met with the same sort of treatment
and kindness at the next village. The house belonged to
the priest, with whom, through the medium of some
mongrel Latin and Spanish, I managed to converse a
little. These quarters are some of the best I have had
since leaving Lisbon; at Togadillo, where the route sent
us, there was only one good house.

At Robedila, a place out of the road, where we got by
accident, finding we had passed Togadillo without knowing
it, all was comfort again. This place the French occupied for some time with ten thousand men. We arrived
yesterday at Salamanca. After the first five leagues from
Ciudad Rodrigo, which were as rough as Dartmoor, we
have passed through a country like the neighbourhood of
Salisbury Plain, only that the villages were much more
numerous, though several only of three or four houses,
now nearly all repaired. Not a single large, or, I believe,
two-storied house, from Ciudad Rodrigo to this place.
Much of the country now quite a fine green, but a very
large part in cultivation. The land looked good; about
midway it consisted of, for five or six leagues, clay, and
knee-deep : in some places a light soil, or reddish sand ;
with water up to the mules' bellies, from the heavy rain,
though it had ceased twenty-four hours. The people
have plenty of bread and straw, but there are no shops in
the villages. They only sell to oblige each his own lodger

for the night. Bread was threepence a pound—it had
been fourpence. All along this country, from St. Martin
de Rio hither, are abundance of acorns, almost as good as
chestnuts; quite sweet. The muleteers and men halt to
eat them. This also gives good fires everywhere. Horses
and bones are strewed more or less along the whole way
from Lisbon. In one place, about seven leagues from
Salamanca, were thirteen heads arranged in a row, as
stepping-blocks for passengers through the water. I
believe there was a little cavalry brush there. Salamanca
stands well, but in a sort of Salisbury Plain. The colleges are destroyed, but the church is most beautiful, and
the entrances much finer than those of our cathedrals—
the figures and heads very fine indeed.

The altered Roman bridge is striking. The town is
so full, principally of sick, that I have got bad quarters,
half a mile out of the town; my direction l'Ultima Casa.

Later, same day.—I have been again looking at the
town. The great church is very fine, and not damaged,
but there are many miserable ruins of noble colleges,
some gutted, some nearly razed. The public library has
a fair supply of books, but too exclusively of sacred,
or rather ecclesiastical literature; there are, however,
good classics, French, and modern learned works, mathematics, and others : it is about two-thirds of the size
of Trinity College, Cambridge. I hope to proceed the
day after to-morrow, to Valladolid, which it is proposed
to reach in seven days. There are good shops here, and
articles not dear. It is curious to see the same effect
of ages and of tastes as in England. Below and behind
the great altar of the church was some old English, or,
as we should say, Saxon architecture, that is, a rude imitation of Greek. Then came a florid sample of Gothic,
not in the best taste, but beautifully ornamented, with
screens, &c., in the style of King Charles and King William; forced Grecian again, of two centuries back.

CHAPTER II.

Arrival at Head-quarters—Ciudad Rodrigo—The Retreat—Its Disasters—
Capture of General Paget—Personal Anecdotes—Scarcity of Provisions
—Courts-martial in the Army—Business of a Judge-Advocate—Wel-
lington.

Head-quarters, Rueda, Nov. 5, 1812.

My dear M——,

At last I have arrived safely at head-quarters, as
they have been kind enough to come half-way to meet
me. From Salamanca, we proceeded on the first day
to Alba de Tormes, a town in a fine situation on the
Tormes, with the remains of a castle of various dates,
extensive and picturesque; part of it, particularly the
entrance staircase, very richly ornamented. The whole
was striking, and the vicinity of the town was interesting, for here it was that the French so completely
beat the unhappy Spaniards, and put them to death by
thousands, almost in cold blood. We saw where General del Parques' cavalry were posted, and the positions
of the French. On our road near Salamanca we also
observed at a distance, on the other side of the river,
the hills where the battle of Salamanca was fought; and
our route lay in that of the pursuit through Alba, then
on to Peneranda, another good old town, and so, through
villages, to Arevalo, where we arrived in four days,
tracing men's bones and bits of soldiers' dress, as well as
horse bones and carcasses, on the route thither.

This country resembles Salisbury Plain, in open cultivation of corn, and is covered very thick with neat

villages, with a general appearance of comfort. Arevalo
is a large place in ruins. There are many remains of
fine richly-wooded brickwork, convents, churches, many
good houses, and the town standing very finely on a hill,
nearly surrounded by the river, which runs in a deep
hollow round it, with four or five substantial and rather
picturesque bridges. Our route was by Valladolid,
where we should have been in three days, and which I
regret much not to have seen, for I hear it is second only
to Madrid, and very little damaged. Had I proceeded
on the route I should have reached Valladolid the day
before the French entered it. Hearing that the army
was rapidly retiring, the road became unsafe. No one
knew where head-quarters were to be; the treasure, and
my mules with it, were consequently halted, and instructions were written for. For four days we remained at
Arevalo. The treasure party were then ordered to
Olmedo to deliver their cargo, and head-quarters were
here at Rueda. I proceeded with them to Olmedo,
rather a handsome and a large town, where I was housed
in the good quarters which had been occupied by the
Prince of Orange. When I arrived here, my beasts
were kept standing loaded in the streets, and all of us
without anything to eat until past six, before I could
get a quarter. The people were civil, but I had to go
to the Quarter-Master-general, Adjutant-general, to the
billet-manager, to the Military Secretary, &c. One said,
"go here;" another, "go there;" a third sent a serjeant
to inquire, and then thought no more about it.

At last I procured an indifferent quarter vacated by a
Commissary, only a shed, and holes through the floor
into the cellar below. My animals, therefore, stood all
night in the entrance of the passage.

This morning, 5th, I heard of a Spanish aide-de-camp
of Castanos', who is here, and who had three small
stables close to me. I found him in bed at nine o'clock,

but he could speak French, and I persuaded him to give me one of the stables for my four animals. Thus we are better off to-day, and, as a favour, I have got them something to eat. I was introduced to Lord Wellington this morning, and delivered my letters. He was very courteous. We conversed for half an hour, and I am to dine with him at six to-day, in full uniform. He is to send me fifty cases against officers, to examine, in order to ascertain whether any can be made out on evidence, which is the great difficulty. There is a caricature here of Johnny Newcome, who makes it out till sent to the rear rolled up in a blanket in an ox-car, creeping on at the rate of two miles an hour to Lisbon. We are in hourly expectation of moving. The bridges are repaired, and the French within three leagues, and able to cross if they choose. General Hill is expected here to-day. His forces are at Arevalo. Soult is in Madrid; whether they push on further is to be seen.

Few reinforcements have arrived; eighteen thousand Spaniards (such as they are) are with us. The lower classes of the people are a very fine race in person, talents, and feelings, and vastly superior to the Portuguese. It is very provoking that rank and prejudice render this of no avail. The inhabitants of the town seem half French. About six hundred French crossed over to us last night, but retired again. The cavalry were off in the middle of the night from head-quarters. I was alarmed for a moment, but all seems quiet this morning. The last five days have been very fine; cold dewy mornings, but clear sunny days, damp cold evenings, but for the time of the year here very fine. There are very queer-looking military figures here, some English, a few Portuguese, many more Spanish. The whole scene presents an odd medley.

Ciudad Rodrigo, November 19, 1812.—To continue my diary from Rueda. Two days afterwards, the 7th,

an order to march at four in the morning came, as soon
as Hill's army was within reach.   I then first saw what it
was to put seventy thousand men in motion, about ten
thousand public, and a greater number of private mules,
horses, &c.   At five we started, and about two that day
I reached head-quarters.   Torricello by four o'clock.
At five next morning started again for Petueja.   Here
the head-quarters had only thirty houses for one hundred and fifty officers.   Lord Wellington and the Prince
of Orange had only one room each.   I was ordered a
league in advance, where I found Castanos, who had
come in for better quarters.   He sent me on another
half-league, but when a mile on the road he passed me,
as he had heard that the next was the best quarter.   So
I returned, and at three o'clock got a little hole and a
stable.   About five came in about three thousand
Spanish troops.   Half my house was down in a moment
for firing, and nearly all the owner's property, pans,
dishes, straw, &c., stolen.   I secured mine, which was
attacked, by swallowing a mouthful and packing up and
keeping guard.   The remainder of the house was also
saved; and, by the help of a Spanish officer, who took a
fancy to the kitchen fire, the house was cleared with fist
and foot.   My animals were not safe, as my man heard
one soldier say he would have one before morning.   I
saved them by putting them in a row in the passage
close to me, where they stood for the night.   Fires all
round us; noises of all kinds; people breaking in.
There were only about six civilians, English, in the
village.   At five next day off again, and at daylight
joined the general train on the road to Salamanca.   It
was easily found, for it extended five or six miles.

The day before we again started three cases were laid
before me on which to draw charges.   Upon these I was
to report to Lord Wellington next day.   I drew them
up, but he was too busy to receive them.   When I went

home and sent for a paper, the answer was, "All packed up;" and it seemed that I ought to be so too, as our position was turned, and we were all ordered to be loaded and ready to start. After much hurry, I was ready soon after twelve. My beasts stood loaded at the door till seven in the evening; then came orders to unload, but to be loaded by four next morning, and to start for a hill a league off, and there wait for orders. There was only one long bridge to pass the whole army, and it was near seven before we were all over.

It rained hard. We stood on the hill loaded and waiting for orders till one o'clock. Nearly the whole of our army was in sight round us, cooking their dinners in the rain, in their new position. The French were all around, about a league off, their fires visible in the woods, and the heads of their columns visible with a glass. They would not attack us, as they might, but manœuvred to turn our right wing. Had there been a battle we should have had a fine view of the beginning at least. At one o'clock we saw our whole army break up and put itself in motion; and orders came to us to march and keep with the second column. This we did, marching in the rain, in a fine confusion, till five o'clock, when Lord Wellington halted at a miserable place for head-quarters, and the men bivouacked on the swampy ground. I was ordered on a league further. Darkness soon came on, and the rain descended in torrents. Misdirected by some Spanish muleteers, I lost my way, and did not reach any village for three leagues, and not till nine at night, wet and starved, as the Salamanca people, in our confusion, stole my bread, &c.

I was the only English officer there, and got the best quarter at the parish priest's, the best house there. Here I procured a loaf of bread, fire, and a bed, which were no small comforts. I got, however, but little sleep, not knowing how to proceed next day, and being aware that the French were close at hand. By my map I found that I was in the nearest road to Ciudad Rodrigo, and, taking a retreat to be the object, I determined to wait till eight or nine o'clock next day, and observe whether any one passed. By that time half the army was on the road through the village, and Sir Edward Paget took my quarter for the last night's rest he had before he was taken prisoner. I then had a short march in the rain again this day to Aldea Quella and to Boleado. In two hours' time I got a quarter through Colonel Campbell's influence; and because the stables would not hold a large horse, all the mules, half the servants, all the soldiers, and most of the officers, were out in the wet. Three Spanish officers burst into my quarters at night, and the people were hammering at the door every moment for straw, shelter, &c., sick and all sorts. In spite of my vigilance, either the Spanish officers or the people of the house stole my pistols out of my room, and finished by purloining the bread and rum of my men. Honesty is not a Spanish virtue. We all of us lose things daily. At two next day we loaded, and at three started for this place, twenty miles, four hours before daylight. Luckily we had some moon. I stuck to Lord Wellington's carriage and baggage, thinking the people in charge of them would be best informed, though my own inquiries elicited other intelligence than theirs.

I was told the rivers that way were not passable, and we found the whole road almost under water for miles, ankle, and even knee deep, and three rivers to pass. Many mules were upset or stuck fast, and much baggage damaged or lost. I had only one load overset, and that at the edge, and we saved all, and not much damage done. By daylight there was a general halt; no one knew the ford or the road. At last we passed the river a mile above; but then, finding the French had been in the village three miles off the last night, we all turned

off by a by-road six miles round, and at last arrived here
at Ciudad Rodrigo, miserably cold, with animals knocked
up, sore backs, &c., about two o'clock. In the confusion
here, at last I got a bad quarter in the same house with
Colonel Gordon, Lord Wellington's aide-de-camp. But
I have a place for my animals, and hundreds have no
room for animals, or even for themselves. We halt to-
day, whether for a longer time I know not. The army
is mostly passing the river to-day. We lost many men
in the retreat, but a very little money is missing. The
sick are numerous. Two officers have died of fatigue on
the road, in which dead mules are to be met with in
plenty, and some men. To-day we are relating our adventures. We get but little barley for our horses, no
hay or straw. The cavalry have been without it for
some days; but this is considered a very orderly retreat.
Sir Edward Paget accidentally fell into the enemy's
hands near his own division, within six hundred yards of
it, between that and another. The French are said to
have ninety thousand men, with nine thousand cavalry.
They pressed hard until yesterday; they then relaxed
when they might have done us most mischief. The
roads and weather, I suppose, and the want of food and
forage, impeded them. I hope they will now leave us
quiet. I am very sorry for Sir Edward Paget on the
public account and on my own, as I found him most
friendly, civil, and good-natured. This capture is also a
triumph to the French.

Malliarda de Sorda, November 26th, 1812.—We are
now in our winter quarters, and fill all the villages and
places for twenty miles round on the Portugal side of
Ciudad Rodrigo, the works of which are still quite out of
repair where our trenches were made, as the Spanish new
work has all fallen in. Wellington's head-quarters are
at Frenada, an old station; the doctors are all at Castello
Bom; and the other civil departments, in which I am

included, all at this place, Milliarda de Sorda. We are distant four miles of most infamous rocky road from Frenada, and eight from Castello Bom. This I fear must shut me off from nearly all society, as it would be paying most dear for a dinner at Frenada or Castello Bom, to return in the dark, along roads compared with which those of Ireland or Cornwall are bowling-greens. We are in three wretched villages, in a country like Dartmoor, but more wood near, all rocks around, and stone-wall enclosures, and rocky roads; then woods, with open wastes for twenty miles round. I have a room opening to the street, without ceiling, only open loose pantiles, with holes to let out the smoke of a fireplace without a chimney; a window tinned up by last year's occupier, except four small panes, two of which are broken; there is a hole in the floor to look through at my five animals and three servants, who all sleep on the straw below me.

The weather for the last three days has been a complete English December, cutting easterly winds; and on the 23rd I will vouch for ice three-quarters of an inch thick. All the Sierras are white with snow. I found Lord Wellington's secretaries sitting with candles at twelve o'clock in the day, in order to stop their holes and windows with curtains, and burning charcoal fires. We have had every variety of weather here in six weeks: I never remember it colder in England for the time of the year. Here are no books, no women but ladies of a certain description; and as to living, you would be surprised what good living is here, except at Lord Wellington's table, and about two more, and even at those no port wine, only thin claret, and the country wines and brandy.

At Ciudad Rodrigo there was starvation: no corn, no hay, no straw, no bread, no rum, for three days, only beef and biscuit; at last we got some mouldy biscuit for the animals, which I mixed with carrot, cabbage, and potatoes; everything was devoured. Tea, 22s. and 25s.

a pound; butter, 4s.; bread, 1s. 6d. a pound, above 6s. the loaf; no wine or brandy; gin, 12s. the bottle; straw, a dollar for a small bundle, and all sold in a scramble. The truth was, the troops, poor fellows! came through the town quite starving; during the retreat supplies had been mismanaged—regiments were three and four days without rations, and numbers died of absolute starvation, besides the sick. Lord Wellington is, I hear, very angry. Till I saw B—'s mess, &c., I had no notion of the loss in this retreat, and the great suffering of the men and horses. From what I hear, not merely were about one thousand made prisoners, but five or six thousand put for some time *hors de combat*, by sickness, starvation, and want of horses, &c. The cavalry were too weak to act, mainly from want of food. A great many animals were killed. A treasure-party had a narrow escape: the French were in sight while they were loading, and much baggage was lost. Lord Dalhousie lost almost all; five horses and thirteen loaded mules, with his name at full length upon his baggage—another French triumph! Colonel Delancy lost three horses, taken at Salamanca; and the men suffered shockingly from the wet. The whole was so unlucky; as had the three days' rain begun at Salamanca, in all probability the French would not have crossed the Tormes and turned our position, and we might still have been there; and had they come three days later, we should have saved our three or four thousand sick. We should, moreover, have had good roads and dry nights, no floods and torrents to wade through by day, nor swamps to sleep on by night; in fact, we should only have lost drunken stragglers. The distress at Madrid, after all the joy and gaiety, was dreadful. When we left the town sixty thousand poor were contending for the remains of our stores—the worst objects had the preference given them. King Joseph's Palace was left by him entirely furnished; and as Lord Welling-

ton made a point that he should find it again the same,
nothing was touched by our army.

The 26th.—To-day is a cheerful, frosty, Christmas-day,
and within an English farmhouse the whole would do
very well : but I go, like others, to bed at seven o'clock,
to keep myself warm. General Castanos and his troops
are gone back to Gallicia, which is one grievance removed
at least. Ballasteros is in disgrace at Ceuta, for dis-
obedience. I fear, upon the whole, the Spanish cause
has suffered much by our advance to Madrid and Burgos.
The people find we cannot support them, and will be
very shy in future; and the misery of the peasantry and
townspeople all the time is extreme. There are few
deceptions in England like that about the life in Spain.

Frenada, Head-Quarters, December 8th, 1812.—I will
now tell you one day's adventure and how I came here.
Two days after writing from Malliarda de Sorda, where I
was lonely and heard nothing, I determined to walk over
to see how things went on here, and put my papers into
my pocket in case I should be able to see Lord Wellington. On my arrival I met the Quarter-Master who
managed quarters : he told me he had kept a miserable
hole for me, if I chose to move; it was much worse than
even my old one, but I instantly said "YES." The next
person I met was Lord Wellington, and I asked him
when he wished to see me, and whether he had any
objection to my moving here? He said I might take my
choice and take the best of the bad. He then asked
whether I had my papers about me? I said, "All."
"Come up," said he then; and in ten minutes he looked
over my papers, which consisted of four sets of charges
against officers. These were all settled with a few
judicious alterations, in which I entirely agreed. I then
came out and wrote them fair in the Adjutant-general's
office, and two were sent off to Lisbon that day.

On my way home I found a Portuguese half drunk,

killing his wife. He had bruised her, and laid her head open with a large stone; this occurred on the open road. As I was not in full strength from the effects of a recent accident, I could only gently interfere, and the brute persisted in his cruelty. A servant then came by on horseback who struck him with a good stout stick; but the fellow turned on him, and hit him with a great stone on the head. Thereupon two dragoons, who saw the whole affair, came up, and were going to cut the Portuguese down, when I begged them only to use the backs of their sabres, which they did sharply, and brought him into the village.

I have dined again with Lord Wellington, and at Castello Bom with Dr. Macgregor, whence I walked home with Colonel Colin Campbell at ten at night with a lantern, over rocks and streams. I have also seen Lord Wellington again, twice, about charges; but I understand I am not to go over to some Courts-martial which he has just fixed to take place in ten days, at two divisions, about forty miles from hence, but to stay here. He is shortly, as general report says, going to Cadiz or somewhere. At Lord Wellington's we had a curious conversation, about himself, Canning and his speeches, and Vetus's letters in the *Times*.* He joined in and indeed led the conversation, as if talking of persons and things he was not connected with, but seemed not satisfied with the Ministry, though he did not favour the opposition. He said he took in the *Courier* to know what government meant to do, &c., and as a decent paper to show General Castanos.

It has not lately been very cold; indeed, we had four or five charming days, but the rain has now begun again; but want of all books and society is the worst. The little conversation here beyond the topics of the day is of

---

* It was generally supposed that these celebrated letters, often compared to those of Junius, were written by Lord Wellesley.

a review a year old, or a pamphlet. The dress here is a
cap made of velvet, cloth, and fur, with a peak over the
eyes (that is a foraging cap); the handsomest are all of
fur, dark or grey fur, the former the best, with a broad
gold band and tassel on the top. With this is worn a
dress great coat, or plain, with military buttons, grey
pantaloons; this is the costume for dinners. Morning
dress—overalls, boots, and white or more generally fancy
waistcoats; in winter blue and black velvet, or cloth,
with fancy buttons of gold, and narrow stripes of gold as
an edging. There are four suttlers here, who sell everything, and we are, all things considered, well supplied.
We have one little Exeter-Change shop, but all very dear;
pepper and mustard dear, a small sauce bottle 7s., tea
three dollars a pound, cheese 4s. a pound, porter 5s. a
bottle, gin and brandy 7s. 6d., port wine 6s. 6d., milk 1s.
a quart, salt-butter 3s. a pound, sugar 1s. 8d., pork (no
other meat) 1s. 8d. a pound, oil 5s. a quart. These are
the prices here at *head-quarters.* Remember that distinction; not the national prices.

Head-Quarters, Frenada, December 31*st*, 1812.—For
the last month I have really been too busy to write. During the last week, before Lord Wellington went away, he
kept me hard at work, and left directions to endeavour
to get rid of all the cases pending for Courts-martial.
About thirty-two cases were made over to me, some of
nearly two years' standing. We have now a Court
sitting at Lisbon, one in the second division at Coria,
one in the seventh at Govea, and another here which I
attend myself four miles off at Fuentes d'Onore. I have
sent six to Lisbon, five to the seventh division, five to
the second, and intended taking seven myself to Fuentes
d'Onore; the rest have in some way been arranged.
Hitherto we have made little progress from the sickness,
which keeps back witnesses. I have only myself tried
one, and hope to finish to-morrow. One charge is of

that of a mad Commissary, whose trial was put off last week, on account of his being raving. He wrote to the Adjutant-general a mad letter, amongst other things telling him that he had ten thousand men, that he might drive all head-quarters to "Nebuchadnezzar's fiery furnace, where," he added, "Lord Wellington and you may sit at the head of the table." I served him myself with his notice of trial; he appeared very wild, and I have great doubts how he will behave.

I have had long instructions to write to the three other Judge-Advocates and summonses for witnesses to send to every regiment and to the Commandants about here, and that over and over again. As fast as one prisoner or witness got well, another became sick, and half the cases are now pending in this way. Then comes a long case to abstract for Lord Wellington; then an opinion for the Adjutant-general by return of post. For these three weeks I have been writing nearly seven hours a day, circulating copies of the charges to prisoners, to the Courts, and to the prosecutors, and much of my labour is thrown away by the sickness of the prisoners and witnesses. I have nine here in the Provost's hands for trial, and five are in the hospital— one just dead. There is one comfort, the reflection that such a press of business is never likely to recur. The *Gazette* and newspapers you sent me afforded me considerable amusement and comfort. Since Lord Wellington has been absent, Colonel Colin Campbell remains to do the honours and invite at the great house. I spent Christmas-day there, and have dined several times. Besides a good dinner and the best society, I there hear the latest news and get honour. The party is now very small.

After ten days of horrible damp, cold, rainy weather, we have now a thoroughly good genuine English frost, with an east wind, quite like an old friend in England;

D

but the sun has some power, so that it is like our frosts in February rather than Christmas. We see here very few of the officers. Just before Lord Wellington went he was angry at all the applications for leave of absence, observing, "A pretty army I have here! They all want to go home: but no more shall go except the sick." As the sick are now fast recovering, I may mention what I did not like to do a month ago, that the returns of the sick were then between nineteen and twenty thousand! You would have no idea of this. I have dined here with Major and Mrs. Scobell, the only lady here. I have also dined with Lord Aylmer, the acting Adjutant-general here, who is very civil. The Commissary, Mr. H——, keeps a good table, and often asks me. Dr. H—— is our doctor now at head-quarters—a sensible man. Lord March has lent me two volumes of Gold-smith's works.

Castanos' army went back in an orderly manner. Our Commissary reports well of them, and of the country, where, he says (that is, in the Tras os Montes), there is an abundance of bread, poultry, turkeys, &c., and of many things we have no notion of here. They have procured two turkeys at head-quarters this Christmas, and have had mince-meat in tins by the post from Lisbon.

We send to the woods for firing, and bring it home on the mules, and send out from four to six leagues, that is, from sixteen to twenty-four miles, for hay or straw. Ten pounds of straw a-day is the allowance for the animals, but I fear it will not hold out, as the villages are now nearly all emptied. We shall soon have to get little bundles of dry grass, which are already brought to our splendid market for sale. The Lamego wine is the only wine which I can drink with comfort, —it is a sort of port. The Sierra di Francia is the next best,—a much lighter wine, from the Sierras towards Madrid, from hence between thirty and forty miles off.

Lord Wellington, whom I saw every day for 'the last three or four days before he went, I like much in business affairs. He is very ready, and decisive, and civil, though some complain a little of him at times, and are much afraid of him. Going up with my charges and papers for instructions, I feel something like a boy going to school. I expect to have a long report to make on his return.

I hear a good account of Ballasteros's army: that it is better equipped than that of Castanos'. I wish it had done more. The French are supposed still to have about a hundred and eighty thousand men in the Peninsula. I do not believe their force in this neighbourhood has increased or diminished. Some have receded to Vittoria, but have been traced by the spies (of whom we have one constantly at Burgos) no further, nor have many supplies of men to any amount been discovered, I believe. We have some difficulty in getting fed; bread in the markets is about 9d. a pound; barley for the horses very scarce: we often go without for two days. A commissary-agent is now in Salamanca buying bread. The villages between Rodrigo and Salamanca, described in my journey, are, it is said, quite destroyed. We did much, the French the rest. Pork is the only thing abundant, about 1s. 6d. per pound, very rich but too fat, and the fat not firm; the flesh sweeter and richer than that of our pork, from the acorns on which the swine feed, and which are like chestnuts.

I was a little nervous at the first Court-martial, but it went off pretty well, and I got the whole over and brought away eight sides of notes in three hours. To-morrow I take my fair copy to be signed, &c. In my way to this Court-martial, Henry and I were puzzled by a river which seemed to be over our necks,—a deep hole off a rock. At last I made out a way zigzag, only about three feet deep; there was no one near or on either side; I should have had a swim, I am told, as people are sometimes drowned there. A ducking the first time of my appearance in public would have been awkward.

Two cases have just been brought in to me; they are for shooting natives, one an alcalde. Adieu.

CHAPTER III.

Arrival of the Gazette — More Courts-martial—The Mad Commissary—
Intentions of Lord Wellington—Social Amusements—Sporting—Wel-
lington's Fox-hounds — His Stud — A Dinner at the Commander-in-
Chief's—Number of Courts-martial—Anecdotes of Wellington.

Head-quarters, Frenada, Jan. 3, 1813.
My dear M——,

In hopes of giving you letters every week, I must
seize every odd half-hour to write in, and you must not
be nice as to my writing, &c., as my hand is quite tired
of the regular official style, and my fingers cold, for we
still have fine, clear, frosty weather; but in the middle
of the day it is very pleasant.

Pray thank John very much for his parcel of newspapers, and especially for that of the 17th December,
with the *Gazette*, &c., and the glorious news. I was the
only person here with a paper of the 17th. Head-
quarters had only that of the evening of the 16th with
the *Gazette*; and though this was, in fact, much the same,
this was an event—and I sent mine up to Colonel
Campbell, by his desire, for his dinner-party at head-
quarters. It has been in constant request ever since.

All the Guerilla party reports here state, that a body
of French cavalry has left Spain for France, for some
purpose. They say that from three to four thousand
men are gone; this agrees with your story; but our
Portuguese Quarter-Master, from his spies, reports otherwise. The forces in this neighbourhood are now but

small; about four hundred men in Salamanca, which, by-the-by, has been much plundered; and the English dollars, which they extorted from the hungry troops by their high prices, pretty well squeezed out of them. At Segovia there are only one thousand men, more at Valladolid, and a force at Madrid, and thus dispersed about; but as to their being starved, their country is much better, I believe, than ours; and as I have already told you, our Commissary goes to Salamanca for bread. The light division near this place, and troop of Horse Artillery, have had scarcely any corn for their horses for the three last weeks, and the cavalry will not be fit to act much before April and May.

Yesterday a great event occurred here—the arrival of a Guerilla chief, who was formerly a sort of smuggler or robber. This man, whose name, I believe, is Sumeil, attacked a French party, carrying despatches from King Joseph to France, at a village near Valladolid, at twelve o'clock at night. He came in upon the French by surprise, and the plan succeeded. The despatches were seized, some of them on the person of the courier, but the most material in a secret place in the pummel of a saddle. A little spring in the buckle of the brass ornament discovered a keyhole, and in the saddle was the pocket to conceal the papers. They are principally in cipher, but some have been made out, and are, I understand, important. I have heard the contents of only one letter from King Joseph to the family in France, full of complaints of want of money and much distress; he states that he cannot get a dollar. From eighty to a hundred prisoners were taken by the party. These prisoners were French, and two English officers were released. The French were much irritated, and sent eleven squadrons of cavalry after the Guerilla chief, but he got off with most of his prisoners, booty, despatches, and party. Only one or two of the officers, and a few of the Guerilla privates, have yet arrived here, but more, with the prisoners, are expected shortly. Sumeil expects to be made a General for this. He was at first very shy of suffering the aide-de-camp and Colonel Campbell to look at his despatches, desiring to show them to Lord Wellington in person; nor could he consent to give up the most important, until General O'Lalor, who was at Ciudad Rodrigo, was sent for, and explained matters to him. I was to have met them at head-quarters at dinner the day of their arrival, but they were busily engaged at cards when sent for; and said they were tired, and declined going out to dinner. I was very sorry for this, as it would have been curious to see their manners at a formal dinner.

I have sent out my mules and Portuguese to forage. They now are obliged to go so far for it that they cannot get home by night, and soon, I fear, must stay out some days. I must get another horse; Colonel C——has a handsome Spanish horse to sell, strong, showy, and, considering the price of horses here, not very dear, two hundred and fifty dollars; it is a sort of a Rubens, sleek, black, manège horse, with a fine, thick, curved, sleek, black neck.

I take my morning walk daily, from eight till nine, to secure some exercise, whilst Henry lights my fire and gets breakfast ready. Instead of the gravel walk at Sheen or in Lincoln's Inn gardens, it is a stroll over the rocks, down towards the Coa river, which is almost two miles from hence, and in parts is wild and picturesque; large masses of rock, rounded by the weather, stunted trees, stone-wall enclosures, a succession of ravines, and ruined fortified villages on the hills at a distance; for Castello Bom, Castello Mendas, Castello Rodrigues, and Almeyda, which, as well as Guarda, are in sight from the rocky hill, half a mile from hence. Behind the whole, the sierras of Portugal and Spain, now generally covered with snow.

By these means, and with a hasty ride or walk now and
then in the middle of the day, my health is certainly
better. The work, except on account of health, I have
no sort of objection to: I only lament the delay in the
proceedings, on account of the sickness of the prisoners
and witnesses. However, I may have been of some use
in law lecturing, and helping the other Deputy Judge-
Advocates; and no trouble has been spared by me in
facilitating matters.

If the news from Russia be good to the extent supposed,
it is thought here that the French will withdraw from
hence this spring, at least behind the Ebro. This, however, I much doubt; though it seems agreed that, at any
rate, we are not in a state to follow, without very great
disadvantage, and almost destruction to our cavalry.

January the 4th.—There are strong reports, as I have
said, that the French are retiring; but General O'Lalor,
whom I have just seen, tells me his accounts are otherwise,
and that no French have left, or are leaving Spain; on
the contrary, he assured me that the intercepted letters
from Soult state that the contest will, in the next campaign,
be between the Douro and the Tagus. D'Aranda de
Duero is therefore to be fortified, and made a good depôt,
until the Emperor can send reinforcements enough to
enable them to enter Portugal. The French head-
quarters are at Madrid, nor does it appear that there is
any intention at present to give it up, though the Spaniards thought otherwise from some letters of Soult, who
ordered some of his men, detachments of his corps, and
letters, to be sent to him from Valencia, but this seems
to be only to complete his own corps. General O'Lalor
told me that a muleteer of Paget's had just arrived from
Bayonne, with a pass, which he showed me, for him to
return to Portugal as Sir Edward Paget's muleteer. This
man says the French on the frontiers were told that our
retreat was a rout, our loss immense, and that sixteen

thousand prisoners had been taken, who were said to be on the road; he added that many were fools enough to go several leagues to see them, and found they were about two thousand five hundred; they also reported that the Commander-in-Chief, Lord Paget, was taken.*

We are trying to send French gazettes of the Russian business to the French army, to give some of them a better notion of affairs in that quarter, as it seems the armies hear little or nothing from France, and at long intervals.

January the 6th.—I am just setting out for Fuentes to try my mad Commissary, and from the fear of not having time before post on my return, I must now close my letter.

Head-Quarters, Frenada, January 16th, 1813.—I was so much occupied last week that I could not find time to give you one of my usual scrawls before the post-day. The business of the mad Commissary's was finished in two long days last week, but I have had a long job in copying it fair, as he put in a half-mad defence of five sheets in folio. He is now off for Lisbon. I have bought Colonel C——'s horse for two hundred and fifty dollars.

Our last accounts from Lord Wellington are Cadiz, the 8th. He was going to Lisbon on the 9th or 10th. He has taken the command of the Spaniards; and is expected here on the 23rd. Lord Fitzroy Somerset seems much pleased with Cadiz; I do not know whether Lord Wellington is. The Prince of Orange is not yet returned from Oporto. He has been very much fêted and entertained; there is dancing every night, and he is much pleased. Lord March is just returned from thence; Colonel G—— from Seville; so we all begin to re-assemble here. I have just been making out on a large sheet the

---

* Meaning Lieut.-General Sir Edward Paget, second in command, who was taken prisoner in the retreat. Lord Paget, afterwards Earl of Uxbridge, now Marquis of Anglesea, was not in the Peninsula at this time.

states of the Courts-martial for Lord Wellington. They
are thirty-one in number, which are now going on, just
finished, or which are to proceed when witnesses can be
collected. At present my place is no sinecure.

The French, they say, have been for some time in
motion here, but I believe only to forage, &c.; their last
movements are southward of Madrid and towards Seville
again, but this is thought to be either a feint or to be for
the sake of supplies.

Doctor M'Gregor has been a tour to visit the sick; of
whom I am sorry to say many have died; more than I
was aware of. He has been as far as Oporto.

I have gone on very smoothly with my Courts-martial.
General V—— is the President, and has been very civil.
They are all light infantry, and have been very attentive,
orderly, and obedient.

January 17*th.*—The house which I now occupy belongs
to the Portuguese lad who is in my service, and who is
about eighteen. It is a droll circumstance to live in the
house of your own servant, who receives six dollars a
month, and is a tolerable groom. These reverses are here
very frequent in the fortunes of this class of people. He
owns three houses here, such as they are—stone barns;
and his family had sheep, goats, and land.

There is plenty of game about, and we now get wood-
cocks frequently, shot by the officers, very good hares,
better, I think, than in England, a few good snipes and
plovers, and a very few partridges; the latter are very
wild. We have had, off and on, frost for this month and
more, and some very fine days, others like a London
November fog, a little snow, and now and then a day's
rain; but in eight hours again, from a sudden change of
wind, all dry and frost. The sun, when out, makes the
mid-day very pleasant; and though the winds are very
cold, and produce very hard ground and thick ice for the
time in a very short period, yet the ice does not continue,

as in England, and accumulate. It never gets much thicker than it is in one night with a cold wind, and in the daytime the ground is soft; the cold, therefore, though for a time very sharp, certainly cannot be near so intense in reality as in England. We go to bed sometimes with the ground entirely wet at eleven o'clock, and at six in the morning find there has been a very hard frost, which is then going off again.

The population here is very considerably thinned, and there is much less land in cultivation than formerly; the people remaining have generally lost their flocks and their animals for agriculture. Few have now means of ploughing and manuring. The vineyards are generally in a very neglected state also; not manured or in any way attended to, and eaten close down by our hungry animals. Yet the labour required is so moderate, and the light soil seems so productive, that the country might very soon recover itself; but we take the oxen over the whole country, buy up, and eat up everything. Out of our reach, in the Tras os Montes, are plenty of poultry, sheep, turkeys, &c. The Portuguese, naturally lazy, never repair the damages of war, never rebuild, clean out, or set to work to bring things round. They despair, and only just work to supply our market with onions, 4d. each; eggs, 3d. each; potatoes alone rather cheap at 2d. the pound; pork, 1s. 6d. the pound, and good. The Spaniards, on the contrary, begin, very soon after the armies go, to restore; they put on their tiles, rebuild their walls, and especially whitewash the inside of their houses; they collect their cooking-vessels, and get to work on their farms. The peasantry recover themselves much more and much faster than the Portuguese, but yet they have not in any one place suffered so much and so often as this part of Portugal has; and in this town they are pretty much as lazy as the other.

The 20th.—A very interesting case of a poor deserter

whom we tried yesterday at Fuentes, I must copy out
fair to carry over to the general president for his signature to-morrow. The deserter, poor fellow! deserted for
love to the Spaniards, with a Spanish girl from the
neighbourhood of Madrid whom he had brought away
with him. She had been most honest and faithful in
very trying scenes during the retreat. On being ordered
to send her off by his Captain, he appeared to have had
no intention of going over to the French. I was not
aware of the merit of his story till I copied the whole out
fairly. It was translated in broken bits, by a not very
skilful interpreter. Three deserters came in here yesterday; they are Flemings. They report that part of the
French cavalry are gone to France, and that all the cars
round Salamanca have been put in requisition to carry off
the sick from the hospital there. But this does not prove
much, as it would at any rate be an unsafe place, and out
of their line of defence next campaign. They state that
the sick have been very numerous, and Salamanca well
plundered.

I have been one morning over to Almeyda to breakfast with the governor and see the town. At breakfast
I met a sawny Spanish signora, with a crying, poor-look-
ing child : she breakfasted on beefsteaks, onions, partridges, and wine, and did nothing all day. Almeyda is
twelve miles off. I rode thither on my new horse. He
is just such a horse as you would admire, prancing,
showy, sleek, like a Flemish picture of a horse, rather
clumsy and heavy; but he went well and quietly. Almeyda is in ruins ; a mere heap of rubbish ! The works
are being repaired, and much is already done ; but there
is yet a great deal to do, and the workmen, though well
watched, seem very lazy. There are very good shops
among the ruins for the materials of all articles of wearing apparel; these from Oporto, and not dear ; cloth and
baize of all sorts, linen, stockings, but not a cup and

saucer to be had, or a drinking-glass. Most of the new work at Almeyda is at present only earth—slanting so that you might run up in a storm, I think ; but the masonry is going on, and it would cost some men to storm it, if we defend it. At present there is only a Portuguese garrison.

Head-Quarters, Frenada, January 23rd, 1813.—I do not quite feel as I did in England, nor can I make out that others do either. There is a languor and laziness which seem in some degree catching from the natives, as they have it in such perfection. We have had almost constant frost or cold, fog and sleet, but in general clear cold days ever since Christmas. It seems that we are likely to have some snow, which hitherto we have only on the sierras and hills (where it lies almost constantly), except a very few storms of snow which melted as it fell ; and then rain in February ; then some warm days in March and in April, with very cold mornings and nights, and some very cold days again, even so late as in May at times. By-the-by, our English post from all the different parts of the army, to each other, and to Lisbon, is now in general in very good order, which saves me much trouble in my extensive correspondence relative to the Courts-martial. I have now also got through the great worry of the number of cases which came upon me at once, and, though fully employed, business comes more regularly. I have persevered in being civil and useful as far as I could to every one, never objecting to anything, answering all queries, and taking everything upon myself. I endeavour to model the whole as it was arranged in England, before the Adjutant-general's offices did two-thirds of the business of Judge-Advocate. As I have no clerk, and am not allowed a soldier, this at times presses me hard, but the greatest stress is now over, though new cases come in regularly. I yesterday sent in one against a Lieutenant-colonel, with six charges and

thirty-seven witnesses. I have another Commissary just
come in here as a prisoner, for purposely burning down a
house, a mischievous freak, when drunk.

I now dine out about three or four times in the week,
generally once or twice at head-quarters—and occasionally
with Major and Mrs. Scobell, who give very pleasant
little dinners, and tender meat, and a loo party afterwards. He is a clever man, in the Quarter-Master-
general's department, and has the command of the corps
of guides, and the arrangement of the English post
through the country.

The report current now is, that next campaign is to
be in camp, and not in towns and villages, as Lord Wellington wants to keep the army more together than he
can do in quarters; and unless he goes into camp, the
other Generals also leave their divisions and come into
the towns. At any rate, it will not be as it was last
year, when the men went into camp in February and
March, as, from general rumour, the army will not be in
a state to move much before the end of April; nearly
one-third are still sick, and this state of things mends
now but slowly; this I observe from the general daily
state of the whole army made for Lord Wellington, which
is kept most perfectly. The horses will not be ready till
they have had a month's green food in March and April;
straw, bad hay, and a little Indian corn do not suit them
for very active service.

I want a neat lantern sent out, to go out after dark in
these horrible villages, where if you go only a hundred
yards in the dark you step from a rock half up your legs
in mud.

There is a shocking set of servants at head-quarters;
idle, drunken English servants and soldiers, almost all
bad, and the Portuguese are every day running off with
something or other from their masters and others.
There has been no chaplain here for these last eight or

nine months, or any notice taken in any manner of Sunday! It used to be, I hear, a very regular and imposing thing to attend divine service performed out of doors with hats off, but the people must now think we have no religion at all, as almost every public business goes on nearly the same as on ordinary days. The English soldiers, however, keep it as a holiday, though the Portuguese will many of them work, particularly after three o'clock. We have had a glee or two with the aides-de-camp of the Prince of Orange and some others. There is also a Spanish Commissary who sings and plays the guitar very well. I wish my violoncello were more portable, and, with a flute or two, we should have a little music now and then here, in the evenings. They have asked me to send for a collection of glees.

People here are all very sore about the Americans and our taken frigates. I think we deserve it a little. Our contempt for our old descendants and half brothers has always rather disgusted me, and with some English is carried so far as not to be bearable. This reverse may set matters right. The Americans have faults enough; we should allow them their merits. Our sailors all thought the Americans would not dare to look them in the face. I think the army rather rejoice, and laugh aside at all this falling on the navy, as they bullied so much before. I will not write to you of northern or English news, for it would be absurd; you would, if I did, receive comments and observations on what was nearly forgotten, or entirely altered, by the time my letter reached you. I keep this paper under my business heap, and take it out and scribble when anything occurs. Lord Wellington is to arrive to-day; and I must get up my lesson for to-morrow, so adieu!

Tuesday.—Lord Wellington arrived last night at six o'clock. I saw him with the rest who happened to be in the market-place when he came. He was looking well.

There is a great quantity of game around us, and the sportsmen supply their tables. It is not mere sport here, but more like the case of Robinson Crusoe, a matter of necessity. Nearly all our luxuries are thus obtained. Commissary H——, two days since, went across the Coa for about five hours, and brought home five hares, four couple of cocks, three snipes, one partridge, and a rabbit. All these animals are remarkably good here, except the partridges, which are nothing in comparison to ours, and I think not so good as the French. Lord Wellington, except presents now and then, buys up all we can get —gives 8s. for a hare, and so on. Turkeys are only to be had thirty miles off: the price, which has been 25s., is now 14s. Powder and shot are very scarce, only a little to be had now and then at Almeyda. This you will think at the head-quarters of sixty thousand men rather strange, but the same stuff which kills men will not bring down birds. We have three odd sorts of packs of hounds here, and the men hunt desperately: firstly, Lord Wellington's, or, as he is called here, the Peer's; these are fox-hounds, about sixteen couple; they have only killed one fox this year, and that was what is called mobbed. These hounds, for want of a huntsman, straggle about and run very ill, and the foxes run off to their holes in the rocks on the Coa. Captain W—— goes out, stops the holes over-night, halloos, and rides away violently. The ground is a light gravel and rock all over the country. From a hard rock sometimes the horse gets up to his belly in wet gravelly sand; thus we have many horses lamed, and some bad falls. The next set of hounds are numerous,—greyhounds. The Com-missary-general, Sir R. Kennedy, is a great man in this way, and several others. And thirdly, the Capitan Mor here, that is the principal man of the place, has an old poacher in his establishment, with a dozen terriers, mongrels, and ferrets, and he goes out with the officers to get rabbits. Lord Wellington has a good stud of about eight hunters; he rides hard, and only wants a good gallop, but I understand knows nothing of the sport, though very fond of it in his own way. There will soon, I hear, be good trout-fishing in the Coa and in the streams in the ravines near it.

Wednesday, January 27th.—It has happened just as I expected; I have no time to add more, for I have three new cases to draw charges in, and most troublesome ones too : one of four fellows, old commissariat clerks I suppose turned off, who have been about the country living by their wits, extorting provisions, forage, &c., from the Spaniards, by frauds, false passports, &c., under pretence of acting for the English and Portuguese Commissariat. There are thirty-seven enclosures sent to me, papers taken upon them, all in Spanish, in general badly written, and no translation. The case, it is to be feared, will never be proved. I have got General O'Lalor to help me in this case. In short, my hands are full again; and my report of the old stories not made out. We occupy from Coria, Guinaldo, Vizeu, Covilhaon, and even almost to Coimbra; hospitals at Celerico, Vizu, Coimbra a few, Abrantes, and Santarem. I fear my Court-martial will be moved farther off. Some additional attached Spaniards are to have their head-quarters at Fuentes d'Onore to be about his Excellency, now that he takes the command of the whole generals, &c., and General Vandeleur and the famous Caçadores are to move from thence in consequence; the arrangements, however, are not yet completed.

Head-Quarters, Frenada, February 2nd, 1813.—Lord Wellington is returned in high spirits and great good-humour with every one; and, in spite of the number of deaths here, which are very formidable (between four and five hundred every week for the last six), declares that he shall take the field this year with nearly forty thousand

E

British, and, on the whole, with a hundred and fifty thousand of one sort or other.

General Vandeleur is to go to Fuente Guinaldo, and the Courts-martial will in future be there. It is about twenty-four miles off. I must sleep out always, and shall thus lose one or two days' post; this will be inconvenient to me, and just now to the service, but it cannot be avoided. The General is very good-humoured, and we are very good friends; he has offered me a quarter, and a dinner, if I will bring my bed. At present our weather is colder than ever, but generally clear frost; the wind is excessively sharp. The ice yesterday on the road would bear my horse; and the thermometer, at seven in the evening, was four degrees below the freezing point; at night sometimes it is much colder.

Two packets have just arrived; the last brought Lord Wellington the last good news from Wilna. I have dined once at head-quarters since Lord Wellington's return, with Sumeil the Guerilla chief, looking like a dirty German private dragoon, in a smart new cavalry jacket, on one side of me, and Dr. Curtis, the Catholic head of the Salamanca college (who has been sent off from Salamanca very lately), opposite to me. The Spanish General O'Lalor treated Sumeil like a child, told him what to do and eat; but he had, I conclude, dined long before, for he ate little or nothing. Dr. Curtis seemed to be a clever, sensible, gentleman-like priest. He said the French knew immediately of Lord Wellington's absence, but were not clear about it, and very anxious in their inquiries to ascertain the fact. General Hill's corps, who did not share in the early siege of Rodrigo last year in January, nor the wet bad work at Badajoz, are by far the most healthy part of the army, and, next to them, the light division here. The fifth and seventh, near Lamego, are the worst, and the Guards (the new comers) very bad. General Hill has only about fourteen hundred in the hospital, and about seven thousand fit for service. I suppose we shall have an active campaign next year, if the whole be not put an end to by peace, which is not improbable, if the Allies are not too unreasonable in consequence of their successes. If Austria will join in dictating the terms with Russia, Prussia, and Great Britain, they should be very good for Europe; but if the devil Bonaparte be driven hard, he will rouse himself, appeal to the vanity of the French, and recoil upon us stronger than ever. The Gil Blas set of swindlers who went about Spain with false papers and passes, raising the wind under pretence of getting supplies for the British and Portuguese commissariat service (one was a German, two Spaniards, and the fourth a Portuguese), I much fear it will not be easy to convict.

February the 3rd.—You must excuse my writing, for it is done at all odd moments, as a relaxation from all my formal letters of business, which require a good deal of method and order in a small compass not to get into scrapes, such as sending witnesses to wrong places, &c. As I have Courts sitting here at Fuente Guinaldo in the light division; at Lamego, in the fifth; at Maimento, in the seventh; at Alter de Chaon; at Coria, in the second division; at Maimento de Biera, in the third; and at Lisbon; letters coming at all hours of the day about each, a witness wanted here, a difficulty arising there, and so on; I can only get on by keeping a book, in which I instantly put down the exact state of everything, and keep copies of all my letters till the business is over; and I make it a rule, if possible, to answer every letter by return of post, as the only way not to get in arrear. I am very glad that I persuaded my Court at Fuentes d'Onore to have patience, and let me take down all the long love story I told you of, of the deserter Prang Neigabauer. It was quite a pretty

E 2

story. Lord Wellington pardoned him, from the good character of his regiment, and that which the Colonel gave him. The Prince of Orange is returned, and we are all here again assembled in this magnificent town!

5 *o'clock.* — I have been sent for twice to-day by Lord Wellington, besides twice last night, and have so much on my hands about Spaniards, Portuguese, and English, that I cannot add more.

Head-Quarters, Frenada, February 7th, 1813.—There never were known so many Courts-martial in this army as at the present moment, and as I have the whole direction of them all, I really scarcely know where to turn, and my fingers are quite fatigued, as well as my brains, with the arrangements and difficulties as to witnesses, &c. I sent out seventeen letters yesterday, and to-day I have one case of thirteen prisoners who have been committing every sort of outrage on their march here. Lord Wellington is now much more easy with me, and seems to trust to me more. Yesterday I was pleased when he said, " If your friends knew what was going on here, they would think you had no sinecure. And how do you suppose I was plagued when I had to do it nearly all myself? "

He seemed to feel relieved, and of course I could not but feel gratified. I can assure you, however, that we have none of us much idle time. Dr. M'Gregor has seven hundred medical men to look after. The Quarter-Master-general, all the arrangement of the troops, clothing, &c. The Adjutant-general, daily returns of the whole, constantly checked by an eye which finds out even a wrong casting-up of numbers in the totals. Lord Wellington reads and looks into everything. He hunts almost every other day, and then makes up for it by great diligence and instant decision on the intermediate days. He works until about four o'clock, and then, for an hour or two, parades with any one whom he wants to talk to, up and down the little square of Frenada (amidst all the chattering Portuguese) in his grey great coat.

General Alava, whom I have seen lately much more about Spanish business, is a very gentleman-like, and appears to me to be a clever man.

We have had constant frost hitherto; but I fear the rain is going now to begin. Some of the days lately have been delightful, like the frosty days in England at times at the end of February, with a fine clear warm sun in the daytime.

I have just heard of five German deserters, brought in to the Provost here; and shall, I suppose, have to try them. They were taken on the other side of Rodrigo by the Spaniards; they are just come out to us from England. Don Julian's cavalry are very useful in this way, and very active. The Cortes want to encourage farming in the country, and will give land to any wounded soldiers of the allied armies, English as well as natives, on condition of building and living on the spot.

General Wimpfen, one of the Chief's new Spanish staff, is arrived, and will be stationed with us.

At Ciudad Rodrigo they are going to set up a Spanish newspaper, which is to come out once in a week : I mean to take it in. My new black horse goes on hitherto very well; I like him much ; but use him little. Whenever I can, I get a gallop and a trot for an hour on the common just close by, and return home to write again.

Excuse this stupid letter. I am very tired and must to bed.

On Thursday, the 11th, I go to Fuente Guinaldo, and shall probably sleep there, at General Vandeleur's.

CHAPTER IV.

More Courts-martial—Bal Masqué—Anecdotes of Wellington—Songs in his praise—Spanish Banditti—Excesses of the Army—Carnival—More Anecdotes of the Duke—The Staff—Grand Entertainment at Head-quarters—Wellington's opinion on Affairs at Home—Murder of an Officer—General Craufurd.

Frenada, February 12, 1813.
8 o'clock, Friday night.

My dear M——,

On my return from Fuente Guinaldo I found instructions for two new Courts-martial in Lord Wellington's rough pencil notes,—a broad scroll in pencil in one corner, " Refer all this to the Judge Advocate," meaning me to draw charges, &c. I must now tell you of my expedition to Fuente Guinaldo. We were to have tried the Commissary for burning a house down, but by my advice he offered to pay all the damage done to General Alava, the Spanish agent here, and in consequence to be forgiven if it was paid in time. This was the best for the Spaniards, the owners, and a tolerably sharp punishment for a man whose only lawful pay is 7s. 6d. a-day, the damage being near fifteen hundred dollars. The night before the trial he had not raised the money. I went to Lord Wellington to know what I should do, as the witnesses were all ready. He told me to give him till Monday next, and have all the witnesses rationed and kept till that time at Guinaldo. Suspecting that this would be my instruction, I had got another case ready for the Court there.

About seven o'clock, after a crust of bread and a glass of rum and milk for breakfast, off we went, Henry and I, for Fuente Guinaldo, and at the same time I sent one of my Portuguese men with my mattress and blankets, coverings, corn and hay for my horses, to meet us there, Henry carrying my papers, Mutiny Act, testaments, and all writing implements, &c., for my Court-martial. The morning threatened much, as the frost is just broken up; but we got there dry and in time, and I found my way without any blunder, which, as the road was entirely across open downs, or through woods without inhabitants, and full of cross tracks, was some merit; I had, however, applied to Captain Wood, the hunter, who knows all the country well, for instructions.

We arrived at Guinaldo in two hours, finished a case and tried a man for shooting a Portuguese, acquitted him of murder, but found him guilty of very disorderly conduct, and sentenced him to receive eight hundred lashes. I then walked round the town, looked into the church, and came back; wrote the whole out fair on six sides of folio paper; dined with the president at six, had a hospitable reception; and in the evening went to a sort of frolicsome masked ball, given extra on account of the Courts-martial. As the General went, I accompanied him. There were all the *equivoque belles* of Guinaldo, and all the light infantry officers, many in disguise and masquerade; some as females, and one as a Spanish farmer, the regular dress. We were all struck with the becoming appearance and picturesque style of the costume. One or two of the ladies were dressed as officers, and so on. The ball went on very well for some time, but the two ladies who were the leading beauties of the evening quarrelled, and the harmony was disturbed. At ten I went home, and left the party half tipsy and rather riotous, so that it was time for Generals and Judges to retire. The Court-room was my quarter. This

morning before breakfast I read over my fair copy of the
evidence, &c., with the General. He signed it, gave me
some breakfast, and I set off home, on a very threatening
day which was as good as it promised; my cloak, however, kept me nearly dry.

Fuente Guinaldo is nearer the Sierra de Gutta, and
several degrees colder than we are here at Frenada, though
we are many, many degrees colder than Lisbon. The
Spanish staff are now all arrived, but scarcely a Spaniard
amongst them—all foreigners. General Wimpfen, a
Swiss; General O'Donoghue, Irish; and so of others.
They all dined two days ago at Lord Wellington's.

Tell John, in answer to his inquiry, that with regard
to the campaign and the siege of Burgos, it is a question
much argued and discussed. Some say we should never
have lost time by going to Madrid, and that was the
mistake; some that if we had taken Burgos, as we
should have done but for the very bad weather, all would
have gone right. General O'Lalor, however, told me he
thought that would have made no difference, but that if
the French chose to give up the South, and unite against
us ninety thousand strong, we must have been off just
the same even though Burgos had been taken.

My quarter at Fuente Guinaldo, having no window,
is rather cool, but being in Spain, is clean. The church
is a fine building, and the town not quite broken up;
I suppose we shall move there next. To-night is a
play-night in the gay light division at Galegos, and
Lord Wellington was to have gone there, but the perpetual rain will probably prevent him. He meant to
ride there, a distance of ten miles, at night. Had it
been very fine I might have been almost tempted to
take my mattress round that way, and go once to the
theatre, which all say is very tolerable in regard to
acting, scenery, &c., the whole carried on by the light
division in a chapel at Galegos. I was not a little

surprised to see common country dances very tolerably performed last night at Guinaldo, and even Sir Roger de Coverley.

Two or three days ago I was somewhat puzzled, when, upon my pointing out the sentence of a Court-martial as illegal, Lord Wellington said, "Well, do write a letter for me to the president, and I will sign it, and it shall be sent back for revision." I did not know his style, but my letter was fortunately approved of. I had yesterday a visit from Colonel ——, of the Engineers, begging for a favourable report upon the case of a complaint against a Captain of artillery; I suppose people think I have some weight in Lord Wellington's decisions, but that is by no means the case. He thinks and acts quite for himself; *with* me, if he thinks I am right, but not otherwise. I have not, however, found what Captain —— told me I should find, that Lord Wellington immediately determines against anything that is suggested to him. On the contrary, I think he is reasonable enough, only often a little hasty in ordering trials, when an acquittal must be the consequence. This, in my opinion, does harm, as I would have the law punish almost always when it is put in force.

Wednesday, 17th.—I have heard no news at all: still strong reports that the French cavalry are partly gone from hence to France; but I cannot ascertain that they are actually removed beyond Vittoria, and that may be only for forage, as our cavalry are wide apart and dispersed. The first division, under General Bock, is at and below Coimbra, near the sea, where I have just fixed a Court-martial to try a set of men of the 9th and 87th for most outrageous conduct on the march to join the army. Lord Wellington has had the whole complaints against this party along the road written out, to send home, with an official copy of his letter, as he finds

that an account of the matter has travelled home, and is
quoted as a specimen of the conduct of our army on the
march. The first division of cavalry is, on the other
hand, at Alter de Chaon, towards Castello Branco, and is
all much dispersed; General Hill, with the second division, Coria; sixth division, Cea; fifth, Lamego; third,
Maimento de Beira; seventh, Maimento; light, Fuente
Guinaldo. These are the head-quarters of the troops.
Marshal Beresford is better, and his wound nearly
healed; he talks of soon joining; his head-quarters will
be Villa Formosa. I now see Lord Wellington almost
daily on business; he one day fell into a passion about
the Courts-martial for not doing their duty, by acquit-
ting and recommending to mercy, &c., and also about
officers commanding parties not being attentive. He
has always been civil to me, though at times quick and
hasty in business. I nearly got into a scrape by saying
a good word for Captain ——, merely from his good
character, as I did not personally know him. However, Lord Wellington so far acquiesced, that he said I
need not draw the charge as yet; but he should send
him word that if the village in question were not satisfied for their forage and bullocks in a week, he should
either have him tried or sent home.

I have just got a letter of reprimand to send out,
according to a written memorandum from Lord Wellington; a little slap at a deputy of mine, and greater at
the Court-martial, with directions how they should act.
Adieu.

*Monday Evening, Head-Quarters, Frenada, February
22nd,* 1813.—On getting up in the morning yesterday,
I said to myself for the first time these two months,
" Well, I do think I have no business to-day, and will
write to M——." In two hours' time, however, before
I had finished my breakfast, and read one of Vetus's
letters, in came three new cases, and old General O'Lalor

to tell me he had sent me a case to try at Guinaldo—a man charged with shooting a Spanish girl through the door, because she would not give him some chestnuts! The wanton outrages of our people are quite extraordinary. There are four poor fellows to be hung this week in the second division; one for desertion, and three for a burglary near Coria about a fortnight since. For the sake of immediate example I hastened the case, by giving full instructions to the Deputy Judge-Advocate there. The men were tried immediately, and three are to be hung to-morrow. The Commissary charged with burning the house was at last let off for a large sum of money. I was very glad when it was settled, for I had more trouble about it than if he had been tried and hung ten times over. An overwhelming heap of Spanish proceedings has just reached me about the man for shooting the poor girl; and yet I have very little doubt, when the Court meets, I shall have much difficulty in proving that the man shot her, and that she is dead. I go over for that purpose the day after to-morrow.

During the last two or three days the weather has been delightful—quite a mild south-west breeze, with a clear sun; but this was, I heard, too unusual to last. I like "Vetus" much, and agree with him in most things; but his style is not by a good deal to be compared with Junius. In parts there are considerable blunders, and often confusion and want of clearness; but there are some curious stolen cuts, if facts. I have just heard from General O'Lalor that we have been attacked at Bejar by a party of French, and have beaten them back. It was the second division, General Hill's corps, who were concerned, and I believe the 50th regiment principally. I am told no great loss, but know no particulars. You will hear more of it from the papers than I can tell you. It is still said that we are to encamp and bivouac this next campaign. We are now consuming our last stock of hay—two great stacks, which have been saved by Lord Wellington's orders at Almeyda. After that we must buy reaping-hooks, and try to cut grass before the green corn forage comes in; and though I can see a plain difference already in the colour of the hills, and the young green corn and spring grass are here and there making a show, there is very little to be got to eat yet in that way.

We have still many sick, and the doctors do not take better care of themselves than of their patients, for no less than five medical men have died at Ciudad Rodrigo since we have been in quarters here. The French have got all about the part of the country near General Hill, near Nava, Morguende, Mentrida, &c., and are moving; but I do not expect anything important for some time. Some say the French will begin this campaign; and I rather hope they may. The 10th Dragoons have arrived, I hear from every one, in the highest style and in excellent order. This is very good news.

We have three Spanish songs in honour of Wellington, one rather gone by now: "The Retreat of Marmont," " Ahe Marmont, onde vai, Marmont," a very pretty air; the other was composed at Cadiz lately when Lord Wellington was there. I suppose you have them in England. Moretti of Cadiz is the composer. One of them is good, and the other very well. Lord Wellington sits and hears his own praises in Spanish with considerable coolness, and calls for it himself at times.

February 23rd, *Tuesday Morning.*—Just a few lines more, and but a few, as I have just been with Lord Wellington, and, having got rid of one batch of papers, have returned with another. I hear the affair at Bejar, or Banos, in the sierras north of Placentia, was not much. We had six taken and a few wounded. It is supposed to have been a French party for provisions and plunder, as they wander about for these purposes, and to have been no serious movement. Our men got a position first, which the French tried to get, at Bejar. We had no cavalry, or an attempt might have succeeded to turn the French party; but without this assistance the 56th drove back the French, and saved Bejar and that country. The 71st were also there, and concerned.

Lord March is just returned from a flag-of-truce excursion to the French. He fell in with their pickets half a league from Ledesma, where the French seemed in force. They were very civil. He dined with a General Goutier, or some such name, and stayed about four or five hours. Their men and cavalry looked well, and clothing very fair; accoutrements, &c., bad and slovenly; horses in good condition; but he concludes that he saw the best, for he found they knew of his approach five leagues off. They kept away all the Spaniards, who were getting round him, and were particularly violent against the canaille, the Guerillas. The latter were close upon the French. He passed them very near the town. They abused Sumeil; said he would rob even the English, and would not believe he dined at Lord Wellington's table. They hoped to see the English in a month, they said. His five hussars and his trumpeter were surrounded by eighty men in a trice, and all communication cut off, and a thousand questions asked of course, but little given in answer. The French officer and escort of five dragoons, who escorted Lord March on his departure, would not go above half a league, for fear of the Guerillas, and was half inclined to accept Lord March's offer to let his trumpeter and some men see him back, with a party of the Guerillas; but at last he said he had a good horse, and galloped back. I do not know what Lord March went about; some say on Sir Edward Paget's affairs.

Guinaldo, February 24*th*, 1813.—From the blunder

of General O——, here I am, after a wet ride, with no
Court-martial to-day, and nothing to do. The consequence is, I must stay to-morrow also, when I really
hope to get this business over, for I have plenty to do at
home. Marshal Marmont had the quarter I occupy
when he was here, as well as Lord Wellington. The
former shut the whole up, and used candles all day.
The latter got on as well as he could in the dark, and
used the General's bedroom, which is rather a better
room, as his dining-room. The owner was once a man
rich in flocks, herds, and lands and houses, and has
another good house at Ciudad Rodrigo. At present I
take it his worldly goods are not sufficient to make him
think too much of this world. Between Pago and Coria
there are banditti and robbers; and two or three murders
have been committed there by armed men, Spaniards,
I believe, and Portuguese, five or six together. What a
state this poor country is in!

Frenada, March 1st.—Several of these banditti I hear
are deserters from our army, and Lord Wellington has
sent out after them. On the Thursday I tried the man
at Guinaldo for murdering a poor Spanish girl. We
had some difficulty in coming to an understanding. The
witnesses were all Spaniards, principally the relations of
the deceased; the only interpreter was Portuguese; the
prisoner a German, but he spoke bad French. At last,
as I had looked into all the Spanish proceedings, we got
on, as most of the Court understood Spanish as well as
the interpreter, and nearly all understood French. The
prisoner's defence was in French. I then read it in
English to the Court as he went on, and took it down.
He had a very narrow escape for his life; I thought it
murder, and the Court were long in doubt; at last they
only found him guilty of a most disorderly outrage and
killing the poor girl, and gave him a thousand lashes.

I wrote it fair, got it signed, dined again with the

General, and came over here on a beautiful day. We have now again fine clear, frosty mornings, beautiful, but really almost too warm days and too cold evenings. I wish this would last; and yet it is trying to the constitution, for there must, I think, be thirty degrees difference between the temperature at three and at six o'clock.

On my return here I found that no less than nine Courts-martial had arrived and plenty of newspapers. One Court-martial had met thirty-eight days, and another sixteen : thus I had plenty to read and report upon. I saw Lord Wellington, in consequence, two days running, for nearly two hours, as I thought four of the cases ought ·to go back for revision, and one only to be confirmed, as it was half illegal—eight hundred lashes and transportation for life—which latter is not a legal sentence for mutiny. In truth, the men should have been shot.

The Courts will not do their duty : Lord Wellington was quite angry. He swore, and said that his whole table was covered with details of robbery and mutiny, and complaints from all quarters, in all languages, and that he should be nothing but a General of Courts-martial. He has given some broad hints to the Courts in general orders. I sent out three new cases yesterday, and have about fifteen deserters just in hand now—in general Poles from the second King's German Legion light infantry battalion.

I made it a rule, whenever possible, to clear off everything as I go, and answer every letter by return of post, which is the only way ; and I am glad to see my pile of papers done with now larger than that in hand. Whilst I was with Lord Wellington, the Commissariat returns came in, and were very confused. That added to his ill-humour ; but he was very civil to me, and gets more easy, as I do with him. He sent orders for fifteen thousand complete black accoutrements to be sent round to Corunna, so I hope the Gallician army is to be increased; some of their regiments got home much more entire than any of ours during the retreat, but upon the whole they diminished very much by desertion when they first got away from home.

The people of Guinaldo, whilst I was there, were almost mad—nothing but dancing and noise in all quarters. They told me it was a particular day, when the women were to rule the Dios de Madre; but it seems to me they are always in this gay state. The people agree there very well with the English, particularly with the 52nd, which is now there, a fine light battalion, seven hundred strong, and in high order. The ladies go about, and tie strings to the coats of the officers, and even of the General; dance about, sup, and drink with them, and are all alive both with them and the men.

The 52nd and 43rd lost part of their baggage in the retreat, and one on the Court-martial told me an anecdote as to his baggage. A French officer and a few men overtook his bâtman with the canteens, &c. "Where's the key?" he said; "come, quick! break it open; out with the tea and sugar, I have had none these three months:" and in this manner he took all worth having, the best horse and mule, and left the bâtman frightened to death.

There is one regiment of the Caçadores that is the constant astonishment of the English. Badly paid, no new clothes for the last two years, almost in rags this winter, and yet scarcely a man has been sick. I wish this was the case with them all. Our men are getting their clothes much better than last year, but still many are sick. Of two hundred men, a reinforcement to the 43rd light regiment Walcheren men, ninety have died; and the Guards have suffered terribly, but still all are in spirits; though the verses I enclose to you (and which

are printed at the Adjutant-general's portable press, used
for printing the army orders, &c.) give a very fair description of the life in Portugal.

I have taken a ride to Malliarda de Sorda, and found
the Deputy Paymaster-General H—— very unwell, with
an attack of fever. One must not think of these things:
that is the best way, I believe, if posible. Sir W. Erskine,
who threw himself out of the window here in a delirium,
came to his senses after his fall, and said he never thought
he could have been guilty of such an act, and that he did
not intend it. This was very melancholy; but I am told
he had been two years confined, and that he should not
have been here as chief officer of the cavalry—it was too
great a risk.

We have a report here of a revolution in France; but
I do not credit it yet, though not unlikely. It seems to
me Bonaparte is a man to run that hazard by his conscription and immense levies, and that there will be either
a revolution, or he will soon be again formidable; and
much is yet to be done. I hope we shall make a good
end of it here this year.

Wednesday.—I dined yesterday at head-quarters, and
sat next to Baron Wimpfen, the new Quarter-Master-
general attached to Lord Wellington. He is a very gentleman-like man, and talks French well. We had much
conversation together, in which Lord Wellington, who
sat next to the General, often took part. He gave us the
whole history of the battle of Fuentes d'Onore, which
was fought some time since near here, in which the
French were three to one, and in which Lord Wellington
said he committed a fault, by extending his right too
much to Poço de Velho; and that, if the French had
taken advantage of it, there might have been bad consequences, but that they permitted him to recover himself
and change his front before their face.

Another new comer at dinner yesterday was a Mon-

F

sieur Saudri, an agent for the Portuguese, a sort of interpreter. He gave an account of the state of the Portuguese provinces. Some are recovering fast, it seems,
Coimbra particularly, but many are still in great distress.

Yesterday was the last day of a sort of carnival here.
We had fools, and pantaloons, and straw bulls, &c., and
masks walking about the streets—much noise but no
great magnificence. I saw poor pantaloon fall in earnest
when throwing his sword after a soldier, and he could
scarcely get up again.

A general order has just been issued for all the officers
to apply for tents for the next campaign. I must do the
same, I suppose, and try that sort of life, which in dry
weather may be well enough, but bad work if as it was
last year, when the little bed-legs sunk in mud up to the
mattress, and the blankets got quite muddy!

Head-Quarters, Frenada, March 6th, 1813.—A man
arrived here two days ago from Madrid in five days, for
payment of a Commissariat bill due to him. He states
that the French are in small force at Madrid, and that
Joseph was packing up. But I believe this is only
because he individually is going away; for I understand
that the French are still in force below Madrid, and that
the only notion entertained as genuine here as to their
troops going homewards is that ten men picked from
each squadron and battalion, or as some say from each
company, are to be sent home to make good the Imperial
Guards. I do not think myself they will withdraw at all
now. They keep the country to support themselves till
we are ready to move, and then I think they will collect
and risk an early action with us, as their difficulty is to
keep together long. If they beat us, they will remain as
they were, and I think that is all, unless we are quite
routed; if we beat them, then they will go behind the
Ebro. The conjecture is, as far as I can understand from
the probabilities, a late opening of the campaign on

account of the Spaniards not being ready, and then an early action when it does begin.

Some say that the Spaniards will not be ready to move before the harvest in July, or not much before. The French have nearly ninety thousand men in their extended positions, with their right on and near the Douro and the left on or along the Tagus. We shall have, when we begin, about forty-four or forty-five thousand British, about twenty or twenty-two thousand Portuguese, and how many Spaniards no one can tell, or what they will do. So do not expect to hear of a march to France—to the Ebro, or very possibly up to Burgos again. The opportunity for effecting this must be by obliging the French to assemble, and then by rousing up all the Guerillas to starve them. Having heard Lord Wellington give his account of the battle of Fuentes d'Onore to General Wimpfen, the Spanish Inspector-General, I rode there yesterday with Lord Aylmer (who was present in the action) over the whole field of battle, saw all the field-works, the positions of the different divisions, and the plan of the whole. I perfectly understood Lord Wellington's blunder, and the risk he had run, and could form a very good notion of the strength of the position, and the nature of it as protected by the ravines of the Coa, &c. Lord Aylmer gave me two striking instances of Lord Wellington's coolness : one when, as he was pursuing the French, in a fog in the morning, he found a division of our men under Sir William Erskine much exposed in advance, and nearly separated from the rest of the army, and the French in a village within a mile of where he was standing, he could see nothing ; but, on some prisoners being brought in, and asked what French division and how many men were in the village, they, to the dismay of every one except Wellington, stated that the whole French army were there ; all he said was, quite coolly, "Oh! they are all there, are they? Well, we must mind a little what we are about then." Another time, soon after the battle of Fuentes d'Onore, and when we were waiting in our position near them to risk an attack, in order to protect the siege of Almeyda, early one morning Lord Aylmer came suddenly in to him whilst he was shaving, to tell him that "the French were all off, and the last cavalry mounting to be gone;" the consequence of which movement was to relieve him entirely, to give him Almeyda, and preserve Portugal. He merely took the razor off for one moment, and said, "Ay, I thought they meant to be off; very well:" and then another shave just as before, without another word till he was dressed. I find, however, it is said he magnifies the French now and then— sees double as to the number of blue uniforms, and cannot see all the scarlet; but I believe most men in his situation do this more or less. I must now proceed to summon some witnesses: so, for the present, adieu.

Monday, 4 o'clock.—You ask me what my house is like, and what Frenada is? Frenada is a village much in decay, very dirty; in the streets are immense masses of stones, and holes, and dung all about, houses like a farm kitchen, with this difference that there are the stables underneath. My last lodging was like a part of a Welsh farm-house, boarded off at one end from the common room, with a hole through the wall and one pane of glass let in. I am now in a distinct building like a granary, with the stables below, in an English farm-yard, in which are my animals of all sorts, servants and all. The kitchen is a miserable shed, not water-tight, where the woman of the house and three children live quite separate. The building I occupy has one opening with a wooden door besides the entrance-door, and the end, about eight feet wide by sixteen long, was boarded off by an officer last year. In this I sleep, eat, drink, write, &c., and live altogether, as it has a fireplace in the corner built by the same officer. The fireplace is so contrived, however, as to let more smoke into the room than up the chimney, and of course my eyes suffer, and all I have looks yellow and smells of smoke.

It is said that Lord Wellington and the Court here are to go to Ciudad Rodrigo, to a fête, to install the new Knight of the Bath, General Cole. I shall not go unless especially invited, and I have enough to do here, for except, probably, the Adjutant-general, the Quarter-Master-general, and perhaps the Commissary-general, I have more correspondents than any one here.

I take it in the army that the officers in the lower branches of the staff are sharp-set, hungry, and anxious to get on, and make the most of everything, and have a view even in their civilities. I have tried not to notice much that I could not help seeing, and which gave me a moderate opinion of the profession, which has not the independence to be seen in all the most respectable at the bar. There is much obsequious, time-serving conduct to any one who is in office, or is thought to have a word to say to his lordship.

Lord Wellington gets angry about the Courts-martial, the difficulty as to getting witnesses, the inconvenience, and then at last the great lenity of the Courts. " How can you expect," he remarked to me, " a Court to find an officer guilty of neglect of duty, when it is composed of members who are all more or less guilty of the same?" He does not like the tribunal. We have, however, hung six men within this month, broken several officers (at least their cases are gone home with that sentence), and flogged about sixteen or eighteen (pretty well, this), and we are still at work. I have now twenty-two cases left on hand, about thirty-six tried, about two or three new cases every week, yet I hope we are getting on better now. I am glad to be made of such importance as you say I am in England; my reputation increases here a

little, several Courts-martial having been sent back for
revision: for this I get in a degree the credit, and in
some instances justly. I am thought a formidable person
to whom it is as well to be civil, and who can often be of
service to others.

The Princess of Wales's letter is good; and I think,
and have always thought, that if she could once dare
inquiry, her case would be unanswerable, and the Prince
in a complete dilemma. We have heard here that
Brougham wrote the Princess's letter: is there such a
story in England?

Wednesday, 10th March.—No more news, and no
more mails, and no more time. I am to be asked, it is
said, to Rodrigo to the fête there on Saturday. Lord
Wellington wants to be very magnificent in his own city,
and has said that he wished to give a supper to a hundred
and fifty, but is told that it is quite out of the question, as
the town and head-quarters would not supply dishes and
plates, &c. There is, however, to be a small dinner first
before the ball. But this arrangement may be a little
disturbed by an event I have this moment heard from
General O'Lalor. A Spanish dragoon is come in, with
news that the French are moving in the Sierra di Francia;
their object, I think likely enough, to rout us up before
we are ready. I know no more; General O'Lalor went
to Lord Wellington to tell him the news. N.B.— Orders
have just come in to prepare charges against nine Polish
deserters.

Head-Quarters, Frenada, March 15th, 1813, 9 *o'clock
at night.*—As to Sir Isaac Heard's coming over here to
invest the Marquis with the Garter, doubtless the old
Garter king would like it; and at this time of the year,
while quiet here, and neither hot nor wet, no mosquitoes,
and without baggage, he might do it tolerably well. If
you travel without baggage, as Lord Wellington did
when he went to Cadiz, with good horses, you get on

thirty, forty, and even fifty miles in a day; avoid all the bad places, only stop in towns, get the best accommodation, and only rest where there are English Commissaries, &c. Lord Wellington came from Lisbon here in five days, with relays of horses; the last day he rode fifty miles between breakfast and dinner.

The movements of the French I mentioned in my last came to little or nothing—it was a mere alarm.

I have had a long letter from Sutton in answer to several queries. He agrees with me in every point which I have had to decide; and I am particularly glad to be right in the great one on which Lord Wellington differed with me, and directed me to send home his reasons. Still Lord Wellington is hardly satisfied, but desires me to wait till I hear officially from Sutton about it.

The day before yesterday we had a hard day's work in the shape of gaiety and amusement. Lord Wellington desired to invest General Cole with the Order of the Bath, in a suitable manner; and as he had never done anything at Ciudad Rodrigo, of which he is Duke, he determined upon this opportunity to give a grand fête in the midst of the ruins—a grand dinner, ball, and supper. All heads of departments, generals, public authorities, Spaniards and English, were invited to dinner, to the amount of sixty-five. In the evening, ladies about forty, and men about a hundred and fifty, came to a ball and supper. The dinner and supper were half cooked at Frenada, and carried over in military waggons and on mules. All the plate at head-quarters was put in requisition, and there was enough to afford a change of silver at dinner. Plenty of claret, champagne, and Lamego, i. e., port, was sent over. A caravan of glass and crockery arrived from the governor of Almeyda, and from a shop just opened there. Almeyda is twenty-five miles from Rodrigo. The whole went off very well, except that it was excessively cold, as a few balls during the siege had knocked in several yards of the roof of the ball-room, and it was a hard frost at the time.

Lord Wellington was the most active man of the party—he prides himself on this; but yet I hear from those about him that he is a little broken down by it. He stayed on business at Frenada until half-past three, and then rode full seventeen miles to Rodrigo in two hours to dinner, dressed in all his orders, &c., was in high glee, danced, stayed supper, and at half-past three in the morning went back to Frenada by moonlight, and arrived here before daybreak at six; so that by twelve he was ready again for business, and I saw him amongst others upon a Court-martial on my return at two the next day. Campbell and General O'Lalor managed the fête. I made cards for every place at dinner, with corresponding ones for each person, with his name, table, and number of his plate, and so there was no bowing and scraping, or pushing for the first table. We got quarters in the ruins. Stables there were none scarcely, and we took over hay and barley for the horses for the night, and our beds to lie down for an hour or two. Several ladies, refugees from Salamanca, were there, and the band of the 52nd.

The house at which the entertainment was given was the best in the town, with some very good rooms; but it had suffered a little by the siege, and had, moreover, only bare walls. Luckily, however, the General O'Lalor discovered that the Intendente of the Palace of St. Ildefonso had brought away the hangings of five or six of the best rooms to save them from the French, and had deposited them at Rodrigo. These were obtained, and the bare walls of the ball-room were hung all over with yellow damask satin with a silver border, with openings at each end in festoons, like a tent, and looked very well. The other supper-rooms were hung with crimson satin and gold from the same palace, and in tolerable condition.

The whole was laid out so as to astonish the inhabitants, and the defects were concealed almost entirely. Near one hole in the floor a man was placed to take care that no one got a leg in, and a mat was put over the whole. The ladies were not very handsome, but two or three good-looking, and several very lady-like in their manners.

I was most pleased with the bolero and fandango dances, which were executed by two Spanish ladies, Chanoinesses as they were called, nieces of two Chanoines, and two Spaniards, one of whom danced very well. The best was the old fellow who was sent for to play on his ornamented paper square tambourine, or rather flat drum, who sang the airs and accompanied himself with great humour, and afterwards gave us a dance in the true style. The enthusiasm of the Spaniards was also amusing, and their eager applause. All the other dances were English country dances, which the ladies execute very well and exactly like ours, except that they waltz the poussets, and generally, therefore, dance waltz tunes, and have that figure. They are also a little more twisted about and handled than our fair ones would like at first; but upon the whole, perhaps our country dances are improved by the change. We had much drinking and toasts given on both sides, at the expense of the French: "Ferdinand the Seventh," "The next campaign," "Death to all Frenchmen," &c. In short, several Spaniards as well as English got very drunk by five o'clock in the morning, and they chaired the Prince of Orange, General Vandeleur, whom they let fall, and several others, as soon as the ladies were gone, and there was nothing else to do. The Spaniards at first began with "vivas," but soon learnt "hip, hip, hip, hurra!"

With great care a few silver spoons and knives and forks only were missing, and it is said one plate. Henry tells me the servants saw one Spanish officer with a turkey's leg sticking out of his pocket; but, like our aldermen, they are given to pocket even at Madrid, and have some excuse, for they are paid little, and find everything very dear. Probably a turkey had not been seen there for months: they were, I believe, all brought from thirty or forty miles down the Douro, near Lamego. Besides the Spanish military authorities, there were some civilians of rank, as the Marquis d'Espeja and a few others. Colonel Gordon was the only officer who would return with Lord Wellington; and though he has the best horses here next to those of the chief, he borrowed another horse which had come over earlier, to ride back upon with Lord Wellington, and left his own, which he had ridden on in the morning with his lordship, to come back later in the day.

The repairs of the walls of Ciudad Rodrigo are going on better, and they are now nearly cleared of rubbish, so as to be ready to begin to rebuild the new work, which all fell down last autumn. I sat at the grand dinner directly opposite to E——, who introduced himself to me afterwards in the ball-room. Colonel Fisher, of the Artillery, was next, a very pleasant man, a great artist, connoisseur, traveller, &c. Except at a grand fête, and the few great men who come to head-quarters, or when crossing a division on the march, which we always avoid if possible, we seldom see any regimental officers.

Tuesday Night (16*th*).—We have flogged and hung people into better order here, I think, but have now got into a little squabble with the Portuguese Government, who will become bold by success. By the Portuguese law a magistrate is only to give evidence in writing by deposition, which our Courts, if it be a fact in his own knowledge, and where he is wanted as a witness, ought not to receive. I fear the Bill proposed at home will be unpopular, and yet inefficient in a great measure.

The Guards, who joined nearly when I did, have suffered most of all by the campaign. They came out a noble battalion of fine men, twelve hundred strong; four hundred are dead, and not above five hundred are now fit for duty. This is very shocking.

The division on Grattan's motion in the House is stronger than I expected it would be after all the outcry on the subject. I had a long conversation while walking up and down the market-place with Lord Wellington here, a few days since, upon that and the Indian question. He has, from what he saw in Ireland, taken up a strong notion that independence is what the Irish really aim at, and he is, therefore, for giving no more, but proceeding upon King William's plan to keep them down by main force, for he thinks that they have too much power already, and will only use more to obtain more, and at length separation. He said he thought his brother and Canning had just taken up the Catholic question when the tide of popularity was turning against it. I hope this is not so; and though I agree with him that the party for separation is strong, his plan would drive them to extremities, and is now too late; the only chance is, to get the higher orders of Roman Catholics and the priests, if possible, by pay or otherwise, and by looking for pay and patronage, to be dependent on the Crown and on England more than they are, and at the same time not to be a degraded class.

Did I tell you the size of Frenada, about which you asked? It is about as large as Ashted, without the three gentlemen's houses in it. Lord Wellington's house is, however, better known than the inn there (the Leg of Mutton and Cauliflower), and more ornamented, though it does not contain more room or as much comfort. This is as good a description as I can give you, only that all the houses are more roomy than in our villages—more like barns—for the straw, corn, and all are left under the same roof.

As Sutton only answers my letters indirectly, and not officially upon the point on which we differed, Lord Wellington says he will not act until he has an official answer. He does not like to be wrong, and yet I am very glad he is so.

Head-Quarters, Frenada, March 19th, 1813.—The day before yesterday we had a most extraordinary arrival here in General Murray, the Quarter-Master-general of the army. He left Plymouth late on the 10th instant, and was here at Frenada on the 18th, in the morning, in about seven days and a half. He got to Oporto from Plymouth in less than five days, and here in three, travelling post on horses, ponies, mules, and anything he could get : he brought London papers of the 8th. His baggage went round by Lisbon. He was to have come out with General Graham and General Stewart, but was sent off here express with despatches in a sloop of war. No one knows what the important news is which made it advisable to send out a Quarter-Master-general as a messenger.

I hear of no movement yet in the army, and as part of the cavalry are down below Coimbra, and part still below Abrantes, near Cabeça de Vide, Aunde Chad, and Monforte, it will be necessary to give some notice of anything like a serious movement in good time. Perhaps head-quarters may move to Guinaldo in a month— I think not sooner, for there is no grass there yet, and the cold is not gone, nor the rain come, though the sky has threatened much for the last day or two. I have now to send above thirty miles for bad hay or straw for my animals, and that I hear is nearly exhausted. We have been obliged to send fifteen miles for some time past, which is hard work for the poor mules during what should be their resting-time.

You ask about our religious duties. There are four or five or more clergymen in Portugal, but no one now at head-quarters. The clergyman stationed there went away ill about a twelvemonth since, I hear.

Sunday, 21st.—The remains of the battalion of Guards which lost so many men, and was so sickly, is going down towards the coast and towards Coimbra, to recruit with sea-air.

I must now away to answer letters. I have only read four of the newspapers out of the last fifteen; you may therefore conclude how much I am employed. I get through one at breakfast-time, and when at home two of an evening; nor have I yet read half through one review. Lord Wellington is as bad; he borrowed my "Vetus" nearly three weeks since, and has not read it.

Wednesday, 4 o'clock, Post-day.—Having got all my proceedings written out fair by half-past six yesterday, I dined with the General. Early again this morning I breakfasted with him; compared the two, got the fair one signed; picked you up botanical specimens of the flowers in the fields in my ride back, and here I am.

Since Rodrigo has been taken, the inhabitants about Guinaldo feel more confidence, and more land is this year in cultivation. They are tempted also by the high price of everything; and near Guinaldo I saw a new enclosure going on, and trees being grubbed up to a considerable extent. The old lady where General Vandeleur is quartered, is doing this to an extent of several thousand acres. To give you a proof of the lightness of their ploughs, I met a man walking off a mile or two to work from Guinaldo with a complete plough on his shoulder, the whole plough fit for use, iron share, &c.; he was walking three or four miles an hour, quite upright. I hear that the inhabitants of Bejar, rather an opulent Spanish town, and where there is a cloth trade, have been so well satisfied with the 50th regiment for having driven away the French and saved their town, that they have given them all round a pair of pantaloons each, and several days' double rations of spirits, and some other presents. The place is now strengthened considerably as a post, it is said, for the French seem to be making some stir, though no one seems to know what they mean to be about.

Head-Quarters, Frenada, March 27th, 1813. *Saturday.*—The statement of Courts-martial, which I shall present to Lord Wellington to-morrow, satisfies me that we are mending, and that we have not tried fifty cases, hung eight, transported eight or ten, flogged about sixty severely, and broke several officers—for nothing. I have now only eighteen left in hand, and three of these very old cases. We had one very melancholy piece of business here last week : a young corporal, Mac Morran, a Scotchman in the 42nd, was reprimanded mildly by his officer, Lieutenant Dickenson, for neglect of duty ; he answered rather impertinently, and was then told to consider himself a prisoner, and to follow. Having walked a few yards, Lieutenant Dickenson looked round, and the corporal, having (no one knows how) loaded his musket, levelled it at him, and shot him dead through the heart. The corporal has been tried, and is to be hung to-morrow. They were both under twenty years of age, I hear, and the most promising young men in their respective stations. The officer was a man of mild, humane character. The corporal made no defence : it seemed an excess of Scotch pride. It is altogether a very painful business.

We have still very cold north-east winds, and to-day a little fall of sleet, hail, and stormy, windy, black sky. Lord Wellington is gone hunting, which gives me a little time.

I hear the French are moving ; two divisions of Soult's army are said to be retiring behind the Douro, near Valladolid : and I am told they are engaged in fortifying all the fords and bridges near the Douro, at Toro, Tordesillas, Aranda de Douro, &c. Probably they will make a grand stand on that river; where, from what I saw, they have great advantages, for the banks on our side are low and flat, and on their side, towards France (the right bank) high and commanding, and the position on that side also strong. It is thought the slight movement in advance of one of our divisions, the fourth, from St. Jean de Piscara, merely for convenience of supplies and change of air, caused this movement on the part of the French, who only stay down about Toledo, probably, for food.

Accounts have just come in from one of our look-out officers, who live close to the French, and act as spies, and have correspondence with them—a Captain ——, who was here a fortnight since. He says that the French are all moving, and apparently towards the other side of the Douro. Joseph has left Madrid. His informers state that the French are going at once behind the Ebro; but he himself thinks not, as they would not willingly give up the fine country between the Douro and Ebro for nothing, and have fortified, report says, the passes. So we stand. Conjectures are made, that our advance will not be the same as last year, through Salamanca, as we have no great depôt being made yet this way at Rodrigo, and should have to force these passes on the Douro; whereas some depôts are being formed in Portugal near the Douro, more in the north of Portugal; and we could in that direction cross the Douro without opposition, turn all these French works on that river, and join the Spanish army in Galicia, but the roads in that case will be much worse. I hope we may go that road, and thus see a new country, and in part, I believe, a fine one. There is one fine pass in the Agava, only five leagues hence, at Barba del Puerto, which I have never yet had time to visit, but shall do so, if possible, after the rain, provided we remain here.

Lord Wellington, in conversation the other day, told

me that some Spaniards of rank had talked to him about educating their children at a Roman Catholic school in England, if there were such. I knew of one or two good girls' schools, but could not remember any good Roman Catholic boys' school.

We have a most furious Portuguese lady now here, the wife of a hidalgo of Portugal, whose daughter was run away with by an English officer. Lord Wellington told her that he would give him up to the laws of Portugal; but as he has now married her, Lord Wellington says he will not interfere at all. The woman swears that she will get the priest who married them transported for life by their law, as well as the officer, and has moreover declared she will kill the daughter if she meets her!

As to Mr. R——, concerning whom you inquire, I know nothing about him: we have a *ci-devant* major of that name just arrived here. He is full of travellers' stories; has been long a prisoner in France: had a prefect's wife for his *chère amie;* escaped with wonderful risks; joined the Guerillas, got to the coast, and off, I believe, to Cadiz. I am told that he is to be an officer in a new horse-police staff corps about to be established.

30th March, Tuesday, 4 o'clock.—I have presented four Courts-martial to Lord Wellington, and sent one back for revision as illegal, and confirmed three, two against one man—together, two thousand lashes. This is absurd, he will bear six or seven hundred, and there it will end. The sentence, however, is legal, which it was not before, when transportation was the punishment. Lord Wellington now addresses me with the familiar " How are you?" So we go on more easily, and I made a sort of proposal to him to insert a passage in general orders now, to be read to the men every day until we march, to let them know that a new police corps was established to catch them, and to tell them that seven officers would be sufficient now to hang them, and that Courts would be held always ready in every division. He said he would think about it, and thought it would be of use.

Dr. M'Gregor told me yesterday, that his sick-list was improving daily, and that if Lord Wellington would give him another month he thought he should bring the greater part into the field. King Joseph, I have just heard, arrived at Valladolid from Madrid on the 23rd instant; Lord Fitzroy Somerset just read it out of a Spanish private letter.

Head-Quarters, Frenada, Sunday, April 4th, 1813.— You will observe that I do know when Sunday comes, although that is certainly nearly all. We, however, have a church and a bell, which goes on tolling for hours in a most unattractive manner. We have a church, too, which is made use of for various purposes, civil as well as ecclesiastical; for instance, one night about one hundred and fifty Spaniards and their mules, officers and all, slept in it. The building is large, considering the size of the village, the floor covered with straw like a stable, but the end where the altar is, is all gold and glitter up to the ceiling. The decorations must originally have been very expensive, for, besides the great expenditure of gold-leaf and foil, and carving, all the ceiling, which is coved and circular, and divided into squares, has a picture of a saint, or a father, a founder, a hermit, or some great divinity hero, in every square. Masses, the funeral service, weddings, and christenings, are also performed there. I just look in now and then, for it is awkward to stand there, when all are on their knees on the floor. There is also a little chapel belonging to the owner of Lord Wellington's house; which is fitted up by Colonel G—— for his quarters. He has hung it with red baize, fitted up the altar as his dressing-table, put up an iron stove, and made it one of the best quarters here.

Lord Wellington looks forward very coolly to another

G

winter here. He said yesterday he should have twenty-five couples of fox-hounds next season. The other day the Commissary-general told him that we had eaten nearly all the oxen in the country, that the cultivation of the lands in Portugal could not go on for want of them, and that he scarcely knew where to turn for a supply of beef, as there was this year no reserve store near Lisbon. Lord Wellington said, " Well, then, we must now set about eating all the sheep, and when they are gone I suppose we must go." And General M—— added, "Historians will say that the British army came and carried on war in Spain and Portugal until they had eaten all the beef and mutton in the country, and were then compelled to withdraw." Without joking, I fear our Commissariat may have great difficulties next year. Talking on this subject, I must add that the Portuguese agent here, a sly, money-making man, who has realized about 25,000l. during the war, said the news was so good, that he now hoped to get a peace, and that the Portuguese would get rid of the " beefs," meaning the English. Communication as to necessary articles and others is so difficult with Lisbon, that one of Lord Wellington's aides-de-camp has been six months getting two bridles up, and C. Campbell four months in getting up a great coat.

Lord Wellington yesterday, talking of his soldiers and English notions, observed that his men were now all so round-shouldered and slouching in their gait, that he was sure, if his regiment here was in its present state to pass in review at Wimbledon Common, the whole would be sent to drill immediately, and declared quite unfit for service. Indeed, he added, that the men had now got into such a way of doing everything in the easiest manner, that he was often quite ashamed of the sentries before his own quarter. He did not mention this by way of complaint, but as showing how ideas here and at home differed. He also laughed at our notions in England about the supply of the army, saying that some corporate body or society in England had once made him an offer of twenty bullocks for the army, which would last head-quarters only about a week. General M—— said it must have been a mistake—the offer must have been for his table only; not for the army.

Orders, it is said, are gone round for the Alicant army to be re-embarked and landed in the rear of Suchet, to compel him to quit Valentia if possible; this will be the first step I conclude. You say you are all looking to us, and want us to move. Our black clouds have all rolled away, and to-day we have again a clear north wind and hot sun, and not a blade of grass growing; without the latter we cannot stir. If the rains will but come soon and bring grass, we may, perhaps, move in the first week of May, but not before: that is, no important move can take place. Our cavalry, though down below Coimbra, are very much distressed for food, and complaints come up without number from the Portuguese that our people will feed their horses with the young corn, which is now great waste; but what is to be done? When we have finished the oxen we may go, as Lord Wellington says, to the sheep, but what are horses to do when hay is all gone, and straw, and there is no grass come? How little you know in England about the real state of things here, and the requisites for moving in a campaign! You forget our ten or fifteen thousand animals for baggage and for food, besides the cavalry and artillery, &c. The Portuguese agent here repeats that another campaign in Portugal will be impossible, for there will be neither animals to eat, nor for transport, unless we bring all with us. I hope, however, not to pass another winter at Frenada; but so hoped those who were here last year.

Did I ever mention to you Lord Wellington's saying how anxious the Prince Regent was that he should corre-

spond with him, and how much hurt he was that he had
never done so. " But," observed Lord Wellington, " I
wrote to his ministers, and that was enough. What had
I to do with him ? However, his late favour was a reason
for my writing, and I have had a most gracious answer,
evidently courting further correspondence ;" but which he
intimated he should not comply with.

I understand the famous Guerillas are much more
dreaded by their own countrymen in the north of Spain
than the French, and I fear with some reason, as they are
(many of them, at least) very much like banditti. The
French, however, suffered so much by them, that they
have adopted the same plan, and have their counter
Guerillas ; some with French officers to conduct them,
and some headed by Guerilla chiefs, who have quarrelled
and separated from their companions in the good cause.
I was sorry to hear this. The French continue moving
about, and their force towards the Tagus diminishes.

You have my news as I hear it : we are now getting
ready ammunition, &c., to the front, to prepare for an
advance when possible ; so, perhaps, we may pass Rodrigo,
and cross the Douro to the left of Salamanca, if the French
stand on that river, as we have now this year pontoons,
which we had not last year. We have also a new and
more portable battering-train, come out from England,
which has arrived as far as Abrantes, where it only waits
for means of transport to come on here. That which we
had here last year, I am told, was excessively clumsy.

April 7th.—I have heard a number of anecdotes of
General Craufurd. All admit that he was very clever
and knowing in his profession, and led on his division on
the day of his death in the most gallant style ; but Lord
Wellington never knew what he would do. He constantly
acted in his own way, contrary to orders : and as he commanded the advanced division, at times perplexed Lord
Wellington considerably, who never could be sure where

he was. On one occasion, near Guinaldo, he remained across a river by himself; that is, with his own division only, nearly a whole day after he was called in by Lord Wellington. He said he knew that he could defend his position. Lord Wellington, when he came back, only said, " I am glad to see you safe, Craufurd." To which the latter replied, " Oh, I was in no danger, I assure you." " But I was, from your conduct," said Lord Wellington. Upon which Craufurd observed, " He is d—— crusty to-day."

Marmont, when he saw Craufurd filing off next morning, could not believe it: " *Diable! voilà Craufurd! ma foi, j'aurais pu deviner cela.*" Another time, Lord Wellington said, " Craufurd, you are going into a delicate situation; what orders do you wish for? I will write what you think best." Craufurd told him his own plan and went away. Whilst Lord Wellington was writing them out, and acting accordingly, Craufurd sent him word that he had done something else. On another occasion, Lord Wellington sent to him to say he should inspect his division, and came accordingly. Craufurd never attended until it was half over, and then said that Lord Wellington was before his time; yet he was very strict with his own division, and would be very exactly obeyed. His division all complained of this, and many officers talked of who should call him out, on one or two occasions, for this. Yet he was so much valued, and the whole division had such confidence in him, that, when he joined them again just before the attack to take the command in the engagement in which he died, the whole division set up a loud shout, so as to frighten a small party of French who were near, who did not know what was the matter, and they ran away. Lord Wellington knew his merits and humoured him. It was surprising what he bore from him at times.

Lord Wellington celebrated the day of the storming of

Badajoz with a grand dinner yesterday; only those present at that event were invited. Lord Aylmer had a rival dinner-party, at which was General Murray, &c,, where I dined also. If the good news brings peace, what will become of your humble servant and many others here? "Othello's occupation's gone!"

General Murray is apparently very clever and clear-headed. In my opinion, he comes next to Lord Wellington, as far as I have seen. We are all full of the news, for a paper of the 22nd has arrived at Oporto several days later than the mail. We now know about Hamburg and Cuxhaven, Berlin, &c. I fear that the French will be driven together into one large body, and may then be more than a match for any one army opposed to them, but they will be considerably cowed and disheartened. When will the Dutch be roused to do anything? Now or never is their time!

CHAPTER V.

News of the French—Castilian Costume—Equipment of the Army—
Melancholy Court-martial Case—Wellington in the Battle of Fuentes
d'Onore —The Chances of War—Anecdotes of Wellington—His Opinions
of the War—The New Mutiny Act—Wellington on " Vetus "—General
Murray—Advance of the French.

Head-quarters, Frenada, April 12, 1813.

My dear M——,

From what I hear, if we could only get grass,
Lord Wellington would move about the second week in
May. There is no immediate prospect of this, as you will
perceive, when I tell you that the Military Secretary has
sent all his horses nearly a hundred miles off for grass.

The news here is, that some more of the French, about
twenty men from every regiment, are ordered home.
Some, but I believe no great number hitherto, are actually
gone : and about three or four thousand conscripts are
supposed to have arrived in Spain to fill up the vacancies
of the old soldiers removed. Head-quarters will not now
probably move until we march ; and, from report, we
shall not go to Guinaldo, but stay here quietly until the
army is drawn up around us, ready to move.

The clergy, both here and in Spain, are in general, I
understand, fortunately of the same opinion as to the
Pope's signing the Concordat, as you say the emigrants
are ; that he did it from compulsion, or that a different
instrument was substituted for his signature. It was
feared that artful plan would have assisted Bonaparte
in Spain.

I hear the same accounts of the state of commerce at Lisbon as George sends from London. Old Colonel Arentschild here says, " She (meaning England) will make enough in Germany, by trade, to enable her, in the first six months, to carry on the war for two years, if necessary." I fear the news in the papers concerning the Prince of Orange was rather premature. He states, that he has hitherto had no offer except from the Continent, nor heard anything from the newspaper. It will prove a prophecy, I hope, instead of a fact. He seems a very amiable, deserving youth, is liked by every one, and has had the greatest of all advantages for a young prince, that of being educated in a great measure with persons who have behaved to him as if he were their equal. So, indeed, he is treated now; except that he has a little more respect paid to him, which I believe is really felt, for he lives nearly on terms of equality with Lord Fitzroy Somerset, Lord March, Colonel G——, &c., and is quite one of the set, and is little or no restraint to any one. I met him, two days ago, scrambling down on the banks of the Coa, three miles off, by himself on foot. He must just now have some interesting subjects for contemplation, and I have no doubt some very flattering visions pass through his brain.

I am looking so much better than when I arrived at head-quarters, that Lord Wellington and several others think I am an exception to the general rule, and that the climate here agrees with me. Lord Wellington says he has had so many ill and dead since he has been here, that he does not like to think of it; many, like General Hulse, &c., whose loss he feels in every way. He says now, he is always ready to let every one go home when first he complains, and is disposed to tell every one who looks ill to be off.

I have just seen some very handsome specimens of the Castilian dresses, male and female, of the higher classes of rich peasantry, made I believe, by a tailor from Salamanca. The three female dresses Lord Wellington means to give to his nieces for masquerades; they are covered with work—embroidery, lace, and gold; he gives two thousand dollars for them. The man's dress was for Lord March, and is certainly most becoming to almost every one.

I must now go and consider the new intended Bill to punish our offenders here, which Lord Beresford has sent for Lord Wellington to consult him upon it, and he has sent it to me—the draught of the intended Act I mean; and as every one makes some observation, I must make a few also. So, for the present, adieu.

I never told you that some of our military great boys here got very tipsy on the commemoration of the fall of Badajoz, and went to a poor *Juge de Fores*, that is a Portugal law magistrate, who was on a visit, and poured a bottle of blacking partly in his mouth, and partly over him, at twelve at night; and then made him dress, and go and help break poor C——'s only pane of glass, and upset his bed, as he had retired. Soldiers, lawyers, and all, I see, are boys at times alike.

April 13th.—Much too hot for hunting I should think; but all the sportsmen are out. Lord Wellington has not got good horses to be idle; he works them well. Besides all the hunting, &c., the day before yesterday, after doing business until twelve o'clock, off he went by himself, without saying a word to any one, across to Ciudad Rodrigo, seventeen miles off, inspected all the works, and was back again here in five hours and a half to dinner. He says that they are now going on very well there, and seems to be a little anxious about his own town. I suspect when we do move that we shall get on fast, for Lord Wellington will like to pass the Douro before the French know his plans.

Wednesday, April 14th, *Post-day.*—This will be but a

stupid packet, as I have no news or events here to communicate. General Castanos arrived here yesterday in a
great lumbering carriage, with eight mules and ropes
from Cadiz, on his way to his division. He called here
for instructions.

We have had in my own line another murder : a
private grenadier of the Buffs shot his officer, on their
private parade at Placencia, in the second division, from
the window of his quarter, just opposite to that of the
officer, and just as he came out to the men, who were all
there. The officer was Lieutenant Annesley. The
grenadier wounded a sergeant at the same time, and was
instantly secured. No quarrel or disagreement was
known, but he said that he was satisfied he had killed
his enemy, and the day before, when another man committed suicide, he said, "What a fool, not to kill his
enemy first, if he had one!" The officer is well spoken
of. The conduct of the grenadier resembles madness
more than anything else, yet they say he was not mad ;
I have just sent out a charge against him, and an order
for his trial.

Our own army is now quite clothed, I believe. I fear
that the Portuguese are only in the middle of theirs, and
will not have finished these three weeks. You have no
notion what there is to be done before an army like
ours is fit to move in such a country as this. We have
been three months getting up these clothes from Lisbon
for our men ; the tents have not yet arrived for
head-quarters, and some say that only the army are
to use them. I suppose, however, that we must carry
them.

Lord Tweeddale continues here as an amateur, and
will probably advance with us. When we march I may
not be able to write so often, as our time will be much
occupied, and pen and ink will not be always at hand.
An order has just now come out to pay everything up to

the 24th of December, that the officers may have a little money to prepare for the march.

Head-Quarters, Frenada, April 17th, 1813.—The corn looks very ill about this place, very thin, very yellow, and indeed positively very bad crops. Whether this is, however, also only comparatively bad as to other years I cannot say; it would appear to be so to some extent. The soil is here very poor, and I suspect the harvest is never very abundant. Several parts of Spain have this year suffered much from the want of rain, and the very early heat of the weather; Estremadura in particular: where the sun has been very powerful, everything has been burnt up. My authority for this is General O'Donoghue.

In my own department I have another rather melancholy story. Mr. M——, a clerk in the commissariat department, had been guilty of fraud and embezzlement of stores (some pork, rice, and milk), to no great amount, as far as I could prove under 20*l.*; but it was sold out of the store at Galigas, in a neighbouring village. By Lord Wellington's orders I made out a charge against M——, and sent it to him at Coimbra, with an order from the Commissary for him to attend under close arrest at Cea to take his trial, as the witnesses were near Galigas. Soon after the receipt of this letter and order he shot himself, and has thus put an end to the whole business. He was well connected in England, it is said, has respectable friends, and was in a good situation there. A woman with whom he lived here, I believe, was the cause of the whole. When he turned her off she stirred up the witnesses against him, and was the cause of its being made known to Sir R. Kennedy, and by his means to Lord Wellington, when of course a prosecution was inevitable. By the Mutiny Act he was liable to transportation for life, fine, imprisonment, or pillory: and he could not stand the disgrace. He partly admitted the charge, but pleaded sickness and distress. It was unfortunate that the discovery fell on such a subject, for it was, I believe, the first falling off from general good conduct.

I have now got a Court-martial in the fourth division, the only one which has been hitherto free, to sit near Escalpaon, and to try three fellows for going out at night and stealing seven sheep, keeping sentry as a guard over the two shepherds, whilst they skinned the sheep and divided the meat; two other men, of better characters, were with them, and they are therefore to be admitted as witnesses against the three. The Court at Coimbra has suffered the two worst fellows to escape almost with twelve hundred lashes; they ought to have been hung, for they are desperate fellows, both Irishmen. They have been most mutinous and insolent whilst under trial, and one of them, a few days since, said he did not know whether he was to be hung or flogged this time, but if the latter, he would take care next time that there should be no witnesses to tell of what he had done.

Lord Wellington said at dinner the day before yesterday, "We must move by the end of the first week in May, that's positive." And then spoke sharply to Colonel F—— of the artillery, because the artillery was not arrived. The Colonel coolly replied, "My lord, I do not think the artillery have been, or will be, the cause of your lordship staying at Frenada. Transport is the great difficulty—animals are so scarce. The Portuguese make much money, but are afraid of spending it, or getting or breeding animals for fear of their being seized or embargoed." An engineer has been appointed and sent to each division, and a messenger or Spanish courier (who arrived three days since in four days from Cadiz post), was last night sent post round through Seville to Alicant. Something, therefore, is in agitation, and all this looks like preparation for moving. He expected to arrive at Alicant in eight days at furthest, if not in seven.

Lord Wellington the other day was again talking of the battle of Fuentes d'Onore. He said that he was obliged to ride hard to escape, and thought at one time, as he was on a slow horse, that he should have been taken. The whole of head-quarters, general and all, he added, English dragoons and French dragoons, were all galloping away together across the plain, and he more than once saw a French dragoon in a green coat within twenty yards of him. One Frenchman got quite past them all, and they could not knock him off his horse. At last they caught his bridle and stopped him.

21st April.—We sup early (as you call your late dinners) here, and are as smart as you are in England in that respect. At present half-past seven is the hour. We cannot change this hour till Lord Wellington does, for business is now going on till six. We also beat the most fashionable in London in one respect, for we have no female society at all here. There is one lady here, Mrs. S——, and that is all the English we see, once in a week perhaps ; and then the men preponderate so that the tone of the society is quite male. There is one Portuguese lady, niece to the Capitan Mor here, or principal resident inhabitant : but she is ugly, and said to be perfumed too strongly with oily salt fish. She is no favourite, and is very little noticed. Her little uncle hunts with Lord Wellington on a little country pony, and does wonders in that way ; he seems an active little Portuguese.

Lieutenant-Colonel W——, in the Adjutant-general's Department here, who was ill when I joined, has now returned. He has had some curious adventures in this country. He once fell in, accompanied by two dragoons, with a small party of French, close to their main body, who were attending some baggage. He, his men con- senting, attacked the French, beat them off, plundered their baggage, and brought off the best mule. The latter he kept himself, and has it here now, and the two soldiers took the money, &c. On another occasion, he was riding quietly with Captain D——, of the same department, on the advance from the lines at Torres Vedras on the retreat of Massena. They were quietly jogging on, and were about to enter a place intended to be English head-quarters that day. When close to it, they found the French were still there in force, and saw three French dragoons close upon them, who, however, did not see them. They resolved to attack by surprise. They knocked two off from their horses, and attacked the third; he got away and they pursued him. In the mean time the other two set off. It ended, however, in W—— and D—— securing one dragoon horse, and some other booty, with which they got safely away. Soon after this Lieutenant-Colonel W—— was himself taken prisoner at Sabugal, when the French advanced during the siege of Badajoz. He was then mounted on this very dragoon horse, which he had kept as booty; the horse was known by the French when he was carried in. He was asked how he came by the horse? He said he bought it of a soldier; and as the three Frenchmen had reported that they had been attacked by a "dozen men in buckram," and had said nothing of two officers, it all went off well, and he kept their secret and his own. He refused to give his parole, and was therefore ill fed, and kept prisoner with privates, and treated like the rest, except that they let him ride Dragon, as he had christened his horse.

Near Salamanca, a Spanish friend to whom he had been kind came to offer his services to him: "Only get me a new pair of very sharp rowels to my spurs," said he, "that is all I want." This was done, and on the next day, the party, a whole French column of infantry, marched on at daybreak about seven. Just near the end of the wood, near Salamanca, in a wide open part of the road, he observed that most of the French horsemen were dismounted; so turning about, he used his new rowels

strongly, got the start of them in some way, and was off.
He galloped till he heard no one behind him. At first
there was a shout of " *Le Mayo, le Mayo*," and some pursued; he then crossed another road where another
French party was, got round by the mountains, reached,
I think, Tamones by eleven that night, and to Fuentes
d'Onore next day safely. The French had fed their
horses in the fields at night on grass, and were soon
blown. He had refused to suffer his horse to leave him,
and gave him only a little bran, yet though his horse
was a slow one too, he thus got safely off. He has since
sold the horse. Lord Wellington asked him "Why?"
He said, " Because, my lord, I was very near being taken
again on him when with your lordship at the battle of
Fuentes d'Onore, and that would be awkward, as the
horse is known by the French." He seems an odd
character.

The Commissaries all live here exceedingly well, the
Lord knows how out of their pay; and that ought to be
nearly their only advantage.

Frenada, Head-Quarters, April 24th, 1813.—Four
Generals have arrived—Graham, Fane, Picton, and
Oswald: Sir Stapleton Cotton, who has received orders
to command the whole cavalry, has, however, not yet
arrived, and is much wanted; but Graham and Picton
are very good officers.

Lord Wellington, a few days since, said that he
hoped the Spaniards were in many respects getting on
much better; that there was a numerous body now well
clothed at least, and armed and tolerably disciplined;
that he was always ordering the drills to go on with
spirit, and by perseverance he thought they were much
improving; that he never interfered with the mode, but
asked what their military rules and laws were, and then
said, " Well, that is very good; now mind and see that
they are put in force, and, remember, it is not I but your

law orders this; I have only to see your laws executed, which are very good, and they must be obeyed." He said, the Staff here seemed well satisfied.

The artillery is what Lord Wellington rails at most. They cannot get on so well as he thinks they ought, or at least as he wants them to do. I do not mean in particular at this moment, but generally. The officers commanding this part of the army are rather heavy and slow, or, as Lord Wellington said himself one day of a late commander, "I took care to let him feel that I thought him very stupid." "That must have been," General Murray said privately, "by telling him so in plain terms, I have no doubt." Colonel F——, who commanded the artillery at the battle of Salamanca, and who is very well spoken of by every one, but at times, I believe, is slow, was once with Lord Wellington at an audience when things went wrong, and Lord Wellington got irate, who told him pretty nearly that his friend concerning whom he was inquiring "might go to h—." Colonel F—— came muttering out, "I'll go, Sir, to the Quarter-Master-general for a route," which Lord Wellington heard, and laughed at well.

General Murray says that on hunting-days he could get almost anything done, for Lord Wellington stands whip in hand ready to start, and soon despatches all business. Some of the Generals, Lord Wellington observed one day, used to come and hunt and then get on business, and get him to answer things in a hasty way, which he did not intend, but which they acted upon. "Oh, d—— them," said he, "I won't speak to them again when we are hunting." Colonel F——'s friend on his route to his destination would have found plenty of fuel but less green forage than we have here.

By all accounts the first day after we were in Badajoz, the scene was very shocking in every way. Nothing but dead and wounded on all sides, and

drunkenness and plunder in all directions. Even Lord
Wellington, when in the street with his staff, was followed by drunken soldiers, continually firing feux-de-joie
over his head with ball-cartridges, and never thinking
where the balls went.

The Portuguese Government have got bolder, and
have tried some of our people by their laws, when caught
in the act, and have sent two or three of them to the
coast of Africa. If this were generally known, it would
do more good, I believe, than our flogging. Lord
Wellington said formerly, that their government always
declined trying our people themselves, but now they
generally accepted the offer when made. Lieutenant
K——, of the Guards, who was tried and acquitted last
week of ordering a sentry to fire and killing a native, was
very much alarmed lest the Portuguese should try him,
as it was at first agreed. It was a hasty act on his part,
but there was a slight riot, and I think in law he was
properly acquitted, for he was struck with a stone by
some one in the mob which was collected.

My cases are now rather increasing again, I think, and
will probably continue until we march. I have had two
very blackguard officers to try in the Royal Drivers' corps.
Sheep-stealing has now succeeded to pig-shooting, as pork
is out of season. The horses are now like mad when
turned out, and are scampering all over the country.

I had a long conversation with Lord Wellington yesterday. After discussing our business up and down the
market-place, he said that " the want of rain began to be
very alarming; but that as soon as the pontoons arrived
he would be off. The heavy artillery have started two or
three days since from Castello Branco, and will be here
by the 31st. The pontoons are stuck somewhere on the
road." He discussed the war here, and in the North,
with me: observing that, " a country ought to think well
before it undertook to do what Spain did; that, certainly,

H

Spain and Portugal were the fittest places to try the experiment of a battle for the mere soil, because in general there was nothing else in the country much worth fighting for, or which could be much damaged."

"As, for instance," he added, "what is this village worth? burn it, and a few hundreds would make it as good as ever with a little labour; but now," he continued, "he believed that a great portion of the Spaniards began to be very anxious to bring the business to a close; they had rather that we should beat out the French and be off, but, next to that, they had sooner the French beat us out, and had quiet possession, than that such a war as that of the last three years should be continued." He said "he thought the Cortes were going on ill; that they were unpopular, knew it, and did not know how to set about becoming otherwise; that he disapproved of their meddling with the royal feudal tithes, or church property, and particularly with the elections of the next assembly, with which he thought they had nothing to do. They have declared the elections of one district all void, from some informality, and as the new elections have run much upon priests, they have been trying to make these void, as being within the clause concerning placemen in their constitution—' that no placeman was to be elected for his own district.' However," he continued, " in the present state of things all the real and urgent business, and what is now the most material, namely, all relating to the army and the war, is done here, at Frenada, and let them squabble at Cadiz; if they will leave us alone, I don't care. Portugal is for some time quite safe and out of the scrape, and if things go on well I think Spain will be out of the scrape also." "But," he added, "he should be almost sorry to see such a war as this has been carried on all over Germany, where there is so much to destroy, and to be lost."

In spite of the poverty of the country and the difficulty

as to obtaining bullocks, we have somehow or other collected one thousand here to begin the campaign with : I hear one hundred and fifty fine ones for the artillery.

April 26th.—I am kept going to the last minute. A number of new cases are come in, and I am very busy again; the more so, as the time is so short, and so uncertain when all my Courts are to break up. I cannot get below a dozen cases in hand, for new ones arise faster than I try the old ones.

I have just heard from Coimbra, that one Court-martial is broken up by a division of cavalry moving down to Oporto. I do not quite understand this, but conclude that they will pass the river somewhere below, and so march through the Tras os Montes, and join us again on the other side of the Douro, and have a good untouched country to advance through—otherwise this does not look like a march. No one knows, however, and probably I know as much as the Adjutant-General. I must now write to Lord Wellington; this movement at Coimbra has disturbed two of my Coimbra cases very much.

The new Mutiny Act has been sent out to me. There are several changes, one I see which I suggested; but the business is very much bungled. The Mutiny Act and Articles of War are now at variance, as the latter have not been altered with the former. By the first, an officer may be tried here by a Court of seven members; by the articles, there must be thirteen.

Some of the fifth division have, I hear, moved across the Douro at Lamego. This confirms the opinion I have given above, especially as D'Urban's Portuguese cavalry are all north of the Mondego, and have been some time there. This will disturb another of my Courts. Lord Wellington says, that the witnesses must follow and try and catch the Court; but I am no hunter, and shall try to remove the case to another place. I dine with Lord Wellington.

Head-Quarters, Frenada, Saturday May 1st, 1813.—
This last week I have again been very busy, and shall
remain so, no doubt, until we move. This will probably
be in a week or so, for our wings are in motion. The
cavalry round by Oporto, as I mentioned before, and some
Portuguese infantry, under Colonel Hamilton, are advancing to Alcantara from near Portalegre and Eloss.
We shall soon be drawing together, but head-quarters, I
have very little doubt, will be the last to move. We have
just got the "*Spanish Gazette,*" of Seville, with Elio's
letter, stating the victory gained by General Murray near
Alicant, and his driving Suchet back with loss, through
Bejar and Villana to Fuente Higuera. I conclude you
will have heard this in England before this reaches you.
We have no English account, but Lord Wellington seems
to consider it very good news. He came running into the
Military Secretary's room, where I was yesterday, to
communicate this, saying, "Murray has beat Suchet,
Fitzroy." I always expected the fighting would begin in
that quarter this campaign. We got also yesterday from
Lisbon the almost incredible good news that Austria had
agreed to join the Allies with eighty thousand men in
Germany, and one hundred thousand in Italy, and that
Davoust and Grenier had been again defeated. Lord
Wellington seems rather to give credit to all this. Poor
Bony will go mad if it should prove all to be true.

A few days since at dinner at Lord Wellington's, he
got upon the subject of "Vetus." He said, "He thought
he knew the author, and that he had been in India—
not Mackintosh, as reported here." He then went on to
say, "he did not think much of Vetus's letters:* that
many of his facts as to this country were quite without
foundation; that neither Vetus, nor the O. P.'s, nor

---

* If the letters of Vetus were written, as was supposed, by Lord
Wellesley, it is quite clear that Lord Wellington was ignorant of the
fact.—ED.

Lord Wellesley, knew anything about the war here, and what could or could not be done; that he fully believed Government had done all they could; that the men who did come could not have been here sooner, and perhaps had better have come still later; that more cavalry he could not have employed, had he had them at Lisbon, for want of transport for food; that when he advanced formerly to Talavera, he left several thousand men at Lisbon, because he could not supply them had they been with the army; that even now he could not have brought up the Hussar brigade into the field, unless by draughting home the three regiments whose men he lately had sent back, and thus setting at liberty their transport; that the Guards, Life and Blues, he knew of some time since, and sent five months ago to Estremadura to collect mules for their supply; that every two dragoons employed a mule to feed the men and horses, and that all this difficulty in the detail was quite unknown at home. In short, he said, Lord Wellesley knew nothing about the matter, and he had no reason to be dissatisfied with Government at home." All this made several of us stare. I am told that Lord Wellington was very angry with Lord Wellesley for his resignation, and hardly spoke to any one for some days after he had heard the fact. Lord Paget has just sent up here two of 'the Hussars, a corporal and a private, to wait as orderlies on my lord the peer; two very fine fellows. This was done out of compliment. They will only be ruined at head-quarters, which is a terrible place for soldiers and servants; over-pay, great idleness, and every third house a wine-house.

I have just read Mrs. M. A. Clark and the Messrs. Fitzgerald's, &c., which Lord Fitzroy Somerset sent me by desire of Lord Wellington. It is a curious production, and very ingenious as I understand it, merely as a punishment on the Chancellor of the Exchequer for not letting her profit by the Treasury, and, at the same time, a strong inducement to all others in her favour, held over their heads *in terrorem*, not to be guilty of equal ingratitude; that is, not to neglect making up her deficiences in cash when a hint has been given them of the necessity.

May 2nd.—Lord Wellington, I hear is to go to-day to General Cole's division, the fourth, near the Figuiera, above Castello Rodrigo, and near Eschalao. He sends his hounds over the six leagues to-day : they hunt there to-morrow. On Tuesday he is to review the fourth division, and return here to dinner at Frenada afterwards. Lord Wellington said, some days since, he would move on the 5th of May : some of the army may, and will, I have no doubt; but I do not think *we* shall before the 10th. No one knows, however; and I dare say no one will know until the day before, when all will be in a bustle. I hope we shall not set out in this weather, however, which continues constant cold, rain, and wind. By watching sharp, I can generally get an hour's ride dry ; but it will be rather dismal work to start on a long march in this wet, and it would, from the state of the roads, knock up the mules too much at first, when I take it they will have far enough to go.

If the news from Austria be true, and General Murray has really beaten Suchet in an English and not merely in a Spanish fashion, the French, when they hear we have crossed the Douro, will probably go at once behind the Ebro, carrying all they can with them that is moveable and worth carriage. At present, however, their plan seems to be, to try to make a stand on the Douro first. They are evidently receding gradually from Madrid.

Later.—I have just heard that part of my gossip of head-quarters is not correct. Lord Wellington has got a cold, and has determined not to go to General Cole to-day, though the weather has now cleared up.

May 3rd, Monday.—Lord Wellington is rather worse to-day, I hear, and does not leave Frenada. I hope his review will be quite put off. He has, I believe, only a bad cold. We have still no further news from Alicant: at Cadiz they had only seen the same account that we have. Mr. Wellesley says that the people were in high spirits about it there, though I suspect that some of the Spaniards did not behave well. The allied loss is reported to be nine hundred, that of the French at two thousand. If we could kill off at this rate, and make the Spaniards bear a fair share, this would do very well. I have since heard from Colonel C—— that it is supposed Elio's troops behaved ill, and threw away their arms. Elio's corps had received orders not to fight, but to unite with General Murray : he was just about to do so, and part of his corps was on his left, but too far distant, and gave way when attacked. The orders were, for all the corps, Elio's, Del Parque's, &c., to unite with General Murray without a battle. General Murray will scarcely be able to do much (if he has beat Suchet) with his small force, if he cannot trust the Spaniards. I hope, however, Whittingham's corps has behaved well.

May 4th, Tuesday.—Lord Wellington has just got eight of the Prince Regent's grey stallions up from Lisbon to draw his carriage on the march : they are small, but showy, little, prancing, round-carcassed animals. They have the same mark as is on my black horse from Machacha; but mine beats them in beauty. To-day they were tried, and not having been for some time, or ever, in harness, or not liking the country so well as Lisbon, they would not for a long time go at all. One reared up and fell backwards twice, clean over, and one got astride the pole. They got on better, however, at last, and did not break the carriage as I expected. Lord Wellington's six old large mules would do the work much better, though they are not so showy for Spain.

I saw Lord Wellington to-day, he said he was much better; but has apparently a heavy, bad cold.

May 5th.—Here we are, still mum, as I expected; and the reason for it is now said to be that the pontoons are not yet arrived. They left Castello Branco May the 1st only, and, it is said, cannot reach this place before the 9th. Monday the 10th is now talked of; I think, however, it may be still Thursday next, the day after the post-day again, before we stir; most people say, however, Tuesday the 11th ; much may depend on news. Of course, Lord Wellington must be very anxious to know the true state of the North of Europe before we start; and the present strong south-west gales are much against our hearing soon; he also wishes to know the exact effect of the fight at Alicant. I dined yesterday at head-quarters, and Lord F. Somerset told me that they had more irregular accounts of the latter business, and that they became less and less satisfactory. It was understood that the Spaniards, when first attacked alone, were charged and quite cut up by the French—*muy mal tratado,* is the Spanish private account; and one whole regiment, I am told, surrendered. Three regiments are considered to be *mis hors de combat.* Our army, it appears, did certainly afterwards at last beat back a French partial attack with loss; but our vanguard had been beaten back before, and the loss in our army, English and Sicilians, without Spaniards, was nine hundred. This will not do; still it is to be hoped that Whittingham's people behaved better.

Lord Wellington dined at table again yesterday, and was much better. I sat next to him on one side and the Prince of Orange on the other, as there happened to be no other grandees there; and we had much conversation. This has happened two or three times lately, when I have been there, and there are few besides his own establishment present. He always calls the two who are on his right and left, and Campbell settles the rest. Lord F.

Somerset sent me yesterday a little pamphlet of Lord Wellington's, containing the account of the Russian retreat—rather a catchpenny, I think; and, though not exceeding the Russian gazettes in the number of French prisoners, adding several rather incredible details, such as the French crawling into the fires like gnats into a candle, without being sensible of their danger, &c.

The French, who had quitted Toledo altogether, have again advanced, and occupied it with much the same force as before, to the great discomfiture of the junta there, who thought the " *Esclaves* " (as they call them in the account of the Alicant battle) were gone for good and for ever. To-day Lord Wellington keeps the anniversary of the battle of Fuentes d'Onore, and all present at that battle are to dine with him.

5th (*Later*).—Since writing the above, I have received a case of a deserter from the Isla de Leon. Two years since he deserted to the French, and persuaded others to go with him. As no time is now to be lost, I have drawn the charge and sent the whole off to Lamego for trial directly. My only Court which has as yet moved, or had orders to move, is that at Coimbra, who are cavalry, and are now at Oporto. I have sent Mr. Commissary D——, from Coimbra, there to be tried, for a breach of orders; and a number of witnesses are all gone with him on both sides to Oporto : I only hope they may not, by any sudden order, have all their march for nothing. We have now, since Christmas, tried eighty cases, and there are still ten in hand, besides about thirty which have come to nothing.

CHAPTER VI.

Newspaper Complaints—Wellington's Comments—Review of the Portuguese—Gatherings at Head-quarters—Reviews—Recommencement of
the March—The Route.

Head-quarters, Frenada,
May 8, 1813.

My DEAR M——,

I HAVE first to thank you for your letter and
paper of the 21st, which was most acceptable, as it happened to be, once more, the only paper of that date at
head-quarters, and of course the only one which had the
accounts from the French papers of Bonaparte's having
left Paris, and of the state of their armies, &c. Finding
this to be the case I hastened to read it, and laid it, with
three Courts-martial, before Lord Wellington; more particularly, among other things, pointing out to him a
malicious letter against him, from Lisbon, stating the
discontent of the cavalry officers at having their horses
turned over to the Germans, and at its being done by a
German officer, &c., and the disgrace at being sent home
dismounted. He read it through, and at every sentence
of that part relating to the general state of the cavalry,
he went on, with a laugh, " a lie!"—" a lie!"—" a lie!"
except as to Lieutenant-colonel Sherlock's being vexed at
the regiment being sent home. " That's very true—all
the rest is a lie!"

I think we are still likely to be here for some days.
The pontoons are only expected to arrive in this neighbourhood to-morrow, and I have then heard it whispered
that we shall not stir until they are on the banks of the

river, or indeed till they are fixed ready. The brigade of heavy artillery, namely, six eighteen-pounders, were encamped about two miles from hence on Thursday, and I went over to see them. The difficulty of transport may be conceived when I tell you that there were above a hundred and sixty of the strongest oxen employed in getting these six pieces, with the appurtenances, along the road, besides spare animals.

The next day the whole proceeded to Almeyda; this, and what I hear about the pontoons, makes me conceive that a part of the army at least will cross the Douro immediately, somewhere in the vicinity of Eschalona; but of course I can only conjecture, and am very much in the dark on the subject. The troops still remain at Lamego, Vizeu, Cea, Coria, Moimento, &c.; the cavalry only round by Oporto, and some of General Hill's, have moved yet. The Hussar brigade are now all up near us, and the Household troops all in the road on this and the other side of Sabugal. Some of the Blues have been here; they are in fine order. I saw some horses as fat as in England; I hear, however, a much worse account of the Life-Guard horses. Colonel H., of the Blues, says that he does not see why his horses should not continue to be in as good condition as they are now, and look as well through the campaign; the other soldiers here, however, say, " Wait for a little duty and starvation, and then talk; you have done nothing but come up in the best time of the year, in the grass season."

I dined yesterday at head-quarters, to meet General Graham. He is a very fine old man, but does not indeed look quite fit for this country work; every one seems to think and say the same, and also that he is broken since he was here. It is really to be regretted that such a fine old man should be exposed as he must .be. General Picton was also there, and seemed in full vigour. All the great guns come here to pay their respects to head-

quarters. Lord Wellington is quite well again; was out
hunting on Thursday, and, being kept in by rain all
yesterday, is making up for it to-day by persisting in his
expedition to the fourth division. He was to set out
at seven this morning for the review of General Cole's
division, on a plain beyond Castel Rodrigues, about
twenty-eight miles from hence, was to be on the ground
about ten, and was to return to dinner to-day by four or
five o'clock. This is something like vigour, and yet I
think he overdoes it a little; he has, however, a notion
that it is exercise which makes head-quarters more healthy
than the rest of the army generally is, and that the
hounds are one great cause of this.

Monday, May 10*th.*—The weather is, since yesterday,
clearing up again, and is just now perfection—a mild sun,
moist ground, and fine, genial, south-west wind : it will
soon turn now to heat. I inquire daily about the
pontoons, upon which our movement depends, and have
now ascertained that they only left Castello Branco three
days since, and that a commissariat clerk went yesterday
to meet them with fresh animals at Sabugal. They
cannot be here, it is clear, before the 13th and 14th, and
so says General Picton, who passed the men on the road.
If they are then to move on to be fixed, we cannot well
stir before the 16th or 17th, and that seems the general
opinion here now, though Lord Wellington appears to be
impatient about it.

I have now to tell you of a piece of gaiety of mine
yesterday. I went to leave a Court-martial with Lord
Wellington about twelve o'clock; saw him, and found
that he was at two o'clock to set out for another review
of the Spanish cavalry of the Conde de Penne Villemur,
who have often been mentioned, and were of use in General
Hill's surprise, &c. I had much curiosity to see these
gentlemen, and finding, after calling upon the Adjutant-
general, that I had only one summons to send out, I

agreed with Lord Aylmer to go with him to this review, ran home, wrote, sent off my summons, dressed, &c., got my black horse equipped in his best also, and at one we set off for Huero, near which the cavalry were ordered to assemble, on the Agueda. It was about twelve or thirteen miles distant, and we got there, riding gently, soon after three, having gone about two miles round, under the guidance of Colonel B——, close to the Quinta de Agueda, a pretty farm and gentleman's house (so esteemed here), in a wild, park-like scene in the wood. I knew the road well, for it was nearly my way to Guinaldo, but I had no objection to see this Quinta, so took merit for my modesty, but only undertook to be guide home. The meadows were quite green, the woods all coming out in leaf, and the thorn in blossom.

At about a mile from this place we fell in with Lord Wellington and his aides-de-camp, who had got over, in about an hour and twenty minutes, by my road. The party then consisted of Lord Wellington, Lord F. Somerset, Colonel C. Campbell, the Prince of Orange, his aide-de-camp, Lord Aylmer, Colonel B——, and myself; and I assure you the black went neighing about in high spirits, looking very sleek and respectable. On the ground we were met by the Spanish generals O'Donnell and O'Lalor, and found the cavalry drawn up in front of the river in open order, about seven hundred in all. The first and best regiment was that of Algarve, the second was that of Estremadura, and then came on the left a single squadron of partizans, to be the regiment de Gallicia. The two first regiments were tolerably clothed, and some of the men fine-looking fellows, all very fierce in appearance, with their dark faces and black beards, &c. The arms, though not uniform, good enough; the greater part with our cavalry broadsword and carbine, but many with our sailors' long straight boarding-sword, and no bad weapon either—I should think the best of the two.

The helmets—black and steel, or rather bright iron—
were serviceable, and seemed to have seen no little
service; many, however, were black and brass, belonging
to other regiments, of Saguntum, &c. ; the belts generally
white, at least those of the Algarve regiment, many black
in the other. The horses, in general, very small, and
some scarcely fit for duty, but for the most part apparently well fed, and in very fair condition; out of the two
one very tolerable set might have been chosen, as good, I
understand, as many French regiments have been when
here.

The left squadron of Portuguese were queer-looking
gentlemen, in dirty brown, blue, and green jackets of all
hues and ages; one fellow among them was quite a
monster in size, and excited much notice. Lord Wellington quite burst out into a laugh as he passed. After
his lordship and his suite had passed in front and in the
rear of the whole, as in England, they passed him in
troops and saluted. The officers then appeared the
worst—they were awkward louts; some did not salute
at all, some in a most clumsy manner; but perhaps this
was not a custom with them, as they had inquired what
was usual with us. They were, many of them, however, round-shouldered, dirty, ill-looking men. Lord
Wellington desired them to form once into close column,
and then to deploy again, and as there was more room
across the river, desired it might be done there. We galloped across, and then the scene of the cavalry passing
the ford was very picturesque, as the day was very fine
and the mountains and country in great beauty. This
was between Huero and Castilegos. They manœuvred
thus much very tolerably, that is, the regiment, for the
squad of partizans remained behind practising the broadsword. The ground on which the regiments were reviewed was quite a bog.

About five o'clock off went Lord Wellington in a

gallop across the country home to dinner. We all followed close for about a league, and then, to save our animals, not having fifteen as he has, Lord F. Somerset, Lord Aylmer, General Oswald, and myself went quietly on, and got here about a quarter after seven, I for one much pleased with my trip. The Conde P. Villemur did not command, and, as I understand, has retired in disgust altogether, because there is a commander-in-chief appointed in the cavalry, and he wished to be appointed if there was to be one, or at least not to have any one over him. He was always, it is said, a person who had a will of his own, and did not like to obey orders. These jealousies and quarrels are much to be regretted. The officer who commanded was Monte Major. His aide-de-camp told me that a number of their men were on duty, and that their real numbers were above one thousand.

The review of the fourth division was, I believe, much more satisfactory to Lord Wellington, as everything was in high order—Portuguese and all, about six thousand five hundred; but having so often seen a good English review, I was much more gratified with these Spanish gentlemen. The Life-Guards, &c., are to be inspected to-morrow.

The messenger who was sent off on the 17th to Alicant has returned to-day, and has been round by Cadiz in his return. He makes our loss less—only about three hundred, I hear from the official statement—and that of the French greater: and I was very glad to hear that Whittingham's men had behaved well, and that General Murray was well satisfied with them. The messenger rode from Cadiz here in three days.

We have here to-day all the grandees—Marshal Beresford, General Alava, Don Julian, General Graham; the latter has been to the review above sixteen miles distant, to see the Household Brigade. They mustered eight hundred and twenty-nine rank and file in the field, that is, Blues and Life-Guards together, and seven hundred and fifty-one horses, and performed very well. The horses of the Blues much the best, some of the Life-Guards' rather skeletonish. I still fear General Graham is too old for this work; at least he must not act as he did at Barossa. Before the battle, I am told, he stood up to his middle in the water for an hour or more, encouraging the troops to get on, English and Spanish; and jumped off his horse on purpose for the example. It is added, some of the men said, "Come, old corporal, do go and take care of yourself, and get out of our way."

Lord Wellington was to-day in his full Colonel's dress uniform of the Blues, and looked very well in it.

Wednesday, 12th, Post-day. Head-Quarters, Frenada. —Still here, and very probably we shall be so for some days. There are symptoms, however, of a move soon, such as the packing of Lord Wellington's claret, &c. The pontoons are expected the day after to-morrow. The twenty-four-pounders are on their march through Gallicia from Corunna. The eighteen-pounders have passed on by Almeyda from hence. The cavalry near the coast, whom I caught for a Court-martial at Oporto sending every witness from Coimbra, have now in part, I understand, passed Braga. I sent a case yesterday to Lamego, but fear it will be too late, and must be tried on the march: there are so many little delays, however, that I may yet be in time. The difficulties now increase. Lord Wellington and Colonel F—— of the artillery do not agree. Lord Wellington complains much of the heads of that department. He sent B—— home some time since, and I now hear F—— is to go to England, and for the present at least Lieut.-colonel D—— is to have the command. F—— is much of a gentleman, I think; draws, it is said, very well, &c., but has a bad memory, is nervous, and raises difficulties, which I sus-

pect Lord Wellington does not encourage, but expects
things to be done if possible. I am now told that
General Pakenham is to act as Adjutant-general to the
army, and supersede Lord Aylmer, the deputy Adjutant-
general, but who has acted hitherto as principal. Every
one speaks most highly of Pakenham.

Head-Quarters, Frenada, May 15*th*, 1813. *Saturday.*
—The first division of the Guards and Germans left
Vizeu for Lamego three days since. The fifth division
have left Lamego, and are marching through the Tras os
Montes. The seventh division have left Moimento, I
believe, on the same route. The sixth have also left Cea.

When the French, who are still at Salamanca, Arevalo,
Avila, Madrid, &c., hear that we have thus crossed the
Douro and turned their position, they must either assemble
and give battle, which I think they will not do, or they
must at once go beyond the Ebro, and then I suppose we
shall attack Burgos, and cross after them. However it
be, I expect a good long march in the outset. The
army, however, on the whole, is in good condition, and
never has had so long a repose, or been so regularly
clothed. The sick are reduced to nearly seven thousand,
and will probably be never much less. A very bad report
has been made of the pontoons : they changed the oxen
for horses, and these treated them roughly. The day
before yesterday so bad a report was made of them, that
yesterday, when they reached Sabugal, off went Lord
Wellington about twenty-six miles to look at them with
his own eyes. I hear he is glad to know the worst,
but that is bad. They are made too slight, were old and
had new bottoms made for them, but now the sides are
very much shaken and decayed. Exaggerated reports
have reached us that the tin covering is knocked in
holes, and that the wood of the sides may be pinched out
by the touch in some places. Lord Wellington may now,
however, act accordingly, knowing the worst. They will

I

not pass this way, it is said, but across by Galegos, a different road from that taken by the heavy guns, the eighteen-pounders. I now think, therefore, that the heavy guns will cross towards Lamego by the bridge, and that the pontoons will be fixed, if at all, further north up the river. We shall probably cross at Zamora, but cannot tell: it is said the bridge is not destroyed there.

On Monday Lord Wellington will review the light division in our front under General Anson—the 43rd, 52nd, 95th, and the Caçadores Portuguese,—a very fine body of men. To-morrow he is to fix his tent in the Praça of Frenada, and will give a dinner to Marshal Beresford, the 16th being the anniversary of the battle of Albuera. To this I am asked, though not a military man, and certainly not present on that fortunate occasion. The town is so full that some encamp; and Captain M——, who is just arrived here, sleeps and dresses in the ante-room of the Adjutant-general's office, where the printing-press is all day at work, and leaves him a fine perfume of printing-ink at night, besides the full smell from the stables below, through the open floor, which he enjoys almost as much as I do myself here in my quarters. The numbers at head-quarters are so increased that I fear we shall find it very difficult to get quarters when on the march. We have now Lord William Russell and Lord John here, the former on Lord Wellington's staff, the latter, I believe, as an amateur. We have also Lord March's brother in the dragoons, and last, but not least, I can assure you, Captain Fitzclarence, an immense young man: he is in the Adjutant-general's department.

The first division from Vizeu are, it is said, to be at Braganza about the 17th. Great part of the army will be there by the 22nd, and by the same day the second division, under General Hill, from Coria, will be within seven leagues of Salamanca; yet the 52nd, who to-day are at Nava da Ver in order to attend the review of the light division at Espeja, are to return to Guinaldo.

I have just fallen in with a dozen of the Life Guards, with their brass helmets, &c. I think before they have lived to October they will have a very philosophical idea of a vacuum—one pound of bony, lean beef will occupy but a little of their long stomachs. I suspect our good allies, the Spaniards, will think that we have sent them a regiment of Don Quixotes, and the horses from present appearances may in a little time make no bad Rosinantes. Five or six of these tall, six feet high men were mounted on mules going to Almedia, to get iron; I pitied them to-day as they were bargaining for a bit of dear cheese and some dried chestnuts in the market. They have some spirit, however, and will not enter the staff mounted corps, a new thing, considering it to be a sort of police, and declaring that they would rather be police at home as before than here, if they are to be police at all. This corps of staff horse is to be two hundred, and to be composed of volunteers from all regiments. Officers do not hitherto take to it, but very good-looking men have volunteered in general; none from the hussars, I hear.

Monday Evening, 17th.—The dinner yesterday went off famously, very well managed in the tent, and very comfortable. Lord Wellington was supported by Marshal Beresford and General Sir Lowry Cole on one side, and by General Castanos and Sir T. Graham on the other; and then all the staff of the three Generals, Wimpfen, O'Lalor, Alava, &c., with the aides-de-camp; the Portuguese Quarter-Master-general, and other staff, Lord Aylmer, Lord F. Somerset, Marquis of Worcester, Lord March, and all the heads of departments. Almost all were with stars, medals, Portuguese orders, or something distinguishing. If I were in the American General

I 2

Harrison's army, perhaps I might get an honourable mention, like his good friend Charles Walker, the Judge Advocate-general, who was of such use in the corps of spies. Then we had Mr. Joe Kelly, of the Life Guards a famous singer, whom I recognised as having heard at Shrewsbury races, and he gave us some good songs; and we " hip! hip! hipped!" &c., to the grandees. I was much entertained at the etiquette observed between the Marshal and General Castanos, who should go into the tent first: at last they went in side by side, as other great men have before determined that knotty point. Castanos seems very easy and good-humoured, and willing to give way, and even to have a little fun, but he is very old. All the fashionables were at the review this morning near Espeja, and a very fine sight it was. Between five and six thousand of the *élite* of ours, and of the Portuguese troops; the line near three-quarters of a mile long, two deep, and they marched in line near half a mile over rough and smooth, and then changed their front three times, and at last passed in review admirably. The German hussars, commanded by Colonel Arentsfchild, were on the right, in excellent style, and beyond them a brigade of artillery : the day was beautiful, and the scene upon the whole very striking. Lord Wellington is indefatigable. He goes six leagues to-morrow another way to Friexada, to review the English hussars, the 10th, &c. He looks, I think, a little fagged and anxious.

Guinaldo, May 18*th.*—On my arrival here at eleven o'clock to attend the Court-martial, I found the President, General Vandeleur, had stayed with Lord Wellington to go over to the review, and had sent an order for the Court to assemble to-morrow, the 19th, instead of to-day, of which he had forgotten to give me any notice. If we march on Thursday I shall be at my wit's end, and it is so provoking to lose a whole day thus, just at such a moment. He is so hospitable, civil, and good-humoured, that, though very much inconvenienced, I cannot be angry.

The fourth division march from Escuao to-day. The light will, I suppose, move with us. The second division are now moving along the Sierras de Francia, the mountains in sight of us here. This air must be aguish; five of the officers and a great number of the men of the 52nd, though such fine-looking fellows, are attacked by the ague when doing no work, and in fine weather. At Frenada most of the sickness was among the natives.

Lord Wellington, at the review yesterday, was on one of his new purchases from General L. C. Stewart. He gave four hundred guineas for the two, and for this two hundred and fifty—a gentleman who has gained some plates in England, and has a name. It is a very pretty animal, but is as troublesome in regard to neighing as my black. They were answering each other all the morning. Indeed this neighing gives quite a character to a Spanish review—it is heard more than the trumpets. I met in my way here about twenty Spanish grenadiers, who, I understand, were part of a treasure escort. They were very fine men, and were well clothed. Individually they greatly surpass the Portuguese in appearance : tall, straight, well-limbed, and with good young countenances. As to their discipline, or how they will stand, I cannot say; but such men can only want good officers to do anything. In the review yesterday, besides the two regiments of Caçadores Portuguese, there was the 17th of the line Portuguese : they really marched and went through the evolutions very nearly as well as our own men. The men, however, are naturally mean, shabby men in general, like the pictures of the Queen's family at Frogmore, which you must remember. The officers look much better than those of the Spaniards, and seem most of them to know more of their duty. The Spanish men, as men, independent of discipline, are wonderfully superior to the Portuguese; and yet we have seen, from want of that knowledge of acting in a mass, and total mistrust of their leaders, how inferior they have hitherto been.

The Portuguese people, though they do not talk so well as the Spaniards, or look so well, have shown much more practical spirit. When the French passed through the Spanish towns or villages, the alcalde went to meet them, the people remained quiet, submitted to the exactions, and the French in general treated them tolerably well in consequence, for they thus got food and forage. In the Portuguese villages, on the contrary, when the French last entered Portugal, almost every inhabitant sacrificed his house and property, and fled, according to orders; and thus it was that the French were so plagued and puzzled for food, and provoked to destroy the houses as they did.

May 19*th, Six o'clock, evening, Head-Quarters, Frenada.* —Just returned from Guinaldo in time for the post. My Court met at twelve. We tried the man by one o'clock. I wrote the proceedings fair, got them signed, and here I am, very hungry, and find that every one has dined, for Lord Wellington began to-day to dine at three o'clock, instead of eight. We do not march to-morrow, perhaps not till Saturday,

Frenada, May 21*st,* 1813, *Friday.*—At last, to-morrow morning we all break up for the march. I go, as a civil department, by the route enclosed; I shall, therefore, see nothing of the greater part of head-quarters for a fortnight. Dr. M'Gregor goes my way; but who else I know not. Indeed Dr. M'Gregor wishes to go to Oporto, and perhaps I may have the whole road nearly to myself. I am told that the road is pleasant; at least it is new all beyond Almeida. The light division is to march to-day. The second are not far from Tamames by this time. Tamames is, I believe, the military head-quarters on the second day's march, the 23rd. The fourth division passed the Douro, I believe, yesterday; the others have already done so, and in two or three days the main body of the army will be at Braganza, Outeiro, and Miranda de Duero; and the light and second divisions and head-quarters on this side of the Douro.

Some of Hamilton's Portuguese in the second division are so ill supplied, that Lord Wellington has, it is said, threatened the Marshal to send them in the rear if they be not better clothed and fed. He says he would rather be without two or three battalions, than have them in such a state as these are. Indeed, he seems either not quite to trust the Portuguese, or they cannot be supplied; for he leaves a full battalion, I hear, at Abrantes, and one or two elsewhere, saying he has Portuguese enough in proportion. He seems in good spirits, but looks worn and anxious. The pontoons have crossed the Douro, so now I do not know where they are to be laid down, unless to let the second and light divisions and head-quarters pass over, whenever necessary, or to bring over the others, if the French should collect.

The French have hitherto always judged of the situation of the main body of the army by that of head-quarters : they were thus twice taken in last year. Before the siege of Badajoz, Lord Wellington had moved away nearly the whole of the army before he stirred, and the whole of the head-quarters were not protected against two thousand men. This deceived the French then, and I hope will now, but they are on the alert; at Salamanca constantly on the *qui vive*, and ready for a run, &c. The Commissary here has already trusted a man with money to go and collect forage, &c., at Salamanca, before the French are gone. Everything is now alive. General Graham, I believe, commands at Miranda de Duero, or at least will very soon. General Picton has the ague, and is too ill to take the command of this division yet, but remains with it. I thought him looking very well;

but there is something in this climate which does not suit the English at all, even when quiet and living well. The natives have their annual ague fit, and seem to think it a part of their existence : they are rather unhappy when it does not come as usual. Lord Wellington's cars with the heavy baggage are off.

Frenada, May 20*th,* 1813.—Route for the head-quarters of the army.

The military department will move on the 22nd instant to Ciudad Rodrigo.

The Civil Department.

May 22nd. Almeida.   Depôt of provisions.
  „ 23rd. Pinhel.
  „ 24th. Cotimos.
  „ 25th. Villa Nova de Foscoa.
  „ 26th. Torre de Moncorvo.   Depôt of provisions.
  „ 27th. Halt.
  „ 28th. Tornas and Lagouça.
  „ 29th. Villa Dalla.
  „ 30th. Sendim.
  „ 31st. Miranda de Duero.   Depôt, &c.

G. MURRAY, Q. M. G.

To the Commandant of
    Head-Quarters.

CHAPTER VII.

The March commenced—Scenes on the Road—Villa Dalla—Toro—Castro Monte—Palencia—Prospects of a General Action—Skirmishing—Massa.

Head-quarters, Civil Department,
Torre de Moncorvo, May 27, 1813.

MY DEAR M——,

WE here halt a-day; on the 22nd, about twelve, I arrived at Almeida—that heap of ruins—and turned out, by the authority of the Governor, two Portuguese officers, to get one miserable room as my quarters. Colonel Le Mesurier, the late governor, was too ambitious a man to remain inactive, shut up in Almeida during a campaign. He therefore applied for a brigade in the Portuguese service, and, though he could not obtain it, gave up his government to command a regiment. I met him at the gate on his way to Miranda de Duero to join his division. The new Portuguese governor was just moving, but as he had not yet got into the present government-house he gave us up all the great stable, which was very good, and he was in every respect very civil and willing to do the most for us. In my way here we had no particular adventures. By the aid of the Spaniard in loading we have much less trouble, and I have always ridden on, and got a quarter before the baggage arrived. My only companions were the Paymaster-general, Hunter, and Mr. Whitter, and nine other clerks with him, and the military chest, &c., and two or three commissariat parties. The weather has been uniformly fine, and at times very hot.

We have daily been roused at five o'clock, and off at six, but have nevertheless suffered from the heat, at times very much, before we arrived at our station.

On the 23rd we left Almeida and descended to the Coa and passed it by a very picturesque bridge, rendered more so from one stone arch having been blown up, and repaired with wood in a rough style. After a mile of steep ascent, we reached a lofty, rough, level common, in a wild, uncultivated country, like Dartmoor; with the Sierra d'Estrella on one side, still partly tipped with snow, and the ridge of hills and Castello Rodrigo on the other. We passed Valverde,—a complete ruin now—a village without one roof remaining! I was sorry to hear that we had begun the destruction of it, and that the Portuguese soldiers afterwards left very little remaining for the French to do. The next village, Periero, was pleasingly situated, and we then soon got down by a river, and observed Pinhel with its old Moorish tower, fort, and walls, and a bishop's palace, and a convent adjoining, a league before us, on the brow of a hill. At Pinhel we were all fixed by the *Juez de Fores* in the bishop's palace, and had a choice of large empty rooms in this now uninhabited but lately handsome house. It was all tight, and Mr. Hunter having a table by means of baggage, and tubs for seats, we fared very well. The stables are magnificent, good ones for thirty horses, and inferior for sixty horses more.

At Almeida there was no green forage to be had; we bought small bundles of grass at about a shilling each in the grass-market for our animals. At Pinhel we however got an order for green barley from the Juge, twenty-eight pounds each animal for the day, and they all fared so luxuriously that my black gentleman was the next day very troublesome. In the bishop's palace at Pinhel, the rooms formed a very handsome suite round a square court in the centre; the hangings, &c., all removed, but the ceilings ornamented; the rooms well shaped, with a tolerable garden adjoining; but the house standing exactly like the Castle Inn at Marlborough, by the road side, at the end of the town. The water is very bad, a nuisance from which we are, it seems, to suffer much throughout the summer in Spain. Last year our men were at times obliged to hold their noses when they drank. At the convent adjoining the palace, which has been much damaged but not destroyed, one or two monks still remained, and I met one as I wandered over the building. He was very civil. The palace is now appropriated as barracks for officers or troops as they pass. The bishop lives at another, at Santa Euphemie, a league beyond Pinhel.

The castle is like all the Moorish castles I have seen here, with the square smooth towers of well-cut hard stone, as sharp now almost as when first built. In the castle lying about are four curious specimens of old cannon, two ribbed, made of beaten iron bars and braced together; one of them appeared to be hollow at both ends, and solid in the middle. The other two a sort of mortar, something in the shape of a very old-fashioned, clumsy earthenware jug, with a sort of handle to raise and fix it for use.

At the convent was a small aqueduct of stone pillars across the garden, to conduct a little stream of water to the monks' habitations; the stream was so small in the pipe that you could scarcely see it run at all, but it was good, and ran constantly all the year, which, as the only good water was a mile off in the river, was very valuable.

On the 24th, our party, consisting of the ten paymasters, three commissaries, and myself, with about fifteen dragoons, and thirty or forty horses, and about thirty or forty baggage animals, assembled at five in the morning in the palace-court and marched onwards.

In less than a league we passed a very pretty village, called, I believe, Valbom, and in another short league came to Euphemia, another village, with rather a large but imperfect house where the bishop resides now; and I believe he was there sitting in his shady colonnade. In a short time we descended again and crossed the Lamego; here we all dismounted, and let the animals graze on the banks, whilst we got some bread and cheese. Half a league further on we turned up out of our road to Cotimos, our destination for the night. It was a bad village, but with a few houses formerly good and still tight. Mr. Hunter, Mr. Whitter, and I, were in a fidalgo's house, and tolerably comfortable, though there was only an old woman there, but we had chairs and tables. We made a great cup with the country wine, brandy, lemons, &c., and were very well off for a dinner by the purchase of a leveret, eggs and bacon, and mutton broth.

On the 25th left Cotimos; and about a league beyond we came to a much better village, with two or three very good houses, of imposing appearance. This was directly in our road, and would have been a better division of the distance. After another league of excellent road we passed Marialva, half a league on our left, a village, with another Moorish castle. After another half league we came to the entrance of a long winding descent of a mile and a half, which brought us into a pretty vale, with another Moorish castle on the hill on our left; and there we again ate and the animals grazed in the meadows near a little stream. Thence we had a league and a half of excessively steep hill to ascend until we got on the high level where stands Villa Nova de Foscoa; this ascent at near one o'clock was tremendously hot work, and very difficult for the baggage.

We here began to get into the army train. About twenty hospital waggons were encamped on the hill near the town, and two troops of the waggon train; and near them were about eighty ox-cars with bales of cloth done up in a sort of sacks to fill with straw for hospital beds, &c. We here got good quarters and tolerable fare.

On the 26th, leaving Villa Nova, we began immediately to descend a winding road to the Douro; this was very fine, one of the best things I had seen here.

I was off as soon after sunrise as possible to pass the ferry before the military chest. I got down to the bank and found about eighty cars drawn up to pass with ammunition, boards, planks, and beams, for the repair of bridges, &c. Two at a time crossed in one boat; and there was another for mules, &c. I stopped some Portuguese; and having waited an hour for the baggage, who had loitered on the road when I left them, we at last got on board this platform as close as we could stick.—Mr. Hunter, and six other gentlemen, about a dozen servants, seven stallions, three mares, and six loaded baggage mules. After some kicking and confusion, we landed safely, and after a league of ascent arrived at Torre de Moncorvo. Both banks of the river were covered on the sides of the road with parties of artillery or baggage grazing, &c.; some bivouacking, and others in camp. The scene was interesting, except that I regretted the obligation of cuting so much of the corn for green forage just as it was becoming ripe.

Here we found the same scene in all the environs; parties picketed and bivouacking, and more artillery drivers; quarters very moderate; but shops very decent; the town not destroyed, for the French have never been here.

The great number of troops which have been quartered here on the march has cleared most of the shops, and injured many of the buildings; even here we cannot buy anything except honey, sugar, bacon, bread, and cheese. The convent of Franciscans above the town is nearly entire, and has two tolerable pictures—the altar-piece, and one in the refectory, by Romano, the monks said, and from the style it may be so. There are some houses here with the furniture remaining; that of the Capitan Mor (the head inhabitant, and a colonel of militia) has painted coved ceilings, and apricot-coloured silk hangings, with old-fashioned wooden chairs and sofas, with bottoms to match the hangings. The church also is handsome. The town is surrounded by hills like Bath, and yet we ascended to it three miles from the Douro. I saw also something like a female to-day, a smart, pretty Lisbon miss going to church—quite a curiosity; and so, I believe, the inhabitants think. My old patrona (or landlady) here came to tell me to look out of the window, as "The Lady" was going by.

Head-Quarters, Civil Department, Villa Dalla, May 29th, 1813.—On the 27th, the night before I marched from Torre de Moncorvo, we had some heavy rain, which cooled the air, laid the dust, and made our journey onwards much more agreeable.

On the 28th, the road to Lagouça was very rough and hilly, and the distance four long leagues. The country is fine; the distance very like parts of Somerset-shire and Devonshire in its general features, but the valleys are less rich, and there are some large pine-woods on the hills. About half way we passed Carvacies, a large village; and at the end of four leagues, Tornas, a poor place, where we had the option of stopping, but preferred Lagouça. A part of the staff corps were en-camped near the pine-wood, with several cars and mate-rials for bridges. They are, I understand, about to lay down a bridge somewhere on the Douro, very near that part, as a safe retreat in case of accidents.

At Lagouça I got a tolerable quarter, and bed, at the padre's. House dirty only. I found books which he

could not understand, and I believe never looked at.
There was the 'Recopilacion of the Spanish Laws,' a
book of authority in Spain. He asked me if it was
mine—the authority I acted from ; had I known how to
carry it I would have bargained with him for it. There
was also a Horace, Bourdaloue's Sermons in Spanish,
and a few other sermons. He gave me some wine, and
was very civil; and honestly sent after me something
that I left behind.

Within a mile of Lagouça, but out of the main road,
you look down on the Douro, which runs down in a
deep rocky chasm, very fine and wild, with a very picturesque convent, which was once Mas Bonito, half way
down on the Spanish side of the river, and the Spanish
town of Miesa above. The French had long been at
these places, and had much injured the convent; but
had never got over, as there is only one little bark ; and
the brave Portuguese had a sort of battery. The scene
was very fine.

To-day (the 29th) I started again after breakfast (but
before six o'clock, being always called at four) for this
place. The road was in general good, though rather
hilly and in parts boggy. We passed to the left of
Brosa ; to the right of Majaduero, and near two or three
other villages. The country is finer, and still more
approaching Somersetshire. I have here, at Villa Dalla,
got a decent quarter in a great farmhouse, where there
are five or six beds about my room, which has, however,
only a door, no window or ceiling. In winter I should
have been starved ; it is now well enough. I got a table
and chairs, and have bought one small fowl for a dollar,
and two little chickens, nearly as big as pigeons, all
bone, for half a dollar. We get eggs, and sometimes
milk ; and though this country has never seen the
French, the houses do not seem quite in a state of
English repair. The whole road is covered with marks

of the encampments of troops, &c. The back of the village Lagouça was just like a drawing of an Otaheite village, and not much better, with bad thatch instead of tile, the general roof. The villages, however, are numerous, and much more populous than in the other parts of Portugal I have seen, and rather cleaner, being nearer Spain. There was bread from Zamora in the market at Lagouça regularly for sale.

Miranda de Duero, May 30*th.*—I came on here to-day a very long journey, meaning to have two days' rest, but found Lord Wellington's head-quarters had passed through here this morning; that his lordship left Salamanca yesterday, and was to be six leagues off in advance, near the Esla, to-day, the 30th. The French absolutely ran away, near Salamanca, and a small party were taken. Spanish head-quarters here to-day, and all in confusion.

Head-Quarters, Toro, June 3rd, 1813.—A day's halt will enable me to give you a few lines to let you know how we go on. The day I sent my last from Miranda de Duero (May 30th), I learnt that head-quarters were to be that day and the next at Carbajales, near the Esla, to superintend one great object of the movement, the passage of the Esla, a formidable river in a military point of view. Fearing to be left behind, though without orders, I determined to march again the next morning (31st), at four, six long leagues to Carbajales. I tried to find the nearest road, the longest being round by Constantia, and, though the best, I did not wish to go above a league out of my way. My directions were to pass Val d'Aguia, Aldea Nova, Fonfrio, and Vermilho. I got right to near Fonfrio and then, through a wrong direction given me by a little miss who sent me by mistake for Carvajosa, I found myself two leagues out of my way at Pino, and had to cross straight over the country for Vermilho. The consequence was that I arrived late and tired at Carbajales, where head-quarters still remained, and at last got a very bad quarter there, but a good stable, which General Graham had just left.

In the evening of the 30th I went down part of the way to see the ferry over the Douro at Miranda. The scenery was very fine, and very like that at Lagouça; the river very deep and narrow, running violently through a chasm of rocks not unlike Chedder cliffs in Somersetshire; and the little ferry-boat almost invisible from above the road down and up above three miles, though the real distance across seems not above a quarter of a mile. Lord Wellington and a part of the staff only came over there. Heavy baggage, printing-press, &c., were left with the light division near Salamanca.

In my way to Carbajales, the road I kept near the Douro towards Aldea Nova was very picturesque, but bad. For the rest of the way the road became better, but the country was ugly, like Bagshot Heath, only with several villages—and the mountains in Gallicia, still tipped with snow, on our left, or nearly behind us. The morning of the day I got to Carbajales (the 31st), the pontoon bridge was placed, and made passable on the Esla, in less than three hours. The Hussars passed a bad ford of above four feet water and bad bottom early in the day to protect this operation, and two divisions of the army passed before night and encamped. Lord Aylmer, who had forded in the morning to go over and look about him, found the bridge ready, and the troops passing as he returned. These were the pontoons which had travelled up from Lisbon, and had been the cause of so much anxiety. About nine of them were used, and the river about the width of the Thames at Windsor. This being the state of things, the orders were to have all head-quarters' baggage down at the water-side by six, and to get them over before the other troops should arrive and the guns. As I had got into a quarter with

K

Spaniards, and they were lazy, I had some trouble to get
mine off, but succeeded at last, and afterwards rode with
Lord Aylmer.

We soon fell into the train of head-quarters' baggage,
the whole of the eighteen-pounders with their ammunition, &c., and one hundred and sixty oxen and their
spare horses; and also the whole of the fourth division
of the army—a train of three miles length in the whole.
The scene presented by the winding down the hill to the
bridge, and the order with which everything was managed,
and the winding up the opposite bank, was very interesting. We passed about eight o'clock, baggage and all,
and the guns and two more divisions of the army were
safely over before five o'clock in the evening, with baggage, &c. We then had about three more leagues of a
Bagshot Heath road, sand and pines, until we suddenly
came in sight of Zamora and the Douro. The latter is
here about as wide as the Thames at Kew Bridge, rather
wider—more perhaps as it is at Fulham. It winds along
a large plain on the south side under the ridge of higher
ground to the north, on which, boldly and well-placed,
stands Zamora with its Moorish church.

The town pleased me much. It is nearly the size of
Salamanca, and having been much less destroyed, is, at
present quite as good a town: the convents alone have
suffered and been gutted. Some of the French had not
left the place until the very morning our troops entered;
the greater part, however, went off the night before. The
castle was rather strong, and would, if defended, have
delayed us two or three days, but the garrison would
have been sacrificed. It was fitted up very regularly in
the inside by the French for troops, places appropriated
for everything, with the names inscribed. There was
also a large foundling hospital, and a general hospital for
the poor. In the former were only about ten or twelve
babies, and about sixteen children, for they had now

scarcely any funds. Nearly opposite was the general hospital, with much space and good wards, but not above six or eight sick, partly from the same reasons, and partly because the French had only left the people the use of one small ward, and the room of the intendant, and occupied the rest with their sick and wounded. They had also now in this last retreat carried off all the linen, &c., and only left bedsteads and bedding. They had not, however, done any wanton mischief in Zamora when they left it this time.

The bridge is handsome, but in our retreat last year we blew up the centre arch out of about a dozen; it had been repaired since with wood. This the French had burnt on the 30th, but by to-day it is repaired and passable. The people received us very cordially, scattered roses over our heads, cried *viva*, &c., and hung all their counterpanes and the hangings of their rooms out of the windows. The lady at my quarters embraced me, and was very kind, but—she was old. There was another like a plump Englishwoman, to whom I passed on the compliment.

The people entertained Lord Wellington and the staff with a concert, lemonade, and ices, &c. The former did not admire the time lost in singing psalms to him, as he said. I met him in the evening, in his Spanish uniform, riding down to the bridge to give directions. In the morning he was on one side of the pontoon bridge, and Marshal Beresford on the other. I almost knocked myself up running about to see Zamora, for we were to march again next morning. I could not attend a little dance given by Lord Wellington in the evening, and except for the iced lemonade should have been in a fever. A thunder-storm in the evening cooled the air, and a good bed made me ready again to march for this place (Toro), five long leagues, the next morning, June 2nd. The French having left Toro on the 1st of June, it became an object to take possession, and open a communication with the light division, and the second from Salamanca.

The road was admirable; a flat sandy level, by the river nearly all the way, until we came to the ascent on which the town of Toro is placed, standing still more boldly over the river than Zamora. The only village we passed, and that a poor one, was Fresno; but we saw several on our left, and across the river in the flat on our right.

Toro is very old, surrounded by ruined mud walls, and though it covers much ground has not many good houses, and is not to be compared to Zamora; there is, however, a market, with a little mutton and beef, and vegetables, pork, eggs, &c. The Moorish church here is much smaller than at Zamora, though that is not very large; there are a few tolerable pictures in both. The castle here is stronger than the one at Zamora, and appears almost new: it stands on the hill above the bridge, and is rather formidable. The two centre arches of this bridge had been blown up by us, repaired by the French with wood, burnt again by them now, and is now being repaired again by us.

We passed, two miles from hence, the sixth division and the seventh, taking up their encamping ground on a fine meadow by the river side, near a small wood. It was a very lively scene, the men marching with music, and as regular, without any disorder or loiterers, as if going to a review; the whole in high order. Yesterday evening the light division arrived from a place within three leagues of Salamanca, a march of nearly eight leagues, and encamped in a meadow near the water side, close to the bridge and ford opposite this town: they only left six men behind in their march. This morning the horse, the baggage, and the artillery, have all come over, passing by the ford; and though it is both wide and deep, I believe without accident, except wet baggage. The infantry crossed by ladders across the breach in the bridge—that is, down one side, then up the other—one by one. They encamp at Morales to-day. This was also a very interesting and animating scene from the hill, which is a humble imitation of Richmond Hill in point of beauty.

The Hussars have commenced famously; they brought into Zamora an officer of the 16th (French), and about thirty prisoners, whom they dashed at, and knocked over in fine style, with little loss. The officer came in here prisoner on horseback, which offended the Spaniards, who were disposed to insult the prisoners, whom they dared not fight, and who had been with them now nearly four years or more.

Yesterday the Hussars again came up with the 16th French cavalry and some others; the latter had only a small bridge to pass which would only carry four abreast. Two squadrons of the 10th formed and charged; the French stood at first well, but were broken, and then formed again. The 10th formed, charged again, and again broke the French; the latter then still made another effort, but at last ran for the bridge. The 10th killed a few, and brought about a hundred and ninety prisoners in here; no horses were taken. Twelve or fifteen men badly wounded were left about two miles off, where it happened. Several of those who came in here were much cut and wounded, covered with blood, wounds neither washed nor dressed; but they were fine-looking men; their horses thin, and smaller than ours. Another officer was taken, to whom I spoke. He said he had advised that they should not remain on this side the bridge, but his superior officer ordered otherwise, and afterwards ran away when attacked. We lost a Captain, who was taken prisoner, and a Lieutenant killed, both of the 10th; and about five or six men killed and wounded.

The Captain passed some way over the bridge, where the French had artillery and infantry in force, and they came down and cut him off.

The French had yesterday, I hear, nearly ten thousand men about five miles off, and nearly thirty-eight thousand or more in the vicinity of Valladolid. This made us halt to-day. The second division are still between this and Salamanca, but are expected. The whole are now within eight leagues of this, I believe; most of the divisions very close. The Spaniards are near Benevente: Don Julian's cavalry, between this and Salamanca, have sent in about thirty prisoners and two officers here to-day, who were marauding, I suppose. The French told the people here that they were only moving to make room for other troops.

The Portuguese troops are generally in very high order, as well as ours, quite as well clothed, and hitherto well in health, though they bivouac when ours encamp, their Government not furnishing them with tents. Yesterday was a pleasant cool day for a long march. I met Lord Wellington again last night, walking about in his grey great coat alone. We have a hundred pieces of field artillery with us, besides the eighteen-pounders.

A French commissariat party were caught in a wine-house on the 1st of June; one was brought in prisoner, and nine were killed in the house, as they would not surrender.

Lord Wellington reviewed the sixth and seventh divisions near Morales to-day. They did not perform well, and the poor aides-de-camp were galloped all over the country in consequence: the Portuguese were stupid.

Head-Quarters, Castro Monte, June 5th, 1813.—On the 3rd, we started for La Mota, three long leagues of good road. I was late, for my careless fellows had allowed one of the mule-saddles to be stolen in the night, and we were a long time getting off in consequence, and vainly endeavouring to replace the loss; but upon the whole, when I hear of all the sore backs, lost animals, &c., around me, I am lucky. I looked at the two hundred French cavalry horses which were sold, with a view to purchase one, but they were all half-starved, and the service having seized upon the best hundred and fifty for Government, the remainder, which were sold by auction, were most miserable.

The road from Toro was full of animation: it was one train of baggage and soldiers the whole way, three leagues, as we are now in the midst of the division. La Mota is a very good, large farming village, in a productive corn country, and the quarters were very good in consequence, the inhabitants being comfortable; the French, however, who had left it the day before, had carried off all the bread and fowls, &c. My landlord, Don Fernando Granado, was very gracious to me. Lord Wellington was in a large and elegant palace of the Duke of Berwick and Alva, and, in order to celebrate the King's birthday, had the band playing, &c.

At five this morning we marched for this place, three long leagues again only. It is a miserable hole; with only eighty houses of all sorts, and we require a hundred billets. Several are doubled up, several are encamped, which, as we have now a thunder-storm and rain, is not very agreeable. I have an humble quarter, with mules and all close.

We had a hot but cheerful ride to-day, as we were in the midst of the march. I first passed the Household Brigade; the Blues look very well, the Life Guards fair enough; then the third division, then the fourth, the seventh; I saw also the light division; five are within a league of this. The second crossed the Douro yesterday, and are to-day about a league on our right, under General Hill. I saw Picton with his, looking tolerably well. The French left Madrid the 20th or 28th of May, finally, and have by forced marches joined their army near here. The French were off again yesterday from Valladolid and Tordesillas, and were to be to-day at Duennas; it is thought they may stand at Palencia, or near there; I suspect not, however, though we all wish they would, and fight whilst our men are in health and spirits. I have just heard that their right is at Placencia.

To-morrow we move for Amputia, a good town, it is said, five leagues off. On our road to-day, about half way, we passed one of the finest convents in Spain—La Espina—in ruins; situation good, domain considerable; a large building, handsome, as far as it remains, but the walls only are standing. Adieu: I shall finish and send this off to-morrow.

Amputia, 2 o'clock, 6th June.—I arrived here at ten, having left Castro Monte at half-past five, and seen my baggage off, after breakfast; of course I was up soon after three. The road was by a bye-way over the common, but tolerably good, and covered with troops and baggage the whole way, for the third, fourth, and light divisions of infantry, with their baggage and artillery, head-quarters, the Household Brigade, and the Hussars were all on our route, and passed in their way; they are now in this neighbourhood.

We passed Villa Alba de Alcor, three leagues further; an old ruined village rather, with a castle and walls all around, but nothing particular; after that Villa Real, a little village, and then here. This is a large old-fashioned town, with the houses in the streets projecting, and standing on wooden pillars, so as to form covered footways, a tolerably large church, and a castle nearly perfect, where our police corps and the cavalry are quartered. The people are apparently more cordial and zealous. I have been over the church, spire and all, and castle, and have taken two sketches, for the rain has made it rather cool and pleasant to-day. The country round this town onwards, towards Sahagun, Placencia, &c., is a dead flat, covered with villages and towns, but no trees. Another large castle on a hill, half a league off, and on the whole rather striking.

The French left Palencia the day before yesterday, and are off again in advance, with a good start. Report says they have also left Burgos town, not the castle; they are seventy thousand strong, but think us, we hear, too much for them, end are consequently retiring to strong positions. By very long marches we might perhaps press them, and take some prisoners, and part of the cattle and provisions they are carrying off; but this might put our army out of the high order and condition it is now in, and Lord Wellington does not seem to think this worth while for such an object. So the Hussars and Household are both kept quiet in this neighbourhood, and not sent in pursuit; indeed they could do little without strong support.

Head-Quarters, Amusea, June 9th, 1813.—Another halt to-day enables me to proceed with my journal. The night I sent my last from Amputia, our orders were to have all the baggage ready to start, at the end of the town, by five o'clock on the following morning; and that I should fall in, and proceed on the road towards Palencia, in the rear of the column of the third division, but at the head of the baggage of all the light, third, and fourth divisions. This was because the French had shown twelve squadrons of cavalry at Palencia; and Colonel Waters who went on there that day, could not enter, so that it was not certain that it should be safe to give out in orders, "head-quarters, Palencia." The cavalry had marched early; and as they entered one end of Palencia at about six in the morning, the last of the French were off at the other.

I passed the third and fourth divisions, went through

Paradilla, and entered Palencia with the light division.
On getting my billet, I wandered about to see all that
was to be seen before my baggage came. The city is
old and curious, in size much about the same as Zamora.
Lord Wellington passed us on the road soon after six,
and went on through Palencia, some way, to reconnoitre.

We passed through a good open corn country until
about a league beyond Paradilla, and then descended a
long hill, with a deep clay soil, into the green and rich
valley in which Palencia stands. The city appears to
great advantage surrounded with meadows, and some
trees, but mostly young ones. The Carrion is a respectable river, and we passed the canal near it, about half a
mile from the city, where a very considerable paper
manufactory remains unfinished; and the French having
taken down windows, mill-wheels, &c., for firing and
shelter in their huts for their bivouacs there the day
before, the work will, I take it, be for some time interrupted.

The bridges into Palencia were handsome and entire.
The streets are rather narrow, and the main one, the
" Calle Mayor," about a good half-mile long, contains
about three hundred houses, all old-fashioned, and standing upon stone tall pillars over the footway, on each
side, with the shops under, like Covent Garden. The
houses are in the old style, like Excter, or Chester, and
Geneva; the streets badly paved, with a most offensive
gutter in the middle; the whole dirty. The bishop's
palace is a large, plain, neat stone edifice, quite modern,
of 1799, being built round a square, complete only on
one side and a half however, the rest being bare walls.

The cathedral is Gothic and very handsome, the arches
lofty and rich; but the custom all over Spain of having
the choir in the centre, with very high double screens,
deprives you altogether of the fine main aisle, so magnificent in our churches. This spoils the effect, though the

screens and sides of the choir in the centre were most richly wrought, with Gothic masonry, like some of our monuments of Henry VIIth's time. The side-aisles above are left open, and as there is a range of chapels the whole way down each side, and at the end, filled with gildings, saints, and pictures, the whole striking. There were also a few good pictures.

I afterwards went to the top of the spire, to survey the town, villages, and roads around. On my return, I was sorry to find orders to march again for this place, Amusea, next morning.

The town was all hung with counterpanes on our arrival, which made it look gay, and the people cheered us much. The general cry, however, is everywhere, " *Viva Espana!* " though there is scarcely a Spaniard to be seen in our line of march. Now and then, however, we hear, " *Vivan los Ingleses!* " and " *Los Portugueses!* " or " *Las tres naciones aliadas!* " The Portuguese are in the highest order, the men really look at least equal to ours, better than some ; the officers are well dressed and gay, and have the advantage of language ; the infantry and the Caçadores in particular. The whole army marches very fresh hitherto, but the Portuguese in particular : they come in even to the last mile singing along the road. The cavalry are not nearly so good, and, I suppose, are not much to be trusted. From what passed last year near this place, when they turned short round and ran away, they are called the Vamuses, for they ran off with a general cry of " Vamus! " Their infantry are termed Valorosas, from their having hugged and cheered each other early in the war, when they had for the first time behaved well and beat off the French, each patting the other on the heart, and saying, " *Mucha valorosa!—Mucha valorosa!* "

I hope the latter will support their name ; and indeed they are disposed to do so, for we have put so much beef into both men and officers, that they are quite different animals, and will not submit at all to what they used to do, even from the English.

Our horses finished the half-eaten meal of the French, and I believe that has been all they have left behind for us hitherto; not a store of any kind, sick man, or anything else, has been discovered at Valladolid or anywhere; they must have been well-prepared for this plan.

The young avenues of trees round the town suffered a little by the French bivouac; and our men laid waste many a field of wheat in their march and for forage. The former is particularly wrong, being quite unnecessary, and merely to save perhaps a few hundred yards, or to get before others a little. I was glad to see General Picton stop a party, and about to punish them on the spot. The taking the wheat for forage is also very bad, for the commissaries regularly buy a field at each place, and allow us to take each our proportion, cutting the whole fairly and properly; whereas the fellows who go and steal, cut patches all about, and tread down more than they cut.

King Joseph left Torquemados, three leagues on the right, the day before yesterday, and it is said, peeped in again afterwards. The last French troops left it yesterday at five in the morning, and I believe General Hill's head-quarters were there afterwards from Duenas. Castanos and his Spaniards are on our left all the way; they came by Benevente across the Esla and so towards Carrion. Their head-quarters were yesterday, I believe, at Villoldo, on our left. The Life-Guards and Blues looked well on their entrance into Palencia, and on their march yesterday the former, however, seem dull and out of spirits, and have some sore backs among their horses. The Blues seem much more up to the thing, but they are neither of them very fit for general service here. Lord Wellington saves them up for some grand coup, houses them when he can, and takes care of them. To be sure, if many of the French cavalry are like some specimens we have seen, particularly two deserters yesterday, who were on ponies I could almost jump over, one of our Householders must upset them like an elephant, if they come fairly in contact.

A French officer, a deserter (the third officer), came in two days since, with a pretty woman, daughter of a General, with him; he calls her his wife. Another starved scullion came here yesterday, and says he is an officer, and has some papers, but I think he stole them. He is a little dirty beast, in rags and without uniform. The cavalry who have been taken and deserters are quite new-clothed, and the men very fine; the last who has come in is a Fleming, and had they not persuaded him to enter our corps of guides, I should have taken him as a groom, and bought his pony.

Tamarra, a village a league from this, was deserted by the inhabitants, with their provisions; the French, in consequence, made an example of it, and it is as bad as the Portuguese villages now, almost a heap of ruins. Indeed, all the houses and villages on the high road to Torquemada have suffered terribly, and the villages generally are now becoming worse, more dirty, and *à la Portuguese*. I hear this is now the case all round Burgos, and till we get across the Ebro, if we are destined to do this. We are eleven leagues now from Burgos. The weather has been cool and excellent for the march this last week, and rain often in the night; it has now rained the last sixteen hours, and I hope will be fine again for the march to-morrow. I dined with Lord Wellington yesterday, for the first time on the march, and gave him your Roman Catholic book, with the lists of their schools and establishments in England. He looks well, but anxious, as you may suppose just now, for a false step may be fatal. All prospers hitherto. The eighteen-pounders are near, the twenty-fours still at

Corunna, and if wanted will, I suppose, go round by sea
to St. Andero. For the present, adieu.

June 11*th, Head-Quarters, Castrogores.*—The church
at Amusea is large and handsome : a room 150 feet by
50, and 70 feet high, without a pillar, and the whole
end one mass of gilding. Yesterday morning, after the
violent rains of our halting day, we started at five on a
fine day, the roads in a terrible state, for Mergan de
Fernamental, head-quarters, on the 10th, five long
leagues. Our way was near the noble canal, and through
Pino (one league), a large village. From thence another
league through Fromista, a larger place ; then another
league to Requena : then another to Lantidillo, where
we crossed the Pisuerga over a large bridge, left entire ;
and then after another long league, Mergan de Fernamental.

The country was flat, and rich in corn, meadows, &c.,
nearly all the way, but low and boggy, and a hard march
for men and baggage, &c. ; mine started at five, and did
not arrive till about two. There were villages thickly
set all around us, and all with large churches. The
latter, compared with ours, are very much superior, considering the size of the places : all possess a considerable
church of rather curious construction, and all somewhat
different, though in general appearance alike. The
church at Mergan was particularly handsome, and more
like our Saxon at Gloucester and Tewkesbury. It had
some decent pictures, so indeed have several of the
quarters, though perhaps not very valuable. Many are
to be bought very cheap, and I should have purchased
some, had I known how to carry them home.

At Mergan we were in the right road for Reynosa
and St. Andero, and the first division were two leagues
in advance the same way. I conjectured we were going
to open a communication with St. Andero, and to cross
the Ebro as soon as the French from Burgos, and thus

turn them. There seems now, however, to be a change of plan, as to-day we are come three leagues here, nearly in the right road again for Burgos, which we had before left on our right. Here we have fallen in with General Hill's division, who are now within half a league of this place. We are thus all now quite close together, and report says that the French have united their army of the north to the rest, and are now between this and Burgos eighty thousand strong, about four leagues distant.

They thus seem to make a stand here, and we are, probably, assembled in case they should persist, but many think it is still only a plan to make us assemble and draw up, to see what we have, and also to give time for their baggage and plunder, oxen, &c., to withdraw without loss : time will show. The sooner the battle comes for us the better, I think : and so do most, but it will be more tremendous, probably, than any hitherto fought in Spain. The numbers now approach those of the great continental armies on both sides, and we are at least equal, if you reckon all that are well dressed and ought to fight on our side ; as to the Spaniards, hitherto we must put a query to that. Don Julian's cavalry have sent in about forty or fifty infantry stragglers of the French, and have killed a dozen or more,—about fifty or sixty in all; several with bad pike or lance wounds.

Mergan is a very dirty old town, but this town, Castrogores, though larger, and the quarters better, is in that respect much worse ; the streets so offensive, that you must hold your nose in passing through them, and everything about the place filthy. We passed the German hussars in quarters half a league off on our way here, and crossed the line of march of the light and fourth divisions, meeting General Hill's army on our arrival here.

The scene is now very animated. This place is above
a mile long, round the botton of an insulated hill, with
a castle at the top of it, which looks over a rich country
for some way to a ridge of hills which bound the whole,
about a league off; trees, however (except just round a
few quintas or villas, and about the several ruins of the
old monasteries), are very scarce; corn most luxuriant,
but not much forwarder than with us in England.
Weather, hitherto, scarcely at all too hot, and that only
for a few hours; at times very cold. Lord Wellington
has gone through again on in front.

Castrogores, June 12*th.*—As we halt here to-day, instead
of marching to Eglesia, as was intended, I determined
to finish this, and seal up to-day for Lisbon. Colonel
A——, of the German hussars, told me that he saw
about two or three thousand French cavalry the day
before yesterday, but they filed off as we came in sight.
Colonel Waters went on yesterday to within a league of
Burgos. He only saw about fifteen thousand French in
a valley near there, near Quinta della Duennas. They
were about to march, and the reports are that they are
off again, and the whole of the second division of General
Hill's army have advanced hence this morning. They
began at daylight, and about eight o'clock the Spaniards
began to file by, just below my house. This was General
Murillo's corps: I went down to look at them. There
were about ten regiments, I think, but most of them
small ones. The men looked very well, though a great
many were quite boys. They were singing, joking, and
in good spirits : the artillery with them in good order,
the draft mules quite fat. The clothing and equipments
of some very good, though unequal to ours, or to the
Portuguese; others moderate only. They wore a sort of
flannel jacket and trousers not at all alike, and some
were ragged, here and there a man barefoot,—very few ;
all with good caps, in the French style, and the officers

more respectable than usual, and generally mounted; some very fierce-looking pioneers, fine grenadiers, and all with good English town muskets in good order, brighter than our own, being, most probably, nearly new: in short, the whole was respectable. If they will but fight as well as they look, it will do. Doyle's regiment was one of the best; but the very best, I think, was the Regimento del Unione.

General Alava, the Spanish great man at head-quarters, is in high spirits, thinks all going on well, and is beginning to ask one or two to dine with him at his mansion near Vittoria, where his estates lie. He only begs that he may have a guard to preserve his green forage from our soldiers. The Spaniards are astonished at our baggage. The French carry very little, as they make the people at the quarters furnish everything they want, which is not so much as we require. We carry everything with us. An English captain, therefore, has (plunder excepted) almost as much baggage as a French colonel. Barley is already scarce, and not to be bought, though we pay in guineas. Bread is also scarce, as well as beef. I hope soon to hear through St. Andero, but the French have Castro and Santona. We still have reports that the works at Burgos are being destroyed; it may be so, if the French resolve to go to the Ebro, for the garrison will otherwise be sacrificed. We have only six eighteen-pounders, about the same as last year; the twenty-fours are at Corunna. This will not do for the siege well, and I hope that will not be necessary. For the last thirty miles and more the style of the houses has changed. They are generally now mud or cob walls, like those in Devonshire, whitewashed, but not in the best repair, or else they are unburnt brick, or dried mud bricks with mud plaster.

Miserable Head-Quarters at Massa, June 14*th*, 1813.— The regular English post-day was yesterday, but I had

L

not time to write then, and as it is ten to one but that this will be in time for the same packet, though you will have, I hope, a long letter by the same mail, yet, wishing to give you the latest news from hence, and to let you know the events which have occurred, I write again.

At four o'clock on the 12th, as I told you, Lord Wellington had not returned from the front when my last letter was sent off. He came back at seven o'clock; he and his horse and his comrades well tired. The enemy were found about fifteen thousand strong, two leagues south-west nearly of Burgos, with cavalry and artillery. We had up the hussars (heavy), and General Fane's brigades of cavalry. Manœuvring went on a considerable time with skill. Our infantry could not get up in force in time, or much would have been done. We had a gun, however, close to a French column, and killed a few. We also took an officer and about ninety men prisoners, some desperately wounded, and one gun. A charge of cavalry was ordered, but the French moved off.

There seems to be considerable confusion at times in the intermixture of the French and English. The light divisions were at hand; the second near with the Spaniards, but not up. The Prince of Orange galloped about well, with orders; he knocked up his horse, and was in some danger. Lord March met a French dragoon, took him till he came close for an English soldier, turned short round, was struck at by the Frenchman, and his horse slightly hit below the ear: in short, something material was very nearly happening.

The next day (the 13th) we had orders to march to Villa Diego, where head-quarters were yesterday; a dirty place, but quarters tolerable. The country between is rich and good, and covered with villages. We passed, among others, Ormillos, Villa Sandine at a distance, and Sasamon, in perfect ruin; the whole place, church and all, both of considerable extent and size, having been burnt by Romana and his army for some real or supposed treason. The destruction was certainly well performed; the punishment severe, and very impartially inflicted. The next place we came to, which had been a very neat village, was nearly in the same state, from the same cause. Villa Diego was nearly six or seven leagues from Burgos. Lord Wellington, &c., went round that way, to see how matters went on. They could not find any French, and at last ascertained that the works, castle, &c., of Burgos, had been all blown up and destroyed by five o'clock yesterday morning. This news caused no little joy to every one, and most particularly to those who expected to have to knock their heads against the place. Many good lives have thus been saved. This news met us about four o'clock yesterday, and in consequence to-day we had a long march to this place, Massa, on our way to the Ebro.

We shall probably nearly all get across about the same time; I think French and all. Some of the Spanish army of Gallicia pass to-day up towards Reynosa. The first division do the same to-day or to-morrow. We met one cavalry brigade on their road to cross at St. Martine to-day. General Murray told me that we should probably cross to-morrow; but I find we are here five leagues from a bridge or ford. The first two leagues here to-day were through a productive country like Wiltshire; round smooth chalk hills, well-watered meadows, and rich pasture valleys, with abundance of grass: draining and better farming, with cleanliness, were all requisite. We then entered a rough, wild country, with rocks, &c. We nearly all lost our way, including General Murray, the Quarter-Master-general, with whom I was riding, Lord Wellington himself, and nearly all the baggage! We were near a place called Brulla, ought to have passed Cuirculo, near Urbel de Castro, whereas we got through a rugged pass in the rock, came down to a picturesque village, called La Piedra (so called, probably, from the rocks around it), and there we fell in with the fifth division. At last, after passing another little space called Fresnoy, and leaving Urbel de Castro, in a valley on our right, with a curious small castle on a pointed hill close to it (from whence the name), we arrived at this wretched place. The houses in this place would not in any way hold half of us; so the Spaniards have been sent back to Fresnoy, the artillery, commissaries, paymasters, and doctors to Vilalda, or some such place, a league off.

I was forgotten, but have, from there being one spare quarter, got a wretched dirty hole here: it is the worst of dirty cottages. My baggage is all in the entrance. I have no place but a dirty passage to put up my bed in; I have a table and chair, but am surrounded by baskets, hampers, tubs, boxes, sheepskins, dirt, &c. Cobwebs and dirt are dropping upon me continually. Most have encamped. Lord Wellington and Marshal Beresford are walking up and down the street, and the Military Secretary is writing under a wall, upon his knees, whilst his servants are pitching his tent. In a little field where General Alava is about to encamp, there were just now the Military Secretary, Colonel Scovell, the Commander of the Police Corps, Fitzclarence, General Alava, the Spanish Aide-de-camp, Colonel Waters, the Prince of Orange, and your humble servant, all lying upon the ground together, round a cold ham and bread, some brandy, and a bottle of champagne. And no bad fare either you will say. The Prince and Lord Fitzroy, like two boys, were playing together all the time.

The people in this part of the country are as bad, if not worse than in Portugal. There is nothing but filth and laziness. They are not good-looking either. They live in dirty mud houses, and fleas are so abundant that

I cannot sleep from their annoyance. I suppose we shall cross near Puente Arences, or Rampalaise, to-morrow, or next day at the latest. The French have left about ninety sick or wounded at Burgos, and the bedding of the hospitals, about eight hundred beds. No cannon, &c. We are already short of forage or corn for the horses; bread scarce, as well as spirits, and the country we enter produces little or nothing.

CHAPTER VIII.

March continued—Quintana—Anecdote of Wellington—Morillas—Vittoria
—The Battle—Its Results—Plunder—Kindness to the Enemy—Madame
de Gazan—The Hospital—Sufferings of the Wounded—Estimated Loss.

Head-quarters, Berberena,
June 18, 1813.

My dear M——,

My last left me at Massa, on the other side of the
Douro, in a miserable quarter. On the following morning (the 15th) we marched for Quintana, on the same
side. For about four leagues we proceeded through a
rough hilly country, barren, but at times picturesque.
We passed troops all the way, and at last came to a
tremendous long hill which led us down to Quintana,
near the banks of the Ebro. Troops were descending
the hill, infantry, cavalry, and artillery, from eight or
nine o'clock until past four; and at last the baggage,
which was kept waiting on the banks around the road-
side, moved on; the scene was very striking. The
artillery was much shaken; some guns were lowered by
hand, with the wheels locked, without horses, and all
very gently; four wheels gave way, and the 18-pounders
had to go round by St. Martine.

The valley in which Quintana and six or seven other
small villages were placed, and through which the Ebro
passed, was very rich and beautiful, surrounded with
rocky heights and covered with corn, beans, fruit, vines,
trees, &c., and the villages externally very picturesque.
Internally, however, they were most wretched, and my

quarter was misery itself. The people had not seen the French in the valley for two years, until about ten days before we were there, when they had been through to collect contributions, and to seize part of a magazine formed there by Longa. The head-quarters' house was, however, good, and near it was a large but unfinished and unoccupied college, for young persons of both sexes, founded about twenty years ago by the owner of the head-quarters' house, by the desire of his deceased wife, for the education of children of the valley. The great man of the valley, however, was the owner of the Adjutant-general's quarter, and only a Procureur there—a poor abode. I think he was called the Marquis de Villa Alta. There was a small castle, and the whole scenery, particularly along the banks of the river, was very delightful. I longed for a tent, for I could not live in my house in the daytime from the smoke, and could not sleep in the night from the fleas. The light division and the fourth were encamped in the meadows across the river, and added, by their fires and tents, much to the interest of the scene; the cavalry and artillery passed through the valley. The river runs in this part about as wide as the Severn above Shrewsbury—less than the Thames at Maidenhead.

The next day (the 16th) we crossed the river, and proceeded with the troops between the lofty rocky banks of the river, above the valley, on a road cut close to the water, and winding alongside the river for about a league and more, most beautifully! in some respects like the Wye, the cliffs almost like Cheddar, and wooded to the water's edge. The constant line of cavalry and infantry, whenever the eye caught the winding road, was very picturesque. In two places were the remains of walls across the road made by Longa or the French—I do not know which.

The road afterwards turned from the river, and through

a fine country brought us to Medina de Pomar, leaving Villa Cayo on our left. Medina de Pomar, our next head-quarters, was a straggling dirty town, and the accommodation very moderate indeed. I got a tolerable clean room for myself at the apothecary's, but my stable was down a cellar with dark stairs, and I could scarcely get my animals in or out. The alcalde was not civil, nor did the people appear glad to see us. The town was very full, for the Spanish Generals Mendizabel and Longa (the *ci-devant* Guerilla chief) were quartered there on our arrival, and did not seem disposed to move for us.

I saw Longa in the street; rather a stout man, well dressed in a sort of hussar uniform, and looking civilized enough. I was in hopes of meeting him at Lord Wellington's, where I dined that day, but he did not stay. The party of cavalry attending him were all uniformly dressed, and seemed to me to be more regular than most of the Spanish regulars. They wore scarlet jackets, and appeared not unlike some of our volunteer yeomanry cavalry, but they had quite an air of consequence which was amazing. Longa has left thirty of them and two officers at head-quarters, as part of the corps of guides, to assist in keeping up the communications of the army, in which way I have no doubt they will be very useful.

Lord Wellington was at Medina in a large nunnery where there were twenty-five ladies, who came and played at bo-peep with us in the chapel, which was a handsome building. The altar was very rich, and in the centre was a piece of clock-work of small moveable figures describing the crucifixion.

On that day General Jeron arrived, the General of the Gallician Spanish army acting with us, and he dined there. Castanos, the former General, is now a sort of General of two armies, and amuses himself by parading through all the towns and places in the rear of the army, Burgos last: I suppose he is employed somehow in this way. Jeron is a man about thirty-six, I should think, and looks very much like a gentleman and a man of talent; he is very well spoken of, and considered as one of the best of the Spanish leaders. Through Corunna we have news to the 6th of June. Talking during dinner of the late accounts from Bonaparte, and of the sentimental story about Duroc, which Lord Wellington was laughing at, General Jeron said, " If there was such a place as hell, he thought Bonaparte quite right, and that he and Duroc would most certainly meet again there."

Yesterday, the 17th, we started again (having had no halts) for Quincoces, five long leagues almost, towards Vittoria, but to the left : there our head-quarters were yesterday, in that and the neighbouring villages. The troops I think were pushed on in this way, from an account received from Longa and others, that the French rear was still at Pencorbo, and part even at Briviesca, on the other side of the Ebro. Longa gave great hopes of doing something. We have, however, our difficulties from this. We get no corn for the horses, and bread is very scarce; stores gone for the present, for we outrun our supplies, and there is very little to be bought. We have bought some and baked it, to supply us as we go, but some divisions have been for one or two days entirely without, and others on short allowance. We hope now soon to get into a better country, towards Vittoria, but Longa and the French have cleared everything about this country.

Longa, when we came to Quincoces, was ordered on to Orduna, having had all he could from this place. On taking leave he collected all their oxen for the plough, ninety in number, all they had left, and drove them off. The people received us with tears and lamentations, and with no small fear, not knowing what we should require next. My patron seemed quite stupified and melancholy. We told this to General Alava, and he galloped off with

two dragoons after Longa's people and the oxen, overtook them, and compelled them to restore them to the
owners, to their no small satisfaction. At last we found
eight hundred pounds of bread, that is, flour; half a day's
rations for head-quarters only. We bought it, paid for
it with guineas, and baked it—*voilà la différence!* But
this cannot last or be general; the divisions cannot do
this.

We last night heard that the French were over the
river Ebro, and as near Vittoria as we were. However,
we advanced in hopes of something arising, and head-
quarters were ordered to be at this place, Berberena, and
the neighbouring villages. It was intended that Marshal
Beresford should have been at a village half a league in
front of this place, but when we arrived near here, about
nine o'clock, we found two divisions of the 1st and 5th
halted here until further orders. We heard a cannonading in the front, at this village, and found that the
French were making some stand in a narrow pass near it,
and in the village. Beresford was put into a village to
the rear of us, and an order soon came out for all baggage to proceed to that village for security. Mine was
unloaded; but as I saw the French just before us, only
about a mile off or little more, I made my people all load
again and stand ready to be off, whilst I went with my
glass to the end of the village, to a rising ground, to
witness the skirmishing, and to be ready to act accordingly.

A brisk cannonade was going on, a few shells were
thrown, and a light infantry attack. The French I saw
very plainly in the churchyard and village on the hill
beyond. They advanced under a ridge in the ground
and some bushes, where they stood above an hour and
more, when I saw our men and the Portuguese advance
gradually and drive them back. The cannon advanced
also, and the French by degrees went out of sight round

the hill, our guns and soldiers after them. Very few I believe were killed on either side ; but our light division I find went round by Espeja, and, falling in with another division early in the day, routed them so completely, that two battalions dispersed, and the light division got a quantity of mules and baggage, with a good deal of money ; some privates got two or three hundred pounds. About three hundred prisoners were taken, and some of the runaways are still coming in. One French battalion fled towards Frias, and some Spaniards are sent off after them.

Morillas, Head-Quarters, June 20th.—Our orders yesterday morning (the 19th) were to set out at eight o'clock through Osma, where a little affair took place the day before, and so on to Escorta, following the fourth division. We did this, and I was riding with the doctors just before that division on towards Escorta, when we were told that the French were only two miles in advance, and that there was nothing between us. Upon this we turned out of the road into a field of vetches for the horses, and let the fourth division go by, and have the honour of preceding us, as we did not quite think the French would run away at the sight of us civilians. When this division came well up we went on, passed through Escorta to another village half a league beyond, and then, by the advice of an officer, who told us they were going to attack the French, who were strong at this place, Morillas, and that the passage of the river was to be forced, we ascended a high hill on our right, which commanded the whole scene of action, and there with our glasses we could distinctly see everything.

As soon as the light division had got almost round the hill on our right, from the direction nearly of the Frias road, in order to be ready to advance and turn the French position, the fourth division advanced to the village here, and the skirmishing began from the houses and a chapel on the river. In about half an hour our men entered the village, and we got about three field-pieces into play close to it. We then saw the French, who were in considerable force on the other side, and formed into a crescent on a hill near, begin to move off, at first gently, but soon in quick time, and a part of our division was very soon formed beyond the village over the river. The skirmishing thus went on all the way up the road and hill beyond to another village half a league further on the hill, where the French were drawn up in greater force. When our men got up, however, the enemy went off pretty quickly, and were last night in great force, some say fifty thousand, in a plain about a league and a half from this, and about half way to Vittoria.

The pass here was very defensible, and not easily turned; but the resistance was very slight, and few fell on either side. I suppose the French were afraid of bringing on a general action by further resistance. They had not any artillery with them near here, I conclude, from the fear of losing their guns, as just through and near the village the road is so bad and narrow, that our baggage, without any resistance, did not pass through to the two divisions beyond until dark at eight o'clock, our head-quarter baggage having all followed on here.

Lord Wellington walked into a house and made it head-quarters. I have a sort of barn here. We have had wet and cold weather for these three days; I can scarcely keep myself warm to write, though with my cap on and double waistcoats This is considered extraordinary here for the 20th of June, though the climate is always much colder and more subject to wet than in the more southern parts of Spain.

There is a large plain near Vittoria, and then all beyond is hilly to France. An officer of the 95th was killed on the 18th, and about seventy men wounded, I hear. Yesterday an officer of the Fusileers was wounded badly in this village, and lies in a house here : in another house a very spirited Portuguese (Caçadores) serjeant is also lying wounded.

3 o'clock.—The French remain in the valley, but it is thought will be off to-night.

Vittoria, June 23rd, 1813.—My last was of the 20th from Morillas, and on the 21st I arrived here after a scene never to be forgotten. Our baggage was that morning ordered to remain ready to load until further orders. The French were very strongly posted at about a league and a half distance, directly across the road to Vittoria, about sixty or seventy thousand strong, and extending about a league ; their centre supported by a wood and a small river, their left by strong wooded hills, and their right on another hill not so strong. The attack was ordered in the manner you have seen before this in the *" Gazette."* General Graham was to turn the French right flank ; General Hill their left. I mounted my horse about nine to see the result, leaving Henry and everything behind, with directions to do exactly the same as Lord Wellington's servants. I got, with Dr. M'Gregor and a few others, on a hill about a mile from the French, which commanded nearly the whole scene. At about half-past ten the firing began very briskly on the hills on the French left. The different ridges were well contested ; but our people con- stantly, though gradually, gained ground, and advanced along the top ridge to turn the French. The cavalry were nearly all close under us to be ready, some in the rear, and one division of infantry also. General Paken- ham's division was not up at all—it was four leagues in the rear.

By the ground gained on the French left, and soon after from General Picton having got up quite on the ridge of the hills there with his division, a steep and dif·

ficult ascent, the centre were enabled to advance a little also, and much skirmishing began there near a little village before us, which was for some time contested. At length, some guns being brought to bear there, and one also half way up the hill, the village was passed by our people, and we saw them lying sheltered under a hill beyond, nearly opposite the wood at the French centre. A smart contest then ensued. The cannon and a few men from the hill and village fired into the wood, and a constant firing was kept up from the wood on our men; the main contest being still, however, on the hills on the French left. By this time, about one, we on our hill all advanced to another nearer, to observe more distinctly with our glasses. Soon after this, General Graham's attack began on the French right, and a very brisk cannonade was then kept up right and left. The French line on the hill on the right and left (for we saw the whole of their line) began to give way a little, and to put itself in motion, and the plot then thickened. Still we gained ground, and some of our men also got close to the wood, and, lying down, kept up a smart fire. The cannonading lasted two or three hours, the English constantly gaining ground. Our party moved a second time to a third hill within the original French picquets, and in front of our cavalry. At last we saw our line forming gradually under shelter of the rising ground, within half a mile of the French line and guns. They then advanced, and the cavalry began to move up—some say rather late, as Lord Wellington was not there to give the orders.

We then left our hill and advanced with the Household Brigade constantly as they moved. We now began to see the effects of the guns. Dead and wounded men and horses, some in the most horrible condition, were scattered all along the way we passed. These were principally cannon-shot wounds, and were on that account the more horrible. It was almost incredible that some could live in the state we saw them. From my black feather I was taken by some for a doctor, and appealed to in the most piteous voice and affecting manner, so that I immediately took out my feather, not to be supposed so unfeeling as to pass on without taking any notice of these poor creatures. Our hospital spring-waggons were following, and men with frames to lift up and carry off those near the roads. Some in the fields about crawled by degrees into the villages; but hundreds have lain without food or having their wounds dressed until now, two days afterwards. Parties are sent all over the contested ground to find them, though the peasants are continually bringing in the wounded.

On the hill in the centre of the French position, at a village where we first came in full sight of Vittoria, and about two miles distance, the contest was very sharp, and the three first guns were taken, with several tumbrils, und there the first charge of cavalry took place. The sufferers there were principally Portuguese of the 11th and 21st regiments, and we had all along seen more of our people wounded than the French. We now found swords, muskets, knapsacks, &c., in all directions. The stragglers and followers were stripping and plundering, and a scramble ensued for the corn, &c., which was in the tumbrils with the ammunition. The Hussars in their charges suffered much. The Life Guards I kept close to all the way to Vittoria, and to that time they were not engaged.

We could hear the whistle of the cannon-shot, and saw the ground torn up where they struck. Tumbrils and guns were now found upset or deserted at every half-mile; and when we got near Vittoria the road was absolutely choked up with them, so that our artillery was some time stopped. Some of the Life Guards were placed at the gates and in the streets here, to keep soldiers, &c., out, and to preserve order as far as possible; and we rode into Vittoria amidst the cries, hurras, and *vivas* of the mob, which consisted chiefly of women. We looked into the stores and found little left, and then passed through the town, at the further side of which we stopped at a very curious scene. The French so little expected the result, that all their carriages were caught, and stopped at this place—three of King Joseph's, those of the Generals, &c.; the Paymaster and his chest, the *Casa real*, hundreds of tumbrils, the wives of the Generals, all flying in confusion; several carriages upset, the horses and mules removed from them, the women still in their carriages, and the Spaniards (a few soldiers, but principally the common people) beginning to break open and plunder everything, assisted by a few of our soldiers. Upon the whole, our people got but little of the plunder, except by seizing and selling a few mules. The seats of the carriages were broken with great stones and ransacked, and gold, silver, and plate were found in several in abundance. I took a case of maps, part of Lopez' provincial set, and a horse-cloth, which I bought of a Portuguese soldier as a memorial, but would not meddle with the rest. Maps, books, &c., were thrown aside; brandy, &c., drank.

In the midst of this, a lady in great distress, well dressed and elegant, with her carriage in the ditch, and she herself standing by, appealed to me, and, asking me if I could speak French, said she was the Countess de Gazan, wife of the French General, and that she wished to get back to the town, and, if possible, save her horses, mules, and carriage, and those of King Joseph, which were by. With the assistance of two hussars, after above an hour, I at last accomplished this in a great measure; that is, I got the lady, her woman, the carriage, and four out of six of the animals, to the house of a friend whom she pointed out to me, and also a few loose things out of the carriage. The other two animals and the three trunks of clothes had been plundered before I arrived. I also put King Joseph's carriage and horses in their way to the square of the town; I then went and tried to find out amongst the prisoners a little boy of two years old, a son of the General, whom some French gensd'armes had taken from the carriage to carry off, and who had not since been seen, and whom the mother thought was taken prisoner. I could not find him anywhere; but I met Lord Wellington returning to the Palace at ten at night to his quarters there; and as Madame de Gazan was most anxious that he should know she was taken, I told him, and also about her boy. He desired me to say that he could not then see her, but that she might rely on his doing what he could to find the child, and that she should be immediately at liberty to join her husband. This I went and told her. I also found an English aide-de-camp of General Hill, who had been released only the day before, having been prisoner, and to whom she had been very kind when he was with the French, and who had, on taking leave, promised, if the fate of war should make a change in their relative situations, to return her attentions.

My return and message made her more easy: I fear, from what I have since heard, that her boy was killed between two carriages; but still hope he may have escaped. The confusion lasted all night, and indeed, has continued until now. The event was also so little expected on our part, that for a long time there were no guards for the prisoners, and many escaped in consequence, and several are still wandering about the country.

The next day (22nd) the head-quarters followed the French to Salvatierra; but I was advised by Colonel Campbell and others to stay quietly here, and proceed afterwards. I did so, but already repent, for no place is so certain of news, and so secure, as head-quarters, though

M

the accommodation is often most wretched. I have been over the hospital, and the scene which I there witnessed was most terrible; seventeen or eighteen hundred men, without legs or arms, &c., or with dreadful wounds, and having had nothing to eat for two or three days, the misery extreme, and not nearly hands sufficient to dress or take care of the men—English, Portuguese, Spaniards, and French all together, though the Spaniards and Portuguese had at first no provision at all for their people. Half the wounded have been scattered round the villages in the neighbourhood; and there are still many to come in, who arrive hourly, and are lying in all the passages and spare places around the hospital. A Commissary is just established.

Six hospital waggons are just now setting out for another load of these poor wounded fellows!

I do not know what now to do as to proceeding to join head-quarters; for, to our great surprise, last night Lord March was sent over here to tell the Commandant, who was just appointed, that it was discovered that from ten to twelve thousand French, supposed to come from Bilboa, were in our rear, and might be in here soon; that a division of men (I believe General Pakenham's) was left for our protection, but that every man here capable of bearing arms must be kept in readiness, and every one must be ready to leave this place at an hour's notice. I now, therefore, do not know what to do exactly, and wish myself at head-quarters. The pay-chest, with about a hundred or a hundred and twenty thousand dollars of French prize money in addition, is still here, and several of the doctors.

In the blue coach was a box of gold in different shapes, which a servant of King Joseph stayed behind to give up to Lord Wellington, and which report says he has given to his own personal staff. But everything was in confusion; even the ammunition waggons were left unguarded, and were broken open to be ransacked, and we have had accidental or intentional explosions almost every hour since. One tumbril with twenty shells was set fire to by the foolish Spaniards yesterday, and several persons were hurt in consequence. Every one is taking and wasting the musket cartridges, notwithstanding Lord Wellington is really in want of some. All, however, are now busy in trying to remedy this confusion.

I hear that nearly one hundred and forty pieces of artillery have been now taken in different states and places between Morillas and Salvatierra. The French, however, have comparatively lost fewer men than we did; the Portuguese more than their proportion; the Spaniards, several. Some corps behaved well, though General Picton said some liked best to fire away and make a noise at a distance.

I fear that few prisoners are taken—as far as I can learn about a thousand; and I suppose they had a thousand killed and wounded, having done us much mischief with their tremendous artillery firing. Their line would not stand at all when Graham advanced to turn them, but they were off so quick that our men opposed to them could not get up to them. Had they waited for a fair attack, the prisoners would probably have been numerous. As it is, the French still have numbers, and, though the equipments of the army are gone, they may, if they can fall back on supplies, be again formidable. Report also says that Suchet is moving fast to join them. Last night, when our head-quarters were at Salvatierra, the rear of the French was three leagues in advance; they are off so quick, the weather is so bad and wet, that I fear we shall have many sick in the pursuit. The result of the whole is, however, the most glorious possible, whatever may be the consequence; never was there for the time an army of sixty or seventy thousand men, as we say, more completely routed and put to flight. Several

M 2

French Generals are killed, wounded, or prisoners; in officers of rank the French have suffered much.

It is so very difficult to be at all certain as to our own loss, unless one is in the secret, that I shall say nothing but that General Colville, who had a slight knock in the arm, is the only officer wounded of whom I have heard. The 18th Hussars suffered much. I must now see the Commandant, and settle whether to move or not. The reports when not at head-quarters puzzle one very much. A dragoon (Spanish) rode into the town yesterday, and came up to me in the square to ask for the mayor of the town, to tell him that six thousand French were only two leagues off. I took him to General Pakenham, whose division had just arrived. He carried the man off to see what he knew, and said, if true, he would have a dash at them. I suppose this was in part true, from what passed afterwards about the French in our rear; the division of men is still, however, close to us.

Suchet was endeavouring to join the other French army, and was, as the prisoners say, in the neighbourhood of Logrono for that purpose, so that he will soon be with the others. Tarragona we hear is taken, and I conclude Murray is after Suchet. I have had much conversation with the Commissary-general of the army of Portugal, a talkative perfect Frenchman. He has lost everything, and has neither money nor a change of linen, but he seems tolerably happy. He says he had orders to pay out of the Treasury when the fire had commenced, which was madness, and he described the confusion of the fight most eloquently and most truly I am sure. Joseph had sent off a caravan of valuable pictures only the day before, and various kinds of baggage, and a heavy train of artillery. Some of this will, I think, be caught in the confusion, but the pictures probably destroyed.

Head-quarters are to-day at Echarva Aramaz, and I mean to get as near that place to-morrow as I can, or even there, if I can get my baggage over the nine leagues in the bad state of the roads, for it has rained constantly these ten hours. Lord Wellington has not given the box of treasure to his private staff. It has not yet been opened, but is here. Colonel Campbell, who is just come into the town on business, says that the French have committed great ravages on their route from this place, destroying property, committing every excess. A girl at Lord Wellington's quarters at Salvatierra accuses even King Joseph of an attempt at violence; but I do not believe it. Some very strange things were found in the baggage. I was sorry to find that, except stragglers and more baggage, we have got little more by our pursuit. There are tumbrils I am told to the amount of five hundred, and carriages and carts as many. King Joseph had neither a knife and fork nor a clean shirt with him last night. The loss to the French must be very considerable, though our gain is not nearly so great, from the destruction of many, and the quantity of things taken, to us of little use.

CHAPTER IX.

Pamplona—Pursuit of Clausel—Wellington on the March—Prospects of more Fighting — Effects of the War—The French Position turned—Anecdote of Wellington — Ernani—St. Sebastian—Wellington's Movements.

Head-quarters, half a league from
Pamplona.

My dear M———,

I have repented staying two days at Vittoria. The consequence has been that I fell in with all the fagged division of the army, and found every hole full of troops, and nothing to eat or drink. The roads were poached up knee-deep with clay, and I have almost knocked up both myself and my animals. Yesterday I had no dinner, and to day no breakfast, and the first day I was twelve hours on the road going six leagues to a place two leagues beyond Salvatierra; from thence I got in thirteen hours more to Orunzun, eight leagues. There my baggage did not arrive in time, and I went to bed without dinner and without anything except the comforts of a Spanish cottage.

I set out this morning for head-quarters. Now we start fair again; to-morrow we march. Pamplona is invested, but I fear that we have little means for a very regular siege; and accounts state that Clausel is, with fifteen thousand men, on his road from Logrono, endeavouring to escape towards Suchet. It is hoped that we may intercept him, or at least his guns; and so we march, though the army is terribly fagged, and the animals also. General Graham is at Tolosa; Mina at Tudela to assist against Clausel. From Vittoria to this place we have constantly passed at first stripped and unburied dead, then baggage and animals without number, but the French have got off to France, and march away like monkeys, scrambling over everything, consequently there are few prisoners. Lord Wellington is in the highest spirits. King Joseph was within two hundred yards of our dragoons, and had a narrow escape. A few more cannon have been taken.

It is one continued pass, or valley, all the way from Vittoria to this place; the road infamous, villages every mile, but much damaged by the French, and the people, from affluence, reduced to misery and distress. Oh war! war! little do you know of it in England. At Orunzun the French had spent much in a blockhouse and fort; they withdrew the garrison for the battle, and the peasants destroyed it immediately.

One league from Sanguessa, Head-Quarters, Casseda, June 29th, 1813.—Thus far we have arrived in pursuit of Clausel and his division, who were at Logrono, on their way to join King Joseph. Had the battle been delayed two days longer, we should have had these fifteen thousand men, in addition, to contend with; for by that time they would have joined the king's army. As it was, they were in some degree cut off and separated from their friends, and might have been in some danger; for had it not been for the information of some treacherous alcalde (I believe), these men would have proceeded towards Pamplona, and would then have fallen completely into our net. As it is, hearing of our approach, and having the start, there is no chance of doing anything with them, I think; they have full opportunity of joining Suchet, and nothing material in their way, though Mina may harass them much. Our army, by this pursuit, already is terribly harassed and out of sorts.

In marching, our men have no chance at all with the French. The latter beat them hollow; principally, I believe, owing to their being a more intelligent set of beings, seeing consequences more, and feeling them. This makes them sober and orderly whenever it becomes material, and on a pinch their exertions and individual activity are astonishing. Our men get sulky and desperate, drink excessively, and become daily more weak and unable to proceed, principally from their own conduct. They eat voraciously when opportunity offers, after having had short fare. This brings on fluxes, &c. In every respect, except courage, they are very inferior soldiers to the French and Germans. When the two divisions, the fourth and light, passed through Taffalla the day before yesterday, the more soldierlike appearance and conduct of the foreigners, though in person naturally inferior, was very mortifying. Lord Wellington feels it much, and is much hurt.*

The 23rd and 11th Portuguese regiments, who behaved in the field on the 23rd as well as any British did or could do, are on the march, though smaller animals, most superior. They were cheerful, orderly, and steady. The English troops were fagged, half tipsy, weak, disorderly, and unsoldierlike; and yet the Portuguese suffer greater real hardships, for they have no tents, and only bivouac, and have a worse commissariat.

---

* Mr. Larpent's opinion on the moral deficiency of the English soldier has astonished many; but it should be remembered that he was a non-combatant, and his professional practice as Judge-Advocate-general brought him more in contact with the *delinquents* than with the real steady soldiers of the army. Let any reader who inclines to think that the French can outmarch the more robust English, remember the advance of the light division to Talavera under General R. Craufurd, so justly eulogized in Napier's History. An English soldier becomes sulky, careless, and insubordinate in a *retreat*; but let a battle be announced, and spirit and discipline reappear together. Witness the conduct of Sir John Moore's army, when he offered battle at Lugo, and afterwards when he was attacked at Corunna.—ED.

I think we shall to-morrow retrace our steps to Pamplona, and give over this pursuit. Lord Wellington, I think, sees it will not do. We had a very long march the day before yesterday to Taffalla. The road was, however, very good on the Canuria Real from Pamplona to Tudela. Thinking that the French were making to Tudela, we proceeded that way by this forced march. The country was very fine. About two leagues from Pamplona was a handsome, plain, elegant aqueduct, of one hundred arches, light and simple. We passed several villages, and, near Taffalla, a quantity of well-managed orchards and garden-ground; the consequence was, fruit and vegetables cheap and good, plenty of cherries about 1d. a-pound, pears and plums, &c.; onions, beans, peas, lettuce, pork, cheap; in short, a most plentiful Spanish market.

Taffalla is a good town, and the people civil and hospitable. They had never seen us before, and gave us a welcome. I should have liked another day there, for both my men and animals were knocked up, and wanted it. The next day, however, we proceeded by a mountain-road over a little sierra to this place (Casseda), changing our direction of march, though the object was the same. Last night, I believe, it was found that the French had much the start of us, and had crossed the Ebro. In short, I presume from this, and from the very harassed and bad state of the men to-day, we halted here; and I suspect to-morrow we shall return.

Lord Wellington himself seemed knocked up yesterday; he ate little or nothing, looking anxious, and slept nearly all the time of sitting after dinner. I think he was not quite well, and anxious, no doubt. Lord March was sent off to General Graham, at Tolosa; he returned yesterday, and reports that General Graham had entered Tolosa, which might have been well defended. He blew open the gates with a nine-pounder, and so got in.

General Foy, however, had taken a position beyond, with eighteen thousand men, in such a strong country, that Graham dared not attack him, and Lord March thought the loss would be great if we did, unless we could turn it by a circuitous march. He said the country was in that direction full of positions; in short there is much yet to do.

Tarragona is, I believe, not taken at last. General Murray re-embarked when Suchet's army came that way. This, as a plan to free Valencia, has, I believe, answered, and Elio, &c., have advanced. Longa's people have behaved well in another affair since the battle. The day after to-morrow I expect to be either in sight of Pamplona again, or to be on the way towards the Tolosa road; but time will show.

From this place, which is a large village on a hill, we have a full view of a long range of the Pyrenees, which I have been spying at with a good glass. They are fine mountains, but much less so, I think, than the Alps. I see much snow on them, but no glaciers. The shapes are more picturesque, but less astonishing and sublime. We are, however, far off, and perhaps I do not do justice to these hoary gentlemen. There is no snow summit so far as I can see, only great lodgments of snow.

Huarte, July 2nd, in front of Pamplona.—As expected, we yesterday set out on our way back here, a short cut over the sierra, to Monreal—the day before yesterday sending the guns, &c., round by Taffalla, and from Monreal here yesterday. This is a wild road, and yet not very picturesque. About this place we have a fine plain, in which Pamplona stands. The town is invested, but I believe that is all, and no steps have yet been taken for the siege; the place is strong, and we have as yet no guns for the purpose. We yesterday found the suburbs burning, the work of the French, and more women sent away from the town. The town looks handsome, but somehow has disappointed me. A French party also still holds out at Pancorvo; the worst of all, however, is the bad news from General Murray. It is said that he went off in such a hurry when he heard of Suchet's approach, that, without waiting to know his exact danger, or where Suchet was, he embarked, leaving all his battering artillery, or as some say twenty pieces, with all the ammunition, &c., belonging to them, in a perfect state for the use of the French; and this when, in fact, he had four days to remove it in, and when the Admiral offered to undertake to bring it off. I am glad, however, to hear that Lord William Bentinck has arrived to take the command. The odds are, however, that the Spaniards will get a beating under Elio before our men join them again; it is now said that Suchet left five thousand men at Valencia also. In short, in this game of chess we are playing, there is almost always some bad move to counteract Lord Wellington's good ones.

It is now said that we are not to wait here for the siege, but to move towards Bayonne, and the King's army, which is said to have taken up a position on the frontiers. We expect to move towards Roncesvalles to-morrow; but this is not settled. In my opinion we should have done this immediately, without going after Clausel; but no doubt Lord Wellington knew best what to do. We have to-day cold rainy weather again, bad for men in camp. This place, Huarte, is rather a large village with tolerable market. Villa Alba, half a mile off, where some troops are posted, seems better still. We are about two miles from Pamplona, across a little stream, now from the rains become a respectable river. The great distress at present is for horseshoes, and to-morrow I expect a mountain march.

It is now stated that we took fourteen hundred prisoners altogether in this late battle, not wounded, eleven hundred wounded, and about seven hundred and fifty were found dead; the prisoners reckon their own loss at eleven thousand. However, as they say, thousands ran away over the mountain, and left the army altogether, this must be exaggeration. If the armistice produces a Russian and Prussian peace, and we are left here to Bonaparte's sole attention and undivided care, I fear we may again see the neighbourhood of Portugal before six months are passed, notwithstanding the late most glorious victory.

Head-Quarters, Ostiz, July 3rd (*Civil Department at Boutain*).—Here we are now within five leagues and less of France, and on our way, at least, towards Bayonne. General Hill is, I believe, to be to-day at Estevan, and we have some men in France, at St. Jean Pied de Port. General Foy's (French) eighteen thousand have left their position beyond Tolosa, having given the great convoy three days more time to be off. This convoy had the pictures, immense service of plate of the King, three hundred pieces of heavy artillery, &c.: I think we might have caught it had we known how things were going on. They have now retreated to France, and I believe Graham after them. All cars and wheel carriages remain at Orcayen, near Pamplona; I guess, therefore, we shall soon be back again, and perhaps proceed against Suchet, if he joins Clausel at Saragossa, as his orders, from intercepted letters, were supposed to be. Your proverb, however, *vedremo co'l tempo*, applies here as well as everywhere. Dr. M'Gregor is very much engaged, and if this wet weather continues will, I think, be more so. I am so cold now that I am writing with my coat buttoned up, and my hat on, and we have constant showers. For about three hours the day before yesterday it was excessively hot. So we go on! As yet we have seen nothing very beautiful on this road, but it may mend. I am hungry, tired, and worried, and must send this off to Ostiz: so adieu.

Lord Aylmer has now a brigade, and has joined it as Major-general. General Pakenham is the Adjutant-general. Three thousand of our men wounded at Vittoria.

Head-Quarters, Lans, July 5th, 1813 (*Civil Depart-ment, the Spaniards and Artillery at Arriez*).—We were yesterday ordered to proceed to Lans, but not very early, as the French were in the neighbourhood. It rained all the way, and was very cold and uncomfortable, and what added much to the unpleasantness of the journey, was the horrible road and the loss of my horse's shoes. The first league of this *camina real* was a narrow lane of large loose stones, nearly the size of my head, with all the interstices filled with good Brentford slop, half a foot deep; baggage constantly stopped the way. About half way, however, I bribed a Spanish farrier to put me on three Spanish shoes, with the heads of the nails half an inch square, upon six of which heads in each shoe the horses walk, as the shoe never touches a stone; these skaits are, however, much better than nothing. Having stopped an hour in the rain for this, I proceeded, and at Lans found an order to go on half a league on the left. We are almost all here, or close by, except the Adjutant-general's and Quarter-Master-general's departments, and except Marshal Beresford. The latter was to have been in my house, but did not like it, and found a place at Lans. The quarter being vacant, I popped into a large rambling black place, with long tables and benches, like your servants' hall, great stables, &c., all under one roof.

The villages are nearly all alike in general shape and accommodation;—scarcely any cottages but farm-houses, and I suppose the great tables and benches they all contain have been in better times used for the workmen to dine. This has been the character of all the villages for the last ten or twelve miles, and they lie very thick, four in sight here, and probably ten within a league. The hills around are all covered with wood; the valley almost knee deep with grass for hay, and abounding in corn; the walks further on towards the mountains very pleasant; fine oaks and rocks, &c.; the climate very cold for England in July, and wet; the verdure like that of Ireland; plenty of sheep on the mountains, but little to be had here except milk. At Lans there was pork at a penny a pound, and French brandy.

To-day we halt here, for the French are disposed to stand a little further. Our cavalry moved last night to Almandos, two leagues on,—the 14th, and some Germans, and General Hill's head-quarters, to Berueta, whence the French retired. The reports now are that General Hill sent word last night that the French were strongly posted a little farther on, and that the peasants said they were eight thousand; but though he could not see so many, he did not much like the position. Lord Wellington sent him word that he would be there by ten o'clock this morning, and he is gone with most of the military staff. We have heard firing very plainly, but know not where it is. This is famous ground for sharp-shooting, as you cannot see in general a hundred yards before you. General Byng, with some British and Spanish, is gone along the Roncesvalles road, toward St. Jean Pied de Port, and Graham proceeds by the great road. Some stores are ordered round to land at Deva; I conclude we shall only secure the passes, and that we shall not enter France. Ground is broken up before Pamplona, but I think only for form sake; very few men at work. Only the six eighteen-pounders are at hand. An artillery serjeant I hear deserted from Pamplona two days since, and is supposed to have given important information. General Wimpfen tells me that the French have some works at Elisondo, which is, I suppose, the place General Hill is stopped by, and that they seem disposed to make a little stand there. I wish Suchet would either come up by Sara-

gossa and fight near Pamplona, and thus save us that
long trip, or that he would be off at once, like the rest;
the latter is, however, I fear, more to be wished than
expected. With Clausel, he will have probably, including garrisons, about forty thousand men. If after
all a peace should be made, leaving out England and
the Peninsula, we must even now still be off, and I only
hope it will be settled before the autumn bad weather;
another rainy retreat from this part will never do. I
think we may at least stand towards the Astrinos and
Gallicia, and not go back to Frenada, for Bonaparte,
with all his energy and activity, can scarcely be ready to
follow us in force this autumn.

My old witch of a patrona came in just now, into
the place where I am, and moving the heavy bed, disappeared down a trap-door under it to get up a little
clean linen from her hiding-place, where she conceals
things from the French. She also produced a guerilla
soldier's shirt, which he had left to be washed, and
called for to-day. She was very much frightened
at us yesterday, as all here are, but is more sociable
to-day.

We have turned about three hundred mules and
horses into the meadows here, and have cut down two
or three fields for the feeding at night, instead of the
green oats or barley, for that is scarce here. How
would you like all this in England? The peas and
beans also are pretty well pillaged by our soldiers, and
frequently the cattle get in besides. I do not pity the
Spaniards for this; but as they are obstinate, they will
not pick and sell to us officers who ask them, consequently the soldiers and our muleteers pick for themselves
gratis. I do not think the crops here are so forward as
in England; we are, therefore, luckily for the horses, just
in the grass season. If we go back to the barren, brown,
southern plains, it will be rather a disagreeable change.

We shall then, however, probably, get corn for the horses, which now is very scarce. For the present, adieu.

If the French do not move, probably we may halt here to-morrow again; but I doubt we shall proceed. Twelve Portuguese field-pieces were following us up this horrible road; the French got two guns by the same road to Pamplona last year. For the last fortnight we have found the people of Navarre very stupid, and their language unintelligible. They do not understand good Castilian, but have a lingo of their own, very barbarous; the little Spanish I have picked up is here, therefore, of no use, and I am nearly reduced to the state of the deaf and dumb, to have recourse to signs and acting.

Head-Quarters, Irurita, July 7th.—From Lans and Arriez we proceeded on the 6th to Berueta, through Almandos, across a part of the Pyrenees. The first league was through a fine oak wood, and very hilly; the next there was more hill, and, if possible, worse roads, and in particular a very long descent. The hills were, however, green and wooded to the summits, rounded, and not wild or savage, in short it was hilly scenery and not mountain—this is the Lower Pyrenees. From one part on the Lans road, the sea, I am told, was visible. Some Portuguese artillery followed us all the way, and have arrived safely.

We then reached Almandos, which contained a few very large houses for head-quarters; there the artillery, engineers, and Spaniards of head-quarters remained, and we descended a zigzag hill, and then ascended to Barueta. I there got a very bad quarter, but staid, in order to be at the head-quarter village, to inquire into some complaints of public money taken by a Commissary at Vittoria. On the night of the 5th I was sent for at nine at night from Arriez to Lans by Lord Wellington about this business. It is a most horrible road even in the day time, and in my way back alone, I lost myself on a boggy common, and did not arrive until nearly one o'clock, having for about an hour and a half splattered about in a bed of wet clay, up to the horse's knees at times, and having some notion of wolves, &c. This made me anxious to be at the head-quarters village, where I dined with Lord Wellington, and examined the Commissary in General Pakenham's presence.

Berrueta was a small French post against the Guerillas, and the ground was strong; the church and about four houses, and a wall near were cut with loop-holes for musketry, and a little round bastion built in front with a double row of loop-holes commanding the roads, and a little tiled roof for one sentry at the top. The house had a rough eagle in black drawn upon it, and the inscription " Place Napoleon." The little street or alley within the enclosure was called Rue Impériale. In spite of this the French, about three thousand strong, had the day before been driven from this ground and position by about five hundred of the second division, and had left us in possession, allowing General Hill to go on to this place, Irurita, a good league further, where we have now the head-quarters. General Hill has proceeded this morning to try and drive the French from a position about two leagues and a half further on near the French frontier at Maya, where they have made a semblance at least, with about eight thousand men, as if they meant to defend the pass there.

The road from Berrueta to Irurita was over one long hill of a league, but good enough, and then brought us down to this place at one extremity of the valley of Bastan. This valley is a very rich tract, surrounded by cultivated hills, well built and peopled, and terminated on the other extremity by the pass of Maya.

General Hill has moved on his head-quarters from hence to Elisondo, full a half league further, near the

centre of the valley; and if the French give way, is
to proceed further. Lord Wellington and all his suite
are gone on forwards to watch the event. This place
contains a number of large houses, but is in general
dirty and bad in the interior. Lord Wellington's house,
and that of Marshal Beresford, and a few others about
here, are in the French style, with glass windows in
folding doors, and French blinds, &c., and they are clean
and comfortable; at Elisondo, there is more of this,
I hear. This valley has a sort of nobility of its own,
and most of the numerous good houses belong to an
inferior nobility. They almost all sport arms, and most
the chequers. I understand this valley is also famous
for the number of men of talent who have at different
times issued from it. There is also trade in the valley,
and commercial connexions even with Cadiz. These
second-rate nobles have had the sense not quite to
despise that mode of getting money, and thereby all
other comforts. The effects of the war and of the times
are, however, equally manifest here, but on a higher
scale than in the ruined cottage, or the farmer stripped
of his cattle and corn. Lord Wellington's patron, whose
house is now opposite and very handsome, was a native
of this place, and went as a merchant to South America:
he was engaged there in trade twenty-six years, and
then returned to enjoy himself, like our Scotch Indians,
in his native place. He, however, foolishly bought no
land, and continues engaged in trade by means of an agent
at Cadiz, and another at Vera Cruz, living here on the
profits. One rich vessel we took from him before the
declaration of war; this shook him a little: since that
his Vera Cruz agent turned gambler and failed. We
have taken another vessel of his since, and he thus was
reduced nearly to his moveables. To supply French
contributions, and to find the *à quoi vivre* for himself
and two sons, he has sold all his plate, &c., and jewels.

He has now only some tolerable bedding in twelve bed-rooms, and straw chairs and deal tables. The little man, however, told all this to General O'Lalor in my presence with much good humour, and did not seem very unhappy. He was very anxious to please Lord Wellington in his quarter.

Here we see the miseries of the contest in another shape. The old mad Marquis d'Almeida left this to-day to go on with General Hill, very anxious to beat the French in their own territory, and give them back their own again. He has attached himself to General Hill's corps all along.

I believe King Joseph's gallantry in trying to seduce a young girl at Salvatierra, the night of the battle of Vittoria, was mentioned in a former letter by me. In this valley he performed a most noble feat: after the dinner given him by his patron and the neighbours, he permitted or ordered his servants to sweep off and carry away all the utensils, table-cloths, spoons, &c. The Padré at Arriez, our last place, told General Wimp-fen that he had there carried off the sheets. This is a noble exit; and all his suite were without a change of linen.

The papers taken at Vittoria make it appear that nearly a million of property was taken after the battle —250,000*l.* in gold. Only about one hundred and twenty thousand dollars have been paid into the chest. Much was certainly plundered by the natives and soldiers: the latter were offering nine dollars for a guinea, for the sake of carriage. Lord Wellington, however, has his suspicions of pillage by the civil de-partments; has heard various stories, also, of money taken on the road back from Vittoria. I do not know what may come of this: I have made out but little satisfactory as yet. One gentleman, however, whom I examined yesterday intended to keep two thousand dollars. At the same time, the understanding that this was all fair seems to be pretty general.

Captain Brown was knocked off his horse by a sabre cut on the head and taken prisoner, but as he had his sword left, he cut down his guard, who was pricking him with his sword, and ran into our dragoons and escaped, changing his own horse for a French one in the confusion.

Lieutenant-Colonel May had a musket-ball in his belly. It passed through his double sash, his waistcoat, and pantaloons, and then, by striking the button of his drawers, was so deadened as only to give him a swelling the size of an egg, and he has been long with us again. I dined with him at Arriez the day before yesterday.

In the skirmish on the 5th, at Berrueta, we had about twenty wounded. The Spanish peasantry are a fine, stout, tall, well-made race of mountaineers, and behaved that day with spirit. Several would act with their fire-arms with our light troops, and brought in two prisoners ; and one set would go on with a picket of six of our cavalry, and when told by Major Brotherton that they were acting foolishly, as he could not protect or support them if the French cavalry turned on him, they said they could run as fast as those French horses, and would not be caught so. The rulers here have also been forward in offering supplies, a good part of which, I believe, they were ordered to have collected by the French, and by which collection we have profited.

More Portuguese troops and artillery are now passing this way. I believe no English artillery has come this road. The Portuguese guns are not so wide in the wheels, having been made for their own roads, and are therefore more adapted to this.

Irurita, Head-Quarters, July 9th.—Still here. The day before yesterday, the 7th, the French showed fifteen thousand men in the Maya pass, two leagues and a-half in front, a line of nearly two miles. It took much time to climb the hills to turn this position. About four, we got possession of a hill which had that effect; the French saw their error, tried three times to recover it, drove back our men a little, but it would not do; they just now will not stand against us. A battalion of Caçadores behaved well, and drove them back once. A close column of theirs was opposed on the hill by two columns of ours, the 39th; our fellows, when near, shouted and came down to the charge, and the French were quickly off. It was dark, however, before the pass was abandoned, and past eleven before Lord Wellington and his staff got home to dinner, as he lost his way for some time in the fog, despising guides, &c. Yesterday the French, in part, came back to a little village near the pass, and stood some time against our light infantry; but the third shot of our two guns which were brought to bear, sent them scampering off. They little think that we have some eighteen field-pieces in this valley.

Yesterday Lord Wellington came in early, and left the French in another pass in the last Spanish village. They were, I hear, to be driven out to-day unless they retired. They had yesterday, however, nearly succeeded in surprising some of our men. They appeared in rear of our advanced troops, through a pass on our right, which communicates with the Roncesvalles pass to St. Jean Pied de Port, drove in a small picket, and came, about fifty of them, down very nearly to a village in which we had much baggage. The peasants said they had five hundred men there: they however went back again, and one of our serjeants, by himself, caught one of the stragglers when the others were gone. Just then there was only a small body of cavalry between their party and our baggage, and even between them and our head-quarters here. This was soon looked to, and a Caçadore regiment ordered into the neighbouring village. The peasants here continue to behave with great spirit

and activity, and want to enter France to take some revenge. They had been told by the French that we were
ten times worse in regard to plundering, &c., than themselves, and so the French are told now. The French
respect their own people, and do not treat them like the
Spaniards. In Spain a French encampment was covered
with all the doors, window-shutters, beams, trees, &c., of
the Spanish villages near; in France, though in rain, they
are now seen without any such shelter on the bare ground.

The French peasants in these parts, I hear, are as fine
men as the Spaniards here, and formidable. If we enter
France, we must not wander and ride about as we do
here, nor let our baggage cover leagues in extent. It is
said that they disposed of four of our soldiers, Portuguese
I believe, whom they caught stealing cherries. I do not
think head-quarters will enter France, here at least, but
enter down towards the sea: this is, however, only my
speculation. General Byng sent an invitation yesterday
to dine with him in France. The Spanish troops are in
France in part also.

The day before yesterday Lord Wellington ordered
young Fitzclarence to go and bring up two Portuguese
companies to attack. He went. It was close by; but
he was highly pleased with the order. When he had
given his instructions, he saw a cherry-tree, and went up
to break a bough off, and eat the cherries. When Lord
Wellington lost his way the other night in the fog
(returning to head-quarters), Fitzclarence told Lord
Wellington he was sure the road was so-and-so, as
they had passed the place where he found the two Portuguese companies. "How do you know that?" quoth
Lord Wellington. "By that cherry-tree, which I was
up in just afterwards," was the answer. It amused
Lord Wellington much; and yesterday he called to him,
with a very grave face, and desired him to go and get
some of the cherries, as if it were an important order. I

believe we only lost about seventy men killed and wounded, Portuguese and all included, on the 7th.

I misinformed you some time since about General Jeron, the Commander of the Gallician army. I understand he was not named at the suggestion of Wellington; there are two opinions about him.

We have had stories against several of the civil departments in regard to the plunder. One or two I have saved from suspicion by an immediate inquiry and explanation, which I stated to Lord Wellington directly. It is always best to know the whole openly at once, as ten suffer in reputation from reports for one really guilty. One Commissary, I believe, will have leave to resign.

Yesterday the chimney of the house of Lord Wellington's patron was on fire, from the dressing of Lord Wellington's dinner. I was much afraid that it would spread and complete the poor man's ruin, by destroying nearly all he had left. It was with difficulty at last put out, when the fire-bell had collected all the town buckets full of water, and a wet blanket had been pushed down the chimney, which, being half wood, made the event very uncertain. I was really glad when it was put out. Lord Wellington was out in the rain with his hat off, and a silk handkerchief over his head, giving directions, as well as your humble servant.

P.S.—*Head-Quarters, Zobieta, July* 10th.—We arrived here this morning, in the direction I expected, about four leagues from Irurita, on the road to St. Sebastian, through a very pretty wooded valley all the way, the road good, and by the river side, with villages every two miles. We passed St. Estevan, the largest place, and perhaps the only one you will find in any map, except Lopez' provincial ones. Some of the other villages were large, containing some thirty or forty good large farmhouses, and some mansions. The light division was dispersed on the road, and in one village I found George Belson and his artillery. I do not, however, expect to hear any more of him for some time, as he is not likely to follow us any farther, from what I am told of the road.

To-morrow head-quarters move eight or nine leagues of mountain track road through Gaygueta to Ernani, in parts it is said scarcely passable for a mule; so at least Colonel Ponsonby reports, who came last night from Ernani. In consequence of this account, civil departments and baggage are, if they choose, to stop at Gaygueta, which is half way. At Ernani we are on the high road to Bayonne from Vittoria. Something is now, I believe, going on at St. Sebastian. I understand a convent near it was to be attempted to-day or to-morrow, preparatory to the grand attempt. The heavy guns are, I believe, landed, and are, it is said, at Deba for this siege. The garrison is two thousand strong, about sixteen hundred of their own, and four hundred from another fort near, now blown up. Santona is left with a strong garrison, and well supplied, and would be a more difficult affair, from what I learn. Pancorvo was taken by O'Donnell and the Spaniards: they took an outwork by storm, and the men then surrendered.

Pamplona is more closely invested by means of some redoubts, and I believe nothing more will be done there. These redoubts will be of use, if this undertaking is left to the Spaniards. Though we have thus to-day gone away from France, I conclude we, or rather some of the army, are to be within France soon, as Lord Wellington has published some long and good general orders on the subject of well treating the people, &c., and not copying the French in Portugal and Spain, as we are at war with Bonaparte, and not with the inhabitants, and that *recevos* are to be given for supplies, &c. Still I think we shall only keep on the frontiers. Clausel, it would appear from the Spanish authorities, has, since we left him, made off for France by the great Tacca pass in Arragon, instead of joining Suchet, as I supposed, and Suchet was at Tortosa when last heard of. Zobieta is but a miserable place, and the people quite unintelligible. We shall soon be in Biscay again.

Head-Quarters, Ernani, July 16*th*, 1813.—My last was from Zobieta, a little village in the lower Pyrenees. Our next day was a tremendous journey to this place. I started at six o'clock in the morning, and we immediately began to ascend near the bed of the stream, which ran by Zobieta towards its source, in order to cross the mountain at the back of the town, which divides that valley from the one in which the river is situated, which runs down by this place to St. Sebastian.

In less than half a mile the road became choaked with baggage. There was only one path winding zig-zag up the hill, and every mule whose load got more on one side, or out of order, discomposed and stopped the string. I had one mule lightly loaded, and my man, foolishly eager to get forwards, led it up straight from one path to the cross one above, instead of following the track. He got on safely, but this tempted three of Colonel Dundas's mules to do the same. Just as I passed below, the hinder one fell backwards, with a heavy load, and the whole three being tied together, he pulled both the others down upon him, and they all lay in a heap at my feet kicking in the path. With some difficulty I got an ass out of the way in time, and scrambled upon foot, leading my horse to get away, that I might not be pushed down the side of the hill; by this means I also gained ground, and by continuing on foot for about two miles of the steepest ascent, I got up tolerably quick. Two of General Murray's mules rolled into the river below.

We then continued to the highest point of the mountain, whence we were told Bayonne was visible. When

we arrived the fog was so thick that we could not see a
yard, and we went on two leagues more in this mist
through the clouds, along the top and side of the hill,
until we got over Gaygueta. Then we had a very bad
descent of about two miles to that place. Near the
town we passed General Longa and his suite going to
meet Lord Wellington, and we found the town full of
his troops all drawn up to receive the English General.
They looked very well, fine men, tolerably well dressed
and equipped; about five thousand in the whole. One
grenadier company looked very fierce and military.

I here found every quarter occupied, and could hear of
none; after waiting an hour, I determined to proceed.
After an ascent of about half a league again, very steep,
we went along the top of a hill for another half league
to Eranos; here I found another thousand of Longa's
troops, and all the houses occupied. I therefore went
to a shop where they sold bread and wine, and we got a
large loaf and some wine, which, with the help of the
horses, for whose sake I principally stopped to procure
this feed, we soon finished, and then proceeded refreshed.

Whilst I was thus employed Lord Wellington and his
staff passed. I was sorry to hear Longa had missed
him, and that he was much mortified at this, especially
as his men scarcely knew Lord Wellington and his party,
and he had almost passed before they irregularly presented arms to him. The one thousand men at Eranos
were more fortunate, for at a hazard I told them, when
they inquired, that he would pass in about twenty
minutes, and he actually passed within the half hour.
I followed in Lord Wellington's train to this place,
Ernani, over a road still worse than the last, a mere
water-channel, with irregular broken steps and slippery
clay; most of our horses got more or less on their
haunches. The road ran up and down on the side of a
thick wooded hill on the banks of the river, near which

we saw two or three works for iron, in which this country abounds.

We arrived safely, about four o'clock; very little baggage got in that night. All mine came in by seven o'clock, except one mule load and man, who stuck, knocked up, at a house two miles back. I bought some eggs and bacon and went to bed. About eight, next day, my stragglers arrived, the mules strained in the shoulder and scarcely able to move. Dr. M'Gregor had two mules killed down the mountain, and many have suffered as well as myself.

The next morning after my arrival at Ernani, I walked off to see what was going on at St. Sebastian. Not knowing how long we might be here, my horses being tired, and having no shoes, I made this survey on foot. The road is a wide *camina real*, a rough sort of pavement, but a good road. About half a league distant I saw the fort or citadel of St. Sebastian, and the smoke of the guns, the noise of which I had heard before. I proceeded on by our heavy guns, which were near on the road side, passed about four thousand Spanish troops of the Gallician army drawn up to receive Lord Wellington, and then our reserve park of artillery, with some small works around. Here I began to hear the distant whistle of the balls, which occasionally got near the road. At about a league from Ernani, just at the brow of the descent to St. Sebastian, and about half a mile from the latter, a barrier of tubs of earth was placed across the road and sentries posted, our advanced sentry being at a turn of the road a hundred yards forwards. I went to the left to take a sketch, and soon heard a musket-ball whistle by me, which I took at first for a rocket behind me. I thought this an accident, but soon came a second, and a third. I then concluded that I was the object, and leaving my sketch rather in a hasty unfinished state, I

returned behind the barrels as the last shot came into a
bush close to me.

Our trenches were open about fifty yards to the right,
against a convent on the side of the hill, which was full
of French, and from which almost all the musket-shots
proceeded. I determined just to peep into them before
I went off, and having been cautioned how to proceed,
I looked in : but having had one more shot whistle close
to me, and passed a bloody hole where a shell had just
fallen, which had carried away a man's arm, I walked
home, to dine at Lord Wellington's at three o'clock.
At dinner I met Castanos, Jeron, Alava, Mendizabel,
and a number of inferior officers, amongst them the
Major who had been left as a Captain to defend Villa
Alba de Tormes, when we retreated last year, and who
held out the time he was ordered to remain, and brought
off two hundred out of three hundred of his men to Frenada. For this he was made a Major, I believe, at Lord
Wellington's request. General Alava also introduced an
officer who came to present to Lord Wellington King
Joseph's sword—his dress sword set in steel and dia-
monds, and very handsome. Where taken from, or
whence obtained, I did not learn. Lord Wellington
just looked at it as he took his seat at dinner, and telling
his man to put it by safely somewhere, fell to at the
soup and said no more.

On the following day the alarm was spread that we
were all to go back to the mountains the next day by
the same road. At last, however, orders came out that
Lord Wellington was going, and that only his immediate
staff, and those who could be very useful, were to attend
him. Even General Murray, the Quarter-Master-general,
the life and soul of the army next to Lord Wellington,
staid here, not being quite well. He appears to me
decidedly the second man ; and it is thought that with-

out him, and perhaps Kennedy, the Commissary-in-Chief, we could never have done what we have; even Lord Wellington would be, in some degree, fettered and disabled by a bad Quarter-Master-general and a bad Commissary-general.

Not to lose a day, Lord Wellington, the first day he was here, rode all about St. Sebastian to examine it in all directions, &c., and was provoked at the Spaniards parading for him, when his object was to be unobserved. The second day he went to Irun, on the frontiers, on the Bidassoa, to see how things were going on there. The day before yesterday, having waited till eight o'clock (morning), just to receive the " *Gazette*," with his battle despatches and his appointment of Field Marshal, away he went, nine leagues over the mountains, for St. Estevan. He is going to see more of the mountain passes that way, and says that he shall be back the fourth day, if possible, though many think it impossible.

We have heard of Lord Wellington eating some trout at Gaysueta at twelve, and arriving at St. Estevan at five, the day he left this. All baggage nearly is left here. The day he went I was occupied all day, by his desire, in examining some gentlemen on a report which had got about concerning some of the captured money, which report Lord Wellington had been caught by, and had suspicions. I hope I have sent a very satisfactory explanation. To me it is so, at least. I sent it off by express the same night to General Pakenham, who is with Lord Wellington on his tour. One idle day, since I have been here, I went to see Passages, about five miles distant, but an infamous road. There are two towns of that name, the Spanish and French, as they are called; one on each side of a narrow deep stream, or inlet from the sea, which forms rather a picturesque basin within. I should have thought more of it had I not seen Exmouth, Dartmouth, and some other western

English scenery of the same kind first, which I think superior. The towns were built with the same kind of narrow alleys, only fit for a horse to pass through; these standing up the side of the hills. They were, however, a better description of houses, and four stories high, with balconies. The scene was more enlivened than usual by our transports, by the landing of biscuit, rum, shot, ammunition, the twenty-four pounders from Sir George Collier's ship, and other great guns, with their apparatus, for the siege; two Portuguese regiments at work, and about three hundred mules, besides the oxen, &c., for the guns : gabions and fascines were making in every direction by the Portuguese. The road was so narrow and slippery in one place, that my horse, as I led him, nearly slipped into the sea.

Yesterday, having a few hours again to spare, I went round to look at St. Sebastian by the right, where I witnessed a sharp conflict, and saw more than I had done before, with much less risk. I was out of the way of the musketry, and only had one cannon-shot, which went over the intended mark from the town, and, whistling along, dashed into the water just under me. It was nearly spent, as I heard it, I think, long enough to have got out of the way had it come up higher. If it clears up to-day, I mean to go to the lighthouse, on the left of the town, or the cliff, where it is said the view is very fine, and where, with a glass, you see much and in safety.

There was almost as much firing yesterday as in a battle, cannon-shot and musketry, particularly on the French part, and many shells; and we made a feint to obtain the convent with only a few men, yet I hear that only four were killed on our side, and about ten wounded.

The convent is almost in ruins, but we have in vain tried to burn it with hot shot, and the French continue to pepper from it. A shell of ours fell amongst their men in a redoubt in rear of the convent, and they ran. I believe this led to our attempt, but it was soon found that they were strong just behind, and several men still in the convent; and three new parties were pushed along the causeway from the town—about two hundred and fifty men—to strengthen the convent party. Ours, therefore, were off very quickly, not being supported. One shell of ours fell just into one of the three new parties, and killed one man and dispersed the rest. Several wounded French were seen carried back over the causeway and bridge. The number of cannon in the town is very considerable; and though our works proceed fast, the town is considered formidable.

I have heard more stories of King Joseph from the Paymaster of his head-quarters, Mr. Frayre, who was taken. He said that the King was in the town until our dragoons were close upon it. He then rode quietly along, through the train of carriages and baggage, with Jourdan and his guard in a walk, in order not to give any alarm, until he was out of the bustle. He then changed his coat for a nankeen jacket, and away they all went, galloping off for Salvatierra, on the road to Pamplona. In the first village, a mile or two from Vittoria, there are two turnings, and he was heard to call out, " *Par où faut-il aller?*" " *Tout droit, tout droit,*" said Jourdan, and away they went again as hard as they could go. Of the twenty-seven Generals who met in the house at Salvatierra, a great proportion were slightly wounded, and their greetings at seeing each other alive were very loud and sincere. Joseph's servant had a sort of saddle-bag with him for the King, and that was all their baggage.

I hear that there are two millions of dollars on the road. Just now we are without anything in our military chest to pay for our daily food and expenses, which

are very great. Corn for our horses, we got none.
Bread is not dear here, or scarce, as yet. Bullocks, I
hear, we have bought enough for nearly forty days for
the army, in this part of the country, mostly from the
mountains. Nine hundred head have been bought within
these ten days.

Head-Quarters, Lezaca, July 18*th*, 1813.—On the
16th I went up to the lighthouse in the evening. I met
Baron Constans coming down. The French did him the
honour of a cannon-shot, a proof they were touchy. I
proceeded within half musket-shot, but at a trot, and
they left me quiet. I stayed an hour on the hill; view
beautiful, evening clear, scene very interesting. I saw
all the French sentries, troops, inhabitants, &c., in the
town, and on the island near, in the convent, redoubt,
&c. I could see our advanced sentinels and pickets,
and those of the French near the convent, within sixty
yards of each other in some places, behind ruins, &c. I
could also see a long extent of French coast, and many
other objects. The ruined convent, and the French
sticking to it in several parts and firing, was, however, the
most curious and novel.

I came down at seven and rode home quietly by nine
in the dark; when, lo! I found an order for head-
quarters, baggage, &c., to join Lord Wellington at this
place on the mountains, on the frontiers, six leagues of
bad road distant.

I was off, however, by eight yesterday morning, baggage and all. The first two leagues were by the high
French road, the *camina real*, through Astigarraja and
Oyarjun. At the end of the last town we turned from
the great road, which is a broad, well-laid road, and has
been very good, though now broken up a little, and very
rough. We then went along a paved mountain road, up
a valley for half a league, and then began climbing a
mountain path over two long hills until we got into this

valley, and to this place. There is a great sameness in the scenery—round hills, wooded in part below and a stream—nothing very fine. About a league from hence we saw the camp of the 95th regiment, on a hill above Vera, which is lower down in this valley, and near the immediate frontier division. We also saw the seventh division camp near and the French cantonment bivouac on the opposite hill; for a short time they kept half Bera or Vera; now we have the whole.

We halt here at Lezaca to-day; the Commissariat baggage is ordered a league and a half in the rear in case of an attack. I believe when reinforcements arrive we shall make one. I was sorry to leave St. Sebastian, for an attack was to be made that morning. We heard and saw a violent firing throughout all our route, and I last night heard that the convent had been taken by our men, and some ruins below, &c., and that the new battery had been opened. The French stood firm when the Portuguese advanced, who behaved very well, but when the English regiment which had been ordered up to assist was seen advancing, the sight of the red coats made the French soldiers run, and the French officers were seen in vain beating and pelting them to make them stand. The causeway (as I had seen) below was cut by the French in two places. This stopped our men for a time, and the French attempted to return, but did not succeed; thus matters stood last night. Some of the first division returned from Oyarjun yesterday to help, and we met them on the road. The French surprised about one hundred of the Spaniards in this place a few days since. The noble inhabitants of Saragossa have contrived to open one of their gates, when the French were in the town, and to let in Mina and his men. The Spaniards now have the town. I believe the French still stick to a fortified part, and have destroyed the bridge; this comes from the English Captain who is with Mina, and employed in procuring intelligence. A flag of truce was sent in to the French, carried by Colonel Gordon, this morning —" *Pourquoi?*" "*Je n'en sais rien.*" Lezaca is rather a good village, and has a running stream in it, which might be more used. It was plundered by the French, and now contains nothing, no bread even, only some straw; and we have now been seven days without corn for the poor horses; even grass is here very scarce: we want the course of the Bidassoa to keep up our communications with Irun, &c. The French now interrupt this—the river runs in part through France.

Soult, the great Soult, the Marshal, is said to have arrived, and taken the command against the allies: so say the country people, &c. To-day it is very hot. A report is circulated that the French have attacked us. So adieu for the present.

July 19*th*, *Lezaca.*—No fresh news. I am going to ride up a hill, a league off, to the seventh division camp, from whence Bayonne and much of France is visible.

CHAPTER X.

Movements of the Army—Wellington on the Portuguese—His Personal Habits—St. Sebastian—The Siege—Miseries of War—Wounded Officers —The Prince of Orange—Vestiges of the Retreat—English Papers— False Accounts of the Campaign—Incidents of the War.

Head-quarters, Lezaca,
July 21, 1813.

My dear M——,

Here we are still, deluged with rain almost incessantly, accompanied at times with violent storms of wind, hail, and thunder. This is terrible for the troops in camp, and for every one more or less, and indeed for everything except the Indian corn, which thrives here most luxuriantly in consequence of this perpetual wet. I took a ride (the 19th) up to the hill above the seventh division as I intended; it was a league and a half, the latter part very steep. The French were in sight all along the hills on the other side of Bera, all around one ridge, but quite quiet. When at the summit I saw the sea-coast around Bayonne (though not the town itself), and the low country in France, for probably thirty miles inland, with the enclosed fields and villages. It was a very fine prospect; I was only sorry to see that the French had apparently so much more productive a country immediately in their rear than we had. They must now, however, be supplied at the expense of old France. We are but ill off here for everything just now, until our supplies come regularly to this coast.

Passages is to be the depôt and landing-place, I hear,

o 2

for our infantry, and Bilboa for cavalry. Major-general Lord Aylmer is to-day setting off to take a command at Passages; he expects nearly four thousand men there very soon. We still hear the battering guns of St. Sebastian continually roaring at a distance; I fear we may lose many men in this siege. Good luck, however, may do something for us, and the French seem everywhere dispirited; sickness, at present, if this weather lasts, will be our most destructive foe.

Suchet, I hear, left a garrison at Murviedro, when he crossed the Ebro. They seem to have intended to give us some tough work until they were ready to return; I hope here, at least, that will not be so easy. Both sides are now strongly posted, and the assailant must have the worst of it. Soult is said to have refused to take the command of the army here unless the pay of the troops was more regular. Talking of this, Lord Wellington paid the highest compliment to Bonaparte, by saying, that if he came himself, he should, as he always did, reckon his presence equal to a reinforcement of forty thousand men, for that it would give a turn to everything.

Lord Wellington, talking of the Portuguese, said that it was extraordinary just now, to observe their conduct; that no troops could behave better; that they never had now a notion of turning; and that nothing could equal their forwardness now, and willing, ready tempers. I am sorry to say that some of our foreign corps do not go on as well. Of the Brunswick corps, ten went off from picquet two nights since to the French, and fourteen from the camp, and others have gone off also; and some have been surprised, so that I believe they are ordered to be sent more to the rear, and cannot be trusted. I do not wonder at it, as Government have taken men from the French prisons, who were only taken last year, and who, no doubt, only enlisted on purpose to desert the first opportunity.

Lezaca, July 22nd.—To-day Lord Wellington cele-
brates the batt e of Salamanca by a great dinner. His
victories and successes will soon ruin him in wine and
eating, and if he goes on as he has, he had better keep
open house at once every day, and his calendar of feasts
will be as full as the Romish one with red letter days.
This morning the guns have been thundering salvoes.

I think the breach at St. Sebastian must be ready
soon. I only hope that we shall not lose many of our
fine fellows. Pamplona is invested more closely—that is
all that is attempted. Two sallies have been repulsed;
there are about fifteen thousand Spaniards there. I was
sorry to hear that bread was, very lately, in the town at
the same price as when we were first there, and that a
low Spanish price; this does not look much like starving
the garrison out. For a regular siege we have no means,
and the place is formidable from the very circumstance
that makes it look otherwise—the citadel is all flat, there
is nothing to fire at, and no ground to approach it by.
The scenery all about this lower Pyrenees and coast, is
like the north coast of Devonshire and Somersetshire, a
little enlarged as you get inland, and so increasing in size,
but the same character remaining for a considerable extent,
only that the valleys become deeper, and the hills higher.
There is nothing, however, so striking here as the passage
of the Ebro, and the valley near where we crossed it.

Major D—— has still got his prize here taken on the
field of battle, namely, a Spanish girl, a pony, the
wardrobe, monkey, &c., the property of one of King
Joseph's aides-de-camp. I am still kept at work. We
yesterday tried two men for plundering Lord Aylmer's
tent in the night whilst he slept.

Out of 500,000*l.* sterling, the supposed plunder at
Vittoria, only about 30,000*l.* has found its way to the
treasury, or military chest. Lord Wellington seems to
think the best of Mina, Longa, and the Empecinado;

amongst the Spaniards there is much to be done yet,
to make them like our vagabonds or the Portuguese, in
regard to fighting; for plundering and the "*savoir vivre*"
here without money or rations, they beat us both already;
we cannot improve them.

Castanos, the other day at dinner, asked Lord Wellington how Madame Gazan had been treated, as she was
accustomed to have a considerable number of lovers?
Lord Wellington looked rather drolly at me, and said,
she had been treated, he believed, very properly and
respectfully. Castanos said, "*Elle en serait bien fachée.*"

Last week some of the light division had rations of
wheat in the grain instead of bread. One fellow, who
was sulky, said, he supposed he should have "long
forage" next, that is, straw. Another more good
humouredly said, he was as strong as a horse now since
yesterday? How so? "Why, they have given me a
good feed of corn you see, so how could it be otherwise."
We had one very ingenious device by two of our fellows
last week; they were employed to take care of two thousand dollars prize, for the benefit of the regiment, and to
carry it on a mule or ass given to them for that purpose.
General Cole passed this donkey on a bridge, and being
irritated from the obstruction caused by the baggage, &c.,
swore he would upset the whole over the bridge if they
were not off. When he had passed, one said, "That will
just do, let's divide the money, and say the General upset
it in the river." This was done, and the report made;
something, however, was overheard, and this led to an
inquiry, when one of them admitted that this was the
case, and that a serjeant shared and proposed the plan. I
said that they could only be flogged for this. Lord
Wellington therefore said they might as well be tried in
their regiment, for three hundred lashes was as good as a
thousand, and that to publish these things was only to
put similar ideas into other people's heads.

Lezaca, Head-Quarters, July 23*rd.*—Lord Wellington and all his party went off at eight this morning for St. Sebastian to see how things are going on. He intends returning to dinner, a late one, though they all have fresh horses on the road. It is feared that his hints have not been attended to, and that the breach has been made too soon before all other things were ready, so that the place of danger is discovered to the enemy in time, perhaps, to enable the French, who are ever quick and ready on these occasions, to let in some sea, and make a wet ditch behind, or to throw up new works, &c. The breach may thus, as at Badajoz, become the worst place of the whole to attack. It is to be hoped that this is only a false alarm; but things do not appear to go on well, unless Lord Wellington or General Murray are on the spot. Lord Wellington is not so easily roused from his bed as he used to be. This is the only change in him; and it is said that he has been in part encouraged to this by having such confidence in General Murray. I understand he was always naturally fond of his pillow. He had rather ride like an express for ten or fifteen leagues, than be early and take time to his work. Upon the whole this may fatigue him less, as being a less time on horseback.

Head-Quarters, Lezaca, July 25*th*, 1813.—We have now been some time stationary in these mountains, and I am at work again, and have little time, and less to write about. We have been in hourly and nervous expectation of news of the storming of St. Sebastian. It was first to have taken place the day before yesterday, but we were not quite ready; then at five yesterday morning; but either from our shells firing a house near the breach, and the French encouraging the flames to spread, or from their originally setting fire to that part of the town, there was such a considerable fire all around the breach, that it was thought too hot to attempt the storming. It was then, by Lord Wellington's order, I believe, fixed for this morning, and he has been as usual very anxious about the event.

He was very fidgetty yesterday, when I went to him about two poor fellows who are to be hung for robbing Lord Aylmer's tent; and to-day he came out to the churchyard, where we were listening, about eight o'clock, to judge from the noise of the guns whether our batteries had ceased, and what the firing was. He has been once over himself, but appeared to wish to leave it to Graham, and not directly to interfere. At eleven this morning, however, Colonel Burgh came over with an account of our attempt having failed; that our party (consisting of English, too, and I believe of the 9th and 38th) went up to the breach, then turned, and ran away. This will terribly discourage our men who have to go next, and encourage the enemy. Lord Wellington has ordered his horse, and is going over immediately.

Nothing can be done, however, before the evening or to-morrow morning, as the attack must take place within two hours before or after low water, in order to pass the sands for the breach. I am told the latter is wide and easy, and we cannot tell what possessed our men on this occasion. The object, St. Sebastian, is most important for the army; first, to enable us to keep our ground here, as an *appui* to the left flank, and secondly, as a safe place for stores, sick and wounded, where, in case of retreat, they may be all left to be brought off at leisure by sea, and also as a refuge for Guerillas, &c. A few things are now beginning to be brought to us in these wild inhospitable regions, but still they are sent from Lisbon by land, with the six weeks' carriage on a mule to pay for. If some one would speculate to Passages direct, it would fully answer, for Irish butter is 4s. 6d. a pound; sugar, 4s.; ham, 3s.; tea, 20s., the same as that sold at Lisbon for 8s.; and so on.

To-day I am going about three miles up the Bidassoa river to a posada, in which the artillery of Colonel Ross's troops are quartered, to dine with them. Part of the way to their present quarters from St. Estevan they had to cut their road with spades and pickaxes for the guns; but there they now are safe.

I am sorry to say several of our men (English) desert as well as the foreigners. I have just heard that the cause of their failure at St. Sebastian this morning was partly the same as that of Badajoz formerly—a deep ditch behind the breach, and nothing to fill it up with, if indeed that were possible; but it is said to have been very deep. Our men looked, came back, got for shelter under the wall, and were then ordered back, and they ran a little. This is a much better account of the business. The attack was also too soon, so that the tide prevented one attack from being attempted, and it is feared that our artillery even fired from that cause on the attackers. The French certainly understand sieges better, I think, than we do.

Head-Quarters, Berrio Planca, in front of Pamplona, half a league, July 31st, 1813.—To my great surprise, here I am again, and now tell you how and why.

Head-Quarters, again at Lezaca, near Bera, in the Mountains, August 3rd, 1813.—I had just taken up this paper, and headed it as above, to begin my history, when a turn of good fortune, arising from the courage of our army from the superior manœuvres of our General, have in eight days brought head-quarters back to our old place, whence the first sheet of this letter was dated. I have been too much occupied in this interval almost to sit down, much more to write; but I will endeavour to detail the important events I have witnessed in them in the best order my recollection will permit.

On the 25th July I went over to dine with the artillery. About seven I mounted to return home, Colonel Ross, Captains Jenkinson and Belson riding with me.

On our way we met a messenger. I asked him to
whom he was going? He said to Colonel Ross. The
Colonel was thereupon called back. It turned out to be
an order to march that night, and rather to the rear.
There had been a distant firing all day, on the right
wing near Maya. Lord Wellington was over at St
Sebastian. Belson was sent to General Alten with orders
by Colonel Ross. Jenkinson galloped back to order the
troops to get ready. Colonel Ross begged me to tell
General Murray he would endeavour to reach Sambillo
that night; and giving a receipt for the letter, was off.
On my return I found Lord Wellington still absent, and
reports flying about, but no orders. I soon found, however, that matters were not going on well, and ordered
everything to be ready for the march next morning.
Lord Wellington returned to dinner at eight, and found
the following account of matters on our right just arrived
to greet him on his return from the failure of St.
Sebastian.

The French had collected a force both at the pass of
Roncesvalles against General Cole, and at the pass of
Maya against General Hill. In the morning of the
25th they pushed a strong reconnoissance against General Stewart, commanding Hill's advance brigade near
Maya, made a show, but gave way again. This report
we had heard, and thought all was over. About three,
however, the French advanced against Cole and Hill.
About twenty-two thousand against Cole's force, about
sixteen thousand against General Stewart's brigade; the
force of the latter are scattered on the hills round the
pass. The French came up in one close body, and
gradually ascended the hill. Our people fired on them
the whole time, and the destruction was very considerable. Still, however, they gained ground. Twice
were they charged by a single regiment of ours, and the
head of the column gave a little, but the press of numbers

urged them on, and as our force was only about three thousand men, and that acting only by small bodies of regiments or companies, the French drove all before them after a most gallant but fatal resistance, before a sufficient reinforcement could be brought up. Four Portuguese guns were abandoned. Our loss in killed and wounded you will see in the " *Gazette.*" It is said to be twelve hundred British, almost all in three or four regiments—principally the 50th, 92nd, 74th, and 28th. In the 92nd, I am told, there was no officer except the Quarter-Master in a state to march off the men at parade. Colonel Belson (28th) had only four officers left besides himself on duty, as he had been thinned at Vittoria. To add to this disaster, General Cole thought he was not justified in opposing the superior force against him, and gave way in the pass of Roncesvalles. This left an opening for the enemy to get in the rear of General Hill in the valley of Bastan at Elisondo. Of course, therefore, he was obliged to fall back also, and the result was that Lord Wellington on his return found his right wing forced, and his position completely turned. Retreat, and that a rapid one, became necessary, in order to take a new position, and to fall back on the divisions near Pamplona.

After I was in bed on the night of the 25th the order came to march, as I expected. Lord Wellington was off early straight across to the second division. The light divisions fell back from our front; the seventh also toward St. Estevan towards the second; the artillery proceeded to St. Estevan by Sambillo. Head-quarters were sent over the mountains by Yanga and Aranor to a little village called Eligarraga, just as you descend into the valley of St. Estevan, there to wait for orders.

We had a wild and tedious road of four leagues, up and down the mountains like Blue Beard's procession, in which we should now all be adepts. A road ran round

the bottom through Sambillo, but probably it was not
thought safe, and that it might interfere with the artillery, as it was narrow the whole way, and nothing could
pass.

About two o'clock on the 26th we reached Eligarraga,
and there found Major Canning sitting by the wayside
to order on everything three long leagues further
through Estevan, and then after keeping the road along
the valley about a league beyond towards the pass into
the Bastan Valley, near Trinita and Elisondo, we were
to turn at Oronoz through a pass on the right, which
brought us into the rear of the valley of Bastan, and into
the rear of General Hill's division, to a place called
Almendoz, on the road to Pamplona from Elisondo,
General Hill's head-quarters being half a league in our
present rear as we retreated, at our old head quarters,
Berrueta. In the meantime the seventh and light divisions got down into the valley of St. Estevan that night.

At Almendoz we found the effects of the battle at
Maya. The wounded had just reached that place, and
there those who had not been dressed, had their wounds
examined, and all were urged on to the rear over a
mountain pass to Lanz as fast as possible. The village
of Almendoz was very small; the wounded lying about
in all directions, till cars and mules could help them on.
It was near seven o'clock, and we had nothing to eat
since seven in the morning; quarters very bad of course,
and the inhabitants all in the greatest distress, beginning
to pack up, to desert their houses, as the people in the
valley of Bastan, at Elisondo, &c., had done already, the
French having got possession. A retreat is a most dis-
tressing scene even at the best, and when conducted with
perfect order as this was.

About nine o'clock that night orders came to march at
daylight for Ulague, a place about half-way between
Lanz and Ostiz. After a five o'clock breakfast, away we

went for the mountains again. The road was choked
with baggage, and artillery, and fugitives, amongst others,
fourteen or fifteen nuns in their dresses, who were reduced by fatigue to beg some rum of us as we passed,
which unfortunately we had not with us. We got on
by scrambling along the paths near the road, and arrived
about twelve. On the 27th we arrived at Lanz. We
there found General Murray and several officers, all looking very serious and gloomy, and orders given for everything to be turned off that road to the right, and not to
go to Ulague, as Cole had been pressed. The firing was
very sharp, and the French were urging on to that road,
besides which, by taking to the right we got towards the
camino real, from Pamplona to Tolosa, and could have
made for General Graham's if necessary. We were
turned through Arayes (where I had been on the advance,
and by the road where I had lost myself before in the
night), on through a rich valley and several villages to
Lissago, or Lisasso.

Here (the 27th) we were placed very snugly, only about
two leagues and a-half from the Tolosa road, about three
from Pamplona, and in the midst of the divisions.
General Cole, with the fourth division, had fallen back on
Pamplona to some hills near Villa Alba, or Villalba:
there he joined the third division, General Picton's, and
some Spaniards. General Hill fell back to Lanz. From
Berrueta, the seventh division got a short way over the
mountains, from St. Estevan to near Lisasso, our head-
quarters, and thus got near the sixth. The light division
fell back more towards Goigueta, or Ernani, to communicate with Graham and protect the Tolosa road, and
thus we stood all night.

The scene at Lisasso was dreadful! All the wounded
from Lanz had just arrived there, in cars, on mules,
crawling on crutches, and hobbling along: all those with
wounds in their hands and arms, &c., walking. Finding

that they had orders to stop there, all our quarters, except Lord Wellington's, and about four more houses,
were given up, and we all dispersed to the villages round.
You may conceive the scene, both on the road and in the
village. I thought one of my horses had lost his shoes
on the road, and desired my servant to ascertain this. A
soldier walking along, apparently one of the best, said
that I had not ; that he was still, as a farrier, able to see
that, though he thought he should be some months before
he could put another shoe on, as he had been shot through
the back. I went with Colonel and Mrs. Scovell to a
little village half-way up the hill towards Pamplona ; and
Colonel Scovell and I climbed up to the top of the hill
to listen and look about until nearly six o'clock, when
we expected our baggage. The curé of the village and
three peasants went up with us. We could see beyond
Pamplona, and beyond the firing, but could not perceive
the place itself for the smoke. By five o'clock, however,
we all agreed that it slackened, and receded a little ; we
therefore descended, got a beefsteak, and waited ready for
orders.

About six that evening the wounded were ordered to
move on towards Irunzun, on the Vittoria and Tolosa
roads ; but we remained quiet. About seven, a furious
thunder-storm came on, and caught all our poor wounded
men on their march : they could not get on to Irunzun,
but got to Berrio Planca, near Pamplona. Two officers,
one sick and one wounded in a house half a mile from us,
heard of this order, left their beds, packed up, and were
proceeding ; but came first to us to inquire. We told
them that head-quarters were not to move. They then
went back to bed, keeping a guide in the house all night,
to start in case of alarm. At nine came an order to
march to Orcayen, near Pamplona, the next morning.
Thus passed the 27th.

At five o'clock on the 28th I began to load to proceed

to Orcayen, when Mr. Hook, who takes quarters, came back and left word that we were to go to Irunzun instead; but the sergeant, by mistake, told us he would call again when he had made more inquiry. In consequence of this Mrs. Scovell and I staid until past ten before we marched. Then, finding every one gone, and the baggage of General Hill's division arrived at Lisasso, we started over the mountain. For the first league we were quite right; but afterwards, in a wood, got too much to the right, and entered a wrong valley: as it was all safe, however, to blunder on that side, and the country was picturesque, we proceeded on that road, and by this means got through to Oscoz, and came into the high Pamplona road to Tolosa, about three-quarters of a league from Irunzun towards Tolosa, instead of half a league on the Pamplona side of Irunzun, which would have been the nearest; it was not a league round, and very picturesque. We were, therefore, not sorry for the mistake. At Irunzun, however, came a difficulty; it was quite crowded with wounded; and of head-quarters we could hear nothing, nor of our baggage.

Leaving my servant to bring on the baggage if it came, we proceeded forwards towards Pamplona, near where we heard head-quarters were—somewhere at least that way. At Berrio Planca, a place on the *camino real*, we found all our baggage and the nominal head-quarters, Every one, however, was absent, and the place full of wounded, the effects of the preceding day. I got a room in the Prince of Orange's quarter, as he had sent for his bed away that night; but Henry had all my keys. About eight I found Henry and went to bed.

The next morning, the 29th, I heard that we had the most severe work on the 28th; that the French attacked our position on a hill six or seven times, which I believe our troops had only occupied a few hours before the French came up near Oricain or Orquin. These attacks were very desperate: and I understand that such a fire for a short time was scarcely ever known, for four French corps all bore upon one point, and General Pakenham told me that he scarcely dared show any of his men. These attacks were, however, all unsuccessful, and we kept our ground. The French were generally driven down with the bayonet, having been suffered to come close, and then received with a volley, a cheer, and a charge. I hear that some of our officers were once very much alarmed for the result. The French remained close and steady, and one regiment (I believe the 40th) went at them rather loose and straggling. However, at the cheer at the last moment the French broke and ran. The Portuguese behaved in general most inimitably, the 4th, 10th, and 12th regiments in particular. The 10th did, indeed, once give way, but rallied; and the 4th charged twice, I think, on the 27th June, in good English style.

Our loss was very severe; that of the French, of course, much more so; but as their cavalry carry off the wounded to the rear, and they have an hospital corps also for that purpose, no one knows their losses; their prisoners aad deserters say nearly five thousand, Lord Wellington's staff were never so roughly handled. The Prince of Orange, who was sent to thank one regiment by Lord Wellington, was very much exposed while executing this order. His horse was shot under him, and he was grazed in the sash. It was near this place that General Cole's aide-de-camp had been killed, and also Brigade-Major A——, one of my Deputy Judge-Advocates. He was trying to rally a Spanish battalion which was quite broken. The Adjutant-general Pakenham had his coatsleeve much torn by a ball. Colonel Waters, A.A.G.C., was shot in the head, through the hat, on the temple, but somehow was little hurt. It is thought that the ball glanced under the hat, against the head, and passed out through the hat. He was out again the next day. Lord Wellington was near at the time, and told him that his head must be like a rock.

Lord Wellington said, I hear, that he had never seen the French behave better. He staid and dined at Picton's on the 28th, and few returned to head-quarters. All the 29th was quiet; both sides employed in burying the dead and getting off the wounded. On the 29th also the staff and light canteens alone remained at Villalba with General Cole; and I was left with scarcely anything except wounded men and baggage. All the stores were ordered to be unloaded, and all spare mules of the head-quarters and of the second and seventh divisions likewise. Two troops of Portuguese cavalry were employed from daylight to dark, in addition to cars and hospital waggons, in carrying off the wounded to Irunzun, to be out of the way in case of attack, and on the road to the great hospital at Vittoria.

I made myself of some use in assisting the arrangement, and as there were not hands to move the men from their mules, to get their rations, &c., and then remount them to proceed, I asked an artillery officer close by, to lend some of his men to assist, which he did directly, and everything went on as quick again. I was sure they would not stand upon form on such an occasion, and the men were standing about waiting for orders; they only regretted that they did not know it sooner, for they would have given men all day. The scene was a busy one. I suppose nearly twelve hundred went through in this way; they were provided with rations for two days to get on to Echani, mounted and sent off, their ammunition having in the meantime been taken from them to be better used, for that was getting scarce more than once. Some had two, some one ball still in them. Besides this, Colonel Campbell, of the Portuguese service, who had been wounded, was lying in my ante-room all

P

day. He was shot through the shinbone, a painful wound. He could not get into my room, which of course I offered, but he preferred the cool passage. I was at breakfast when he arrived. I gave him tea, and some newspapers to try and read himself to sleep. A friend was with him, a Campbell, who shared my bouillie; he ate as good a dinner as I did, but objected to a second bottle, upon which I discovered he was also wounded in the side, and feared that the end of his rib was broken.

The next morning, the 30th, we were all in suspense, as Lord Wellington had determined on a general attack. The firing began at daylight. At nine o'clock I determined to go and see what was going on, and mounting my black, proceeded up for the hills, where the sixth and seventh divisions were, on the opposite side of the valley from our grand position, where we had been attacked the day before. I met many wounded, crawling back all the way, and on the top found only the pickets left in the camp of the morning, and that the seventh division had just driven the French from the adjoining hill, and were after them up the valley on the other side. I went on to the point of the hill and saw the battle still raging strong, just opposite on the hills below, on the other side of the valley opposite our position. The French still steady and firing very briskly all round the side of one hill and in the village below us, and our people creeping on by degrees under ridges towards the village and the hill, and also advancing round the back of the hill. We had two mortars and a gun also upon our position-hill constantly at work, playing upon the French, and we saw the shells continually fall and burst close to the French line, whilst the wounded were carried off to the rear.

This went on for some time, above an hour after I came up, and we had men in reserve all round. I then saw our men in the village, and immediately under the French, and appearing at top also. The French gave way, but went on firing all over the hill. In half-an-hour, I heard the loud huzzas of our soldiers, and saw no French left except on the next hills, where they seemed very numerous and strong, but in confusion. The first huzzas were I believe for a body of about eighteen hundred prisoners, who were caught, being headed every way. There was soon a shout on our side close by our positions. It proved to be Marshal Beresford and Lord Wellington proceeding down to the village to water their horses and proceed on. I should have wished to have pushed on also, but I knew head-quarters would move, and had told my people I should return, and not to stir until they saw me. I therefore went back to Berrio Planca, found as I expected all loaded and on the move to go towards Orquin; got a mouthful of mouldy bread in the market, and went back again close to our position at Orquin. There we got orders to halt loaded, until orders came to proceed to Ostiz. We took off our bridles, turned the horses into a field of Indian corn, where the French camp had been four hours before, and where their dead of the 28th had been buried. We waited thus, hearing a distant firing, until near dark. The reason of this halt, as I learned from General O'Donnell, who passed, was that D'Erlon had attacked General Hill in the morning, and that he had been rather too much in advance, and was in some degree obliged to give way; that he had now taken a new position, and expected the second attack without alarm, as he was to be supported.

About four or five thousand Spaniards moved by us whilst we halted and went up that way. I conclude that this was part of the support alluded to. General Hill was attacked again, and I understand beat Count D'Erlon (Drouet) back with great loss. When this had put all matters straight again, on that side, at least, we were to proceed. At last came orders to advance to Lanz, and we moved again. We drew up first, however, on one side to allow eighteen hundred prisoners to march to the rear,—a very pleasant sight. I spoke to several, and found all of the 17th regiment, who were numerous, to be Italians, principally Genoese. They said that they hated the French, but were forced to fight in Spain against their inclinations. All the prisoners seemed quite tired of Spain, and were as anxious as most of our people never to see it again. They said that Soult was more in the rear, and did not intend to fight that day, which was true, I believe, for he waited for General D'Erlon to get up from St. Estevan towards Lanz. General Monceau, I believe, commanded.

We were again a second time stopped under some trees, for Lord Wellington had ordered the French to be moved from their position beyond Ostiz, and driven to the vicinity of Lanz; the baggage was halted till the result was known. In the villages and on the road, which was strewed with pouches, empty knapsacks, and broken muskets, we passed several bodies all stripped, and in some places could scarcely avoid treading on them, by the horse stepping over a leg or an arm. In one place on the road was a half-buried Frenchman, which the horse had again laid bare. The doctors determined to halt, and encamp under some trees; and if my baggage had been near me to stop it, I should have bivouacked with them, having no tent. As it was, I proceeded, got a wretched quarter at Ostiz with Colonel Waters and seven country-men, just come from the mountains, at about nine o'clock, got a beefsteak at eleven, and to bed at half-past twelve.

The next day, 31st, orders came to proceed to Lanz, and wait further instructions. There we arrived about ten o'clock, and I turned my horses into the forage remaining in the French camp of the night before, and got some collected for the mules. Thus we remained loaded until four o'clock without orders. Lord Wellington then sent on for fresh horses and his light canteens, and of our own accord we unloaded to relieve the animals, but for a long time durst not unpack. At last, General Murray came in, and ordered some dinner; but telling us that he had no authority to direct others to do the same. We were all to go to our old quarters; but, not liking in this state of things to go over to Arriez, my old place, where I had lost myself in the night, I got a room at Haines's, and some dinner, hung my baggage cover up for a door, and went to sleep on the table to avoid the fleas.

The next day, 1st of August, about six o'clock, orders were issued to advance to Berrueta, and there to remain, waiting orders again. We returned over this mountain thus the third time, and got to Berrueta about one o'clock. I called at Almandoz in passing, to remind the patrona of the house that I had told her we should beat the French, near Pamplona, and be back in a week. I was so in five days, and found her more miserable than before, having been plundered by the French. I gave the green Indian corn the French had left to my horse, and wished her good-bye. About two o'clock, we heard that we had driven the French off the hills above St. Estevan, and also through the town, and head-quarters were to move on to St. Estevan directly. We did so, and got there by five o'clock; the French having been driven out between twelve and one. We saw about a dozen French, just killed, close to St. Estevan. So we go on, you see.

The French being driven in, about two leagues towards Lezaca and Echalar, Longa and the Spaniards, and the light division, made a long march back that day, the 1st of August, towards their own ground above Lezaca, going more round, however, towards Echalar. By this, the 95th fell in with the French at the bridge, where the road to Lezaca turns off from that to Echalar, headed them, killed and wounded about a hundred, and, without discovering it, before dark, drove much of their baggage up the valley round again towards St. Estevan. By this movement, the French being then headed at the Lezaca valley, went the Echalar pass and road instead, and in confusion; and the baggage walked into the fourth division just as they advanced next morning.

Yesterday, the 2nd of August, our orders were to proceed again to Lezaca. We started, and got into all the baggage of head-quarters (three divisions) eight miles extent of loaded mules in a string. There was a halt of about four hours, and no one could move. This continued until we got near where the baggage had been caught, which was the cause of the stoppage. After fighting by all the baggage, and leading my horse along some very dangerous places, where, if he had slipped, he must have fallen down to the river (and four to five mules actually did so), I got to the scene of the captured baggage, and then went quietly on. For nearly two miles there were scattered along the road, papers, old rugs, blankets, pack-saddles, old bridles, girths, private letters, lint, bandages, one or two hundred empty and broken boxes; quantities of intrenching tools, rags, French clothes, dead mules, dead soldiers and peasants, farriers' tools, officers' boots, linen, &c. There were also the boxes of M. Le General Baron de St. Pol, and several private officers' baggage; the principal thing taken seemed to be the *ambulance du 2ème division*; that is, the field hospital of the second division. There were still more things worth picking up, and some soldiers digging up three live mules out of an old limekiln near the road-side. This caused stoppages and confusion.

Just beyond the bridge of Yanza the French were crawling off, who were wounded by the 95th the night before, and we twice met small parties of prisoners going to the rear, abused not a little by the plundered and exasperated villagers. The prisoners told me that the country people about these mountains were *"diablement méchant,"* and treated them very ill. The truth was, however, that the French began this treatment; for though they had behaved well in advancing, they had plundered and destroyed considerably in their retreat, and much wantonly. I told them they ought never to have come and entered Spain, to which they replied, "We never wished to do so; it is not our fault."

About three o'clock, I went round to see what was going on, but my horse was tired, and I was not able to get up, to see the French driven from the hill above Echalar, and also from the hill occupied by the light division. In short, all our old position, and a little more, was gained last night.

In our advance again, we also saw some of the effects of our own retreat. In one place was an ammunition-waggon, with six dead mules, which had all rolled down the mountain together. I ascertained that it was English by sending a muleteer down for some papers in the waggon, which turned out to be our printed blank artillery returns. I also saw four other wheels and parts of carriages, and it is said that we lost a howitzer. Colonel Ross's troop suffered the most in this way. The French seemed to have made this advance as a desperate push to relieve Pamplona and St. Sebastian. The garrisons of both sallied; that of Pamplona was driven back directly, as I hear: that of St. Sebastian (as we are told) surprised us in the trenches napping, as the heavy guns were all embarked for security, and nothing going on, and carried off three companies of Portuguese. This, it is to be hoped, is exaggerated. Near Elisondo, I hear, we took thirty cars of bread and brandy, and some baggage also— a day's bread for two divisions; and many are now fighting without it on both sides. There is no delivery of bread to-day, even for head-quarters; corn for the horses we have had none this week.

Head-quarters have stray papers to the 19th, which I am reading whilst the fighting is going on. One great amusement in these papers, to me at least, is the excess of lies, the impudence, the abundance of them, and then the blunders, and ignorance of what is going on. You will be surprised at the contents of this, when you get the *Gazette* account, as you will probably long before you receive this. I told you that the beaten army would return in a month : whether they will muster again this year, and attack, depends, in my opinion, upon the fall of Pamplona and St. Sebastian, and the northern war. Pamplona is starving ; at least it is without meat ; but I still doubt, except that this sudden effort proves it to be in danger. It is merely more closely invested by small gun redoubts—no battering gun has ever been near it, at present only about six thousand Spaniards watch it, and I think if they choose they might be off, only much harassed by our cavalry.

The charges made by the Life Guards were the most ludicrous. They were never near the enemy, until beyond Vittoria, as I was before them, and was almost run down twice by their anxiety along the road, galloping away without occasion. I leaped a ditch once to avoid them, not wishing to blow my horse as theirs were, at a time when we were on one side of Vittoria and the French on the other. They were afterwards ordered on, but never came up with the enemy. They could do nothing in such a country, with six-foot ditches round the inclosures. Very few of the Spaniards have behaved well this time. They have been generally in the rear ; one regiment stood fire well on the 28th, but some ran, and in general I hear they have done little. Longa's people tolerably here. There has been sharp work on the whole. I should put down the allied losses at six or seven thousand, and the French nearly at eighteen thousand, provisions and all, that is somehow put *hors de combat.* If the Spaniards will not fight, we can scarcely stand even this advantage long ; we shall be ruined by our victories. The French under D'Erlon behaved very well to Colonel Fenwick, who was left wounded; no one was allowed to go to his house as a quarter, and every attention was paid both to him and the surgeon left with him. The latter became so popular that the French liked to be dressed by him, better than by their own surgeons.

August 3rd, six o'clock, evening.—The great men are all come in; and I am told nothing has been done more to-day. The last push over the hills, and out of their position has not been made yet. So at least says General O'Lalor. I suspect the Prince of Orange will carry home these despatches, and I think it but fair now, that he should go and see his intended as a conquering hero. He certainly promises very well. An old man just returned home, is thrashing out his wheat over my head, and has been thus employed all the morning, giving me his dust as well as his noise.

Later, nine o'clock, evening.—Nothing has been done to-day; the French remain in their strong ground above Bera, a league and a half from this. It was found, I believe, necessary to turn it in a regular manner to avoid great loss ; for though one brigade of red coats yesterday turned two French divisions off one high hill, we can scarcely expect this to be always the case. I think, therefore, we shall remain here some days at least. I have just heard an anecdote of General Picton. General Cole on the 17th ordered General Byng to retire from a post on a hill which afterwards formed a part of our good position on the 28th. Byng sent to Picton to say what his orders were, and added that though very important, he felt he was not strong enough to justify his keeping it. Picton said to Byng's aide-de-camp, " No, by G—, he shall not give up the hill ; I will bring my division up to support him ; but no, your horse is done up, I'll go myself and tell him ;" and he ordered the division to follow. This saved that hill. Another time, General Cole was by orders leaving a hill, when he received fresh orders to occupy it. His men found a few stragglers on the top, and the French main division half way up; but they gave them such a volley and warm reception, that they soon turned back and were off.

We were very nearly destroying some of the French cavalry, and taking two divisions. Two circumstances prevented this. The night we were at Berrueta two of our men straggled, and got taken, and they told the French where head-quarters were. This made them conclude we were strongly posted close by, and they decamped at night instead of the morning, as they had intended. Thus several hours were gained. The next was, that our light division got their orders seven hours later than was expected. Had they been that time sooner up, they would have headed the French division on their road to Echalar, as well as to Lezaca, and from strong ground might have been able to drive them back upon the other divisions, and have surrounded them. Their cavalry also would have been caught on this narrow winding road down by the river, where the baggage was destroyed, with a path in the wood just on the opposite side, from whence our men might at least have picked off the horses if the men chose to run away. This was just missed, however, from these causes, and remains one of the *ifs* and *ands*; it is very provoking, for that would have completely crippled them for this year.

A Spanish priest told me to-day that all the priests, nuns, &c., in Spain, were constantly putting up prayers for Lord Wellington, thinking almost everything depended upon him individually, as I believe most people here really think. They were sorry he was so often exposed as he is to fire.

Lezaca, August 4th, 1813.—Nothing is to be done, I believe, to-day. Everything *in statu quo ;* the Prince goes to-night or to-morrow morning with despatches to England, and I shall send this with them.

P.S. It feels, as you may suppose, very strange, after the whirl about to Pamplona, and all the scenes I have witnessed, to be again quietly drawing charges at Lezaca. I have just heard that the French have increased their force much in our front above Bera on the hills, but I think nothing more will be done immediately on our part or on theirs.

CHAPTER XI.

Rejoicings for the Victory—Sufferings of Cole's Division—Complaints of the French—Statements of a French Prisoner—Decay of Spain—Characteristics of Wellington—His Opinion of Bonaparte—Prospects of a renewal of the Attack—Exchange of Prisoners—Wellington's Spanish Estate—His opinion of Picton—Disposition of the Army.

Head-quarters, Lezaca,
August 7, 1813.

My dear M——,

Here we are still, quiet, and *in statu quo ante* our last run to Pamplona. I have sent you a long account of all this business with the Prince of Orange's despatches.

Our cavalry have been moving up, both to St. Estevan, and towards Irun. From the former place, however, for want of forage they begin to retire again. Much are left still round Pamplona, where there is only a Spanish infantry force to watch and invest. They have tried in vain to burn the corn just under the walls of the town, for this partly supplies the garrison. Marshal Beresford is gone for a week to the sea side, for bathing; I conclude, therefore, that nothing is to be immediately undertaken to turn the French out of the remaining hills near this place. I should like to have them clear out in the plains below, for I expect in about three weeks to have them plaguing us again. Something is still in agitation for this purpose, but for the present delayed. We fired, at St. Sebastian, a salute of twenty-one guns for our late victory. The garrison regularly returned two for every gun fired. They are very well supplied, it is said, and are very impudent. I fear that all our former breaches will now be quite useless, as they are, probably, before this, made the strongest points. Saragossa, or Zaragoza (the fort) has surrendered to Mina with about forty guns, and, it is said, nearly five hundred men ; this will be good, if Suchet intends to come that way towards us. I think he is now retreating a little, and perhaps this late business may make him go back quicker.

Lord Wellington was on his bed yesterday, and could scarcely rise from the lumbago ; but was in good humour and good spirits. His position near Sorauren and Oricain, or Orquin, was a near-run thing (this was where the last two battles were fought). General Cole was there with the fourth division. In the course of his retreat, Lord Wellington was falling back on him with his staff, saw the importance of the position and galloped over the bridge, and up to General Cole, to form his division, and take up the position at first sight. Pamplona must otherwise have been relieved. The French were so close upon Lord Wellington, that a part of his staff rather behind could not follow him over the bridge, but were cut off by the French, and obliged to find their way round. This position was afterwards strengthened by the third (Picton's) division, and the Spaniards, and this at least saved the communication with Pamplona. I hope we should in any case have beaten the French at last, but it must have been further back certainly, and probably on the Tolosa road. General Cole's division has had, on the whole, nearly nine days' constant fighting and marching. It is terribly cut up in consequence.

The French vow vengeance against the Spaniards. An officer, prisoner here, told me yesterday, that the Spaniards had always complained of the French, and often with reason ; but if they came again as he expected, the French were resolved to show them the difference, and let them have some reason to complain of them in earnest. He said, that France had lost nearly four hundred thousand men in Spain, in the war, and much more than half from sickness and unfair means, assassination, and treachery. He said there was not a family in France which had not put on mourning for this Spanish war, and yet scarcely any of the Spaniards had fought them like men. He said the notion the French had was that in the general peace which was expected, England and France would make arrangements to divide the best part of Spain between them, and that we should keep Cadiz, Carthagena, and all the useful maritime parts, and leave them to the Ebro. He smiled much at my disowning any such honest and honourable intentions on our part. He told me that the French armies had suffered more in their *morale* here in the last campaign, than by their Russian losses, for every Frenchman laid the latter disasters entirely to climate, and was satisfied he still could conquer a Russian as formerly; but here, the troops were fairly beaten, and in general would not stand. Only two brigades, he said, behaved really well at Vittoria, and Jourdan was sent to Paris under arrest for his conduct. As to the money, baggage, &c., they behaved much better on the 18th of July.

He also told me that not even an English or Spanish officer, in the best of times, had ever been so well treated as the French were when they first came here. He appeared not at all to feel how much worse this made their conduct appear since. This was drawn out by my telling him that Bonaparte had contrived now to make the French detested, almost by every nation in Europe, and that power was all he had to rely upon. The part Bernadotte had taken the French officers seem not to have known, so much are they kept in the dark about every thing. The Frenchman also said, that had it not been for the jealousies of the Guerillas, they might, by acting in concert (which they never would do), have sometimes almost annihilated whole French divisions, and that the French could scarcely have kept their ground some time since; but by local and individual jealousies the finest opportunities were lost. He considered that the good or bad behaviour of an army all depended on their having pay and food; or, on the contrary, the want of both; and I believe so much: that he rightly considered that the French discipline was the best when they had both, but that not being here ever the case, plunder was the consequence. " But why come here at all? " quoth I. " *L'Empereur le veut,*" was the answer, "and we as soldiers have only to obey." " Try and enter France," said he, " and you will soon see how the people feel, and whether your stories of a readiness to revolt, and dissatisfaction are true. So far from it, that there has been considerable zeal shown every where in replacing the Emperor's Russian losses." The French think there must be war, and therefore the further from home the better. We have heard before you, by French papers, of the extension of the armistice in the North. This is bad for the campaign here.

The English reviewers and others may say what they please as to Spain not having been on the decline during the last century. It has at least stood still when almost every other country in Europe made rapid advances in everything. In Spain and Portugal, no town is now, or has been lately, on the increase; but several have manifestly diminished. The decay of houses is seldom made good, even on the same ground, by new ones; I do not recollect to have observed, in the whole country, four new houses building, notwithstanding the thousands destroyed of late; nor does this seem owing to the events of the last five years and the present times, for you see no houses commenced before that time, and left unfinished, at least extremely few. In France, almost

every large place had its new town as in England, only
in a less degree, and evident marks of new buildings, &c.,
stopped by the Revolution. In Spain there are no
appearances of new towns at all, nor of parts of towns,
or scarcely even of houses, or unfinished buildings
stopped by the present confusion—some in Vittoria, from
French excitement I believe, but nothing to speak of.
The churches are every where on a large and expensive
scale; a few modern, but in general they are old. The
Spanish towns have nearly all the appearance of what we
should take to be decayed manufacturing towns. The
inhabitants appear to have been asleep as to the rest of
the world, and not to have made any progress whilst
others made great advances. This is a sort of decline.
There can have been little demand for manufactures, for
the same few chairs and tables seem to have been in use
these fifty or hundred years. Whitewashing and new
placing the tiles seem the only repairs of the houses.

Yet, I think many districts seem to have been uncommonly happy and comfortable before this war—
large tight houses, abundance of food, good clothes,
cleanly habits, a general equality of rank; no rich among
them at all; no very poor; and no manufactures. Almost
every man could make what he wanted for his farm, and
a shoemaker, a tailor, and a farrier, were nearly the only
tradesmen, except farmers, in work. Occasional pedlars
supplied the other wants of a people who had but few.
Such must have been the independent, happy state of
many large districts away from the influence of the cor-
ruptions of the large towns, where all the idle, lazy,
pauper nobility lived: they were alike free from the
effects of the misgovernment and oppressive conduct of
their rulers. Other districts certainly were very different, and more like the dirty and ill-provided Portuguese. In Portugal, the higher classes seem, I think,
to have been generally better off, and to have enjoyed

themselves more in their quintas, or villas, and the poor to have been worse off. There are none of the districts in Portugal such as I have described in Spain.

I have just met General Cole, who commanded the fourth division; he is quite knocked up. He says that his division alone have one hundred and four officers killed and wounded.

Lezaca, 8th August.—Yesterday I rode up to the hill at the point of our position above Bera, from whence you see Bayonne. I stood on the top until it was nearly dark, and returned down the mountains by moonlight. The French fires were very numerous, and were burning all over the sides of a tremendous hill, which they still occupy opposite to our position. I passed the boundary stone, and got half-a-mile into France, to the highest summit of the rock, where the outlying picket is. I saw the French relieve their pickets, heard their drums as plainly as ours, saw the men at work at a redoubt to oppose us if we should advance, and, lastly, saw five thousand Spaniards come up to occupy the ground in the place of our light division, &c., who were ordered to go elsewhere. These were O'Donnell's regiments; they were thin in numbers. A brigade, nominally three thousand, mustered eighteen hundred, but were well-dressed and good-looking men. I only hope they will fight—at least that they do not steal as adroitly as Longa's people. We have had the latter near this place, and nothing is safe at all from their fingers—from a horse or mule down to a bit of biscuit. In my letter from Vittoria, I told you that the French as an army had escaped, and that we should hear of them again in a month. So it proved; and so I think it will be probably again, unless the two places surrender to us in a few weeks.

This small, dirty place, Lezaca, is a curious scene of bustle just now; crowded with Spanish fugitives—the

head-quarters no small body, with all our stragglers and
those of Longa's, who are more numerous (he having a
quarter here now, and looking like an English butcher in
a handsome hussar dress), with abundance of Spanish and
Portuguese officers (for both troops are near), as well as
with English, with wounded and prisoners passing, with
mules and muleteers innumerable, besides all the country
people who come here to turn all they have got into
money. Noises of all sorts; thrashing all going on in
the rooms up stairs; the corn then made into bread and
sold in one corner; " *aguardente*" being cried all about;
lemonade (that is, dirty water and dark-brown sugar) the
same; here a large pig being killed in the street, with its
usual music on such occasions; another near it with a
straw fire singeing it, and then a number of women cutting up and selling pieces of other pigs killed a few hours
before. Suttlers and natives with their Don Quixote
wineskins all about, large pigskins, and small ditto, and
middling ditto, all pouring out wine to our half-boozy,
weary soldiers; bad apples and pears, gourds for soup,
sour plums, &c., all offered for sale at the same moment.
Perpetual quarrels take place about payment for these
things between the soldiers of the three allied nations and
the avaricious and unreasonable civilian natives; mostly,
however, between Spaniards and Spaniards. The animals
eating green Indian corn almost against every house here
and in the churchyard, which contains four tents, from
the want of stables and of quarters. Not the least curious
or noisy in this confusion, are about fifteen men and
women with fresh butter 4s. the pound, who are come
from near St. Andero and beyond it—a stout race dressed
in a curious, peculiar manner, who contrive to bring
butter on their heads in baskets for above a fortnight
together, and sell it at last in a state that I am very glad
to eat it for breakfast for ten days after it arrives. It
forms a sort of very mild cream cheese, in fact.

Head-Quarters, Lezaca, August 9th.—You ask me if Lord Wellington has recollected —— with regard? He seems to have had a great opinion of him, but scarcely has ever mentioned him to me. In truth, I think Lord Wellington has an active, busy mind, always looking to the future, and is so used to lose a useful man, that as soon as gone he seldom thinks more of him. He would be always, no doubt, ready to serve any one who had been about him, or the friend of a deceased friend, but he seems not to think much about you when once out of the way. He has too much of everything and everybody always in his way, to think much of the absent. He said the other day, that he had great advantages now over every other General. He could do what others dare not attempt; and he got the confidence of all the three allied powers, so that what he said or ordered was, right or wrong, always thought right. "And it is the same," said he, "with the troops. When I come myself, the soldiers think what they have to do the most important, since I am there, and that all will depend on their exertions. Of course, these are increased in proportion, and they will do for me what perhaps no one else can make them do." He said, " he had several of the advantages possessed by Bonaparte, in regard to his freedom of action and power of risking, without being constantly called to account : Bonaparte was quite free from all inquiry, and that he himself was in fact very much so. The other advantages which Bonaparte possessed, and of which he made so much use," Lord Wellington said, " was his full latitude of lying; *that*, if so disposed," he said, " he could not do."

You ask about my health—I think this hole in the mountains unwholesome : the place is so full, and without drainage ; the air heavy and oppressive ; it is like Devonshire, warm moisture constantly. I long to be on the mountains, to get air and braced up. It has rained nearly all the last twenty-four hours.

August 10*th*.—I have just seen Lord Wellington, about some more than usually important business : he is better, but not well. He has given me an immense bundle of English and Spanish papers to peruse and examine. The enclosed plan may help you a little to understand the *Gazette*, and my letter ; remember it is only my hasty personal sketch in pen and ink, on no scale, and taken from no regular document.

11*th, Post-day*.—I worked very hard all yesterday, and could not get through Lord Wellington's papers. I am still at work at the last part of them : a Spanish narrative of all the Spanish operations of a Spanish army for a month, by their General Copons. It consists of sixty-four sides of foolscap in a Spanish hand. There is nothing new. Lord Wellington will give a dinner to-morrow, in honour of the Prince Regent's birthday, to all the heads of departments, to which I am invited. There are reports of the French moving already, but I believe all lies as yet. Do not be too sanguine about Suchet. He may retire, but will hardly be forced out of the country, for there are forty thousand French on that side of Spain. The Spanish Government have given Lord Wellington a handsome royal estate near Granada ; he told me this yesterday.

Head-Quarters, Lezaca, August 13*th*, 1813.—Here I am, and very busy still, and with no events to communicate. All is now quiet for the present, as at Frenada, though this cannot last long. Having the paper by me, how-ever, I determined to place this letter upon the stocks, against the next post-day.

Yesterday I dined at Lord Wellington's, with a party of thirty-six, to keep the Prince Regent's birthday. Eight mules had arrived in the morning with prog and wines from Bilboa, and we had therefore a good feast, and some very good claret of Majoribanks and Paxton. The party was very dull, though many grandees were present—Castanos, O'Donnell, the General of the army of the reserve (the best Spaniards I have seen, and now on the hill above us, with something like a Commissariat, &c.), their aides-de-camp, &c., Generals Cole, Anson, Murray, Pakenham, &c. Two bands were in attendance those of the Fusiliers and the 7th. Fuento, the Spanish Commissary, gave us "God save the King," and Lord Wellington's favourite, "Ah Marmont, onde va Marmont?" but it was very hot and stupid; every one here, in fact, is fagged, and half done up. Lord Wellington could scarcely rise when he sat down, or sit down when he rose, from lumbago, and was in great pain, but is much better; all around him looked pale and worn. I think, however, we shall be up to another brush again soon.

We are soon about to begin again at St. Sebastian; but it is to be feared that it will be hard and bloody work, unless some piece of good luck should arise in our favour.

Later.—I have just been to Lord Wellington, with the result of my labours, which have amused him much, and which he thinks I cannot be correct in, as to facts; or if so, the whole, he concurs with me, is most extraordinary. He has now got the papers and my statement to examine. It is not, in my opinion, the Spanish General who was to blame; I must not explain more at present; he seemed pleased, and asked me to dinner again to-day. We have a stray paper to the 4th, which has set us all agog; but I have only heard the news concerning Lord Aberdeen, and it does not seem quite certain that there is to be an ambassador from England to the Congress. The French nation, or rather the news through France, is I hear all for peace, and the Rhine and the Pyrenees are to be the boundaries, Jerome King of Holland, and Joseph King of Italy; this is only French rumour.

I am told that Soult says he will be here the day after to-morrow, the 15th, and has two bridges ready near Irun, to come on our left; he would only come there, for I think we should be able to do something. We are well up for an attack there; four hours would put the divisions here on that flank, Spaniards, &c.

The 14th.—We had last night a little firing, but I believe it was only the Spaniards. The latter and the French fire at each other at every opportunity, and when neighbours, are never at peace. Our sentries and the French, on the contrary, are within one hundred yards of each other, and are relieved regularly without the least molestation on either side. This is the way. Unless an attack is to be made, what is gained by killing a poor sentry? Our new brigade is not yet at Passages, although expected for this fortnight. Some reinforcements have, however, come up, and the brigade of Guards, which were left behind, have, by easy marches from Oporto, now joined us—about fifteen hundred out of the three thousand who came out at that unlucky time last year. The French have also reinforcements, and must in honour do something if the two places hold out. The French gentleman who came over to us near Pamplona fourteen days since, dined at Lord Wellington's yesterday, and talked away. He seems clever, and, like every Frenchman, professed to know everything— the secret history of everybody and of every event. He calls Bonaparte *un tigre*, &c. I cannot say that I like him much, and would not trust him; but I am not much afraid of Lord Wellington doing so. Lord Wellington told him the following fact, concerning the exchange of prisoners in this country. He said that Massena once agreed to exchange three hussar officers and one hundred and twenty men, rank for rank, and when he had got his own three officers and the men, sent back only twenty soldiers, and the rest countrymen and Portuguese militiamen, and three officers of militia scarcely embodied. Lord Wellington vowed never to trust his honour again, and in every proposal always excepts Massena. Indeed he said he was so little inclined now from experience to trust any of them, that a short time since, when an exchange was proposed, he said, "Yes; but first name the officers and men you offer, and their regiments, ages, &c., and then I will treat, but I will not have Spanish peasants for French soldiers." To this they sent no answer.

Lord Wellington also tells them, that until our travellers, civilians, &c., who were detained are released, he can never listen to non-combatant pleas. All must be exchanged; but he is very liberal. He also said Soult once complained that six of our officers had escaped from their guard near Oporto, on that retreat, and had committed a breach of honour; but that he (Lord Wellington) having inquired into it, found they were placed in confinement under a guard, and their parole not relied upon, and that they had got the better of their guard. Lord Wellington, therefore, told the Marshal that the parole being abandoned by the imprisonment, the point of honour was gone; and that there were two ways of prisoners and their guards separating, and that he believed the guard had run away from their prisoners, not the prisoners from their guard. To this also he had no answer.

Lord Wellington also talked of Grant's case, who lately got away from Paris. Lord Wellington had advised him not to give his parole in Spain, and had provided persons to rescue him in several places on the march to France. They offered this to Grant in consequence, but the offer was from honour declined, as the parole had been given and acted upon. The moment he was in France the French placed him under a guard, and at Bayonne he got away from them and went to

Paris, remained there nine months, and got to England at last. Lord Wellington yesterday was excessively stiff and sore, but in high spirits. He seems to have a notion that the Continent will make a peace, and leave us and the Spaniards in the lurch, and I believe this prevents any very forward movements here on his part, for the French would then soon come down upon us with decidedly superior numbers ; and if we had quite passed these mountains a hasty retreat back through them would not be a very easy or agreeable manœuvre.

I rode last night to Bera or Vera, where our out-posts are in the valley. The French pickets are in two houses on the hills opposite, a few hundred yards up. Several of the houses about there are destroyed, gutted, and burnt, and most of them deserted. It was only a month ago a pretty little town. Longa had also, since we were here last, burnt two neat farms on the road, and knocked off the parapet of the bridge, and dug a trench across it, for the purpose of annoying the French. We have headed nearly all the green Indian corn in this valley for the horses ; it is cut short off, half way, leaving the fruit below ; and this is said not to do much harm to the corn. But then we cannot eat our cake and have it also. There will be no dry forage for the animals in autumn and winter. The little wheat straw about these valleys is nearly all eaten already, and much of the wheat and Indian corn itself has been either destroyed or taken by the irregularity of the thousand muleteers around us, in spite of their being occasionally flogged when caught in doing so. The inhabitants will, I fear, be half starved in the winter, unless they migrate, which many will, no doubt, and we must be supplied from other parts if we stay near here. Spain in general will, however, have been released from the supply of, nominally, two hundred thousand French ; and as we drove them away before harvest time, most of this will be in the market somewhere, except what has been destroyed on our immediate line of march. Much has been of course trodden down, and from the want of forage and corn our horses have been obliged to take the ripe wheat and eat it—straw, grain, and all—to serve both purposes. This is dangerous food, and if drink is given carelessly, often kills the animal; but otherwise it answers well.

We understand here that it was not until three days after the news of the battle of Vittoria arrived that any one durst inform Bonaparte of it. This last battle will very probably be almost entirely concealed from him. As we are now both *in statu quo* as to place, this may perhaps be managed: though the enemy are about fifteen thousand men minus to what they were before the attack at Maya began. From intercepted letters we find that, in reports even to each other, the French lie considerably, or at least misrepresent, for the good of the service, and this will present a good opportunity, as Bonaparte is so far off.

In this little town, or rather village, there are about twelve priests at least, walking about in their shovel hats. These hats would astonish the most orthodox bishop's chaplain in England, and our coalheaver's hat is nothing to them. The only fine cloth in the shops here is black, you may guess for whose use.

The estate which the Spanish Government has given to the Marquis of Wellington is, I understand, a very desirable one; and the best proof that it is so, is that it was one which the Prince of Peace had given to himself, and doubtless he chose the best he could find. It is nominally thirty thousand dollars a-year, a castle, I understand, and about a league from Granada, in a fine country.* Lord Wellington seems very much pleased with it. He says that he hopes the house is a good one, as he should

---

* It is situated in the Val de Soto.

not like to have to build, and that he hears there is hunting, coursing, fishing, and everything near it. There was a fine wood, but I fear the Prince of Peace cut most of that down. General O'Lalor, who is in a bad state of health, is to have the government of Granada, and will superintend this estate for Lord Wellington. The latter had got the papers concerning it before him when I called a few days since, and said, " This relates to the estate they have given me."

The 15*th*.—I have been very ill all night and this morning, but am now rather better, and the doctor tells me I am saved a fever by this bilious attack. We are all most anxious for news from the North, for all must depend in the end upon that, at least in a great measure. Next to General Frost, I think, our General has done the most for the common cause. General Villa Alba, the Spanish Inspector of Cavalry, dined at head-quarters to-day. He is a queer-looking creature, anything but a General in appearance, and much less a cavalry officer. I know, however, nothing of his real character. We now feel the effects of our work through these valleys ; for we cannot ride a few miles without the alternate smells of dead horses, dead mules, and dead men. Bonaparte's birthday has passed over very quietly, except a tremendous triple salvo of all the St. Sebastian's guns and mortars upon our poor fellows in the trenches at daylight. The garrison are amazingly pert, from their success hitherto ; but we have some hopes they will soon want water. Adieu.

The 16*th*.—Much the same to-day, the attack continuing all night. Cannot think what it is in this country that affects us. The thermometer has never in the shade, in my room, been beyond 72° in this part of Spain. General Sir T. Picton is attacked again with a violent bowel complaint, and is fallen to the rear. He would be a great loss, for he is one of the best here.

Lord Wellington, the other day, said, "Why, even General Picton did so-and-so the other day," as if surprised that he should not have acted quite right.

Our soldiers are quite unaccountable; all is going on right, and they are just now quiet and well fed, yet desertion, and even of British, to the enemy, was scarcely ever more frequent. It was not surprising that one hundred and forty of the Chasseurs Britanniques went off when we were falling back to Pamplona, and, as they thought, probably to Portugal; but that the English soldier should desert, is astonishing and unaccountable. Three went off from pickets together the other night, towards the French, and were all caught, and are to be tried. Several must be hung for this. Two new regiments have at last arrived. I wish the French would come fairly on now, if at all, but every one talks of a general peace. Adieu.

The 17th.—We have this day a strong French report that peace is signed, and that the Pyrenees are to be the boundary of France on this side. Nothing said about England; but even at this rate, we must be off if this prove true. The news you told me of the fifty thousand men, under Soult, you will have seen was tolerably correct; it was intended he should have been here sooner, to prevent the mischief which happened at Vittoria. As soon as the report came that we were threatening to cross the Ebro he was sent off, but he did not allow sufficiently for Lord Wellington's rapid movements, and was a little too late. It is clear, from many circumstances, as Lord Wellington says, that he intended to drive us back to the Ebro this last push, and that his measures were all taken accordingly; his cavalry, which he brought with him, and which, as regards the country as far as Pamplona, would have been useless, has suffered much from the roads, want of shoes, &c., and had no employment except that of carrying off the wounded.

Our army is now nearly as follows : first and fifth divisions, Oyarzun and St. Sebastian, under Graham ; Jeron, with his Spaniards of Gallicia, in their front at Irun ; Longa between them and this place, with his diminished Guerillas ; here the fourth division and the light division in front, and the Spaniards of O'Donnell the reserve next, on the right of the others, in front ; then the seventh division above Echallar, &c. : then the third and sixth in Maya and Roncesvalles Pass, with Spaniards I believe also, and General Hill's second division behind them in the valley of Bastan, Elisondo, &c. ; six thousand Spaniards watching Pamplona, and our cavalry about there principally or in the rear of Graham.

The 18*th, still Lezacá.*—O'Donnell is unwell, from the wound in his leg, from which thirty splinters have been extracted : he is going to the baths.   He is the Conde de Bispal, commanding the army of Reserve.   Jeron is to take his command now, and give up the Gallicians ; our men, however, I am glad to learn, are in general considered as very healthy : General Cole told me that his division was particularly so, after all their fatigues.   The army have Lord Wellington to thank principally, even for this.   Last year the mules per company allowed by Government were employed in carrying the heavy iron camp-kettles, and our men had no tents ; though they were allowed them, they could not be carried.   This year Lord Wellington had light tin kettles made, one for every six men, for the mess, to be carried by one of the men, each having a small cooking machine of tin besides.   This plan sets the mules free and disposable, and thus three tents have been carried for every company, and allowing for absentees, guards, officers' servants, sentries, &c. ; this now nearly houses or covers all our men, and contributes much to the health of the army.   It was entirely an arrangement of his own.   The Portuguese are still without tents, as are the French and the Spaniards.

The French, however, are very expert at making wood huts, with fern for the top and for the bedding, tolerably comfortable except in heavy rains. So are now the Portuguese indeed, and many of them (as well as our men who happen not to have tent room) join two together, and giving up their blankets for sleeping on, make a good tent of them, which holds two very well, and only consists of their two muskets and two blankets; and now, since we have obtained so much plunder, generally a good sack or piece of carpet at the rough weather side. Orders were given before we marched from Granada, by Lord Wellington, to have all blankets looped and strengthened at the corners, for this purpose, all ready, as an excellent defence from the sun, even better than a tent, for it is cooler, and a very tolerable one from rain.

I am to dine with General Cole, who is quartered here. My people in this house are up all night, making a noise, and baking for Longa, and all day the children are shaking the dirt from above down upon me.

CHAPTER XII.

Reported renewal of Operations against St. Sebastian—Effects of the War
  on Spain and Portugal—Wellington's Account of recent Proceedings—
  Courts-martial—Prisoners Shot—Discussions on War between Wel-
  lington and a French Deserter — The Siege resumed — Work of the
  Heavy Batteries — Trial of General O'Halloran —Volunteers for the
  Storming-parties.

Head-quarters, Lezaca,
August 21, 1813.

My dear M———,

SEVERAL of our Vittoria sick and wounded now
begin to return and join their regiments. Major Free-
mantle came back just in time for dinner yesterday, and
amused us with an account of all your madness in
England about the battle of Vittoria.

General Cole, with whom I told you I was going to
dine, lives very comfortably. To do this, even in his
way, he has now travelling with him about ten or twelve
goats for milk, a cow, and about thirty-six sheep at least,
with a shepherd, who always march, feed on the road
side, on the mountains, &c., and encamp with him.
When you think of this, that wine and everything is to
be carried about, from salt and pepper and tea-cups to
saucepans, boilers, dishes, chairs, and tables, on mules,
you may guess the trouble and expense of a good establishment here.

I mentioned to you the iron-works all about this
country, and their simple construction; they make, however, I believe, excellent iron. For this purpose they

mix the ore of this country, which is too brittle, with the ore they fetch from near Bilboa, which is rather too ductile and soft, and of the two form an excellent compound, which used to supply much of the southern part of France.

Our great guns are, I am told, to begin pounding to-day at St. Sebastian again, but I have not heard them yet. The old breach will not do at all; it is, we are told, mined and filled with little intended explosions. A seventy-four and some frigates are now near. I wish they would let the sailors try the sea side when we storm. I think they would get in somehow at once into the castle.

August the 23rd.—I have now a fresh set of Courts in every division again, as my last are broken up. One Deputy Judge-Advocate sent me, out of curiosity, a history of his Court-casualties, &c., nine members out of fifteen, and the Judge-Advocate, killed or severely wounded, since the 22nd of May, two prosecutors and three witnesses, all officers. We are trying to clear as we go, and to prevent all arrears, and we hang away to prevent desertion. I am told that the French do the same and still more, but their people will go home to the rear; this is more natural. We are told that ten men from each company are gone by orders to the rear also— some foolishly say to quell riots, for which purpose ten old men would be the most useless possible; but the most plausible account is, to drill new conscripts. Some deserters say they are sent even to Italy for this; I believe just now that they are not prepared to move, and will be content to remain quiet. We have alternate accounts, of course, of war and peace. To-day two women (one French, the other Spanish,) of the French prisoners from Vittoria, came in here on their way to join the French. Lord Wellington, however, has stopped them, and says he will have no more sent over until the

French release about three hundred mothers and wives,
&c., of the Guerillas, who were carried off by them as
hostages for the return home of the Guerilla relations, so
they cry and think this very sad to be put upon the same
footing as such creatures. One of the ladies asked the
Adjutant-general whether she had better write to her
friends openly, to propose an exchange, or in cipher?
Upon which he thought a cipher lady should not remain
here, at least long. We now give some flour to Longa's
people for bread, and try to make regulars of them.

It is very terrible that our people, muleteers, soldiers,
&c., do more mischief by far than the French, except
when the latter do it by way of punishment and revenge;
at ordinary times their discipline is much better than
ours. The heads of the Indian corn are now nearly all
eaten off about here by the cattle, and cut by the soldiers
to roast, as well as the leaves for our animals. The
Spaniards, however, in some degree have their revenge;
we bring a quantity of money into the country in spite
of our bad pay, and this they fleece us out of in high
style. They sell everything like Jews, and are naturally
exorbitant, greedy, and avaricious; this seems the general
character. So we go on! They cheat our men as much
as they can, and our men get all they can gratis; upon
the whole, however, if we remain stationary, we benefit
the country.

Lord Wellington yesterday said it was stated in his
letters from Lisbon, that Portugal was miserable without
us. No money, no markets, nothing doing. I believe
he was half joking with the Portuguese agent here; but
he really meant that we were much missed there. The
muleteers with us are the worst. Their terms were, a
dollar a-day each mule, and one for a man for every three
mules, and rations. They have gone on four years, and
more; they are now, I believe, sixteen months in arrears
in their pay, having just got one month lately. If paid

up they would make fortunes, and have no pretence to behave ill. As it is, they steal, plunder, turn out their mules in the corn, &c., and from one of the most orderly classes in Spain, are become the least so. There are about ten thousand of the mules in this state, and I suppose four thousand muleteers. Their pay is almost more than the army; and when is it to be paid or how? there lies the rub.

The people say that we have brought the plague of flies, and I really believe we have increased the swarms by the number of dead carcasses, and various kinds of filth caused by the density of the population at present. We do not bury so regularly as the French, either our offal or dead animals, or anything; the Spaniards not at all, unless we do it for them. To give you a notion of the flies, they eat up all my wafers, if left open, and spot my letters all over if left one day on the table.

Nothing can look better than the condition of the Portuguese troops. They are cleaner than our men; or look so, at least. They are better clothed now by far, for they have taken the best care of their clothes; they are much gayer, and have an air, and a *je ne sais quoi*, particularly the Caçadores both the officers and private men, quite new in a Portuguese. It is curious to observe the effects of good direction and example, how soon it tells. The French seem to do the same with Italians, and with every one; or rather have done so, for I hope this may not cease in part at least,

Head Quarters, Lezaca, 24th.—Having been writing nearly all day yesterday, I took an evening stroll, and then went and sat down on the churchyard parapet wall. In ten minutes who should come there but Lord Wellington, alone. After one turn he came and sat on the wall with me, and talked for more than half an hour. Amongst other things I said, I hoped that you in England would hear Soult's account of the Maya business

R

first, as you then would be alarmed, and value the latter account by the Prince of Orange as it deserved.

He said, "Why, at one time it was rather alarming, certainly, and it was a close-run thing. When I came to the bridge of Sorauren, I saw the French on the hills, on one side, and it was clear that we could make a stand on the other hills in our position on the 28th; but I found that we could not keep Sorauren, for it was exposed to their fire and not to ours. I determined to take the position, but was obliged to write my orders accordingly at Sorauren, to be sent back instantly, for had they not been dispatched back directly by the way I had come, I must have sent four leagues round in a quarter of an hour later. I stopped, therefore, to write accordingly, people saying to me all the time, 'The French are coming! The French are coming!' I looked pretty sharp after them, however, every now and then, until I had completed my orders, and then set off, and I saw them just near one end of the village as I went out at the other end; and then we took our ground."

I then observed that the only time I felt a little uneasy was, when we were stopped at Lanz, and sent across to Lisasso, for all faces seemed very long, and the removal of the wounded was very much pressed. This led him to explain more; and he said: "Had I been as regularly informed of how matters stood on the 26th and 27th as I was of what had passed on the 25th, that need not have happened; but General Cole never told me exactly how far he found it necessary to give way, or let me know by what a superior force he was pressed, and that he intended giving way, or my arrangements would have been quite different; and the French might have been stopped sooner than they were. In truth, I suspected that all Soult's plan was merely by manœuvres to get me out of the hills, and to relieve one or both of the besieged places, as things should turn up and succeed for him;

and I expected him to turn short round towards St. Sebastian accordingly. I had then no notion that with an army so lately beaten he had serious thoughts, as I am now sure he had, of driving us behind the Ebro. The consequence was that the second division halted a day and a half at Trinita and Berrueta, on the 26th, and till three on the 27th; and the seventh division only took a short march to St. Estevan, as I was unwilling to lose a bit more of the mountains than was absolutely necessary, from the probable loss of men in recovering such ground. On the night before we marched, or at three in the morning of the 26th, I knew all that had passed on the first attack, and acted accordingly. Had I been as well informed, and had everything been communicated to me as punctually on the next evening, the march of several divisions would have been different. I should and could have pressed them more on the 27th; there would not have been the risk and apparent alarm as to headquarters, &c.; and we should probably have stopped the French sooner. As it is, however, and as I had men who could fight, as the English did when they recovered the hill which had been lost, it has all ended very well."

We then got upon the expedition on the other side of the Peninsula; and he explained some of the reasons for his instructions there. He was rather stiff with the lumbago; but in high spirits. He said that the Spanish Generals thought the reason the French beat them was, that they had no good cavalry; and that whenever they had our cavalry with them, they wanted to fight. This was what he was anxious to prevent, " For," said he, " our cavalry never gained a battle yet. When the infantry have beaten the French, then the cavalry, if they can act, make the whole complete, and do wonders; but they never yet beat the French themselves."

Talking on this subject another day, Lord Wellington and all the officers present seemed to agree that a cavalry

regiment did not know what real infantry fire was.
They talk of a sharp carbine fire, which kills ten or
twenty horses and half as many men ; but they could
not exist ten minutes in a fire to which our infantry
battalions are at times exposed ; they would be annihilated if they did not go threes about very quick indeed.
Even in the infantry at times it was said, that in less
than half an hour every mounted officer would be dismounted, from his own or his horse's wounds, and
perhaps not six men in a company out of sixty, would
remain.

Head-Quarters, Lezaca, August 25th.—We are as
quiet here as at Frenada. Desertion is terrible. I think,
however, Lord Wellington must stop it. We have only
as yet tried five out of sixteen sent for trial : they are all
sentenced to death, and all shot ! This will, I think, at
least have a good effect on our new reinforcements. One
of our officers did an odd thing to stop it ; and it
answered, or has done so hitherto ; he called his men
together and, addressing them, said, " I want no men
who wish to go to the French, and if any now will
say they wish to go, I promise to send them in with a
flag of truce." No one stirred, nor has any one stirred
since ; but as to the legality of this plan there may be a
query ?

Our great guns have now just begun pounding again at
St. Sebastian ; we are to demolish everything this time ;
but still I fear we shall scarcely get in easily at last.

As to Pamplona, the reports are, that they are now on
half-rations, and have enough at that rate to last till the
15th of next month. It is provoking how much they
have picked up. They have tried to send out another
batch of inhabitants, but these have been sent in again
to help eat ; a hard fate to be made a mere tool for starvation ! and I conclude they will not have the best commons even Panplona can afford.

Head-Quarters, Lezaca, August 28th, 1813.—Here we
are still quiet, and very busy; and Courts-martial all at
work.   In these hills, however, our Provosts are not the
most secure; and common precautions will not do against
men who know they are probably to be shot in a day or
two.   A Court was adjourned till yesterday morning, for
a witness for the prisoner, and in the night he was off.
Another man under sentence of death, near Maya, and
three other deserters just taken as they were going over
to the French, were put foolishly under the care of a man
and a lad armed to convoy them a little way.   They rose
on them, took away their arms, and went over with them
to the French post.   I am sorry to say, however, that we
have still enough to hang.

The French deserter, the talkative Lieutenant-Colonel,
is here again, and has one great merit—he induces Lord
Wellington to talk and discuss his old battles, &c., when
this man was on the other side.   Thus from the two
I pick up a little of the cause of things.   Yesterday the
conversation turned upon the retreat of the last year.
The Frenchman said that all their officers blamed Soult
for his conduct after crossing the Tormes; that he was
in fact nearer Rodrigo than our army, and might and
ought to have cut us off, if he had pushed on.   Lord
Wellington observed, " I fully expected to find him on
the high road : and I ordered nothing at all that way in
consequence on the first day; afterwards, when I found
he was not there, I took to it."   The French officer
replied, " From the rain and hazy weather, and bad
roads, Soult was puzzled and afraid—he did not in the
least know the English plans.   He heard of some troops,
and did not know whether they were a rear-guard or the
main army, and so on; but when he found your lordship
making a stand collected at St. Munos, he said, ' *Ah que
j'avois tort.*' "   He then tried to pump Lord Wellington,
and said, " If he had cut you off, perhaps you would

have recrossed the Tormes, and made for the Benevente
road? but you would have suffered much." Upon which
Lord Wellington observed, " No, I certainly should have
done no such thing : that would have been ruin. But if
you must know what I should have done, I should have
done that which many thought I ought to have done as
it was—I should have fought, and trusted to the bravery
of my troops to get me out of the scrape." The Frenchman then said, " No one ought to have blamed you for
not doing that, unless it were absolutely necessary, for
the French were twenty thousand stronger than you
were, and their cavalry was then very numerous, and in
the highest order.

These conversations give a value to the Frenchman
which he does not otherwise possess, though a clever
man. I found Lord Wellington the day before yesterday busy with all the Spanish staff and General Murray,
with a dozen great Spanish drawings and plans of the
mountains about them ; they were comparing our several
labours together. The Spanish staff draughtsmen have
a good character. I should like to have been called in,
but I was only waiting an audience at the other end of
the room.

Yesterday, Lord Wellington went off on horseback
over the mountains, for Irun; he then went on to St.
Sebastian, and was not back here till nearly nine at
night. They are pounding away at that fortress from
fifty-one pieces of ordnance, mortars and all ; but nothing
is done yet.

The 29th.—No news yet. Still battering away at St.
Sebastian. We had a ridiculous event here yesterday :
an enraged bull—belonging, I believe, to the Commissariat—broke into the quarters of the Commissary-general, Sir Robert Kennedy, and contriving to get to the
room of the clerks, put all to flight, one this way, the
other that, in the greatest alarm. All were dispersed in

an instant. After upsetting a few things, the bull retreated into the garden, and jumped over the wall, without doing any serious mischief. The joke was, that the owner had contrived this, on account of nonpayment of his demand.

Our fifty-one battering pieces have now been at work three days, and have laid open one end of the entire wall of the town of St. Sebastian, and to-morrow is talked of for the assault. Two days since the garrison made another sortie, and carried off a few men ; and, upon the whole, I think people are not quite satisfied with the conduct of the fifth division, who are employed. Ever since our retreat and the former sortie, they seem to have had in some measure a sort of panic. We have had a general Court-martial on Major O'Halloran, for neglect on that occasion as field-officer in the trenches ; but he is acquitted on the ground that the orders he gave were correct, but that he was disobeyed. The facts on the trial were these :—

A sortie was expected all the night, and peculiar precautions were taken accordingly ; every fifth man sentry, &c., by order of the General. All was quiet until an hour after daybreak and more ; then a Captain Canvers, of the Portuguese service, who has since shot himself, seems to have suffered the sentries to enter the trenches, and rest on their arms for security, without orders, or rather against orders. At a little after six out came the French, and another Portuguese captain seems to have misunderstood his orders, and did not suffer his sentries to fire instantly, thinking that he had no orders to this effect ; he was made prisoner. In short, the consequence was, that about fifty French were in an instant in the trenches, when half-a-dozen of our people fired and fell back. The Portuguese were mostly in a panic, and they were nearly six hundred out of seven hundred then employed. They did once attempt to get up the bank and form, but the sandy ground gave way, and in they went again. This increased the confusion, and no exertions of our or their officers could rally the men, until they had been quite driven out of the trenches, and pursued to the little village in ruins under the convent. There Major O'Halloran rallied them, and, with a fresh English working-party just arrived, drove the French back again to the town, but in the meantime many prisoners were made.

Lord Wellington himself, I think, is not pleased with the fifth division ; and, as some proof of this, has ordered three hundred of the first division, one hundred and fifty of the light, one hundred and fifty of the fourth, and, I believe, one hundred and fifty of the third (of each of which one-third are to be of the Portuguese regiments), to march to-day to assist in forming the storming-party to-morrow. This is a cut at the fifth ; and these men are all volunteers, and the orders are to send men who, by their cool courage and good conduct, will be likely to succeed. In a measure the success of this will depend on these qualities. The fifth division ought now to volunteer, trying first alone, I think.

There was nothing but confusion in the two divisions here last night, (the light and fourth,) from the eagerness of the officers to volunteer, and the difficulty of determining who were to be refused and who allowed to go and run their heads into a hole in the wall, full of fire and danger ! Major Napier was here quite in misery, because, though he had volunteered first, Lieutenant-colonel Hunt of the 52nd, his superior officer, insisted on his right to go. The latter said that Napier had been in the breach at Badajoz, and he had a fair claim to go now. So it is among the subalterns ; ten have volunteered where two are to be accepted. Hunt, being Lieutenant-colonel, has nothing but honour to look to ; as to promotion, he is past that. The men say that they don't know what they are to do, but they are ready to go anywhere.

I fear we shall find the French have run a ditch across and a new second wall behind those we have destroyed, and that we may have tough work yet. The shells, however, which are sent every ten minutes into the castle, and shake the dust out of its roof in a fine style, must make the place rather too warm to hold just now ; and I heartily wish it would induce them to give in before all the bloodshed begins. They fire now but very little. Lord Wellington and every one is gone over to St. Sebastian to-day ; and having nothing to do, I have made up my mind to be off also.

August 30th.—I was on the point of setting out when I heard that the storming was put off a day ; as the French are in motion, and making pretence at least to relieve St. Sebastian, and as the fourth division marched accordingly this morning, and head-quarters may, therefore, suddenly be off, I determined to be quiet here, especially as I do not feel quite well. Lord Wellington came home at nine o'clock, and was off again before eight this morning. We remain here much in the dark, of course, when he is away. General Murray stays here to protect us with the light division in our front.

CHAPTER XIII.

The Author taken Prisoner—Kind Treatment by the French General—
Life of a Prisoner — Release — Details of the Author's Captivity —
Curious Scene at General Pakenham's—A Basque Squire.

Bayonne, September 5, 1813.

MY DEAR M——,

WHEN you told me, some time since, that you
expected to hear from me from this place, I never expected
to have realized in this way your prediction. But as the
French all tell me with a shrug, "*c'est le sort de la
guerre, Monsieur,*" I must submit to as great a piece of
ill luck as generally falls to a poor man, "*dans le meil-
leur des mondes possibles.*"

On the evening of the 30th August I was, as I mentioned to you in my last, stopped from going over to see
the storming of St. Sebastian the next morning by the
general report that the French were in motion ; that an
attack was expected on our line at daylight, to relieve
that place if possible, and that therefore head-quarters
would probably move. So it turned out ; at six we
heard that the French had all crossed the Bidassoa, and
were moving on. The baggage was all ordered half a
league up the mountain Yangi, there to wait orders either
to proceed further for security if we were pressed, or to
return if we repulsed the attack. At seven, Lord Wellington, &c., were off. By nine the town was nearly
cleared, and every one in motion.

Nothing can be more stupid than thus waiting a whole day standing with the mules and baggage, to hear the result, without a creature to talk to, and knowing nothing that is passing. One of the officers advised me to go up the hill just above Lezaca, to observe a little what was doing near, assuring me that it was quite safe. Just afterwards Major Canning returned from Lord Wellington with orders, and said he would show us the way to the hill and then go on. I mounted, and set out with Mr. Henry, having sent off my baggage. Mr. Booth, the principal Commissary of Accounts, Mr. Jesse, his assistant, and Captain Hook, the officer who takes all the quarters for every one at head-quarters, determined to join the party. When we had got a little way Major Canning remarked that by going up the first hill we should see sooner what was doing, and could then return to Lezaca, or stay and proceed as was found advisable, and that we should be thus sure of not being cut off from Yangi. This we accordingly did. When half up the hill we observed two battalions resting under arms quietly on the top and having examined them some time with our glasses, thought that they were Spanish; but not being certain (for they are so alike as scarcely to be known at fifty yards distance), we thought it advisable to keep to our left, towards the rear of some of our own red-coats, whom we saw engaged with the French in a wood further on. We did this, and then waited to see whether those two battalions advanced and fired or not, to enable us to be sure, by their fire, to which party they belonged. As they remained at rest, we could not determine this point; and as there was much fern and wood, and we were only about a short half mile off, we determined, for fear of a surprise, to go back, and follow up the mountain Major Canning's road, where we saw our own red-coats. We did this, and just before we ascended, ascertained that our people were still there; we trusted firmly to their not giving ground, as the French were already much advanced, and this road was the common communication of all our army through Lezaca to Oyarsun and San Sebastian.

About half-way up the hill, or mountain, is a wood, from whence we got a peep at the two battalions. We saw them moving towards the English position, but not firing, and Captain Hook remarked that there were several red-coats amongst them, so they must be friends; but that, however, about a hundred yards further on we should be able to ascertain, and if it were not so we must return.

At the end of the hundred yards the woods ceased, and the two roads up the mountain joined, when to our great astonishment, just as we came one way to the place of junction, two French battalions came up the other, and we found ourselves within twenty yards of each other; Mr. Jesse was still nearer. I heard a cry of *qui vive*, which put an end to all doubt as to who they were; and after a sort of short pause and drawback in the head of the French column, thinking, I believe, that they were the head of an allied column, several moved towards us, and two levelled at us. Mr. Jesse, the nearest of us, dismounted, and surrendered instantly. The other two jumped off their horses, and, as the side of the mountain was very steep, and no one could well ride after them, they ran down, and the French having incumbrances, I believe they escaped. I now think that was the best plan I could have adopted. At the moment, however, as I was in the road, and nearer to the French than they were, I determined to turn about, and try my horse down the road again the way we came, thinking it a great chance that the only two who levelled, and seemed ready to fire, would hit me. They never fired, but some pursued, and one or two officers on horseback. I galloped down, however, nearly a mile, at the risk of my neck. The road then got steeper, and I looked round to see if any one was nearly up behind me. I pulled up a little, as I found they had not reached my servant, who was above a hundred yards behind me ; but, on turning round again to proceed, I saw, in the narrow part of the road just before me, where the descent was steep both ways, one up and one down, six Frenchmen ; two in the road, two on each side, all ready with their pieces up to their shoulders. Upon this I pulled up and we had a parley. On my pulling up, and addressing them in French, they seemed in doubt, and spoke some bad French. I then looked about me, to see what chance remained, but seeing that they all levelled again, and cried out " *prisonnier*," the risk was then too great for the remotest chance of escape, so I dismounted, and they instantly took down their pieces, and ran up. In a moment, my two horses, and cloak, pistols, sword, telescope, handkerchief, were all gone.

Having received some money just before, and fearing some theft from my Portuguese servants, I had about fifteen doubloons about me, as being the most secure place. One-half they found instantly, and were so pleased that they scarcely searched more, except to take my knife, comb, &c. I then told them that I was no General, having heard a cry before from the battalion of " *voilà le Général ;*" that I was only a civil officer, a noncombatant ; but that I had some more money, and if they would then, when they had got everything from me, release me, I would tell them where it was, and give it to them. This I did, thinking as they had got so much booty, they would perhaps wish to keep it secret, not to be called upon to refund any part, and that therefore they would not be sorry to say that I had escaped, and let me go that I might not have to tell the story.

They promised to do this, so I produced the rest, and at the same time contrived to give my watch a twist up above my waistcoat, that when they felt for it, they found nothing, and by this means I contrived to save that.

The other speculation did not answer so well, for I believe they still took me for a General. They would not release me, and I was carried into the battalion, and then to General D'Armagnac (I believe), who was behind their attacking troops. They were leading me into the fire of our own people, when an officer ordered them up on one side. I said it would be very hard to get me killed by our own fire, and that they had better let me run across, and shoot at me themselves. Upon the whole they all behaved very civilly, and without any violence. I there met Mr. Jesse. I told our story to General D'Armagnac. He said we were very unlucky, and seemed good-humoured, ordering the captors to give me back two doubloons. After telling his aide-de-camp to take us to General Clausel, who commanded in chief there, and then to the rear, he said he would apply to get us exchanged (as that was now the fashion, and not to release civilians gratis) for two civil officers, friends of his, in England : and then lending me one of his horses to ride back upon, took leave of us. The soldiers told me that he had bought my horse for a trifle, and thus ended the fate of poor Blackey!

The whole was the work of half an hour. Whilst we were in the wood, our people had just given way across this road to superior numbers, and had thus left us exposed to this misfortune in a place where every one had passed in safety all the morning, and so again from an hour later all the evening. A little sooner, or a little later, we should not have been caught above a league within our lines of the morning. Such, however, was our fate !

We were then taken to General Clausel, and were instantly ordered back to his former head-quarters. There was then a great outcry for ammunition, which delayed the French some time, and, as they said, saved our last position on this hill. I found that they did not, however, know the country well, and tried to pump me as to what was beyond, both as to men and mountains, &c. I always pleaded ignorance as a civilian. They had contrived to get four small two-pounder field mountain-pieces up this difficult ascent, and kept them constantly in use, asking me why we, who were so ingenious, did not adopt the same practice? I said they had taught us the art of war, and I believe they had found their scholars had made very rapid progress, so that if these guns were really worth the labour, I had no doubt we should soon have some, but that such things were not to be found ready-made in the mountains, therefore they must wait a little. I soon gave up my horse to a wounded man, as they abounded on the road, and we descended and crossed the Bidassoa by the ford below the bridge, as I found our light division were still maintaining their ground near the bridge at Bera (or Vera,) and had kept the other side of the valley all the time secure.

A tremendous storm then began. We took shelter till five o'clock in a hovel, but at last proceeded, the storm continuing, up the mountain of La Rhüne, to the French position, and head-quarters.—those of General Clausel. Mons. d'Arnot, an officer belonging to the latter, was extremely kind to us. He said our best prospects were not to stay and sleep in the hovel, where we should be starved and crowded by wounded, &c., but to go with him to the General's hut on the top, where, if anything was to be had, we should have it. He also lent me a horse part of the way up again. We passed the French position to the entrenched camp, where amongst a variety of huts of boughs, earth, &c., were three rather better than the rest, consisting of a few feather-edged boards at top, and earth and fern on the sides and bottom. These were for Generals Clausel, Taupin, and D'Armagnac, for the attendants, &c. There were only two places where it had not rained in considerably, and we were wet through, without a change.

The General's canteens were unpacked, and the aide-de-camp said, "If he returns, you will have some dinner, if not, we have some bread." That and sour wine was all our fare for the night, and we laid down in our wet clothes on the ground. They first gave us up General Clausel's dry inner chamber, but on a notice coming that he was returning, we were removed to the attendants' hut. There I passed a sleepless night, our party being the two aides-de-camp, a colonel, a major, five of the gens-d'armes, or police corps, Henry, the General's cook, a friend, two or three attendants, and about four wounded men who staggered in, and lay in the middle. The horses were all tied to the boards, out in the storm all night, and making a noise against our heads. The wounded were groaning; then came an oath from an officer against them as cowards, and asking how that noise made them any better? At last came a poor creature with a violent colic; this last filled us as close as we could lie, and constant quarrels ensued between those near the doors, or those who came every minute for shelter from the storm and rain, and to get help for their wounds. The lightning gave us a glimpse of the scene every five minutes. Now and then an observation escaped as to the rain swelling the Bidassoa, &c.

At three o'clock the firing began again close to us; at four the drum beat to arms, and at six we got a little cold meat and bread and wine, after the General's breakfast, and about seven we were marched towards St. Jean de Luz with a party of prisoners and deserters. Amongst them were several of the Chasseurs Britanniques, who, with their red jackets, had, by deserting to the enemy, and then advancing with them, contributed to our being surprised and taken. We stopped half an hour in the wood below, and got a little brandy from the post of the gens-d'armes in the rear, and arrived at St. Jean de Luz about one o'clock,—three leagues. This was Marshal

Soult's head-quarters. Thither we went, and merely saw him in a crowd. We were then taken to Count Gazan, and then to the Commandant of the Police, &c. We were quartered at an inn with some gens-d'armes in the outer room; got some supper at seven at General Gazan's, to whom I mentioned what had passed at Vittoria; was allowed to write to head-quarters to let them know where we were, and to ask for money, clothes, &c., if we were not exchanged, and we were allowed to stay till next day to wait for an answer.

No answer came. It was intended to give us horses to carry us to Bayonne the next evening, but all were engaged in carrying away wounded men, including some troops of cavalry, so we marched on foot about three o'clock, five under a guard. We were delayed by the bad walking of some deserters, and were then again caught the last half league in a most furious thunder-storm, which soaked us through in five minutes. At nine, we reached this place, three long leagues, and were taken to the Nouveau Fort. The Marechal-de-logis gave us a bed between us, on the ground, in a room with two midshipmen and a sick and wounded officer of the 34th; and having got some bread and cheese, we went to bed, with a dry shirt which he lent us. I have ever since had rheumatism. We occupy a round tower here, and our soldier-prisoners are in the court below; the Spaniards are above, and some sailors in confinement, as their dress would enable them to escape. The two midshipmen were exchanged the next day. From Mr. Babou, the banker, a most liberal and generous man, we have got money, and therefore now go on well. How officers manage who have no money I cannot guess. Only three of the numbers the banker has given money to have had their bills protested, and he says that if it is poverty he shall never complain, otherwise he should wish to be paid. If I get

s

back I have undertaken to speak to Lord Wellington on the subject.

13th September, Mont de Marsan.—On the 8th I received a most kind letter from Lord Wellington in his own handwriting, as to an old friend, telling me that he authorized me to tell the Duke of Dalmatia he would send back for me any one named by him, to be given in exchange.* I had just before received a notice to set out next day for Verdun. I went with a gens-d'armes instantly to the General of Division, Baron d'Huillers, and to the Commandant-general Sol. To them I told my story, and showed my letter. They advised me to send my letter to the Duke of Dalmatia, and engaged to detain me until the answer came back. I also asked to write to the Duke myself. The other officers, who had already been to Moulins (where General Paget is), wrote also for leave to go to a nearer depôt than Verdun, on account of the expense they had been put to; they were of the 34th

---

* Head-quarters, September 4, 1813.

DEAR SIR,

    I WAS very much concerned to hear of your misfortune, which, however, I don't doubt will have been alleviated by the Comte Gazan as far as may have been in his power, as soon as he will have known that to your humanity in the first instance he owed the safety of his wife.

    In former wars a person in your situation would have been considered a non-combatant, and would have been immediately released; but in this war, which, on account of the violence of enmity in which it is conducted, it is to be hoped will be the last for some time at least, everybody taken is considered a prisoner of war, and none are released without exchange. There are several persons now in my power in the same situation with yourself in that respect, that is to say, non-combatants, according to the known and anciently practised rules of war; among others, there is the Secretary of the Governor of St. Sebastian, and I authorize you to tell the Duke of Dalmatia or the Count Gazan that I will send back any person in exchange for you that they will point out.

    I send you, with this letter, the sum of two hundred dollars, of which I request you to acknowledge the receipt, and that you will let me know whether I can do anything else for you.

Ever yours, most faithfully,
WELLINGTON.

F. Seymour Larpent, Esq.

regiment, and they also were allowed to wait the answer. The other five officers of the 60th were dispatched with a *feuille de route* for Verdun. On the 9th, about seven o'clock, I went to the play with two Dutch officers of the 130th regiment, one of whom was with me when at La Rhüne in the camp, and had been all along very civil, and had called upon us and volunteered going with us to the theatre. I did this in order to pass the anxious time away till the answer to my letter came. The play I did not much enjoy, as you may suppose, though our two gens-d'armes were very well behaved, and went into a box opposite, leaving us with the officers.

At nine o'clock came an account that my letter was arrived. I ran home and eagerly opened it. I found it was a very civil answer from Count Gazan, full of good wishes, &c., but stating Marshal Soult had never had any proposal made to him for my exchange by our General, or that it would be done instantly; again assuring me that if any such should arrive I should be instantly sent back, and that in the mean time orders should be given that none of us should for the present cross the Garonne.

The next morning (the 10th) came an order to be at Mont de Marsan in four days, about seventy miles off, the chief town of the department of Landes, and there to wait orders. We also got a letter to give to the commandant there, to halt the others there, or to bring them back if they had passed that depôt. I prepared a letter to Lord Wellington, encouraged by his letter to me (I had before only written to the Adjutant-general), and stated to him how matters stood, thanking him for his kindness. This I enclosed in one to Count Gazan, in French, and begged him, as a last favour, to forward it by a flag of truce through the lines to Lord Wellington. I then hastily bought a few necessaries, and engaged with the other five officers to be conveyed to this place (Mont

de Marsan) in a large coach with six mules, Henry in
the driver's tilt-cart in front. When I went home to
pay our gens-d'arme, he was most unreasonable and broke
his agreement; we would not pay him, so he locked us
in. I said I had the General's orders to march at one
o'clock, and called upon him at his peril to release us, and
to go with us to settle the matter. He would not, but
released us, and would then take nothing. I then went
off to General Sol, and told my story. He sent for the
man in a hurry, but as he did not come instantly, asked
what we proposed to give. I told him. He said if we
were willing to pay that sum (which was according to our
agreement), "Very well, leave it here, and you may set
out; had you left it to me I should not have made you
pay nearly so much." Accordingly at two o'clock we
started, and got, in four hours and a half, over four
leagues of the country, or sixteen miles, to a small village
on the river side, where we dined and slept. Our route
was through Dax, but we had leave, as that was knee-
deep in sand, to pass by Orthes.

Next morning (the 11th) at four o'clock, we proceeded
to Orthes to breakfast, and got there, six leagues, by
eleven o'clock. There we sat down to a *déjeuner à la
fourchette*. We then, at one, started again, and before six
got to Hugemont, where we dined again, and slept four
leagues further.

On the 12th, at seven, we set out for this place, through
the heavy sand in some places, and over a ruinous
bridge; we did not arrive until twelve. All along the
road we found everything in a state of the greatest activity for the supplies of the army—everything in requisition. I longed to have some of the Spaniards with me,
to teach them what was to be done in this way. The
love of coffee is much diminished, and the lower classes
are excluded from it by the high price of that and of
sugar. Other things are cheap, and we got our dinner,

beds, and all for five francs a-head each night. Our mules were very fine, and each had a name, which we soon learnt, by the constant dialogues of the old driver and his boy, one of the two latter always running by the mule's side, as there were no reins to the other four in front.

We met with every attention and civility here, were in time to stop the other five officers, and we are now all in officers' billets, the same as the French officers themselves, and have received for our days of march the same as they do on the march,—a captain three francs, a colonel five, a lieutenant two and a half, &c. I am at the house of the principal engineer (from Paris) of some works going on here, Monsieur de Beaudre. Great improvements are nearly completed in this little departmental capital: a new wide stone bridge of easy access, instead of an old narrow Gothic one, and an open space cleared around it; a new Prefect's palace, with departmental offices, &c. A new chapel, new official houses, and much private repairs, are in progress: this is very unlike Spain. I breakfast alone in my billet on my tea, which I have discovered here, as the others have only meat and wine. I dine with the rest—and to please them, but against my will—at six; we have a good cheap dinner at four francs each. The poor officers do not know what to do with themselves. I immediately applied to my patron for books, and he gave me the range of several. After a play or two of Racine's, and a few of the *Contes Moraux*, I have attacked La Harpe's *Cours de Littérature* at the Lycée, and am as yet well pleased; I walk as much as my rheumatism permits. Thus goes time; but I suffer much—I feel as if I had been broken on the wheel.

Poor Henry is more bewildered than ever, but flatters himself that he shall soon learn French. If he could copy the activity around him, he would be wonderfully improved. We are here full of the *Moniteur's* victories, and the little check the French appear to have sustained latterly under Vandamme, in Bohemia.

Before I go to bed I get my cup of coffee, a small one indeed, for my ten sous, at the café, read the news, and then retire home. This place is very full, from the wounded being in part here; from the exertions making as to supplies, for we have two hundred cars here in a day; from some artillery drivers being here, and from the constant passage of everything to and from the army. The Commandant has been particularly obliging. We have a mile round the town to walk in, and are never troubled by any one.

20th September, Mont de Marsan.—Alas, poor Seymour!—[Hiatus.]

On the 21st, at Mont de Marsan, arrived my mules, pony, and baggage: no letter. I gave up all prospect of exchange, and was stupidly ill and tranquil. The lady where I was quartered, was very attentive and good-natured, and I had begun my literary course, and had made up my mind to my fate. On the 22nd, however, at nine, came an order for us all to set out at eleven for Bayonne again. We did so, had some little misfortunes, overturns, &c., but got to the Chateau Vieux, at Bayonne, on the 25th September, and had the honour of being confined in the same room where Palafox had been for three months, and all the great Spanish prisoners—the Duke of Gravina, Prince of Castel Franco, &c. We staid there, seven of us, until the 1st, in anxious suspense—the room too noisy for reading, and I too ill for it, so we played whist, and killed time in that way quietly. At five o'clock on the 1st, when at dinner, came an order for Mr. Jesse and myself only to set out at six for St. Jean de Luz, in the dark. We got a coach at six, the only vehicle to be had; and I packed all my baggage, and mounting Henry and my Portuguese on the mules, we

arrived all at eleven at night, at the Police at St. Jean
de Luz. We were sent to an inn for the night, then the
next morning (the 2nd) taken to Count de Gazan, at ten.
I found him very civil, had much conversation with him
for an hour, breakfasted with him, and at twelve we were
all packed off with an escort for Endaye, to be sent over
here.

The gens-d'armes took us first to Count Reille, whose
quarters were half a league on from St. Jean de Luz.
He sent us on to General Maucale, who was half a league
further. He gave us a fresh escort, and sent us round
the end of the lines, down to the water side at Endaye.
All very civil in every way. At Endaye, about four, we
were with some danger sent across, mules and all, in a
little flat-bottomed boat to Fontarabia to the Spanish outpost. There also much civility, but much delay. At
five we got to Irun with a Spanish escort, were taken to
General Frere, found him at dinner—very civil. I then
went to General Stopford; he was at dinner. No
quarters to be had, so I sent my baggage on here, but got
some dinner. At eight, came on in the rain here: found
General Graham; very kind. He gave me a bed in his
quarters, and some tea. Breakfasted here this morning;
baggage gone to Lezaca; I am to go there in half an
hour. I have grown very thin, and am in very crazy
condition, but must get patched up at head-quarters,
and go to work again. This last month has been like
a dream. I hear there has been much difficulty about
my exchange; but it is now over, I am happy to
say, and Lord Wellington has been very kind. I
hope to do something for my fellow prisoners when I
see him.

Count Gazan asked me to get for him the following
print or caricature to complete a collection he has. Will
you do your best to find it, and send it out if possible.
The Count's description :—

" Une caricature qui a paru il y a douze ou quinze ans à Londres, au sujet d'un voyage que fit dans cette capitale Le Grand Rabbin Juif d'Hollande, dans l'intention de reformer la manière de vivre des Juifs de Londres dans ce temps là."

[N.B.—It was not possible to trace or find this print, though every inquiry was made.]

Oyarzun, in Spain, at the Head-Quarters of General Graham, October 4th, 1813.—Once more again at liberty, as far as my rheumatic limbs will permit: the will, at least, is free, and I hope soon my arms and legs will be so likewise.

Lezaca, Head-Quarters, October 7th, 1813.—To-day I have a little leisure, as every one is engaged out, and a grand attack is to be made on the French position to drive them quite off that mountain, La Rhüne. It will be, I fear, tough work : I dare not go and peep again, even if I were well enough, so have taken up this paper. Baggage and all for the present remain here, only ready to load in case of necessity.

Lord Wellington had much difficulty in procuring my exchange, and has been very kind ; indeed every one here has appeared very much interested in my return, and "my French value." The Commissary-at-War was treated here like a prince, to procure me every favour, when he went back, by his representations. In short, if my pain goes off, I shall not regret my other losses, which amount to about 230*l.*, but shall feel myself a very fortunate man upon the whole.

Monsieur Babedac, the banker at Bayonne, is most liberal and kind to all the English officers taken. I hear a hundred have had money from him; only five bills of 110*l.* in the whole have been sent back unpaid; this, I hope, Lord Wellington will pay, though the banker said, if distress occasioned it, he did not wish it. Nearly all my baggage is now collected safely, through the kindness of friends. I have been, as you may suppose, much questioned by Lord Wellington, &c., and many now seem to envy me the trip, as it has ended so well.

I will now fill up my former French letter a little more freely. On the morning following, the scene at the French head-quarters at St. Jean de Luz was very curious. First came rumbling back from the attack seven brigades, or about forty-two pieces of ordnance, with the ammunition-waggons, about a hundred, looking very gloomy, almost all drawn by mules, and generally in good condition. You will here observe how soon the French come about again. Then came the pontoon bridge, and, lastly, perpetual strings of cars, with the wounded; the poor country people shaking their heads and lamenting all this misery, all wishing for peace, and all saying that it was their Emperor who prevented it, from his unbounded ambition. This was the talk of the officers, and of all. They said the Allies, if successful, would rise in their demands; that Bonaparte was too proud to yield, and peace would only be further off than ever. This was the conversation, when they heard of the check in the North.

When the account of the first victory of the 25th came (which by-the-by was the first information received as to the quarrel with Austria), they were all in high spirits, and exclaimed—" Ah! le pauvre beau Père, il sera chassé," and " Peace from the North will either give us peace here also, or enable us to drive you all back to Portugal with the reinforcements which we shall obtain." Things changed afterwards, and three weeks after the bulletin of the 25th, &c., and only the day before the bad bulletin came out, a Te Deum had been ordered at Bayonne, and a hundred coups de canon for the first victory! The people almost laughed at this themselves, though very miserable.

At the inn at St. Jean de Luz, where I was billeted

with a gens-d'arme at the door, we were allowed to dine
with the officers, who were all returning starved from the
lines to get a belly full. I here met with men of a
superior description, Colonels of the Guards, Chief Medical Officers, Post-Masters, Commissaries, &c. They
were civil, some of them gentleman-like and free in their
conversation, much irritated at having been beaten by
the Spaniards, which, with a tirade about numbers, they
admitted to be the fact. Monsieur D'Arnot, a young
man attached to General Clausel, and a young Dutch
officer, gay, tall, and handsome, were the most attentive
to us, and without any object, which most of the others
had in view, to get a wife back, or a lost portmanteau,
their letters, &c.

The people all told us that had we been quite prepared
to advance into France at first, Bayonne was open, and
without guns, dismantled; that we might have walked
in and gone on to Bordeaux. I believe much of this,
but not entirely, and our men were nearly as much
harassed as the French. The French troops in the first
confusion behaved very ill, and plundered the inhabitants,
throwing away their arms, and absolutely flying. Marshal Soult's orders on this subject were stronger even
than Lord Wellington's were here. The inhabitants
generally said that they would remain quiet if the English came alone, and would leave the armies to settle it,
for all they wanted was peace; but as they knew how
the Portuguese and Spaniards had been treated, and what
they might therefore expect in return, they must all fly
if the Allies came with us.

Count Gazan is elderly, and I believe quite sick of his
trade; he said he wanted peace, and to go to his villa at
Nice for life after twenty years' war. He gave me an
invitation there. In general all the officers and men
were attentive and civil; some looked sulky, but most
noticed us by touching the cap, which is more than we

do by them here. In a dispute which Captain S——
had with a stupid old fool, the *Commandant de la Place*
at Bayonne, General Sol, the French officers present
seeing that the General was in the wrong (as he afterwards admitted), all bowed to Captain S——, and the
General's own sentinel carried arms to him as he went
out. This is flattering. The curiosity is very great
about Lord Wellington, as one of the great men of the
age.

From the questions put to me when taken, about the
grand position, and on the way to St. Sebastian, I am
sure that the French had a very imperfect notion of the
exact state of that part of the mountains. My being
a civilian was my excuse for giving them no information.
Their loss in getting back again would have been greatly
increased, had they got on to the next hill. As it was,
from the river swelling, and the men not being able
to cross the ford at which I passed, but being obliged to
go round by Vera bridge, which was under our fire, the
loss was very severe. Had I not been put across early I
should have had that fire to pass through with them.

The country all the way to Bordeaux is barren and
unproductive; mostly sandy heath with vines, and a few
meadows near the stream. I saw no corn, only the
Indian corn, and that much less luxuriant than here, and
with very little head of green for forage. The consequence is, the French provisions and forage come from
an immense distance, and the supplies are very difficult
to procure; the exertions, however, are in proportion,
and very unlike those in Spain of the Spaniards. Everything, for two hundred miles and more round, is in
requisition, all the corn taken, and only *bons* given in
return; wine the same; hay the same; every merchant's
car in the town, and all the country cars with oxen at
work for the public. The districts off the roads send in
to the depôts on the high roads; and from thence the

corn, &c., is forwarded to the army, to the depôts at
Bayonne, &c. The hay for the staff horses and cavalry
comes, as Gazan told me himself, one hundred leagues,
that is, nearly three or four hundred miles, from above
Toulouse, &c., partly by water, but much by land. The
people now feel for the first time what it is to supply
their own army in their own country, and the grievance
is no small one.

The army have had a half month's pay; twenty
months are due. The prospect of payment of the *bons*
for the supplies is very remote indeed, and yet though
they all grumble they act with zeal and spirit, and I still
think, with the feelings of Frenchmen, would all unite
against invasion. In spite of all this, things in general
are still comparatively cheap; dear to Frenchmen, as
they say exorbitant—to us reasonable, except colonial
produce: bread about 4 sous a pound, or 2*d*. English;
and good meat about 8*d*. English retailed; vegetables
and fruit very cheap; wine equally so; oats and hay
tolerably cheap; even as I fed my animals (three) at the
inns for the day for about 12 or 14 livres travelling,
three feeds of corn—small ones, to each—about 6 livres,
or, as I generally gave them, 8 livres. Hay about 6 or 7
livres and good—cheaper when I bought the articles at
Mont de Marsan. A good dinner at the inns, with a
bottle of light wine, about 5*s*. each. This sometimes also
covered the beds where we slept. Tea only to be had by
ounces at a time as medicine; coffee, very dear; sugar
(brown), from 4*s*. 6*d*. to 6*s*.; white sugar, 7*s*. the pound.

The consequence has been, in a great measure, to put
an end to the great use of coffee: it is now a luxury for
the rich, and even they generally breakfast *à la fourchette*,
and drink little of it. Of *Syrope de raisin*, I bought a
basin-full for about 9*d*. This is a sort of vinous treacle,
and gives a taste to tea as if it were taken from a dirty
wine-glass. The *betterave* sugar was to be had some-

times at Bayonne, but I did not meet with any. On some bad sugar being brought to him one day, a French Lieutenant-Colonel, by way of abuse, called it *betterave*, and said, it was only from some small sticks being in it, as really he had seen *betterave* sugar as good as any other: they still, however, give 6s. a-pound for brown island sugar.

The Chateau-Neuf, at Bayonne, was just like an English sponging-house. With money we were very well off. The man, however, cheated us; we quarrelled; I got redress from the General; and on my return got into the Chateau-Vieux instead, an old English castle, where we were in the same room where Palafox had been; the Commandant, a gentleman-like man—his wife a troublesome skinflint. The Commandant at Mont de Marsan was uncommonly liberal to us all, so were the people there; equally so, my patron and patrona; the civil engineer, Baron d'Huilliers, who first commanded at Bayonne, was also civil, but more distant. He is now gone to Bordeaux, and General Thevenot, the late Commandant at Vittoria, has succeeded him. Their reports were, that Soult was going to the North to replace Berthier, who was sick, and Suchet was to succeed in command here. Count Gazan, however, did not admit this, but never positively denied it. It was also said, that the Etat Major would remove to Bordeaux for the winter-quarters. Perhaps the events of to-day may hasten this. The firing is brisk all this time. We met three cavalry regiments on the retreat towards Pau and Toulouse for forage; the horses in fair order, but generally very inferior to ours in size; the men very fine, which was so much the worse for the animals that had to carry them. At one place, near Lain, the depôt of forage was empty. I met a man running hard with orders, the Major's messenger; he was charged to inform the few neighbouring parishes, that unless they furnished and provided ready at the depôt so many rations of forage for three days for two squadrons of cavalry who were about to pass by twelve next day, all fit to move on immediately, the squadrons would be halted there that day to help themselves in the vicinity.

Small horses and mules were very cheap, as the forage rations were stopped to the subaltern officers in France, and they all consequently wanted to sell, and many of the country-people from the requisition wanted also to sell. Bayonne was declared in a state of siege for the purposes of police. One order of the police posted up in the Café Wagram at Bayonne directed, that no politics were to be discussed under pain of arrest. Out of the town, in the suburbs of St. Esprit, was a magnificent hotel, quite in the English style; there our party stopped, but were marched off to the Chateau. The activity exhibited by the French Commandant about Bayonne has been very great; one hundred and twenty guns have now been mounted, of one sort or another, instead of about three. This number has been collected all round the country, and new works are rising round the place every day. The young conscripts of the usual levy were being drilled; they were fine young lads of about seventeen or eighteen; too young for Spain, but who in a short time would make excellent soldiers. At first they appeared dull and a little unhappy; but in a few days they became gay like the rest.

The newly-raised thirty thousand for the twenty-four departments for Spain were not yet out, but are to be out this week. I understood they will be better men, being taken from the old lists of those who had previously escaped, some of them twenty-five years old. This grievance is very great, but the conscripts seem to forget it themselves, and the old parents can do nothing. It will tell, however, some time or other, I think; and I hope soon. My patrona told me that her sister's husband had been drawn five years since, got off on payment of two thousand francs, and two francs per day since; he is now married, has two children, and is still liable to be called upon again. A wish for peace follows the relation of all these stories.

On the whole I was well treated, and it appears to me that in general the treatment of prisoners by the French is very good. Officers are allowed fifty francs a-month to live upon, and on marching, the same *indemnité* as the French; 5s. a Colonel and Major, 3s. a Captain, and 2s. 6d. a subaltern. Our being able to obtain money makes all the difference almost between our treatment and that of the Spanish officers, whom they dare not trust on their parole, so many having broken it. The worst treatment I experienced was being marched on foot from St. Jean de Luz to Bayonne, with our own deserters, after having been promised a horse, and kept back until we were caught in a thunder-storm, because these fellows could not or would not march. The soldiers are like themselves to the last; when marched as prisoners, they jumped over the fences to get apples. The French guard stared, but permitted it to be done.

October 7th, three o'clock.—The officers passing from the front tell me that all is going on well—that the French have given way almost everywhere, though they still hang to the high rocks on La Rhüne, near where I slept on the 31st. They say that the Spaniards have behaved well, but that the 52nd and second battalion of the 95th have suffered, while forcing the position through which I was marched in that thunder-storm. We have no orders to move here at present. The reports confirm the news that I brought in to Lord Wellington, that Soult has gone, and that Suchet commands. I know nothing accurately now, however, as I must not go and peep again for myself.

To return to France, and my dream there (for such it
has appeared), I must give you a notion of a French
placeman in a little way, not like our great sinecurists.
My running friend, who carried the message about the
forage, accompanied me side-by-side for a league. The
people wished him joy of his prosperity; I asked him
why? He said, "They think that I am making a fortune, having a place in the hospital; and what do you
suppose it is?—I am the hospital-sexton; I bury all the
dead, four or five in the twenty-four hours, and all at
night, digging half the night. And for what?—for
eighteen sous (or ninepence English) a day. This is
not the way to make a fortune, you will allow. My
companion makes a better thing of it: he is always
tipsy, and leaves me to dig, but he always sings as
he goes to the grave. The people who know his voice
say, ' There goes poor silly John !' and give him a
sous."

Now for a trait of a gens-d'arme—a private in the
ranks. We went to the play at Bayonne with a gens-
d'arme, and our friend, the Dutch officer. On going
down to the coffee-room, my companion, Mr. Jesse,
meaning to be generous, but not understanding the
method of treating a revolutionary gens-d'arme, told
him to get anything he wished to drink as we did.
Upon which he flew into a rage, said he had drank
with his colonels, majors, captains, and had never been
sent out to drink like a servant before. Our Dutchman
was obliged to explain to him, in order to pacify him,
the difference in our service between officers and privates; said it was once so in France and in Holland, but
that the prejudice was removed there now, though it
remained in England. He then desired him to sit
down and drink with us. With difficulty he was persuaded to do so, and we all knocked our glasses together,
and so it ended amicably. I did not expect this. The

military retain, however, the only remnant of the equality of the Revolution.

The two midshipmen in prison with us amused us much. By mistake, they were at first put in prison with their men for two days on bread and water. Afterwards they were lodged in the same room in which I was. We were five in all at first. They slept in the same bed, and were as often alternately with their heads where the feet of the others were as on the pillow. In the open letter they sent to Sir G. Collier, about their exchange, through the French, they suggested the advisability of bringing in two gun-boats close to St. Jean de Luz, in order to prevent communication with St. Sebastian, and further, advised a little bombardment, &c. The sailors, as they were marched, proposed to the midshipmen to upset the heavy gens-d'armes by their great jack-boots; said they would never be able to right themselves again, and that they, the sailors, might get off. The officers, however, told them that it would not do; so they were quiet.

October 8*th*, 1813, *Lezaca.*—The result of yesterday's operations was, that the French was driven from all the mountainous parts of their position above Endaye, opposite Fontarabia, and so along, opposite Irun, to above Bera. I do not know that we have lost above five hundred men in this part. The French did not fight well, and were not above twelve or fourteen thousand here. What has passed higher up I know not. It is said that the sixth division, near Maya, have lost men. I believe Lord Wellington very prudently stopped short, in this part, near Orogne, on the road to St. Jean de Luz, not knowing exactly the result near Maya and Roncesvalles.

It is thought that the French must be in greater strength there, since they are so weak here. Report says, however, that men have been sent northwards. Our sixty pieces of artillery were all carried across the Bidassoa last night, and are established on the main road. We have

T

not lost many officers. About three hundred prisoners were brought in here, with eight officers, about ten o'clock this morning. How lucky it was that my exchange took place before this, or it would have been at least deferred, or I should have been sent back to the rear.

General Graham has just called on me. He is on his way to England to-morrow; he had called to see Lord Wellington. He was very civil, and assures me that my new mare is a good purchase; and so it ought to be for four hundred dollars. Major Stanhope sold her some time since for a hundred guineas, to take it back at the same if he returned. He did so. General Cole gave him a hundred guineas when he was ordered away again; this looks well.

Evening.—The French still cling with three companies to a rock in the midst of La Rhüne mountain, about half a mile from my resting-place, now six weeks ago. The Spaniards cannot drive them out. Little has been attempted or done to-day.

The day before yesterday, a curious scene occurred at General Pakenham's. A French militia Captain had been taken among the rocks—a *ci-devant* regular officer retired, and now apparently an active, useful man, in organizing the Basque peasantry. He had some regulars with him, and peasants without uniform. Lord Wellington had succeeded in frightening him by threatening to hang him for invading Spain with peasants. He seemed a country mountain squire, and rather simple, though probably useful. He let fall much against Bonaparte, and told us many truths. He was told that I had just come from beyond Bayonne, and made me confirm it by many facts. He was surprised and puzzled, but believed I had been there as a spy, and never guessed the truth. Another officer, who knew about eight words of Basque, was passed off as a proficient in that dialect. The poor militia officer stared, but swallowed everything as easily as his dinner. His own account of the chase of him by the Portuguese, the rocks he climbed whilst they fired, given in the most animated style, was very entertaining. I was almost sorry this unlucky Basque squire was to leave us next morning for Passages, to learn a little English farming.. He confessed that if he had been a single man, and had not left a wife and servants with six of the 6th Light Regiment boarding in his house, he should in these times have been rather glad than otherwise to get away to England, to avoid the present troubles. What he wished for most, however, was to return on parole, as he could then be at home quietly, with an excuse to enable him to refuse to take any part in what was doing. The arming of the country being what Lord Wellington wished to prevent, he could not, of course, favour this man.

9th October, five o'clock.—The French have given up the rock on La Rhüne in the night, and have to-day been beaten out of two or three redoubts; but there has been but little else done, and some say we shall now be quiet again until Pamplona falls. To-morrow, head-quarters move to Bera, only half a league. It is a large ruined village. A letter has been intercepted from Pamplona, stating that the 25th of this month will be the very latest they can hold out; but we have heard this already very often. It draws nearer the truth, certainly, every time. Plunder has begun, and disorder in the French villages, and Lord Wellington is exceedingly angry. He says, that if officers will not obey orders, and take care that those under them do so also, they must go home, for he will not command them here; many of our officers seem to think that they have nothing to do but to fight.

This place, Lezaca, is grown very unwholesome, like an old poultry-yard, and the deaths of the inhabitants are very numerous. So, I think, there is no reason to regret the change.

CHAPTER XIV.

Picturesque Quarters—Spanish Reverses—A Strange Adventurer—Spanish Jealousy—Distribution of the Army—A Pleasant Companion—News from the North—Morale of the French Army—The Artillery.

Head-quarters, Bera or Vera,
Oct. 15, 1813.

My dear M——,

I have now a quarter with a most rural exterior, and a balcony all along the upper story, hung with vines. The picturesque and the comfortable, however, are not always combined, for the room is dirty, and though small has four windows, with only large wooden shutters, and no fireplace.

It will be but a cold winter residence, and I fear even less comfortable in fact than my Frenada habitation. The ground-floor is the stable, the centre devoted to me and to the family, the upper story a great drying-room. The style of the house is, however, pretty.

Several of the best houses are destroyed, nearly all are gutted of furniture, chairs, tables, &c., and many deprived of doors and shutters, for the French camp. The wounded occupy some of the best houses, and in addition to Lord Wellington's staff, head-quarters, and Marshal Beresford's, who has returned from Lisbon, we have General Cole's staff here, and General Alten's. This place was for two months a sort of neutral ground between the two armies, so you may guess that it is a little deranged. It has been populous, and contained a considerable number of spacious houses, though not magnificent; yet the room which Lord Wellington occupies is, upon the whole, better than almost any he has had since he was in Madrid. It is well proportioned, has clean walls, and is sufficiently capacious to admit comfortably twenty-five or thirty persons to dinner. Of course he has furnished it himself, for there are only bare walls. The largest house in the place, and the best in point of situation, on a pretty knoll above the town, was made what is called a strong house of, and a regiment of Portuguese are now in it. The squire, I fear, has not gained by this arrangement.

The Spaniards were disturbed early yesterday morning about two miles from this, surprised, and driven from a redoubt, with some loss in prisoners and wounded. I believe, however, that they behaved well afterwards; but a Spanish regiment gave way. That queer playhouse hero, Downie, who was there as a volunteer, rallied them, and conducted them well, but had his horse wounded. He once more exhibited on the Pyrenees the sword of Pizarro, which had so narrow an escape when he was made prisoner in the south. You may remember that he threw it back to his friends across a broken bridge, when he was wounded and cut off by the French. He is, I believe, very brave, and seems to take with the Spaniards, though with us he can scarcely speak without exciting a smile, or even more. He was first a Commissary in the light division.

The day before this little surprise, the English officers at General Cole's were remarking, that it was only surprising that the Spaniards kept the redoubt and their post; for the officers were never seen there with the men to keep them on the alert, and the men were cooking without arms within twenty yards of the French sentries, quite unconcerned. I hope this little surprise may save us from a greater; but I expect some night that the French will make a night attack upon the Spaniards,

though that is contrary to their usual method, which is
generally to march two hours before daylight, and begin
the attack at break of day.

15*th, later.*—I have just met Downie, and he says Lord
Wellington has admitted that the French were too strong
for the Spaniards, and that he had given them a fort to
defend too much in advance in the French position.
The result, however, is that the French have kept the
redoubt, and are at work on it already, and have recovered every house in the suburbs of Zera, or Sara, of
which the Spaniards at one time had nearly one half.
Many say that this is properly a part of the French
position, and does not signify at all. Lord Wellington
seems to have a bad cold to-day.

Every one appears to have had some adventures the
night I was taken prisoner. General Pakenham's horse
and Captain Eckersley's fell down from a bank into the
river below, and it was so dark that they and two others
thought it best to remain there in the trees till daylight,
and not stir though it rained. Lord Wellington and all
his staff lost their way, and were five hours exploring
two leagues home in the rain and dark, and did not
arrive until ten at night, after various perils. It was a
tremendous night. Mr. Heaphy, the artist, who is now
here, was nearly being involved in my scrape, and it is
said he has, in consequence of these risks, added ten
guineas to the price of his likenesses, and made them
fifty guineas instead of forty guineas. This is too much
for a little water-colour whole length; but he has, I hear,
now taken twenty-six, and some excessively like.

Some of our houses begin to improve much, as many
of the inhabitants, who must be somewhat used to these
events, are returning now with all their doors and
shutters, which they had themselves carried off and concealed. Canning's quarter is suddenly by this means
transformed into a comfortable sort of residence.

Head-Quarters, Vera, October 16*th.*—Here I am still sticking to my post, though in constant pain, and at times bent enough to act the old woman, like Mrs. Sparks. The doctor still says I must, first or last, go to the hot-baths at Sestona, but I fight off as long as possible. Things must mend soon. The ration beef is like shoe-leather; mutton I can scarcely ever get; fowls are 9s. each, and are all snapped up before my man can resolve to give that price for them. Pork, ham, sausages, salt-fish and bacon alone abound.

Every one seems to think that we shall make no other movement until Pamplona falls, which, as usual, is daily expected. The French, in the meantime, are in busy preparation, burrowing and throwing up works, like moles, on every rising ground near them. It does not appear to me that they ever really intended to defend this mountain La Rhüne; they were in some degree surprised, as I told you; they had a notion that we had sent two divisions to Catalonia. They will now probably fight harder for each acre of ground, unless completely turned by numbers, and a decided flank movement from Roncesvalles.

From the reports which are current, the whole of which I dare not mention, it is to be feared that the Spanish Government and Lord Wellington have not gone on well together lately, in spite of outward appearances. The moment any General acts cordially with us, and a measure goes on well, some reason is found for his removal. This ridiculous Spanish jealousy would be endurable if they supported it by exertions of their own, so as to enable us to leave them to themselves; but we are now feeding and clothing their half-starved men in the front, and they are doing very little in the rear to supply those they have, or to increase their numbers. In short, five years' misery has not yet scourged them into reasonable beings, and turned romance heroes into common-sense soldiers and practical politicians. The men, however, seem now to fight well whenever they are well led.

October 17th, Sunday, Post-day.—General Graham has acted wisely in going home just now, his age considered. I told Lord Wellington that the French officers said that he (Lord Wellington) ought to die now, for he never would have such another year, and fortune would prove fickle. He laughed, but did not seem disposed to acquiesce in this. He is better.

I have just got four bundles of English hay, about a hundred pounds weight each, which are to last me for ten days. My next forage must be picked up on the hills, or bought in the market in the shape of baskets of coarse river grass.

Head-Quarters, Vera, October 21st, 1813, Thursday.— The week is already half elapsed, and Sunday, the post-day, draws near, leaving me with nothing to say. I am like the Spanish country people, who without waiting to hear a question always begin " *nada, nada, nada,*" or " nothing, nothing, nothing." They generally add to us " *Francese roben,*" and " *rompas todas,*" and as the French told me, said to them " *Anglesi rompen*" and " *roben todas,*" but always to every one " *nada nada.*"

I have this last week ridden out for half an hour every day before breakfast, and an hour or two before dinner ; and thus exercise myself and my horses in the meadows about here, which are now of course all open, and when it has dried up a little after the rain, make a good riding-school.

The only news here just now is, that Marshal Beresford is to have a separate command of a *corps d'armée*, not to act separately, but to complete our system, which will be—General Hill, right column ; General Sir J. Hope, left column, which Graham had ; Marshal Beresford the right centre-column ; and Lord Wellington the left centre: each consisting of different divisions and bodies of the allies.

The French to-day are collecting upon the rising ground near La Rhüne, and our people, thinking that this looked like a threat of doing something, are all on the alert, but I hear no firing. This is another anxious moment, for the fall of Pamplona is daily expected, and the garrison threaten to blow it up, which will make some desperate work.

Lieutenant-colonel Elphinstone arrived here some time since with Marshal Beresford, from Lisbon. He is now in quarters within a hundred yards of me, across a little stream; my nearest neighbour indeed, except Colonel Ellicombe, in that direction. He is here without his horses, and without much baggage, or many comforts; he is therefore, like myself, buying. His own horses only arrived as far as Ciudad Rodrigo. He has made up his mind to stay till the war is over.

The French, in addition to a few conscripts, who have joined, have called out all the militia in the neighbouring departments. This is a new scene, but I have still great doubts of the policy of entering France at all. The French now suffer severely, and grumble against their own government. Invasion may stir up the strong vanity of a Frenchman, and make him forget his grievances, in order to revenge himself on those who insult his native soil. Five or six subaltern officers have come over here to us; I believe owing to some Spanish connexions generally, or disgust and personal disappointment; and two inhabitants of the village on this side of St. Jean de Luz, Oragne, came over here to avoid serving in the militia, which is now being assembled.

12 *o'clock, Friday, 22nd.*—Nothing was done yesterday. It was all a false alarm in the front. The French, however, say that we shall be astonished with some extraordinary news in less than three days! Some say they

mean from the North, some from Pamplona. If they
are bold enough in the latter to dash out in the night
against Don Carlos and his Spaniards, I think they
would, with the loss of about one-third of their men,
fight their way to Jaca, where they have a garrison, and
escape. They would of course come out with provisions
only, leave mines prepared to add to the confusion, sally
out in all directions, and then push on in a body. Don
Carlos with all his vigilance would not, in my opinion,
be a match for them. He has sent word to the governor
that he holds his head answerable for the safety of the
works of the town, and two Frenchmen liable to death
for every Spanish inhabitant starved.

Saturday, 23*rd*.—As I have dined alone every day since
Sunday last, when I went to Lord Wellington's, I pick
up no news. Your July ' Edinburgh Review' is wonderfully fallen off; in parts very tame, and more like a poor
imitation of the old ' Edinburgh Review ;' and yet some
of the articles are curious.

We begin to feel the effects of this dangerous coast
now. Vessels can even now hardly lie in safety, though
shut up in the close harbour of Passages, and the last
packet was close in on Sunday last, on the same day on
which Major Hare fought his way in, in the *Landrail*,
and was not able to land the mail until yesterday.
Major Hare brought papers to the 9th, but scarcely any
news. He was closely examined by Lord Wellington
when he arrived at dinner-time. He had got up his
lesson so badly, that he could answer nothing clearly as
to dates, but always ended by a reference to the papers.

It is known that Bonaparte was at Dresden up to the
5th instant, and that nothing was done. This some call
bad, some good news. On the whole, I think the latter.
Colonel Gordon states that Bonaparte used our position
here, as a strong argument with the Emperor of Austria
to join him in force, stating nothing could restore matters

here but an entire new army of a hundred and fifty thousand men, who had not known the English, and that he should be invaded unless supported by his father-in-law. This is a queer argument to one who, I suspect, was only hesitating through fear of his son-in-law's strength being too much for the Allies, and would tell the wrong way. He also states, that Lord Wellington's true account of Vittoria did harm in Germany, being much under the notions they had entertained of it.

Head-Quarters, Vera, October 24th, 1813.—Post-day. We remain *in statu quo.* I see the papers have made rather a pretty history of my capture, treating me as an old gentleman (as just now they well may), and that my younger friends got off. In fact, however, the youngest of the party, Jesse, was the first who was taken. There will soon be some dispute here among the artillery and engineers on the subject of rank and brevet rank.

Head-Quarters, Bera, or Vera, October 31st, 1813.— I have been so worried this week with business and other things that I have not been able to write until the very post-day, so this will be short and hasty. The weather has been trying, one day very cold, and I hoped we were to have clear frost, which, in spite of my open room, is, in my opinion, better than wet. The thermometer got down to 36°, close to where I was shaving, three mornings since; but it soon turned to wet—raw, constant, violent cold wet; north-west wind, and rain in repeated stormy torrents. In camp our poor soldiers have had their tents torn, and almost washed away; then we have had hail followed by snow. Colonel Belson has written to me very feelingly, from the mountains, but seems well.

Another drawback as to writing has been this. Three brigades of artillery were moved along La Rhüne mountain, three nights since by night. As they went close to the French pickets, to get from our left to Endage, towards the centre, in our front, they have as yet only reached this vicinity, and have halted here. Amongst them was Colonel Ross's light troops, and Captain Jenkinson, and young ——; the latter came to me here, very miserable, wet, &c. To save him camp I took him in. Here he has been three days, and with my establishment this gives me some trouble. Besides which, one cannot get on well with business with a chum always at hand, in a small room, night and day. He is pretty well, and I conclude will remain at this place until we move—at least until the army moves, which every one expects as soon as the French will give us up Pamplona. This is *en train* I conclude. A proposal came out to Don Carlos some days since, but a most unreasonable one ; namely, to allow them all to go to France, with arms and baggage, and to be on parole for one year not to serve against us. This was refused. They made a great parade of giving our officers white bread and champagne, and Burgundy, &c., at the interview. So much for humbug. They said, " See how *forts* we are." To which we said, " Let us see how your men are." Every day's delay now is very provoking. I hope they will soon surrender.

I wish it were possible to get my chum another quarter, for I work in general at breakfast, at dinner, and in the evening, and a companion is a great inconvenience, though he is very considerate. Pray tell his family, the Colonel, &c., how he is. Captain Jenkinson would not go into a house, but pitched his tent in the wet, and went to bed dinnerless, at four o'clock, from fatigue. He is, however, well now. The work of getting guns along over a clay-road, up a mountain, in the dark, without being allowed to use lights, is no trifling undertaking.

The news from the North is very good, especially the accession of the Bavarians to the Allies ; which, from the papers I doubted, but which Colonel Gordon says his brother mentions as fact; Lord Wellington tells me, also, that Government at home believe it to be correct. The private letters from the Austrian head-quarters which have reached here, do not say much in favour of the Swedish Prince, and seem to think he has much of French humbug in him—*c'est à voir*. It is also said that he saves the Swedes, and is always in the rear, surrounded with guards and twenty sentinels. They speak well of the Russian troops, and very ill of the French lads now opposed to them. You will rejoice to hear that we are to have divine service here to-day in the square with some troops. This will not do for me, standing out bare-headed for an hour in the damp; I must remain a heathen a little longer, I fear. Mr. B——, the clergyman who has lately arrived at head-quarters, seemed to be a pleasant gentleman-like man; I have, however, only met him twice.

Two o'clock, Sunday.—Still nothing decisive from Pamplona. To-day's post brings accounts of no communication for two days, but that the garrison desert twenty a-day, and say that the place is almost in a state of mutiny against the General. To-day the weather has a little cleared up, but our artillery horses are living upon dried fern and corn—no hay, no straw, and very little coarse grass; every one in a fidget to move from hence. Unless we can so maul this French army as to have them at our mercy, and then go where we please, and stop where we please, out of our own moderation, I think we shall not have any quiet winter-quarters this year. As long as anything like an army remains, the French must be doing something to molest us, unless we molest them; and then the great nation can never submit to let our allied army quietly take up their winter-quarters in the French territory—at least I think not. Several of their conscripts have joined them, and they make a parade of drilling them within sight and hearing of our outposts,

even in marching without arms, &c. Their deserters
say they have about fifty-five thousand men ; it is supposed with their conscripts this is rather under the mark.
They are throwing up works in all directions all over the
country, and making breast-works, redoubts, &c. A
breast-work, half round a hill, appears to be turned up in
a few nights.

It must be allowed that they are industrious at least,
but the *morale* of the old soldiers is shaken very much.
It is even said that the young ones fight the best of the
two. This agrees with the story that we hear from the
North : that before the Austrian ambassador left Paris, a
letter from Marshal Soult had arrived, stating, that unless he had fifty thousand new men, who had never
met the British, he would not answer for the South of
France.

I see your papers make Endage a fortified place—it is
a great heap of ruins ; never strong, only once a fortified
village. It was nearly destroyed about the year 1790 by
the Spaniards, and has never recovered itself. In return,
Fontarabia, once really rather a strongly-fortified town,
was soon afterwards blown up by the French, and the
works are for the most part still in ruins. The town has
not suffered much, for this was only a military operation.
Of all the ruins we have made amongst us in Spain, even
including Badajoz, and Rodrigo, and Almeida, it is said
St. Sebastian is the most complete. It was a large,
handsome, and thriving town four months since : one
side of one street alone remains entire ! every street is
barricaded and blockaded ! Rubbish up to the one pair of
stairs windows, and walls half down, make it dangerous
in wind to walk anywhere. Beside this, the large
wooden balconies, hanging about by a few beams at the
two pair of stairs windows, threaten every moment to
fall, even where the walls are sound. Some repairs are
being carried on, however, in a few buildings ; at least

preparations are being made, by clearing, and the works are in progress towards a state of defence. Most officers think the destruction so great that it can scarcely ever be a good town again—that is, as a town ; as a fortified place, with much labour, it may. The French garrison were so disheartened in the castle, that they could not bo made to do more, I understand from the engineers, for it was still tenable for some time longer when it surrendered. When the town was first taken, and our men were all drunk about the place, committing every disorder, the Governor was doubting about a sortie to recover it; thinking, however, that we must have fresh men near at hand, in case of such an accident, kept sober and together, he gave up the idea. Many say, that if he had done so, such was the disorganized state of our men, that it would have succeeded. His own men were very much weakened and dispirited.

Most of the light division tents in front here have been declared unserviceable from rents, &c. The men are still returned healthy, to the astonishment of all, even the doctors, who say the consequences of this must soon appear. Wine is dearer, which is a 'good thing, and I believe our men bear this cold wet weather better than heat.

Tell John his two newspapers of the 20th have been in great request. I believe only Dr. M'Gregor had one besides Lord Wellington. They have been much read, and I have now enclosed one to Colonel Belson, which will probably be the only one in his division. It happened to contain almost all the news of the last week.

Lieutenant-colonel Elphinstone is still here. I understand that he got a queer answer from Lord Wellington when at Lisbon, which brought him here in such a hurry. When he became senior officer of the corps here, he wrote up for instructions from Lisbon, and to ask what Lord Wellington wished him to do, and where he was to

go as Chief Engineer in the Peninsula? The answer
was, that as Chief Engineer in the Peninsula he would
best know where his proper place was. Up he came by
sea in a week, in consequence.

A man to thrive here must have his wits about him,
and not see or feel difficulties, or start them, to go on
smoothly. People wonder at Lieutenant-colonel Dickson,
Portuguese service, and only (barring brevet rank) a captain of artillery in our service, commanding, as he has
done now ever since Frenada, all the artillery of both
nations, English and Portuguese. He has four seniors
out here, but all young comparatively also, who have
submitted hitherto. E—— says it should be a General's
command to be done properly, with proper officers under
him; others say the old artillery officers have rather
changed their sex, and are somewhat of old women.

Lord Wellington seems to favour the latter opinion a
little. I conclude that he finds it answer in practice.
As an instance of this, it may be stated that in the pursuit after the battle of Vittoria in the bad roads, Lord
Wellington saw a column of French making a stand as
if to halt for the night. "Now, Dickson," said he, "if
we had but some artillery up." "They are close by, my
Lord." And in ten minutes, from a hill on the right,
Lieutenant-colonel Rose's light division guns began bang
—bang—bang! and away went the French two leagues
further off. I fear if there had been a General, that we
should have had, instead of this, a report of the bad state
of the roads, and the impossibility of moving guns. In
fact, this same brigade of guns, with their mounted men,
took the last French mortar near Pamplona, and Lord
Wellington passed whilst they were putting it to rights
to proceed. They had killed two of the horses in it the
day before.

CHAPTER XV.

Fall of Pamplona—Deterioration of the Army—Duke of York's Orders—
Orders of Merit—Church Service—Capture of French Redoubts—March
of the Army—Incidents of Foreign Service—Frequency of Desertion—
Wellington and the Lawyers.

Head-quarters, Vera, Nov. 5, 1813.

My dear M——,

HERE we are still, but rather nearer a move than
when I wrote last. Between business and my chum
——, who is still here with me, I could never spare a
moment to write. Even now, at three o'clock, I have
been five or six hours at work.

The weather has improved, however, these last two
days, and now tends to frost. Anything is better than
the incessant wet we have here, up to that part of the
army at Roncesvalles; perpetual torrents from the north-
west, almost night and day, so that the roads have been
nearly impassable. At Roncesvalles they have had snow
in the valley fourteen inches deep. So close as in the
valley of Baztan, at Elisondo, it has been as rainy as
here. We have now cold, thick, November, London,
foggy mornings, until nearly eleven o'clock forenoon,
and then a clear fine day, but not yet absolute frost.
Thermometer about 36° or 37°. Meadows all swampy.
On the whole, however, the snow gentlemen have had
much the best of it, though a little uneasy as to their
supplies just now, from the fear of snow stoppages.

U

Pamplona has at last fallen, as you will have learnt by the last mail, for I believe Lord Wellington kept the packet on purpose back two days. The garrison, four thousand two hundred, it is said, are to embark to-day at Passages if possible, at least as soon as they can be got ready. Don Carlos made them submit to his terms, as we hear, *in toto*. They were even compelled to give up the Juramentudas, besides the fortification artillery. Report says fifty-seven field guns have been found there This shows us the danger we escaped by Lord Wellington's presence of mind, and the bravery of our men on the 28th of July last. Had the French got a league further, they would have found this fine field train all ready, and a reinforcement of near five thousand men in the garrison. No one can tell how this might have changed matters. We have still eighteen guns here, with the horses living on leaves, fern, and corn, but ready to play upon a new star-work the French are every day making more of, on a hill close to La Rhüne, which they still occupy near Sarre. I think these guns will surprise them a little. At present, I conclude, from general report, that we are only waiting for the rains to run down and the roads to dry a little; and if the weather of these last two days continue, every one says that we shall soon make a push on.

Our men have had a miserable time of it lately; and when uncomfortable and idle, I am sorry to say, they always make work for me. We hear of daily losses, plunder, &c., and the Spaniards perform their part well in this respect. General O'Lalor yesterday found his secretary had run away, down towards Madrid, with nearly two thousand dollars, for he trusted him with everything. Last time I dined at head-quarters Lord Wellington got into a long conversation with me for nearly two hours about the poor-laws, and the assize of bread, about the Catholic question, the state of Ireland,

&c., just as if he had nothing else upon his mind. In many points we agreed very well, particularly as to what would be necessary to be done in Ireland—if anything; but he thinks nothing should be done at all. He is still alarmed at the separation spirit which he thinks exists there, and the remains of a Jacobin feeling in the lower classes in England.

6th November.—Poor —— must pass an uncomfortable time with me here, and yet I suffer much more from having him, and he is little aware how inconvenient he is to me.

To-day, 6th November, I received three letters from England. I see there is a magnificent order of the Duke of York about parcels to the army, up to a ton weight, being forwarded to officers by the Commissariat. A few parcels would make the Commissary stare a little, when, with nearly twelve thousand mules, we can scarcely be supplied with bread and corn, and not with forage. You seem to know so little about the real state of things here in England, that I think the General, who came half way up from Lisbon to review, and then gave it up, should be employed to explain the difficulties in the duties of office. The Commissary-general says that it will take him an entire new office, which he must write home for, to keep the accounts which this new plan will require.

Our troops at Roncesvalles have been terribly off; some of the guns are buried in the snow there; some Spaniards, as well as English, have perished by the cold, and one picket was obliged to be dug out. I hear that they are now moving away, and that an attack by that pass must be abandoned; but we shall soon know for certain if this dry weather lasts. Our great men were all in the front, peeping to-day into France from the mountains which surround this hollow. Our army-post to one division, with the dragoon carrying it, was caught

two days since,—picked up, probably, as I was ; he had
got a little out of his way, somehow. I hope no letters
of importance were caught ; but it was provoking. The
French, it is said, sent back one letter to General Oswald,
opened, and said that the rest were all immaterial; however, they did not return them. The aide-de-camp of the
late governor of Pamplona has been here for the last two
days, Monsieur Pomade, a gentleman-like man ; he says
when the Vittoria army arrived at Pamplona on June
the 24th, the garrison was three thousand strong, and
the place provisioned for one hundred days complete, but
that that army, *en passant*, gave them a thousand more
effective men and five hundred sick. This caused them
to give in sooner than they otherwise should. He says
that they never expected their present fate, but that they
knew nothing, and never had any communication whatever with France or Soult ; that they sent out several
times, but never got any one in. This is more than we
can say at St. Sebastian, and does Don Carlos some
credit.

The new crosses for the victories are very handsome—
the medals so so—and the former will look strange with
a whole row of clasps, which I suppose Lord Wellington
must have now, for he has already two, up to Salamanca,
in addition to the cross. I think the thing is either too
general, or not enough so—a selection of distinguished
men, of all ranks, would be better than a general distribution to all of certain ranks and situations. It now
shows little more than that a man had a certain rank in
such a battle, and not that he performed anything more
than his neighbours. A selection might have descended
with advantage even to the privates. Of course many
grumble, and are disappointed that others have more
marks and clasps than they have ; that, however, would
always be the case.

Sunday, the 6th.—Post-day for ordinary men—to-morrow for Lord Wellington; so I proceed. For the first time these fourteen months I have to-day been to a military church; I found that the service was in-doors, and ventured, but was much reproached by my doctor. We were in the newly-repaired large public town room, which has just been made water and wind tight, as well as all the rooms round about it, for an hospital, and will soon, it is to be feared, be filled with wounded. So we go on clearing away one set of hobblers, and destroying houses on both sides, then repairing and cleaning for the new set we are about to make; and then clearing off again, and so on! This town is just now clear of all the old wounded; and the large room was washed, Dr. M'Gregor told me (though I should not have discovered it), for those soon expected. I believe he wished not a little that we had gone somewhere else to pray, and not made a dirt in his department. The service was short, plainly read, but tolerably well; the sermon homely and familiar, but good for the troops, I think, and very fair and useful to any one. Lord Wellington was there, with his attendants, a few officers, and our new staff corps.

On my return home, lo, and behold! I found —— very alert, waiting for breakfast, as he had orders to march on to the front in half an hour, and in less than that time, before breakfast was over, I saw Lord Wellington and his suite all off on horseback to the front, to peep again. It is not likely, however, anything can be done until to-morrow at soonest, and it will be stiff work if the French do their duty as they ought.

I now suspect that the packet will be kept until the result of what is about to be done is known, unless there is another ship ready. My letter must, however, go to-day; but I will try and send a line off, if possible, by the same conveyance as the despatches. As I must not go and peep, for fear of being picked up again and carried off further next time, my communications will be dull and uninteresting now. A move was becoming very necessary, for sickness had just commenced, and in the mountains on the right horses were dying fast. If we can but beat them well, we have a chance of some quiet quarter. Merely beating them back, in my opinion, will not do for us; and if the French defend their new works with as much steadiness as they have shown activity in making them, you will have a long *Gazette*. We all think that their *morale* is much shaken, and that the old soldiers will not stand now; if so, the young ones will not hold out long, though it was observed that they fought best on late occasions.

———, the last thing before he left, was at me again, about procuring his brother to be made a Captain in the Navy by Lord Wellington's interest, though it might be thought I had sufficiently put him aside the first time, as I have no humbug in these matters. It now became necessary to refuse him in direct terms, assuring him that Lord Wellington had continually said to me, " I never interfere with the Navy, when I can help it, in any way; I let them have all their rights, that I may keep all mine; and as I do not wish them to meddle with me, I never meddle with them." I should never have thought of asking Lord Wellington for anything now except upon public grounds, such as repaying the Bayonne banker, &c., as it is not my doctrine that because a man has done you one favour you are, therefore, to ask him to do you another.

Twelve o'clock.—Six more guns are now rumbling by through this place to go up the pass. B———'s have been off some time; six more will, I hear, be soon up, and these eighteen are all to be collected to play upon the French new work, where they had yesterday got about twelve together. It is feared that we must begin from the ground at too great a distance, thirteen hundred yards, but I hope closer quarters will be come to soon, for in my opinion the French succeed best at cannonading and sharp-shooting, and we at the hand-to-hand work.

Two o'clock.—The mail is said to go as usual, so I must close directly, but I have no doubt the packet will be kept, as every one says publicly that the attack is to take place to-morrow morning. General Cole has just told me to go up to the top of La Rhüne, where I must be safe, and must see everything. I shall not go, however, unless I find all the quiet steady ones do the same, for though you may see all, and if knowing, may be down again in time, yet mistakes may be made by the unknowing, and I shall remain quietly here.

Head-Quarters, Vera, November 9th, 1813.—I have this moment received your packet of the 26th ult., with all the kind enclosures from aunts, cousins, &c. The attack never took place on Monday the 8th, as I told you in my last; the roads, from the wet, being so bad that I believe the army could not be collected in time. To-morrow, however, is now said to be the day, as the two last days have continued fine and mild, the wind south, and the thermometer up at 52° again. It now looks like rain, but is fine, and holds up as yet, with a wind south and south-west; whilst all the rain came with a cold north-west wind. It will not do, therefore, to make use of English weather-wisdom here.

Your English mail is thought nothing of. A *Gazette* of the 25th had got here first, and forestalled it; and we have to-day much greater news from the French side, which is believed by every one here, and by the French army as we are told; namely, that Bonaparte is beaten back to the Rhine, with the loss of three divisions cut off by blowing up a bridge too soon, &c.; one General taken, and one drowned, &c. This puts our party in spirits for to-morrow, and will, I hope, damp the French if believed by them, as the deserters report it to be.

The Portuguese are most anxious to enter France, and are in high spirits; the grave ones, however, expect a great number of broken heads, unless the French turn tail shamefully. You ask me about Baron de Trengue-léon, and whether I thought of him whilst I was a prisoner. I certainly did at Mont de Marsan, and found that I was within thirty miles of him; and an emigrant there advised me to apply to go over to see him, but I thought it might do us both harm, and, therefore, never said a word upon the subject to any one. Major D——— had serious thoughts of going as my servant with the baggage to look about; but it would have been a dangerous experiment.

The 10*th November.*—I dined with Lord Wellington last night, and staid there till near ten. He was all gaiety and spirits; and only said on leaving the room, " Remember! at four in the morning." Monsieur Pomade, the aide-de-camp to the governor of Pamplona, was there, and I sat next to him and had some conversation with him. He had been told that operations were going on, and that that was the reason he could not be sent in yet to the French. To show what he expected to be the result, he told me (when I begged him to tell the banker at Bayonne that all his letters had been sent safely) that except from necessity and orders he should avoid Bayonne, as he was not ready yet to be shut up again in another town.

To-day every one was in motion here two hours before daylight; and part of the cavalry passed through here at five o'clock. I got up, and had all packed ready by daylight, and found that every one was gone to see the glorious attack—even the doctors and the two parsons: so I determined to venture up to the top of La Rhüne in the way General Cole recommended. The day was beautiful. I passed the camp of the latter in my way up, and should have heard there of any check. I then pursued my way, and staid on the top from about eight until two, hearing and seeing fire and smoke all the way along the hills from St. Jean de Luz to near St. Jean Pied de Port. The whole was visible at once; and I could see the men even with the naked eye, by the glitter of their arms, for a considerable way. The French redoubts crowned the tops of all their positions with deep ditches; and they had full shelter in woods and houses; but our men slowly beat them on and on, from place to place, forcing their way until all the right of the position seemed ours. Two redoubts on the hill below me I saw abandoned shamefully, when our men got round them. A large star fort on the top took more time. The men from the others tried to make for it, but failed; though mostly got off on our side. Those in the fort I left surrounded by our men, who ran up in four or five directions to within about fifty yards or less, firing as they ran; and then bobbed all down for shelter until all were ready. They lay in this way nearly an hour. When satisfied that the men shut up must be prisoners (as I hear they were) I returned home.

On the ridge of hills all along the right, the rows of huts set on fire added not a little to the scene. By whom they were burnt I know not. The cannon roared away in the mountains. On the hill, amongst others, I met Lord E. Somerset, the Cavalry General, gone up to look out, with Colonel Vivian and Mr. Heaphy. He was there before me, when the fighting was nearer, and declares that he saw one English soldier bayonet two French officers who attacked him when advanced from the others—first one and then the other. I hope that our loss has not been severe, considering what the position was.

I believe we were to have moved to Sarré; but General Giron has taken seventy houses there for his staff; and the rest are full of wounded. From what I have heard, our officers think themselves well out of the scrape. The left of our army towards St. Jean de Luz was refused;—that is, the French were not pressed there much, in hopes of forming the right so rapidly as to cut off a good lot on the left. That will not probably be the case, but that they must move off to-night to a new position, and not having such another line of works, the French must stand to-morrow if attacked openly on the hills, or run for it. I have seen no one yet, so only give you my own views, which may be probably very wide of the *Gazette*. It was a terrible fag for my new mare, and at top cool, and no room to walk about: I have in consequence a new fidget, in her refusing her food. The troops will devour all the forage in front, and I do not know how we shall get on at all. Adieu.

Head-Quarters, St. Fé, November 12th, 1813.—At seven, yesterday morning, we received orders to march; all the baggage to assemble at Sarré, and wait there for orders. We did so; and on our way crossed the first French redoubts and positions, and began to see our wounded and the stripped dead lying about as usual. So starved and weak were many of the animals, and so clayey and deep the roads, that the scene had almost the appearance of a retreat, except that we passed all the wounded and prisoners going to the rear, instead of marching with them. The Spanish oxen were so starved, and thin, and weak, that during the first league I counted probably about eleven lying down to die, whilst every now and then a sergeant with his pike, or a soldier gave them a stab, half out of humanity, and half to see the effect, and from a sort of love of mischief. Then there were ten or fifteen poor women belonging to the baggage of the division lamenting over their dying donkeys and mules, whilst others were brutally beating some to death, because they would not go farther. In every direction baggage was falling off, and the whole formed

a glorious scene of confusion. Near Sarré I was caught
in a violent storm, but got to a house for shelter before
I was wet, and there stood in the doorway of a deserted
house, with three dead bodies on the ground close by
me ; one certainly that of an officer, from his clean
skin, neatly-shaven beard and whiskers, and from every
remnant of his dress having been worth stealing. The
other two were Spaniards.

The Spaniards behaved tolerably in the field, but not
like the fourth and the light division. In plundering
and mischief, however, they excelled them. I found
them, on passing, breaking and plundering one of the
best houses in Sarré. Our own people are grown
expert hands at this, and Lord Wellington threatens
hanging, and, I believe, has hung a few, but in vain.
The people in general have fled, and the Spaniards come
in to carry off pots, pans, dishes, chairs, tables, &c., to
refurnish their own houses. At Sarré, I found the civil
departments were to stop there, and the military to come
on to this place. My baggage had gone by in part
before I knew this ; and besides that, nowhere could a
house be found by me. The Spaniards were in possession, and firing, plunder, and confusion, were all around ;
I determined, therefore, to come on here, and take my
chance.

You will advise me to keep well in the rear for safety;
but the most knowing ones (in which opinion I agree)
consider the rear as the most unsafe place of any. All
the vagabonds, plunderers, and rascals—followers of the
army—stick to the rear, and look about to do mischief
as soon as all the troops are passed. Besides which, it
is not clear here that the peasants, who all fly, may not
return, and knock a few on the head, though at present
they seem terrified and excessively alarmed. I found no
quarters for me here ; but at a little village close by,
where there were only the Commissary-general and a

few of his department, I took possession of a deserted house, which had been ransacked, and cleaned it out a little in one place. Finding abundance of food left for my horses for two or three nights, I thought myself well off, though I was somewhat alarmed at having possession of the last inhabited house on that road, lest any straggling attack should be made, or the owners should come back in the night. There was, however, no alternative. All the immediately useful part of my baggage was behind, and never arrived at all, having been turned out of the road by a Spanish division. Unluckily my neighbours were nearly in the same state. Sir Robert Kennedy had barely enough for his own eating, and went to bed leaving his servants to do the best they could.

H—— had nothing, his baggage not having arrived. Mr. H——n had one half-loaf, and that served us all. Mr. M——, the storekeeper, had got some mutton for Lord Wellington to-day, and he spared us a little bit each; so I got one mutton chop, which was very lucky.

Between four and five, Henry went to inquire about marching, and, finding no orders, we remained quiet. About seven or eight, he found my two stray mules, and I got a loaf of bread and some potted butter out of my stock, and made my contribution to the party, which was very acceptable. I have since been down to headquarters to know what is going on; but can learn nothing except that we are ready now to cross the Nive, and are prepared for that step; particulars I can hear none, for only the clergyman, the doctors, and a straggling civilian, with the provost guard, are to be seen.

I returned, therefore, to my deserted, desolate home. In my way I found one of the owners of a house here who had been shot through the thigh by a Portuguese; I got him to an hospital to be dressed, in the church, where French, English, and all were lying to wait their turn, with now and then a dead man. As soon as they are dressed, they are packed off to the rear on mules, &c. So we go on!

The famous French bulletin has now been seen. Some say Bonaparte is at Paris, and some think that he will come here. Others have a notion that the people beyond Bayonne are ready to join us, if we proceed on. I fear, however, the runaways will not encourage this much with their exaggerated stories of our conduct in their villages. To-day is a very fine day again, and will, I hope, assist our operations much. It is said that when our officers went up to the men in the star fort, to call upon them to surrender, the Colonel commanding said, like the governor of Pamplona, " Yes, on the terms of parole, not to serve for a year and a day." " No, no," says the Englishman; "*prisonnier.*" " *Eh bien, donc je ne me rends pas,*" says the Frenchman. " But you must and shall, or you will all be murdered," says the Englishman, and then turned away. Upon which the Colonel very sulkily returned and consented; and when his soldiers began to rejoice, and to quiz the *ré papé,* and say, dancing about, that it was time it should all end, he was most indignantly sulky, and has remained so ever since, complaining of being sent off to England as a prisoner.

I have now under my window a characteristic scene. A short Portuguese lad, bloated out with ration beef, with an old French helmet on, a great red grenadier's feather, and an old French uniform jacket and pantaloons, with a dragoon broadsword, cutting down cabbages and apples in the garden for his brother Portuguese, who has his apron ready to receive them, whilst a dirty, brown, snuff-coloured Spaniard is looking about on the other side with an old French musket trying to shoot something eatable.

The mixture of the silence of a deserted village with the occasional riotous noise of muleteers and stragglers,

Portuguese and Spaniards, as well as a few swearing English, is striking ; but to a person not actively engaged in what is going on, by which all minor considerations vanish in the dangers and anxiety of the scene, there is a sameness of misery and starvation, of wounds and of death, which, when the novelty of the scene is over, becomes very unpleasant, especially without any rational companion to talk to on what is passing. This appears to be the house of a curé, for there are the remains of many comforts, and of some books, chiefly religious, some crosses, &c.

I just now met a man who spoke English tolerably, and French well, but would address me in Spanish, to say the people were plundering all the flour at the only mill in the place which was at work, and he requested a guard and wanted the Commandant. I luckily noticed by his feather the Superintendent of the provost guard entering a house opposite, and procured him a guard directly. So that one can be of some use without meddling much.

I have just now had a Spaniard at my door to inquire how he could get back safe to Spain, as he had wandered here alone, and dared not return, and had nothing to eat. I have sent him off with a small bit of bread and a shilling, and advised him to go and remain near the provost guard, and keep with the first escort of prisoners which sets out for Spain.

Nearly all the houses about me are empty, and I do not much like my situation, but it is just now like that of a wife—for better, for worse ; so I must submit. I do not think we have a hundred men within three miles, and not one soldier within half a mile, only commissaries and young doctors, and a stray shot is fired every three or four minutes. My own muleteers I have just stopped.

November 13*th.*—Here I am still in my solitary abode. It has rained all night, and the roads are running water-

courses, which will, it is to be feared, impede our progress.
All, it is said, however, is going on well. I have not
seen a creature, or been out; only sent to the Commissary-
general, my neighbour, to ascertain whether we are not
to march, lest I should be left behind here. Several of
the elderly owners of houses have returned, but mine has
not. Lord Wellington has ordered what forage can be
regularly used, and collected, to be paid for punctually,
and I understand has determined to send back at least a
part of the Spaniards, on account of their abominable
conduct, Longa's people in particular. I am not surprised
at it, but it spoils all our plans. We were admitted
quietly into St. Jean de Luz, and the inhabitants
remained there. The mayor offered to exert himself to
get what he could collected, to supply the troops
regularly; and Sir John Hope flogged the two first men
he caught taking some wine—this instantly; so I hope
that town will be preserved.

We can never do well, if we go on driving all the
population before us. The few old people left here, and
who are coming in, speak only Basconee and a little
Gascon, and no French. There is no making them
understand anything.

To-day would have been dreadful in the mountains, so
we have at least that reflection to comfort ourselves with.
I send enclosed Lord Wellington's letter to me and
Count Gazan's. Pray keep the former, as I shall always
value it.

4 *o'clock, afternoon, November* 13*th.*—It has been
raining so incessantly ever since morning, that I have
not stirred from my hole, and have, therefore, seen no
one. I understand that all the grandees were to have
gone to the front at five this morning, but from the
state of the weather, they have all stopped at home—
not for the fear of a wetting themselves, but most likely
from the impossibility of getting through the country,

and across rivers, when in such a state. It is only wonderful how our men got on, as they did up the hills on the 12th. It was as much as I could do with my horse singly on a slippery clay, either so hard that a horse could not stand on it, or so deep that he was up to his knees, between the hard places. We are now, however, nearly out of the Pyrenees, and I hope the roads will mend, but from what I saw of the high road, this is doubtful.

November 14th.—Still here at St. Fé, so the place is called in an excellent old French map. Still rain, and nothing new, except that the French have been well frightened, and mean, we are told, to quit the new position they have taken, with their left on Bayonne, as soon as it is attacked; that is, as soon I conclude as the roads will permit us to move. The communications here are almost as bad as in Spain, and from hence to St. Jean de Luz almost impassable. The Marquis of Worcester, I have just heard, goes to-day in an hour.

Head-Quarters, St. Jean de Luz, November 24th, 1813. —Having a little leisure, I begin my weekly journal. The weather continues beautiful, and I generally get my hour's walk, and my hour's ride daily. A brig from Dartmouth sold off an immense stock of good English moulds yesterday, in the morning, at 2*s.* 6*d.* a pound, by order from head-quarters, and about five tons of potatoes, besides quantities of porter, ale, beef, cheese, &c. The scramble of officers on board to see and buy would have astonished you not a little. We have also some good white wine.

Since our move from the mountains our men are all behaving much better: they were becoming very bad; and desertion, even from the English to the French, was frequent. The temptation of the old gentleman in the high mountains was too much for the men. It has now almost ceased. I hope, therefore, when we are a little quiet, and my arrears are cleared off, that I shall have much less to do. The reports here now are that Bonaparte's aide-de-camp is at Bayonne, and that he himself is expected. If so we may probably have some work to do here again, unless he has been obliged merely to show himself here to convince his army that he is still alive and well.

We had a little affair yesterday. Some of the light division were ordered to drive in the French pickets in one place where they were too forward, and our men being too zealous, pushed too far. In trying to prevent this, a fine officer of the 43rd was taken, and a lieutenant badly wounded, and some men lost. The only annoyance I suffer at present in my quarters arises from the multiplicity of inhabitants, namely, three old women, seven children, three dogs, two cats, and a fair allowance of fleas, whom this late fine weather has revived. We have lately had an arrival at Passages of a hundred and fifty oxen from Ireland for the army, and are promised the same supply weekly. This will do something ; but our consumption is, I believe, about a thousand a week. Our forage in this nook of France is as bare as in the neighbouring parts of Spain ; every field is eaten close down, and all straw of corn and maize consumed. I sent twelve miles for straw yesterday, and the mules have returned to-day empty. I mean now to try bruised furze, to mix with their Indian corn, so as to hold out until some more hay shall reach us from England.

November 25th.—I have just heard that about two thousand of the inhabitants returned here last night, but Soult would not suffer them to carry much with them.

November 26th.—There was no time for more yesterday, and to-day I have nothing to add. I have still not heard anything from you later than the 3rd, but we have papers here to the 13th. I cannot understand how this has occurred. Through France we have news still later, and have heard of the surrender of Davoust's corps at Hamburg, on terms of not serving for a year and a day. It is to be hoped that the terms may be kept. I had a droll *malheur* again to-day. Riding my pony into the sea, into about six inches water, to wash his legs, a wave came, the sand gave way, and he sunk up to his middle, so that my legs were up to the calf in sand. I jumped off, and went over his head to run out, fearing that he could not rise. We thus both got safely out. The poor pony much more frightened than I was.

I conclude that everything goes on well, for Lord Wellington and his gentlemen were out to day with the hounds. He told me that I kept him up reading Courts-martial until twelve o'clock at night or one in the morning ; and this every night. I hope, however, that this will not last long. The Prince of Orange has got a complaint in his eyes, but I believe only a cold, and he seems better. Nearly all our great men except Lord Wellington have been ill.

Send me some law news, and good, for Lord Wellington expects me to tell him who all the new judges are to be, &c., and is very fond of discussing legal subjects. At first I was generally right in my speculations : but I have now no means of knowing how things are going on unless you keep up my credit ; it must not be, however, by loose reports.

I have a poor young Commissary, B——, under charges, who has, I think, been very ill used by a Spanish alcalde. I fought his battle with Lord Wellington to-day to get him released from arrest. He is very well spoken of, and said to support his two sisters. Can he be a brother of the Miss B——'s whom you know ? I detected the Spanish General F—— in a little bit of a fib on this subject. His excuse for not answering my letter for eight days was, that it had been delayed in the post. I complained, and his receipt for the letter was produced the day after it was sent—this on the back of the cover.

Sunday, November 29th.—Still no news, and no accounts from England. We are all anxiety. I have just returned from church at the drum-head, on the sands by the sea. Two brigades of guards present in their best, and white trousers, &c., and Lord Wellington and his staff here. It was rather cold work. The weather is beginning to change again, I fear, for rain, just as the roads were becoming passable. You have no conception how soon fifteen thousand sharp-footed heavy-laden mules in rain, cut up a road in this country, even when at first tolerably good. We have been amused with Cobbett's attributing all Bonaparte's misfortunes to his being grafted into the old stock. If he can now manage well he may, I think, still get his little king Pepin graft to thrive in France, and beat Mr. Knight and our gardeners. The true cause of all is, however, that the *morale* of the people of Europe is changed. It was France, army and people, against mere armies and bad governments, whilst all the people in Europe were indifferent at the least. This is now reversed; and it is now a mere French army against every people and army; and Frenchmen at least quite indifferent.

CHAPTER XVI.

News from France—Lord Fitzroy Somerset—Departure of the Prince of Orange—Exchange of Prisoners—Proximity of the two Armies—Wellington's Cooks—Warlike Movements—French Attack—The Guards—Deserters—More Fighting.

Head-quarters, St. Jean de Luz,
December 2, 1813.

My dear M——,

At last we have got a mail from England. Your papers give us little public news, that is, news to us, for you have no late accounts from the Allies, and French papers we always get sooner this way. Thus we have long known of Bonaparte's arrival at Paris, which you only just now communicate to us. Lord Wellington has, I understand, news of a rising in Holland; and this has been confirmed by our reports through the French, who, in conversation with Dashwood yesterday, when he went in with a flag-of-truce, and a parcel of women, seemed to admit it. We had had this as a report before the arrival of the packet, and Major Dashwood therefore tried to pump them on the subject. We have also had a report here that Admiral Young had taken the Texel fleet; but as no news of this sort has reached us from you, we fear from dates that this must be all false.

This is only a Passages report from some straggling ships, not French news. The deserters who come in also from Bayonne, and the returned inhabitants, all state that the Italian regiments here have been removed to the rear; at least all Italian officers have given up their lodgings and and have packed up. I think now that they will scarcely rely much upon the Dutch either, and there were some fine men and several good officers of that nation here. I told you that the only two officers who were disinterested, and most uniformly civil to us whilst we were prisoners, were two Dutchmen of the 130th regiment.

The Burgundy side of France (Switzerland being with us) is certainly as unguarded as this frontier, except by a naturally strong country in places. Strasburg, almost the only strong place except our old friends Huningen and Kehl, is far removed, and the latter may probably be left on one side, but for all this the French Italian army must be well disposed of first.

If Lord Charles Somerset deserves promotion as well as our Military Secretary here, the grumbling you mention against his appointment must be unfounded. The latter gets through a great amount of business with little assistance, and always quite in public, almost in a common coffee or lounging room, in the midst of talking, noise, joking, and confusion. The Prince of Orange left us yesterday. As he used to be one of the above loungers, this put me in mind of him. He has had a complaint in his eyes, and could not embark before yesterday, when he did so with a fair wind. His arrival, however, and all news about him will precede this. The French, yesterday, when told that he was going off for England, said, " Oh they supposed that it was in consequence of what had happened in Holland." In short, the French seem still (as when I was in France and now even more so) willing to listen to all bad news against Bonaparte, and do not make the least of it at all. All exchange of officers here has now, I fear, at last been broken off, and angry letters have passed. How fortunate I was ! I will send in your French Captain Le Fevre's letter concerning his exchange, if an opportunity should offer soon, and it is permitted.

Friday, December 3rd.—I find Lord Wellington's news about a Dutch insurrection came to him by a telegraphic note from Mr. Croker, dated the 20th ult. This is a grand point. Next for Italy, and then we shall do ; and after twenty-three years of murder, we have a reasonable chance of being able to give the military word when things go wrong,—" As you were."

The Prince of Orange, from all appearances here, where the sea has been tremendous, must have had a most famous passage ; but I should think a quick one, as the wind has been fair. We have a notion that he has been chased by four French frigates which have escaped from some French port. I yesterday gave a grand dinner at the French café here ; the dinner was abundant, and from the paucity of materials the variety was surprising. Ten dishes for the first course, two removes for the soups ; ten for the second course, rotis and sweets together ; ten for dessert ; and we were ten in company, and two excuses—dinner for twelve. Some dishes were admirable, particularly all the patisseries. The champaign excellent ; Madeira and sherry very fair ; port and claret very moderate. I am now paying the bill, and the *tout ensemble* is forty dollars.

I spoke to Lord Wellington this morning about the French Captain's letter you sent to me. He laughed and said, " Yes, when you can, you may send it ; but the whole matter is now at an end, and your companions are all sent to the rear, as Bonaparte has refused to let the exchanges take place, unless three French go for one British, one Spaniard, and one Portuguese. The old squabble in Mackenzie's negotiation, and though very flattering to us as English, very unpleasant to our poor prisoners."

We have a most tremendous sea here—now worse than ever. The waves at high-water break every time almost over an old wall about twenty feet high on the beach, and come over the stone walk; they roar most furiously, and are beyond anything I have seen. A Paymaster here declares that he saw a brig go down, and disappear instantly, about nine or ten o'clock yesterday, near Andaye. We shall be long, I fear, before we hear again from you in England. I do not think that any ships will venture near us now, certainly not to Passages or here.

Post-day, Sunday, 5th December.—The storms have now subsided, and the sea has become calmer; but the mischief already known has been considerable. The vessel which I mentioned was seen to sink got at last into the Bidassoa; but four transports, it is said, have been lost in Passages harbour, together with several lives. One vessel drove into a house and knocked it down; most of the shipping there is damaged, and many of the boats have been crushed between them. An English merchant-vessel, it is reported, also went down at the entrance of Bayonne. The air is now colder, almost frosty, with a dry wind; the mountains all covered with snow; I only hope this may last. No more news from you, and we are here in a very odd state—I mean that our armies are. A few years back the British were uneasy, in Spain, when a French army patrolled within thirty miles of them. Now we have all got quietly into quarters—are nearly all housed; and three-fourths of us go to sleep tranquilly every night, while our front is within sixty yards of the French.

Colonel S——— tells me that he went to breakfast with Colonel H———, the Assistant Adjutant-general of the sixth division, at Ustaritz, and there they were in a house with their breakfast-table within about fifty yards of the French sentry, and within about two hundred of the whole French picket, who, by one volley, might have broken all their cups and saucers, if not their heads.

The other day a Portuguese brigade had a field-day close
to the river in the meadows, and all the French came
down to look at them, and I have no doubt, from the
general report, to admire and approve ; whilst, on the
other hand, in the meadows on the French side, the
French conscripts are brought down to be drilled ; sometimes five or six squads are seen at once, and any of the
sergeants might be knocked on the head all the time by
our sentries ; but this is now all well understood, and we
thus quietly bully or bravado each other.

Another party of inhabitants have come in here—
women and children ; the men Soult detains.   We shall
thus add to our female stock, and to the seven hundred
Portuguese women and four hundred Spanish, who are
already in this place and the environs as suttlers, *vivan-
deras*, washerwomen, &c.   In short, here we are in quiet
winter-quarters, for a time at least, with head-quarters
within seven miles of the French, and yet we are all so at
our ease, even in France, that the baggage animals of
head-quarters are gone now beyond Tolosa, forty miles
and more to the rear, for straw to feed the horses.   Lord
Wellington told me yesterday there was no forage left
here ; and I suppose so large an army never staid so long
in these mountains.   But yet, if a spring campaign comes,
no doubt we shall, somehow or other, find all our animals
forthcoming, and in a state for service.

The Irish oxen sent out for the Commissariat have
proved very good, excellent in comparison, and are served
out as a *bonne bouche*—a pound or two with five or six
of the country beef.   In short, we have occasionally, of
late, had the London alderman's cry of more fat.   Without joking, Lord Wellington's table is now very good in
every respect ; and I think his aides-de-camp will be ill
with excess, who have this daily fare (unless there is a
move), especially if the roads remain too bad for exercise.

Lord Wellington has now three cooks, and an English and Spanish chief share the command, and, by dividing the days, vie with each other.

More rain, more rain! I am sorry to say. I have just seen Lord Wellington; he is much annoyed. A poor Commissary under charges has fallen sick. I reported that he was at Passages, too ill to move to be tried, and that I have two certificates of medical men of the necessity of his going to England. Lord Wellington told me to tell the Adjutant-general not to let him get away; and that if he remained too ill to move, we must try him at Passages. It was for violent conduct to another Commissary.

Head-Quarters, St. Jean de Luz, December 8th, 1813. —A packet is just arrived, and I have letters from you of the 22nd ult. and papers to the same date. Letters and papers are, however, here by the same vessel to the 25th. A most remarkable and astonishing paper!

I hope this fine weather will give us some hay from England, for I have now nothing for forage but furze and bran by way of substitute.

By this packet came a long letter from ——; they want me to ask for Captain ——'s promotion. It is my determination not to ask favours, even if I supposed it would be of any use. One promising young officer has, I trust, been saved by me, by inducing him to make, and another to accept, an apology, and Lord Wellington to agree to this. He would, otherwise, most probably on trial have been broken. My letter ordering the Court to meet was taken by the French. This gave time, and opened a long correspondence, which has given me much trouble; this, however, I shall not regret, if it ends well. I must now go and prepare charges against a German doctor for to-morrow, and against two Portuguese for a highway robbery. So adieu.

Thursday, 9th.—All peaceable business has ceased;

and here I am in an enemy's town quite at ease. All
the troops advanced about four this morning, and we
have here only a provost guard of about forty men, a few
straggling guards, and the muleteers, servants and civilians. The French dared not to have remained so in any
town in Spain, much less in Portugal.

I went out to my morning's walk on the beach. I
had it to myself nearly, and heard a sharp firing of
both guns, and particularly musketry, sounding quite
close to me. Our present object is, I believe, merely to
move up our right, for we are much pinched in our
present position. We are now with our right at Itoasso,
Espellette, and Cambo, on the Nive; our centre at
Ustaritz and St. Fé; and our left by Bidart, Ahetze, and
Arbonne, all on the Spanish or south side of the Nive.
Our object now is to move up the right, nearly or quite
to the Adour, most probably, only making a feint at
Biaritz and Anglet, near Bayonne, on the left, unless
good fortune puts more in our power. We shall then be
more at ease, cover more ground, and open a little
country on the right for our cavalry to get quarters and
accommodation, at least that part which is still with us
in front. This, it is believed, is all that is intended at
present.

Should the report of the French mayor here prove
correct, or the deputy mayor rather, for the chief is off,
namely, that there is an insurrection at Bordeaux, and
that the Allies are within fifty leagues of Paris, it may
soon be *autre chose ;* but at present we are only, as I hear,
taking elbow-room for winter-quarters, and putting ourselves in a position to start when advisable. We shall
also see how the French are disposed to fight, and judge
a little what forces are gone to the rear. How angry it
made me to observe the nonsensical reports in England
of our being not only in Bayonne, but in Bordeaux, and
this given out formally at the playhouse! To exaggerate

just now is so unnecessary, so unreasonable, and so injurious to those who do so much!

Three o'clock.—The firing has continued more or less the whole day, but has now become more distant, and the great guns near Bayonne are heard occasionally. As yet, however, no news, except from a wounded guards-man, just come in, shot in the hand, who says that the Guards are advancing and the French retreating,—I conclude into their lines opposite Bayonne. A fleet of twelve sail, or perhaps fifteen, in sight. Hurrah! for hay and money, we all say! The army is only paid up to May, and the staff to April. It rained much in the night, which was against our movements, but has nearly held up since, though it has just dropped all day.

Friday, the 10th.—Lord Wellington did not return last night, nor the Adjutant-general and grandees. I hear but little except that we crossed the Nive well on the right, but did not make much progress in the course of the day. On our left we did rather more than I expected, and, it is said, pushed on to within a mile of Bayonne, with some loss; so we rested last night, and we have had constant showers, very heavy at times, ever since. This is very much against our arrangements.

Four o'clock.—Here I have remained quiet all day, but in a fidget, for from eleven o'clock there has been continual firing in our front; and, as might be expected, though within six or seven miles of us, we have had all sorts of reports, some rather alarming—to me at least, for I believe Lord Wellington is on the other side of the Nive, with our right, and I have not the same confidence in any one else, especially as only a part of our army is on this side the river. The communication is trouble-some, and the French have evidently made a push here to-day in force, whilst our brigades are all separated. The Guards came back here last night to their positions and quarters, and the 5th division to Bidart and its environs. Some Caçadores were surprised, and some were made prisoners, and the French showed themselves in force in this line, and have pushed us back to our old ground before the troops could be collected again.

At two o'clock the firing was so loud, and so near in appearance, that I began to look to my baggage, especially as an order came from the Guards here to turn out again and advance. I have, however, just seen the Commissary-general, Sir R. Kennedy, and he says there is no danger, for he left the French checked by our works on our old position, and met four brigades on the road advancing to assist. He was, however, a little surprised himself at the end of his ride, to see what was going on, for a fire suddenly began across the road where he was looking, near our cavalry, and when he turned about, our guns began across the other way, and he was obliged to get away. One never can be quite secure in these attacks.

I am told that a note was taken from the French General Gautier to the Duke of Dalmatia, which was sent to tell him that a deserter had come in from us at two o'clock, and told him of the intended attack yesterday, and complaining much of desertion on his side. It is very provoking, that our men should betray us in this manner; but it seems to have been of no consequence.

St. Jean de Luz, Head-Quarters, December 11th, 1813. —From report to-day, there were some slight grounds for my uneasiness yesterday. The French made a bold push with nearly four divisions on the high road. We had only one division, or only part of one, at hand ready. Some Portuguese in advance were surprised, and lost prisoners and baggage. The French regained all that they had lost the day before. At about two o'clock they made a push at our position. A Portuguese brigade suffered very much, and it is said dispersed. An English brigade also is reported to have been unlike the rest of

late : that is all I can say. Lord Wellington had heard
the firing and received intelligence of the attack; he
came across the river Nive instantly, and halted the
sixth division on this side, which was going over by
former orders to act on the other, on the right. The
fourth was ordered up to support the light division.
Wellington himself was foremost in trying to rally the
Portuguese. Both he and his staff were much exposed,
and had not often, I hear, been in a warmer fire.

The French were induced to attack our redoubts and
position by their successes and numbers. Our reinforcements came up; they were repulsed, driven back with
loss, and the ground which we had already gained and
lost once, was nearly all in our possession again last
night, at the close of day. They talk of a thousand
wounded, probably more, on our part. We have taken
some prisoners, and many wounded French; at one time,
however, a whole regiment of Portuguese, and some
English also, were nearly being made prisoners. The
Guards, or as they are called here, "the gentlemen's
sons," were too late, as they had so far to march. They
will never learn their trade of being killed properly, if
they are thus nursed up in the rear. Their great
grievance at present is the order about horses and mules,
limiting the numbers to the old regulations, on account
of forage, and allowing subaltern officers only their one
animal, so that if they ride, they cannot carry anything.
If they carry baggage, they must walk; and then when
they come into their quarters, and their real duty
towards the men commences, they are unfit for anything.
The regulation is therefore severe, and most think that it
is unnecessarily so.

On the other hand, the present establishment of the
Guards is absolutely ridiculous. Every subaltern officer
has his two or three horses, and his three or four mules,
as much as any staff-officer ought to have. He carries

his bed out to the guard-house, or picket, and has his
canteen fit to give a dinner and every luxury, whereas
one set of canteens per company would, in my opinion,
be a liberal allowance. Their General has given them
six weeks to comply with this order, but somehow or
other they will contrive, probably, to evade it, or they
will be the most miserable animals in existence. Whilst
they were in camp, they left one officer with the men in
camp, and the rest got into houses, whilst in many
instances at that time even the Generals in other divisions commanding brigades, were out under canvas (then
in the mountains), or at most in huts. Both men and
officers are only fit for our old style of expedition,—a
landing, a short march, and a good fight, and then a
lounge home again. The men were yesterday all sore-
footed with their march, but at church last Sunday, in
their white linen pantaloons, they looked in high order ;
and the appearance of the men, the care of their dress,
their discipline and general good conduct, is admirable,
when in quiet quarters here.

I met young ——, an ensign in the Guards, yesterday,
a son of Lord ——. He is a very gentleman-like
stripling of nineteen, talks of just remembering Sir John
Moore's death, as the beginning of his political knowledge, and something about General Castanos, and the
first Spanish publication of Cevallos, but is quite in a
wilderness when you talk of the old state of Europe
before the French Revolution. He now principally talks
of the table, and who gives best wines and dinners, and
found fault with General ——'s, which I must say
appeared to me most luxurious, and reminded me of fine
dinners in London.

Ten o'clock.—Hurrah! hurrah! I have just been
called out to see three small battalions of deserters pass
by with drums beating, and colours flying, with their
arms and everything in the highest condition, and

clothing nearly new. Two battalions of the regiment De Nassau, and one of the regiment De Frankfort, in the whole twelve hundred men. This is a grand consequence of our push, and must alarm the French not a little. I should not be surprised now if we advance soon, whatever might have been our former plans. Lord Wellington was out again in the front this morning, up at three and out in the dark. He returns to dinner to-day, and has invited the German Colonels and the Majors, six of them, to dinner, to which he means to return. He has also desired that they may now have their breakfasts, the whole remain in quarters here for the night, and proceed to-morrow for Passages, I presume, though it is several miles off, as the Spaniards occupy all the places between, except Irun, which is voted unwholesome and feverish. Irun will scarcely give a quarter to an English officer, and not to our detachments coming up to join, who have to march through here always; so I conclude that they would not do more for the Germans who have once served with the French. The only drawback to these good tidings is the thought of the poor wounded, crawling in, on foot, or on cars, and on mules, crying with the pain of the motion. It is now quite fine, and I must take my promenade by the sea; so, for the present, adieu.

Later, the 11*th.*—Major D—— has found a friend in the Colonel of the regiment which came over, and who has told him how it happened and was managed. An officer from the North had found the way to him (the Colonel) all through France, with an order from his real sovereign to go over to us, and come and join him. He communicated his plan to no one but the Major (one Major). They waited their opportunity, and when it arose last night, he called the officers together, told them his order and his resolution, and proposed it to them, but said he should force no one; it must be voluntary. All agreed—and the men were too happy to join in the plan. One officer was sent to give us notice and clear the way, and to prevent any resistance or confusion. He was also to make terms that they were not to be compelled to serve, &c. The officer, however, did not like going back, and before any message was sent, over they all came. On their arrival here to-day, just out of the town, they halted, and put on their best clothes to pass through in parade order, and very well they looked I assure you. They say that there are many Spanish, and two good regiments of cavalry who would probably come over if a pardon were held out to them, and that there are a number of Dutch all ready to do the same thing, but they are principally officers, and are not in a body. They are tumultuous and troublesome, and only wait the proper occasion.

The Colonel, K——, has written to Marshal Soult, telling him why he came over ; that he was ordered so to do, and after reminding him that so long as they were French, and he with the French, he had done his duty. In return, he requests (rather an impudent request) that the women and the baggage, or at least the baggage soldiers and servants, may be allowed to join the regiments. He also asks that his band, which he says was excellent, as it was his hobby-horse, and which was of course left behind, may be allowed to join the rest. Of this, however, he has no hopes, for his band was always a subject of considerable jealousy to the French before he left them, and he is sure they will keep it now for themselves.

I also hear that our staff officers were obliged to exert themselves very much in consequence of the dispersion of the Portuguese, and the reluctance of some of our own forces. Colonel Delancey took one colour, and rode on before the regiments to carry them on. General Hope was much exposed, and got two blows ; one on the shin, and one on his side, but of no consequence. General Pakenham had a horse shot under him—his best charger.

General Robinson is shot through the body ; a bad wound. Two of General Sir S. Cotton's officers, his aide-de-camps, who were there as amateurs, suffered. One coming home was shot in the thigh. Many others had narrow escapes, and Lord Wellington remained exposed, untouched! This is really wonderful.

To-day again there was some fighting, but only on our left, a sort of trial of the French strength. We lost, I hear, however, several men, particularly of the 9th. On the whole, with wounded and sick, we shall be much reduced by this week's work, and I still think can scarcely advance safely any further, unless you send men here instead of to Holland, or unless we can get a good corps of Spaniards to join us under officers who will keep them in order. O'Donnell, the Condé D'Obisbal, is come up again, and will do, for he will hang his men until he gets order and obedience. Lord Wellington has also got his full powers renewed by the Spaniards, and may now perhaps try them once more, if tempted to advance after what has happened.

Sunday, 12*th December,* 3 *o'clock.*—Every one has gone out again, but nothing expected to be done to-day. The French attacked us after sunset last night in force, in hopes, probably, of catching us napping again, and getting more baggage, but it did not succeed. The Germans are kept here to-day. My first letter, up to the 11th, I have sealed and sent, and keep this open in case of more news, for which I must hunt, and then come in and finish this, and after dinner divide my prize maps of this canton, and of the whole seat of the northern war— French maps of this year; great prizes. For the present, adieu.

Five o'clock.—More fighting again to-day. The French columns appeared, and we threw some shells amongst them. This brought on a quarrel, and we skirmished sharply for a long time; the Guards were principally

Y

concerned; the Adjutant killed, Lieutenant-colonel, and a
Captain. I hear of no advantage gained on either side
—mere fighting. Our entrenching tools are sent for, so
I suppose we are going to make ourselves snug to remain
quiet.

Six o'clock.—No more news, and no more fighting, but
I have just heard that Lieutenant-colonel D—— W——
is shot in the head, and some say killed; some contradict
it altogether. I had told Miss W—— that he was well,
in a letter just gone to the post. The Paymaster-general
and several amateurs got suddenly into fire without intending it the other day. It is better now to stay at
home, for one fight is much like any other, and I have
now seen some of the best which are likely to happen.

CHAPTER XVII.

French Attack—Plan of Desertion—Excesses of the French—A Basque Witness—Sir John Hope—Movements of the Army—Sale of Effects—Wellington's Simplicity of Character—A French Emigré—Return of Soult to Bayonne.

Head-quarters, St. Jean de Luz,
December 14, 1813.

MY DEAR M——,

As every one is still in the front, and I have now but a few letters to write on business, I shall proceed in writing to you, and, if possible, send this by the delayed packet. Yesterday morning, the French were, I believe, to have been attacked again in our front, in order to drive them back into Bayonne. In the morning, however, they were off, and had disappeared from the disputed ground, and only appeared in the Bayonne works. This made us suspect an attack from them on General Hill, who was on our right, with only some Portuguese, and his two divisions on the other side of the Nive. Reinforcements were ordered accordingly, and all the grandees and amateurs went that way. So it turned out; the French came in large masses and attacked us there, just as we were moving about in our position.

At first they drove the Portuguese brigade there back from a knoll. They rallied, however, returned, and recovered it. By that time the rest of the two divisions were up ready, and the French came on in more force. The attack now became general along the line, and the French were beaten back on all sides with very consider-

Y 2

able loss, and without the reinforcements, which were not in time. I know no particulars at all, for Lord Wellington did not return last night to this place; but some who did, say that the French were very thick, as they came forward in such masses, and some of their own disheartened prisoners talk of four thousand men and more as their loss. These daily desperate attacks, first on their right and then on their left, and the accounts given by the German Nassau officers, make me suspect very much that Soult will after this be off altogether further to the rear after having obeyed his order, by a desperate attempt to drive us back into Spain again. I hear that he wrote to Lord Wellington before these five days' fighting, to say that we must positively quit France, and that, to save bloodshed, he wished Lord Wellington would retire of his own accord. I did not learn this, however, from the very best authority.

The day before yesterday I met at dinner the Major of the Nassau regiment, a very pleasant gentleman-like man, aide-de-camp to the Prince, and the very officer who brought the secret verbal orders to the Colonel K——— to take the steps he has done. The Major arrived six weeks ago, but they never found the opportunity until now. Similar orders are gone to another battalion with Marshal Suchet, and to a corps of Nassau cavalry there, and we have sent word to our army on that side to endeavour to let them know that these three battalions have succeeded. The whole was very near failing even this time: he gave us all the particulars.

The French towards evening thought things were not going on quite well, and ordered up all the reserves. Amongst the rest were three battalions, and that of Baden, which lately had been kept much in the rear. When they were all retiring towards their quarters again at dusk, General Villatte (Colonel Downie's old enemy), who commanded the reserve, was obliged to retire to the rear, being wounded. He left orders with a stupid old General who succeeded him in command. The Colonel of the Nassau regiment was directed by the old man to retire along the great road. He represented the numbers going that way and the delay, and proposed a side road. The old man said, " Well, you will do your best." The Colonel then thought all would do, and was about to march off, when up came the 34th regiment, all French, and their commanding officer said, " *Monsieur le Colonel, j'ai mes ordres de vous suivre sur votre route.*" This was most perplexing. The Colonel then made an imaginary obstacle at the head of the column, and desired the men to file one by one slowly. This tired the patience of the French, who had been out all day. The Colonel then proposed his plan to the officer commanding the Baden regiment. To which he replied, that he had received no orders from his Sovereign, and, after hesitating a little, declined. Colonel K—— then ordered him to take another road, and told the French, as they must divide to get home at all, they had better follow the Baden regiment. The French 34th did so; and the others soon began to incline towards the English, firing away, however, but in the air, to deceive any who might be observing them. They soon found themselves near enough to send in the officer first, and the regiment followed in spite of some shots from our people. The astonishment of many, who not being in the secret, found themselves within the English picket, and fancied they were all about to be made prisoners, was very considerable; and their joy was as great when they were told the true state of things.

The Major told us that they had seen constant service in Spain, that their Sovereign's contingent for Spain was about two thousand men, but that the French kept it up whenever they could to nearly three thousand, and more at times. He was at Talavera, and the bugle of one of the battalions which sounded as they left, and marched through, was English, and I understand was taken from us at the battle of Talavera. He confessed the horrors committed in Spain was " *Nous autres*" (as he was constantly expressing himself), forgetting that he was no longer French, and then correcting himself, said, "*par les Français.*" He said that it was a practice when the orders were issued to plunder and burn places which had been deserted by their inhabitants, to make a great fire near the place so as to make the inhabitants think a battle was about to begin, and lead them to retire to some spot near, out of the way of the fire, but never intending to desert their homes. The troops then voted it a deserted town, and begun first to pillage, then to burn. He described the French army as being now about fifty-five thousand men, after this affair, of which, however, only about twenty-two or twenty-three thousands were soldiers, that is veterans; the rest raw recruits and conscripts, of which Bayonne was full; and there you might now see, he said, even the blind and the lame compelled to come forward and serve.

He said they were ill supplied with everything, and had no forage at all; that one great store of biscuit was spoilt in the church at Bayonne; and that the roads in the rear were so bad that hardly any supplies could arrive but by the river—at least not without the greatest difficulty and labour; that the Dax and Tartas roads were infamous, and the one I went by, Peyrorade and Orthes, very bad. Allowance must be made, I think, in regard to these accounts.

Soult was enraged with the inhabitants for wishing to return home within our lines, and was much provoked at our not having behaved much worse in this country. I have also understood from officers who went with flags-of-truce, that the French are excessively angry with their women for all desiring to come here to us. The Mayor of Biaritz, I believe, is denounced, having given us assistance, and ordered to be seized as soon as discovered. The French were two or three days since in one attack actually in his garden, but could never get into his house. Of course he had removed many of his goods, and was on the alert. He has had a picket always in his house, and been very liberal. Near that house our guns and the French were within three hundred yards of each other, but neither could get at the opponent on account of the formation of the ground. There was a small wood in the neighbourhood, which was a strong point. Lord Wellington, &c., have just returned. I must go and pick up news.

Head-Quarters, St. Jean de Luz, December 15*th*, 1813, *Wednesday.*—We are now all returned to our civil business again, and I have just been to the Adjutant-general and Lord Wellington, as usual, to congratulate them on their safety, at the same time to make my reports, and receive fresh instructions.

All the reports confirm the account that the French got a severe beating on our right the day before yesterday, and that our loss was not that day so severe in comparison with the other affair on our left. Our present position is close round the French and Bayonne, in a semicircle from the sea to the Adour. The advanced posts being from the front of Biaritz and Anglet, on the sea on our left, and so through Arcamgues, Arrauntz, on the Nive, the centre, where our boat-bridge is, and then through Monguerre, Petit, and Vieux, to La Home, on the Adour, on our extreme right. Some alarm us by a report that head-quarters are to be moved in consequence to Ustaritz, as being on the Nive, and more central, and near the bridges. We all, however, hope otherwise. Some Spaniards are come on now also, and more cavalry are ordered up. Our abode here has quite spoiled us for the wretched places we must crowd into at Ustaritz, down in a muddy hole, with the roads almost impassable around it.

Unless you have a good map, you will find but few of the places mentioned by me, and yet I have omitted two or three in the circle.

[The places were all found in old maps by Robert, a French geographer.]

I must go to work to draw charges, so adieu.

There is a most eloquent French, or, rather, Basque witness here, who has been robbed, and whom I am keeping here to give evidence. He pays me daily visits, and acts over the scene in question, and several others, in very high style. The Basques are as proud as our Welsh of their antiquity, and when asked if they are French say, " *Oh, que non Basque.*" He tried to insinuate himself into my favour, by reminding me that this country was once all English, and that the inhabitants had still the memory of that, and favourable feelings accordingly.

Sir John Hope was, including his dress, touched in seven places, besides a shot in his horse, and through his large hat. The skin wound, though slight, is the only wound that gives him pain. Lord Wellington blames him for exposing himself; with what face I know not.

Head-Quarters, St. Jean de Luz, December 16th, 1813. —Though you will have heard from me by the detained mail, which went yesterday, you will expect something by the next, so I begin my work in time; concluding that it will go Sunday as usual again. I have just heard that the packet which went from hence the 22nd, with our letters to the 21st of November, was found deserted at sea, and letters, &c., supposed to be taken, or most likely sunk. I sent you two long letters by that packet, with a plan of my house here, and sketch of it, and the largest proportion of prize Spanish maps, taken at Vittoria; begging you to keep them, and those that come after, safely. It was in that letter that I told you of my narrow escape at St. Fé from being shot through the head by a dragoon whilst I was writing. The ball went between my pen and my nose, and where my head had been two seconds before: one cheek was spattered by the door splinters, and the other by the wall plaster where the ball struck.

We have just got a most alarming report, as far as comfort is concerned, namely, that we are to move to a little dirty village, called Arrauntz, on the Nive, worse almost than Frenada, with the exception of one good house, where roads are impassable—almost up to the knees in mud. I believe this was certainly determined, but Colonel Campbell told me just now he believed the order was deferred; I hope so most sincerely, for we are here rather in a state of civilization and comfort.

I dined yesterday at head-quarters, and who should I meet but Count de Gazan's *ci-devant* aide-de-camp, a fine gentleman-like young man, with whom I dined at Count Gazan's house at that time, Lord Wellington's now. He was then very civil to us. We dined yesterday in his *ci-devant* apartment. He was about to join Marshal Victor in the north, as his aide-de-camp, when I last saw him; but being promoted to a chef-de-battalion, this induced him to stop and take the command. It answers to our Lieutenant-colonel; and he commanded a battalion against General Hill in the last attack. Finding his men running away too fast, he kept in the rear to encourage them, and give them confidence; stayed there too long, and, in a word, was caught and taken prisoner. He is a tall, stout, good-looking man of twenty-eight, and speaks English well, having been in England some time before for education.

I gave him a good breakfast this morning before he set out for Passages, got him a letter to the principal Commissary at Passages, and handed him my father's direction at Somerset House; desiring him to let him know where he is ultimately quartered in England, and whether my father could serve him in any way in London. So be prepared for a letter some time hence from my French acquaintance. He is a stanch Frenchman in everything, but I do not like him the worse for that, or for avowing it openly.

He told me that we were not quite so secure in Holland, and that we were not near a peace, but had much yet to do to obtain such a one as we required, for Bonaparte was ambitious and unreasonable, and we were unreasonable also. In some respects I agree, and only hope the Allies will continue moderate. I offered him money, but he said he had lost nothing, and did not require it, and declined any assistance. He said, at the moment he was vexed that our men did not plunder him, as he knew his own people would have done so by us. He seems a shrewd fellow, and was therefore ordered off directly from hence.*

Lord Wellington looks thin, but was in high spirits yesterday. We have more artillery and ammunition passing up to-day to the front, and, I hear, they are making works to strengthen our position, and to be prepared against any other desperate attack. This may be only Lord Wellington's usual prudence, as it does not look like a move further in advance. Other circumstances, however, do rather look like a movement forwards, and the strengthening this position may be either for the present security, or for a position to retire to in case of accidents, as we have now two rivers in our rear; or, which may be most likely, for both. The fact

---

* He made no application to Mr. Larpent's family, nor did he call at Somerset House.

is, we have above twelve hundred men digging away, and artillery is going up.

My French witness here tells me a friend has just arrived from Bayonne, who informs him, that whilst the movements were going on some days since, Marshal Soult told the leading people of Bayonne, that all who intended to move their valuables to the rear should do so by water immediately, if at all, as circumstances might soon make it impossible for them to do so by water, and the road would be entirely required by the military in certain events. This does not look like much confidence.

Friday, December 17*th, three o'clock, and Sunday, December* 19*th, Post-day.*—A report of more work on the right, and we fancy we have heard much firing. Lord Wellington is gone off. If matters have not gone on well, or the horses get tired, we shall have a move yet, I fear very soon; but hope otherwise most sincerely, that is, if it be a move of head-quarters only. A forward movement of the army will be another matter, as it will prove to me Lord Wellington thinks something is to be done by it. Our cavalry is moving up fast. This looks like a movement. It spreads out by Cambo on our right. I am also assured by a French officer here in our service in the Quarter-Master-general's department, that the French cavalry are fast filing to the rear, and have already passed Mont de Marsan, my former abode; and that many of the old soldiers are from necessity sent back to Bordeaux to compel some refractory conscripts there to move, for they are a little wilful. He also told me that the loss of the French (desertion included) in the late affairs last week, was, in the whole, about thirteen thousand men. He is, however, a sanguine man; remember that. We are also said to have taken two or three boats on the Adour, above Bordeaux.

Head-Quarters, St. Jean de Luz, five o'clock, Sunday,

December 19*th,* 1813.—I have just come from the sea-
side, where we can now scarcely stand for the wind, and
are, on the high walk, quite wet with the spray.   A
violent gale of some hours has caused this, and I have
been watching a vessel off here for a long time which has
been in considerable danger, but is at last safe in Saçoa
harbour.   She was most uneasy at sea, made signals of
distress, and the pilot-boats ventured out, and by their
help and working hard with the capstan on an anchor
carried out, she has at last worked her way in.

I met yesterday at dinner Colonel Barnard, who was
lately shot through the body.   Colonel Rooke is dead.
I feared it must be so, from what was told me yesterday.
He could not eat anything, grew rapidly weaker, and
the suppuration formed a mass clear through his body
from one orifice of the wound to the other, and not
properly round the ball so as to facilitate the extraction
of it.   Lieutenant-colonel West is well.   I saw him
to-day : he was not touched.   The report of his being
killed arose from his having sent a horse to the rear—I
believe to walk.   At the sale of the late Captain Watson's effects, I bought a very tolerable saddle, with
holsters, about half worn, for eighteen dollars, which is
here considered cheap.   I bid 15*s.* for a curry-comb and
brush, bad, but of English make, and in England worth
about 3*s.* or 4*s.*—it went for a guinea !   I also bid for a
Suffolk punch horse as high as two hundred dollars, but
Major Daring outbid me, though it was certainly very
dear.   Captain Watson was of the Guards.

A party of Bayonne sailors have just arrived here I
am told, who have come over to us.   Bayonne envies
this place now.   If we stay, and have money, things will
come in here soon from the French, for the geese they
bring in sell for four dollars instead of 4*s.* before we came,
and so with other things ; we have also got some good
French cattle to eat.

Head-Quarters, St. Jean de Luz, December 21*st*, 1813.
—The furious stormy weather continues, with almost
continual rain, attended yesterday by a most violent clap
of thunder; such repeated gusts of wind I scarcely ever
witnessed. The inhabitants say, that it will last so long
as we have the wind from the sea. At the same time
it is not at all cold, and I have no fire except when I
have been caught in the wet, and am very damp.
This happens if you stir for five hundred yards, as
the rain comes with a gust in a few seconds. The
thermometer in my room, without a fire, has been
constantly almost above temperate, and at times above
sixty. We are at present all quiet again here, and in-
vitations are flying about for Christmas dinners on Saturday next.

Marshal Soult is angry with the inhabitants for being
friends with us. He is now circulating proclamations
on our right, exhorting the people to form Guerilla corps
and to turn brigands. If we continue to behave well,
he will not easily persuade them to do this. The
Spaniards who demand rations and contributions against
orders, and are not so orderly as they might be (the few
that are in France, that is), may perhaps provoke them
to arms, but I hope not. We now go about the roads
here as safely as in Spain; the only marauders indeed
are the followers of our own army and runaway
Spaniards and muleteers. Our own army is behaving
particularly well, and now give me a little leisure occasionally.

To my great joy to-day, and still more, I suspect, to
that of my horses, I have got a good truss of English
hay—140 lbs. weight. This is a treasure. But to
balance good and evil, the Commissary has given us no
corn during the last three days. So we go on! Many
of the cavalry horses get neither, so we must submit.

In spite of the rough weather, we yesterday got a

packet and English mail, and I received a letter from you of the 6th and 7th December, and papers from the 4th to the 7th. You confirm our accounts of the loss of the mail of the 21st November, and of two letters of mine to you. I only hope they are sunk, though I recollect nothing particular in them.

I have no doubt —— plays the great man very well, and puts on all the dignity of a Jack in office. He likes the thing, and has a turn for humbug, of which there is so much all over the world in every line, and which is often of such infinite use to those who can adopt it. I think it very tiresome, and only rejoice that it is not the fashion here at head-quarters. From Lord Wellington downwards, there is mighty little. Every one works hard, and does his business. The substance and not the form is attended to ; in dress, and many other respects, I think almost too little so. The maxim, however, of our Chief is, " Let every one do his duty well, and never let me hear of any difficulties about anything ;" and that is all he cares about. I suppose one should fall by degrees into a love of representation, and keeping one's self up in the world, as it is called (by those who have not much else to float them), by habit and practice. I must say, hitherto, I continue to think it far best to be able to do what you please, as you please, and when you please, provided that nothing is ever done which in the least approaches to a shabby or ungentleman-like action—so that the opinion of those whose opinion is worth having is secured. The sort of incense which is often obtained from the silly majority through exterior humbug is not worth the price at which it is purchased. My vanity takes a different turn, and I pique myself upon other things.

I attended another sale yesterday of Colonel Martyn's effects. It was quite ridiculous to observe the price at which some old things sold. Two second-hand night-caps, which cost about 1*s.* 6*d.* each new in England, fetched 13*s.* This results partly from distress, partly from fun in the bidders. Old towels 5*s.* each; blankets 25*s.* I always feel hurt at seeing all an officer's stock sold in this way, even to his ragged shirts and stockings, tooth-brushes, &c.; everything ransacked. This was very near being my case, also, when I was taken prisoner. Mr. Jesse's stock was sold, and he is not a little distressed in consequence. I have received a note from Lieutenant-colonel E—— to dine with him on Christmas-day, and have accepted, though probably I shall lose a great party at Lord Wellington's by so doing, for he generally asks heads of departments on those days. I own, however, that I prefer his smaller parties, when fewer grandees are there, and Lord Wellington talks more and we drink less. A great party is almost always stupid, unless there is good singing or good speechifying; and I have now seen all the lions likely to be there. By-the-by, our Spanish lions carry their heads wonderfully erect now, and are prouder than any peacocks; or rather, I might say, they are now true Spaniards.

Yesterday I dined at Lord Wellington's, and had another adventure. I recognised an emigré friend at Mont de Marsan, of whom I had been, during my stay there, very shy, fearful lest a malicious report should get about that I was intriguing with the royalists. I reminded him of his questions, &c., and of his speaking to me several times, and I now explained myself and conduct. He was much surprised at seeing me in my red coat, but immediately recollected me, and said I had given him then all the information he wanted. My answers were short, but all true, certainly. He has brought some congratulations to the Comte de Grammont from the persons now on his *ci-devant* estates, and their wishes for old times and old landlords. He had got some money here, and is, I suppose, to go to work somehow for the good cause. He is very sanguine; but though I like and respect the *emigrés*, I always mistrust their view of things.

A foolish Portuguese, who was sentenced to be shot, escaped three days ago, and was off; but like a fool, he boasted in Spain of his performances, was in consequence retaken, and to-day is to be hung.

December 26*th, Post-day*. — Another of my French friends came in from Bayonne yesterday—the principal banker at Bayonne, who gave me money for my bill; was so friendly to us all and to me in particular, and for whom I loaded my pockets so quietly with so many letters, above a hundred in number. He has ostensibly come to receive the 110*l.* still due to him from five of our officers, and which Lord Wellington intended to send him on my representation : but he has also obtained leave from Soult to supply us with claret, &c., and is partly come about that. The French, I conclude, are compelled to try this method of making a little money ; and Marshal Soult being, no doubt, ill-paid, will go halves in the profit. I suspect my friend, however, may have further views also, as he is a Spanish and English merchant as well as banker, and of course a decided enemy to Berlin and burning decrees, and to war in general, which is now nearly synonymous with being an enemy to Bonaparte. Lord Wellington sent him to the Commissary-general to talk matters over.

We have been all quiet here this week, except a little cavalry skirmish on our right. The French cavalry, I hear, had driven in some of Don Murillo's Spaniards, with Hill, in that quarter, and two squadrons of our 18th Hussars were ordered to drive the French back. This they did, as they were ordered, without loss, but as usual would do more, and pushing hastily on fell in with the French infantry support, which is generally near at hand to the cavalry advance, got a volley or two, and lost a captain and several men in consequence.

Our people will suppose that the French lurk about the country without system or order as they do; whereas, however cowed and beaten they may be, the system, order, and habitual rules, remain.

Some more of Don Carlos d'Espagne's troops filed up from Irun yesterday, and turning off about a mile short of this place, went through Ascain towards our right— about five thousand in the whole. Several of Murillo's people are put under arrest by Lord Wellington for misconduct. They complain that the men get sick in consequence, to which he replies, " Then behave better, and that will not be the case."

Some of our artillerymen have by accident burnt one of the best of the few remaining houses at St. Sebastian, worth twenty thousand dollars the Spaniards say, and about to be let for six hundred dollars a-year. This will be quite convincing to the Conciso at Cadiz, and perhaps to the regency, that we burnt the town on purpose, and are now finishing our job. It is unlucky to give this handle to these most unconquerably jealous Spaniards, and already the engineers and few English at St. Sebastian are most unpopular. The weather is now much improved, and has turned to frost for the first time this month, which improves our roads, our spirits, and our prospects. The sea, however, has been for these last two days tremendous, and washed over the stone bulwark where we walk, and has cut off our supply of corn these three days from Passages. I was yesterday caught there when walking with General Pakenham and General Murray : the Quarter-Master-general ran one way, the Adjutant-general and I another; the former escaped, and so did the latter and I, though the foam and surf burst upright, close to us, above our heads, and then

z

washed our legs midway up; but the force was broken,
and we were not moved, only wetted. The natives and
many of our officers think this roaring ocean predicts
more bad weather here again, but I hope it only proves
a storm some two hundred miles off in the main ocean,
as I have always observed there is little connexion here
between our land-storms and the state of the sea, which
seems to be moved by other causes, of which probably
one is the agitation caused by the flood spring-tides.

Monday.—Marshal Soult has returned again to Bayonne. Lord Wellington, &c., are all out with the
hounds.

CHAPTER XVIII.

Reports from France—More Desertion—Anecdote of General Stewart—
Wellington and his Casualty Returns—The Courtesies of War—Scarcity
of Transports—Wellington and the Trial-Papers—Sir G. Collier.

Head-quarters, St. Jean de Luz,
January 1, 1814.

My dear M——,

MANY happy new years to you and all your
party! We are now quite quiet here, and have no news
to communicate. We have repeatedly received reports
of the arrival of an English mail, but it never comes.
This may, however, arise from our having had three of
the vessels at once on this side of the water.

You will be surprised to hear that I had an old French
woman, and a young Spanish girl to breakfast with me
this morning, on their way through to Bayonne, from
Bilboa. I had made arrangements for six mules, and an
ox-car to carry their baggage, but they mistook the tide
in their directions, and the baggage is only just arrived,
so that they cannot go until to-morrow. They are the
wife and mother of a Monsieur Dabedrille, at Bayonne,
ci-devant principal *Directeur de l' Octroi de Bilboa*, who
fled so quickly after the battle of Vittoria, that he left
all his baggage and females behind him. He was very
civil to Colonel Fitzgerald, who had undertaken to
obtain for him the restoration of his wife; and as the
Colonel was not exchanged, I undertook it, got Lord
Wellington's leave, and here they are, so far on their

z 2

way safe. Not having just now much business, I have had time to attend a little to these good ladies, and they are really very pleasant and well-bred, but just now the worse for having been six days on board a Spanish coaster (of Bilboa), to get here.

We have just now got beautiful weather, clear frosty mornings—that is, white frost, the ground just crisp, a little fog early, and a cool breeze from the Pyrenees, from the south-east, and a bright sun during the day.

The only news we have here is a report of the defeat of Davoust, through the French, and an account which General Wimpfen has just given me of the Austrians having taken possession of Switzerland. The French here are hard at work, drilling conscripts, who arrive in considerable numbers, and turning up the ground as usual in all directions. I suppose we shall also, as usual, wait until they have nearly done their task, and by that time, when the ground is dry, turn them out of their laborious defences. It is quite extraordinary how all their former position was covered with the effects of their labour.

The inhabitants continue to come in here to us every day, and now by degrees we get cattle, &c., from them. Desertion from the French has also been common, five or six men a-day, and many French, not Germans, young lads, sick of their work. I now hear that the Swiss have declared against France; that is one step more gained, if true. An officer, who was prisoner at Bayonne, on the 13th, the day of General Hill's affair on the right, states, that the French were most sanguine that morning at Bayonne; they said that two of our divisions were caught in a trap, and that they would, General and all, be taken prisoners. They were quite in spirits, but towards evening, when the officer inquired where our General was, he could get no one to answer him, or talk on the subject. All were sulky. Report says also that

Soult is gone again, and farther back; some say that he has been sent for to Paris.

One of the hay vessels, bringing hay to us, in order to plague us, had got into Bayonne, and the French officers at the outposts taunt us, by saying that they find English hay very good. This is very provoking, for in consequence of this we have now nothing again to give our animals.

Sunday, Post-day.—I understand that there is no packet as yet at Passages, to go with the letters. I have, after three hours' trouble, packed off my party this morning; four great trunks, two old women, and one young one, in an ox-car; and four more large trunks, and a quantity of bedding, and *et ceteras* of all kinds, on four mules; and one lady and a man-servant, on horse-back. My old French woman, now she is safe out of Spain, does nothing but abuse the Spaniards, their language, their manners, their country, and, above all, their stupidity in society.

I must now return to the work of drawing charges, which must be done immediately. I hope there is not another task for me now passing my window, for there is an uproar, and seven Spanish prisoners going along bound to the provost guard.

We have now established a sort of little telegraph of signals to the right and in front, to acquaint Lord Wellington immediately should anything be going forward.

P.S.—I don't think you heard a little anecdote of General Stewart, who is brave, and consequently always gets his aide-de-camp, &c., into some bad blows, if he does not get one himself. The people about him on the 13th were all touched, and he was nearly alone. An officer of the name of Egerton went up to him, and whilst there a shell burst between them. "A shell! sir: very animating!" said Stewart, and then kept Egerton there talking on.

Head-Quarters, St. Jean de Luz, January 4th, 1814.—
Here we are still without any news from your side of the
water, and of course most anxious. On this side we
seem, however, to be preparing something for you to
talk about; at least, appearances look like another battle.
The day before yesterday (Sunday) all was quiet, and on
Monday (yesterday) Lord Wellington ordered out his
hounds, and went off early himself. In the middle of
the day, however, the signal was made that the French
were in motion; Lord March and Gordon went off to
Lord Wellington, and he did not return last night. To-
day the troops have all been on the alert, for the French
are said to be still moving on our right, and in fact
rather on our rear. The Guards were off early from
hence to replace the light division, who went to the
right, and all seems moving in that direction. No firing
has, however, been heard; and I understand nothing has
been done to-day. I went as far as Guethary, and up to
the church-tower, whence the view is very extensive, but
saw nothing in particular. The last report was, that the
French still advanced on our right. If they persist in
this, it is my opinion that we must have a fight, and a
sharp one probably, on that side to-morrow, but as the
staff are all out, I know nothing certain.

Two or three days since we took a little island in the
Adour, almost without loss, which will enable us to
molest the navigation more effectually than we have
hitherto done, though already it is rather impeded, even
at night, and almost totally by day. A contest about
the island was rather expected, but not this bold move of
the French in our rear. If they persist and fail, I think
with the two Gaves in their rear, we may, perhaps, make
them suffer severely for their enterprise. Marshal Soult's
supposed absence looks now rather like a *ruse de guerre.*

We have Spaniards on our right, and in the valley of
Bastan, who perhaps may now come in again for a little

fighting; and it is to be hoped they may, for if the French work constantly on the British and Portuguese, and you continue to send men to Holland, we shall by degrees get too weak for our situation.

Lord Wellington at dinner on Sunday directed some jokes at Major D——, who makes out the returns, because he wanted to make a grand total of wounded, &c., after the late five days' fighting. He laughed, and said that all might go wrong from this innovation, but he was determined he would have no more grand totals until he got another Vittoria without more loss; that the loss was always great enough in all conscience, without displaying it in this ostentatious manner, and that he would not have every drummer and every officer, &c., killed or wounded in the five days, all added up in one grand total, but that at least the croakers should have the trouble themselves of adding up all the different losses, and making it out for themselves.

The weather is just now delightful, and we have had as yet nothing which can properly be called winter. During the last ten days the sea has been quite smooth, and we have not even had a white frost. The people say they think that the first bad season is over now, and we shall not have much more bad weather until near March: I only hope this will prove correct.

A French carriage and a car were waiting at the French outposts to receive my ladies, and they all got in safe. This was managed by sending in a message the day before. A certain communication with Bayonne is also now open; for yesterday we had an arrival of French watches, rings, trinkets, and silk dresses. We carry on war in a very civilized manner, especially if a little anecdote related to me yesterday be correct. One of our officers, it seems, I believe Major Q——, was riding a troublesome horse close to the French pickets, and partly from the violence of his horse, and partly from his own inadvertence, he got close to a French sentinel. The latter called out several times that he was French, and ordered him off, and at last presented his bayonet. The horse still plunging on, and the officer apparently not understanding the man, the French sentry turned the horse the other way by the bridle, and sent him back without offering any harm to either beast or rider, though he might have killed or taken both.

This morning we had another instance on our side. A French officer's wife came in from Bayonne to follow her husband, a prisoner in England. We had a boat in from Sacoa to take her upon the beach, to carry her round by sea to Passages, and an order from Lord Wellington waiting for her there, for a passage to England as expeditiously as circumstances would permit.

Wednesday, 5th January.—No one came back last night, and St. Jean de Luz is almost deserted; scarcely a red coat to be seen. The ladies are in some alarm, and only some inquiring doctors and commissaries are to be seen about the streets. I have in the mean time such an accumulation of business for Lord Wellington that I shall be almost fearful of seeing him—five Courts-martial, one of about ninety pages, another eighty. He always complains, and yet I think he likes to read these cases, and know himself exactly all that is going on. I have just been out to pick up news, but in vain, and have been driven back by a slight shower. Money has been so short here that I could only tempt them to give me some doubloons immediately by accepting a part of my pay on England in another Treasury Bill.

Friday, January 7th.—Lord Wellington is not yet returned here, and we are, therefore, still deserted; but nothing has been done. The French have been manœuvring for these three days on our right flank, but in vain, as our General was ready for them. Yesterday, however, he was nearly bringing them to blows. A part of their force remained on our side of the Adour, between the Nive and the Bidocque. This was too near our position, and they were to have been driven across, but prudently went away in good time of their own accord, consequently nothing was done, and I think nothing will be done just now.

The French head-quarters here are at (I believe) Peyrehorade, a town on the Gave, of some little river commerce. In our present suspense we were at last amused yesterday by the arrival of two mails, and I have got letters, papers, &c.

You kill men for me faster than I do in reality, and that is enough. I am only aware of forty-one having been shot or hung since my arrival in the country; and that is quite enough too, you will say, almost as many as you hang in all England in a year. You were quite right about the lost letter from me; it contained a full description of St. Jean de Luz, and of my horrible muddy journey from St. Fé to this civilized place, with a sketch of my house and its vicinity, &c., a ground plot of my quarter, which, if time and room permit, I will repeat. And as you do not congratulate me on my escape from being shot, I suppose that story was there also.

Later.—As Lord Wellington is still away, I continue to scribble to you. This place has been a very flourishing town, and of considerable trade, but is much in decay; this partly before the late wars, from the bar having increased, so that only small vessels can get in now, and the evil still increases. At low water the river only ripples over the bar of sand, scarcely a foot deep, and at times the river is choked up by the sand, so that it cannot make its way out, and floods the town. This happened twice last year, but has not recurred this year, though at times the bed of the river has been quite changed, and the water nearly stopped.

Sacoa is a very safe harbour; for small vessels drawing

under ten feet, quite safe. They lie there high and dry, according to the tide. The houses of the former merchants are rather magnificent, though some are in ruins, and their number, for the size of the town, considerable. It has been called a sort of little Paris for the Basques. Near the sea the water has been, and is, gaining on the town and bay. There are many ruins; one is part of an old convent, now beyond the sea-wall, and almost in the sea, and some say a whole street has been washed away. The great sea-wall made by Bonaparte, six hundred yards long, was constructed to save the town, and makes a good dry walk.

Sibour is also a very large village, or small town, of inferior houses, where at present two brigades of Guards are, and two other regiments of Lord Aylmer's brigade, besides some staff cavalry, &c. Most of the better houses have French papers from Paris, and it looks very well. The whole wall forms one landscape, like tapestry —sea-ports from Vernet or Claude, &c.; some in colours, some in bistre or an imitation of Indian ink, some Chinese, but in better perspective. The brown and black are very pretty. Most of the walls are papered. The lower parts of the houses are all a sort of warehouse (where they are not shops); this serves us for stabling, but they are flagged, which having no straw is noisy, and they smell much also. Almost all the men of a better sort went away from St. Jean de Luz; several women, for the most part old, stayed, and many have since returned; but no society, or anything of that sort, is as yet set on foot here. The deputy mayor, who stayed, sold all the wine he could appropriate, his own, and all unclaimed, as well as other things, and is, I believe, making money of us very fast. The town is now all a market or fair, and full of Spaniards and Portuguese, as well as French and Bascos, all pillaging poor John Bull, by selling turkeys for 25s. and 30s., and fowls for 12s. and 14s.

The people from Bilboa have been most active. Little has arrived from England or Lisbon as yet, which is extraordinary; but the danger of the coast is, probably, the cause. During the bad weather ten vessels of ours found their way into Bayonne, one with fifty-two Irish bullocks, by which we lost part of the best beef we ever get, and one with seven hundred trusses of hay, others with biscuit, &c. This is very provoking. The Bayonne mayor showed us the post-list of the whole taken in each ship. How we shall get on with our animals I know not, for they tell me that they hear from England, in the Commissariat, there is but little hay on the sea for us, from want of transport, and there is no straw to be got at all now within thirteen leagues, or about forty miles, from hence. I am, however, advised to send for it; and if this movement shall come to nothing, will do so to-morrow.

It is fortunate that we are so near the sea, and have some advantage as to transport in the river Nivelle also, for our transport is much diminished by desertion of the muleteers from want of pay. The army is more numerous than when at Frenada and in Portugal, and our transport is now less. Were we to wander into France (as you suppose), away from the coast, we should find it difficult to live at all. The boats of this place are famous, and the men stayed here, or have escaped here, and are all in our pay now, and thus things are brought round from Passages here by sea, and then up to the division by the river as far as Ustaritz, where they are then distributed to the mules of each division. Even with this help the army cannot be supplied with rum, except by buying it very dear on the spot of the suttlers, for nearly all our remaining mules are required for bread and a little corn for the staff. The meat supplies itself in a way—that is, about two-thirds only of the flesh which leaves Valencia, &c., in Spain, arriving here, falls under the butcher's knife, besides the number which die on the road; and yet all that can be stopped, when fagged or lame, are distributed at the stations on the way. The suttlers, by the great profit they make, can pay the muleteers as high as two dollars a-day for each mule to carry up their produce, making us pay for it in the end. This evil increases, for our muleteers, who only have one dollar a-day for each mule (and enough in all conscience), are tempted to desert and get into the service of the suttlers, who thus supply the men with rum only at a dear rate, when we cannot do it. The pay of our mule-teers is now over-due twenty-one months for each mule : they have, therefore, their own way, and are under no control at all. Nothing but a sort of *esprit de corps*, and the fear of losing all claim to the debt, makes them keep with us at all; and we must submit to their fraud and carelessness, for we have no remedy.

As an instance of this, it may be mentioned that one brigade of mules, which had twenty-four thousand pounds of barley given to them to bring here, five leagues from Passages, only delivered eighteen thousand, and almost openly admitted that they had taken the rest, which I suppose they had sold to raise money. We could only set off the value against their debt, for fear of losing them without getting others. There was a grand con-sultation the other day, at which Lord Wellington, the Commissary-general and his people, General Alava the Spanish General, and most of the principal Spanish Capistras, or directors of the mules and owners, were present, to settle what could be done. They resolved to make the arrears all a debt, to acknowledge it, and then begin a sort of new score. This is in imitation of the Portuguese; only they do not pay the debt at all, but wipe off the arrears. One month's pay was also given by bills on the Treasury at a great discount, still this was something to go on with, and we have not Marshal Beresford's absolute power to control these Spaniards, as he does the Portuguese. Somehow, however, you see we get on.

Head-Quarters, St. Jean de Luz, Sunday, January 9th, post-day again.—As to length, at least, you shall have no reason to complain this mail, though I am at work again at business; for on Friday night all our warriors returned home to their respective quarters, and the Commander-in-Chief to his papers. The latter had so increased upon him in his five days' absence, that he was quite overwhelmed; and when I went in with a great bundle to add to them. he put his hands before his eyes and said, "Put them on that table; and do not say anything about them now, or let me look at them at all."

This week's manœuvring has not this time ended in smoke, but without smoke, as nearly as possible, for our men could not get within a long shot of the French, without following them beyond what our present plans would admit. They remained a short time on our side of the river Arrun, as it is called, in Casini's great map, and Gambouri, in my part of the French National Atlas, a small river which runs by La Bastide and falls into the Adour, near Urt, a place half-way between Bayonne and where the Gaves fall into the Adour.

We collected on the heights above Bastide, and made the signal by a little mountain gun to advance. The French made use of the same signal to commence their retreat across the river, and scarcely a shot was fired. La Bastide, which is on this side of the river, we never entered : but remaining satisfied with that line, the matter ended there. A change of weather, to rain of no trifling kind, will probably, I think, oblige both parties to be quiet for some little time again, until sun and air return to us without wet, and dry roads enable the troops to move a little in this difficult country. It is at present

very hard work to get on, even in the best roads, and
across the country, which is much intersected with
streams and rivers, and has only clayey poached roads,
and strong fences of hedge and ditch; it is almost impassable. Lord Wellington, I believe, always went back
to his brother Marshal, Beresford, at Ustaritz, to which
place he sent for some English hay for his horses. The
Adjutant-general's department remained mostly at Hasparen, which is, it is said, a very pretty small town in a
rich cultivated valley of meadows, where they fell in with
a small stock of excellent hay, not quite eaten by our
cavalry, who are in that part of the country.

All the people at head-quarters have come back safe
and sound; but with horses a little knocked up, and
rather stiff with riding about twelve or even fourteen hours a-day. Most of them, however, look the
better for the exercise. The most fagged of all I saw
was our naval hero, Sir G. Collier, with his lame leg.
He had ridden everywhere after Lord Wellington in
hopes of seeing a fight, and coming in, I suppose, for
another knock on shore, but all in vain. He says, that
the French never will stand when he comes, and nothing
is ever done. He is about to leave this station.

And now for a little account of the Spaniards, in order
to show you how they plague Lord Wellington. We
have undertaken to assist and direct, with our engineers,
in putting St. Sebastian into some order, and into a state
of defence. The actual working-party are, however,
nearly all Spanish. These have nearly all deserted, and
little or nothing is going on but quarrels between our
people and the Spaniards in authority, who thwart them.
At first Lord Wellington thought that we were to blame,
and seemed angry; but he told Col. E—— at last, " If
they go on so, d—— them, they may finish the work
for themselves; but go over and see about it, and make a
report to me."

Later.—Another English mail arrived, and another letter from you of the 27th and 28th, with papers to the 27th, &c. The great news which yours contained as to Lord Castlereagh we had heard through the French outpost five days since ; but the report only stated that he had actually landed at Morlaix, on his way to Manheim, to the general Congress, for a peace. This was believed before your account came, as it agreed with the general tenor of the late English news ; at least I thought so, for one. Whether it will end in a peace, however, is very doubtful, especially if Bonaparte finds that in consequence of this negotiation he keeps all quiet in France, and the conscription goes on without resistance, and his armies in March next will be formidable If he can once assume an imposing position, it is doubtful in my opinion whether he will come into the terms of the Allies. *Mais c'est à voir,* and he has much to do to put himself in such a position.

Many of the French conscripts here join almost without any uniforms or necessaries for a soldier, yet every deserter who comes in has everything nearly new, and is better provided for than any of our men, except the few who have just had their new clothing, &c., of which the Guards, who, by the by, returned here last night to their old quarters, form part. Just now the Italians begin to desert the French, and say it is in consequence of their having heard that their division, which was marched to the rear some short time since, was all disarmed and treated as prisoners of war. This may not be fact ; but the effect is that many Italians come over to us.

CHAPTER XIX.

Rumours of War—The Rival Dinner-Tables—"Slender Billy"—Bonaparte's Trickery—Spanish Violence—Wellington with the Hounds—French and English Aspects; the Outsides of the Nations.

Head-quarters, St. Jean de Luz,
January 11, 1814.

MY DEAR M——,

FINE weather is now returned, and no doubt before we have been quiet another week, should it last, we shall be stirred up a little by the French. At present, all our usual avocations are proceeding, and all is quiet.

The only event in my own establishment which has occurred is my taking into my service a Spanish lad, in addition to my other servants, but it will end in my getting rid of an idle Portuguese, who does nothing. I found the lad begging and in misery, by the seaside, and asked his history. He told me he was without father and mother, and came from a village two leagues beyond Madrid; that he had been under-stable servant to a French Commandant, who had gone wounded from Bayonne to the rear, towards Paris, and had turned him off. He therefore came back here, towards Spain. At first I only gave him food, and then, that I might not have to try him, took him to General Alava, who promised to send him to General Frere, to make a drummer of him. The next morning he called upon me before he started, and, being prepossessed by his looks, I have taken him on trial. He seems active and useful; and I hope will not return my charity by robbing me, of which there is some risk.

A party of our suttling merchants here behaved ill the other night, by insulting a sick officer; the worst among them escaped. One is now in confinement, and I have sent in his charge. They are all in a terrible fright of military law. Most probably he will not be tried if he makes an apology; but it has answered Lord Wellington's intention by convincing these men that there is law here, and that they are followers of the army and liable to that law.

On the neutral ground, on the great road to Bayonne, between our picquets and the French, in front of Biaritz, there are at present, in one of the houses unoccupied by either party, three young damsels alone. They are rather pretty and interesting, and all say very modest. For a time General Stopford, I believe, out of gallantry, put a safeguard there, but it was considered out of our position, and there was some quizzing. So the damsels are left quiet and alone again. They come daily into our lines, to bring milk, &c., and some flirtation goes on; but there they are safe. This is creditable to both sides.

I am told that the people at Hasparem, when the French approached the place last week, and it was thought might occupy it, were manifestly alarmed and dissatisfied, and wished us to stay. This might be from the fear of a conflict there, or from the benefits now derived from us, when the first irruption and mischief are over. Fowls are still, near there, to be had for 2s. each, and turkeys from 7s. to 9s.,; but this will not last, as people here have given, and others now ask, as much as 12s. for fowls, and 30s. for turkeys, or even more. General Cole, as we advanced, bought nine geese, at a dollar each; and this was grand pay, and not from fear. Here they are 25s. each.

Later.—How uncertain everything is with us! Marshal Beresford's aide-de-camp is just come in to Lord Wellington, and there is some stir on our right again. Lord Wellington and several others are off in that direction, and I am told the former stays out all night; this looks as if something was suspected. I dine to-day at head-quarters, and am to go as usual, though the chief is away. He asked me yesterday, but I told him that General Hill had asked me three days before, and expected me. "Very well," said he, "but I advise you to come to me, nevertheless, as you will get a much better dinner, for General Hill gives the worst dinners going." To General Hill's, however, I went; and though plain fare, compared to Lord Wellington's, whose table is just now very good, and much improved, I got a very good dinner.

If any dependence could be placed on appearances, I should say nothing important was going on to-day; for I saw Lord Wellington after he had seen the aide-de-camp, and he read a long letter quietly through, seeming quite at his ease; but he takes all that arises so coolly that this proves nothing. A sudden change again to rain will, in my opinion, damp the plans of the French, if they had any, as well as give all those gone off to the right a miserable ride, as it seems well set in for the day. Wind and wet seem here to be winter.

What a change has arisen for our young Prince of Orange who was here! I only hope he will not be spoilt by success and prosperity. In a little time, after all, it would not surprise me to hear of his looking back to the time he spent here at head-quarters as the pleasantest part of his life. Slender Billy was his nickname with those who were intimate with him, and he knew it; for one day, at dinner, Lord Fitzroy Somerset, not knowing that he was present, said, "Where is Slender Billy to-day?" Upon which the Prince put his head forward, and called out, "Here I am, Fitzroy; what do you want?"

·*January* 12*th.*—Lord Wellington and his party came back to dinner yesterday. The cause of the bustle was as follows. We had in our possession a mill which belonged rather to the French position than to ours; they attacked it, and, after some brisk firing, it was abandoned to them, and then all was quiet again. This news passed Lord Wellington on the road, but missed him, or he would not have gone on as far as he did. Ustaritz is about fifteen good miles from hence, and the road in parts almost up to a horse's belly. Lord Wellington rode there in the rain in two hours and ten minutes, and back in two hours and a half, up and down hills and through the clay: this proves a horse.

The next piece of news you will, probably, hear first: but if you should not, you have to learn that the cunning Bonaparte has been making a treaty with King Fernando VII. privately about a peace with Spain, and that he has sent it to the Cortes for their approval, and has appointed an ambassador for that purpose to Madrid. The gubernador, or preceptor and major domo of King Ferdinand, is either at Madrid or on his way thither. Spain, and Madrid in particular, is said to be in much agitation. The Cortes are to meet the 15th of January. This is a very artful plan to create jealousies between us, if not to procure a partial peace. We shall see now of what the Regency and Cortes are made. They have in professions bullied much, and resolved never to treat at all whilst a Frenchman remained in Spain. How they will act up to their resolution is now to be seen.

Friday, January 14*th.*—We have now French papers up to the 3rd from Paris, and have got Bonaparte's valedictory address, on setting out for the army in France, to fight on old French territory. This, I think, if the Allies persist, must end the business soon, for if he is well beaten, there must certainly be a rising in France; and if he beats the Allies, we shall in my opinion have a peace,

2 A 2

except that he seems determined, even now, not to give up Holland, and that we must at all events retain, if possible. The crisis is, however, apparently approaching, and that rapidly.

We remain here in *statu quo*. French desertion is diminishing, and seems for the moment quiet. The only event of interest has been the folly of two Portuguese officers near the Adour. They had had a long parley with the French, were, it is said, drinking together, but were somehow persuaded by their French new acquaintance to pass over the river for a dance, or wine, or some reason of that sort, under a promise of being allowed to return safe. They went, however, and have never got back. Lord Wellington has written to Gazan, reminding him of his having sent back six French soldiers, who were taken by the Portuguese in the heat of the campaign, owing to a similar promise or understanding, not having been known to them as made to the French. Lord Wellington claims the two Portuguese in the same way, as being taken by a breach of faith in the French officers. If this be not acceded to, he then requests that the two officers may be put for some time into close confinement or arrest, which, he says, they deserve, and might probably meet here if restored. As yet no answer is arrived.

A French dragoon of the 21st chasseurs, a deserter, came in yesterday, giving a curious account of his reason for deserting. He says he had been fourteen years in the French service, and was now a corporal; that his own captain's nephew had lately joined as a private in his troop, and that he, the corporal, had to place this man on duty; that he was not tractable or obedient, and that he was obliged to strike him with the flat of his sword; that the nephew told the uncle, and, when they returned, the captain, as soon as he met the deserter, gave him a severe blow in the face with his fist; and that, in consequence, he immediately got on his horse, and came off to us. He is a fine-looking soldier; and, though he has sold his horse for a hundred dollars, says, that he now repents much what he was induced to do in the heat of the moment; but it is now too late—the deed is done, and he must persevere.

I forgot to tell you, in my last, of an act of Spanish violence at Vittoria, which has caused a strong sensation in the English army, especially at Vittoria. The Honourable Captain G——, of the 94th, was quartered there, and had had some intrigue with a girl. He at first took her home to his quarter. Her friends had recourse to the police. The armed police came, and were in the house to take the girl: Captain G—— resisted, and the police were fairly turned out again by him and his servant. When out of the house, they are said to have formed, as it were, and then to have fired in through the door in cool blood, and with no particular object as to taking Captain G——. The latter was shot, and died almost immediately. Had this happened during the conflict, it might have been correct enough, though rather harsh and unnecessary in an armed police against an individual for comparatively a trifling offence; but as the story is told, it is quite inexcusable, and seems to have been merely an act of spite and vexation, at having suffered themselves to be repulsed by the captain. It was revenge for having exposed their cowardice.

The fox-hounds were out yesterday, and killed a fox; but had not a very good run. Lord Wellington wore the Salisbury hunt-coat, sky-blue and black cape. The Spanish General Frere accompanied him, and as formerly he was a general of cavalry, and the fox soon took to earth, I understand Frere kept up, but all his staff were distanced.

I feel now quite at ease about my animals, for I have collected straw and hay, and furze enough for about eight days, which is with us looking very forward, as much so as is prudent. My Spanish boy, after being here a day or two, told me he would rather set out and try to find his way to Madrid, so I dismissed him, lest he should take a horse or mule to expedite him on his journey.

We cannot prevent the Spanish boats from still getting down the Adour to Bayonne, though it is not quite so easy as it was to navigate the river. If all remains quiet, Lord Wellington talks of giving a ball here on the 18th of January, the Queen's birthday, but nothing can be settled long beforehand. The English ladies will be few, and all married women. We have still only four of the legitimate kind. The mayor of the town says that a number of the ladies who frequented the balls before we came, and of whom I found a list in my quarter, are still here, and will be forthcoming if called upon.

I find my French "seat of war" a most useful acquisition, as it now contains the whole war, except our own, and that I have in the map of this department, which is on a superior scale.

From four to six o'clock our promenade on the wall is quite gay, for all the great men of business, including Lord Wellington himself, generally appear there at that time, and the Guards also, though the exertion of walking, to which we men of business are accustomed to take at a true twopenny postman's long trot, is too great for them; yet they are formed about in knots and groups, sitting on the wall, or gently lounging on it, and add to the gaiety of the scene. We soon perceive when their turn of duty at the outposts takes them away to the front for a week.

As a proof of the supine and inactive state of the Spanish government, bread and corn are so cheap and abundant this year in the Castiles, that they are quite without demand, and it even answers to bring Spanish bread up here to sell, above fifty, and, I believe, a hundred miles; and yet the Spanish nation, relieved from the French army and our own, cannot supply the few men we have in front with us, in France and on the frontier, with money or anything. To prevent their plundering, we now not only have clothed Don Carlos's soldiers, near Hasparen, but have given them a month's pay, and provided them with rations of biscuits from England. With such a nation, and such a population, the state of the Spanish army, and the supplies, which get, I think, worse instead of better, is most provokingly disgraceful to their government and leading men.

I have been much struck with the change in the appearance of this town, when French head-quarters were here, and now that it has become the head-quarters of the English. It shows the difference between the two nations. When I was last there, all was gay and glittering, full of chattering officers in their best uniforms, with gold lace and ornaments, and prancing country steeds with housings and trappings of all kinds. The shops were crowded with sky-blue and scarlet caps embroidered with silver and gold, and pantaloons the same, smart cloaks, trinkets, &c. The road was covered with long cars, bringing in supplies drawn by mules gaily ornamented, and with bells, and waggoners with blue frocks, and long smacking whips, whilst the quay was nearly deserted, only a few boats to be seen which had just returned from an unsuccessful attempt to send in shot and shells to St. Sebastian; the sailors idle, and scarcely the appearance of a port visible. Bread and vegetables were abundant; other eatables, not so.

Now we have, on the contrary, a different scene; not a piece of finery is to be seen, no gay caps, no pantaloons, no ornaments. The officers all in their morning great coats; Lord Wellington in his plain blue coat, and round hat, or perhaps in his sky-blue Salisbury hunting dress.

The streets, full of Spanish mules, with supplies, and muleteers, &c., all running against you, and splashing you as you walk ; every shop crowded with eatables—wines, sauces, pickles, hams, tongues, butter, and sardines. The quay is now always a busy scene, covered with some rum casks, and flour casks, and suttler stores ; the sailors all in our pay, at work constantly and making fortunes ; the pilots in full hourly employment, bringing in vessels here or at Sacoa. The latter is full of masts and sails from Passages, Bilboa, Lisbon, or the West of England. The prices are still enormous, and of course the activity is the result. The French peasants are always on the road between this place and Bayonne, bringing in poultry, and smuggling out sugar in sacks on their heads.

The Basques must have been a very happy race twenty years since, for though generally a poor country, there is plenty of their usual food—Indian corn, and excellent meadows by the rivers, which are numerous. Fish is easily procured—the houses are spacious and comfortable, and the children seem numerous, well-grown, intelligent, and healthy. The men are tall, straight, and active ; the women, stout and useful, and rather good-looking. Nor was any great deficiency of young men observable ; the proportions seemed much the same as in England, though certainly there are not so many tall idle fellows about as in Ireland. The town, however, had evident marks of a tendency to retrograde and decay.

Later, the 16*th.*—By the last French papers (which we now have to the 8th, and which bring us the good news from Genoa), I find the accounts of Bonaparte setting out to put himself at the head of a hundred and eighty thousand men near Dijon or Mâcon, is at least premature, for he is still reviewing at Paris. We have stories of disturbances arising out of the conscription, but nothing certain seems known about them. The French, a few days since, surprised a few of our forage mules near

Lahoupon; I believe only eight. Lahoupon is a place which neither party is fixed in, but both patrole through occasionally.

P.S.—Notwithstanding Cobbett says, we men from the Peninsula must never think of marrying English women, we may at least be anxious about our friends; for we are not, I conclude, worn out for friendship, as well as for love. Tell me all you can, as usual, about every one in your world.

CHAPTER XX.

State of Feeling in France—Rocket-Practice—The Prince Regent's Hobby
—The Mayor's Ball—The Flag-of-Truce.

Head Quarters, St. Jean de Luz,
January 18th, 1814.

My dear M——,

AFTER two or three days' continual rain, we have at last a clear beautiful day; thermometer in my room at 63°.

In the midst of a terrible storm the day before yesterday a little cockle shell of a sloop arrived in the open bay here, with the Count de Grammont on board and Colonel Abercrombie, with despatches and a paper of the 10th. This told us the principal news. We have thus heard that the Danes are with us; ideas of peace thrown aside, and the Allies across the Rhine. This is popular news here; for almost all are against a peace with Bonaparte, partly from public feelings that such a peace would be injurious to England and the world, partly the fact that any peace would not be desirable to our military men, especially to those on the staff, whose splendour would be much shorn by it. The civilians and regimental officers, who are not on the eve of a step, are alone inclined to a peace; to many it will be ruinous.

We again hear of refractory conscripts, and men refusing to march, in the right of the department de Landes and elsewhere, and I believe it in some degree. But this alone will not do without a more general feeling

and even then scarcely, unless a portion of the army
takes a part and declares its views against the common
enemy Bonaparte, whom all Europe are now hunting like
a mad dog.

The Count de Grammont has made a most expeditious
trip. He had had communications with the persons on
his former property here, and I suppose his visit home
was connected with this, to know what line to pursue,
&c. The feelings of this part of France seem, as yet, to
be still the same : all desire peace, and for that purpose
are eager to get rid of Bonaparte ; but there is no feeling
manifested towards the Bourbons, not hitherto, at least ;
and I really believe the military men, and even many
civilians, would rather have Bonaparte if they could be
sure of a peace with him. He has done much for them,
and on a great scale. The Code Napoleon has been a
great work, and from what I hear is much liked. Instead
of being governed, and oppressed in fact, by the rich, as
they were before, they are now governed by the law, and
that a good law ; and as the mayor here and several
others say, well administered, when the state was not
concerned. The only defect seemed to be that the
magistrates having been latterly ill-paid, a temptation to
corruption on their part existed ; and this was a change
from anarchy, and therefore the more felt, as then the
strongest (I mean in means and territory) was everything
and the poor man nothing. In short, the only really
great grievance felt at this distance from the court of the
tyrant seems to have been the horrid conscription and its
tremendous increase of late, and the want of commerce.
Nor would the French feel either of these so much as
any other nation in Europe. The first she would not
feel so much, on account of the natural tendency of the
inhabitants to a military life and habits ; the last, from
the great internal resources of France in other respects,
making loss of commerce of much less importance to her

than to almost any other power which had been accustomed to enjoy them. I do not mean less than
Austria, which has been so generally shut out from commerce to any extent, but compared with England, Holland, or Sweden.

Thursday, 20th.—Another change again in the weather.
Yesterday it was quite a fine, sunny, warm day, till one
or two o'clock, like our May, and we were all out,
witnessing some experiments made with the rockets,
about two miles off, when a storm gathered, and soon
the rain and wind came, and has continued to this time.
The night has been very boisterous, and one of our
Commissariat transports has been on shore in the bay
here, stranded, and it is feared that five or six lives are
lost : all hands are now at work moving the stores—corn
and hay.

All the military men in the vicinity were here with
Lord Wellington, including General Frere, the Spanish
General. The ground-rockets, intended against cavalry,
did not seem to answer very well. They certainly made
a most tremendous noise, and were formidable spitfires ;
no cavalry could stand if they came near them, but in
that seemed the difficulty, for none went within half a
mile of the intended object, and the direction seemed
extremely uncertain. The ground was very bad, and on
a flat, or along a road, where they would ricochet or
bound along straight they might do very well, but in the
present experiment they went bang into the ground,
sometimes within two hundred yards, and sometimes one
way and sometimes another. Some of them, instead of
going fourteen hundred yards, as intended, were off in a
hundred, and some pieces of the shell came back even
amongst us spectators, one very near Dr. N—— and me,
whilst we were standing on one side, out of the way as
we thought. The fire, however, seemed very strong, as
one got into a green hedge, and set it in a blaze directly ;

the furze and heath were on fire, and only put out by the rain. Those which were let off at an elevation supposed for burning towns, &c., were much more successful, and some went very near the spot, compared with others; that is, I think they would have hit Bayonne, for instance, somewhere or other, and no doubt have set fire to the town; but the part of the town you could not very well choose, for their power seemed very different, and the wind at times carried them three hundred or four hundred yards away from the direction intended.

Upon the whole I do not think they were much admired, though in certain cases they might be useful, especially when the enemy are in a mountainous track, like at the battle of Pamplona, and near us. Where guns could not be got up without great difficulty, these rockets could be carried by hand, or on mules, and being let off near, would have tremendous effect even upon infantry when in column. General ——, who is very wise and knowing in the secret views and springs of everything (or at least would be thought so), says that all that fuss of the Crown Prince and Sir Charles Stewart, as to the effect of the rockets in the North, was to please the Prince Regent in England, the great patron of the rockets.

The stranded ship was, I hear, driven out of the harbour of Sacoa by the gale. This is quite extraordinary, for the vessels are there quite shut up. The place is, however, too full by far, for no transport likes to move again when once safe there. The packet lost in the harbour of Passages last week shows you the sort of gales and seas we have here.

This morning, a French picquet of about thirty men were marched off from hence, prisoners; they were surprised by us two nights ago. We got close, and when challenged, an old Highlander called out " deserter," so the sentinel did not fire, and our men got in among them and carried off the picquet. I am not very glad of this, for I fear it will lead the French to try and return the compliment, and make the outpost duty much more dangerous and troublesome than it has been. If it only leads to their shooting our next deserter, so much the better. Deserters continue to come in and tell strange stories. They say that Marshal Soult has issued orders, that whenever a foreigner is to be on outpost duty, all his necessaries, knapsack, &c., are to be taken from him, and he is besides to be watched and placed with others. They even say that a German posted on sentry has his shoes taken away from him. This, barring exaggeration, no doubt is nearly true.

It is reported that last week three hundred young conscripts belonging to one regiment were employed to carry bread to the brigade, and that when near one of the French sentinels, they were challenged by him, but from not understanding matters, they made no answer, and advanced; upon which he fired at them, when the whole three hundred threw down their bread and ran into camp, crying, that the enemy were coming.

But the best story of all, if true, was told by the mayor of Biaretz, who states that he understands three French divisions are under orders to proceed direct to Lyons, whether to meet Schwartzenburg or on account of disturbances does not seem clear, even if the story be true.

Friday, January 21*st.*—In spite of the wet yesterday, Lord Wellington having heard of the surprised picquet, set off to the front to inquire about it, or, as he said last night, to know if it was worth while to surprise it again, as it has been renewed by the French; but he thought not, and was back here to dinner, and in the evening at a ball at the mayoralty. This ball was an attempt to ascertain how far anything of the sort would answer. The mayor was to manage it, and ask all the ladies, and a list of the officers to be asked was given to him, and tickets sent out, and he was to provide the best entertainment he could for a dollar-a-head from the gentlemen only, which will be collected accordingly. It went off, however, but ill, and will not in my opinion be renewed. There were about a dozen or fifteen elderly women, French, who have remained here, and who seemed of the better order, but who came in our country town fashion, with the cloak, the woman servant, and the large lantern, only many of them brought the maid in with them to sit behind and look on. Then there were about sixteen or eighteen younger ladies, French, but who seemed to be nearly all the tradesmen's families in the place, none of the better sort, but from behind the counter in the morning. They were, however, well dressed, and danced tolerably for French—for English very finely. About half a dozen old Frenchmen, some respectable; and about eight young beaux of the place, who had escaped the conscription, and who had remained here, made up the French party. There were six English ladies altogether, but who, excepting one, declined dancing French dances or waltzes, and there was nothing else but one country dance, which went off ill. I have no doubt the French either thought them excessively fine, or that they could not dance. There might be quite as much of the latter as the former. Then to complete the assembly, came about two hundred officers, all in their best, and forming a very smart squeeze. What would your fine ladies in London have not given for such a display of gentlemen? All the field officers of six battalions of the Guards, and about fifty other guards' officers, and all the head-quarters' staff, generals, aides-de-camp, were there.

I think Cobbett would have admitted that, with so many fine young men there, the whole Peninsula squad could not be quite so despicable in the eyes of the English fair. Three sets of cotillions were formed, and some waltzes, but the whole went off but indifferently.

A Frenchman of about forty or fifty, one of the police of the town, volunteered a hornpipe, which was tolerably good.   About 12 or 1 o'clock a long table was opened for the ladies, covered with pastry of different shapes : no meat—the wine, claret.   At half-past one I came away, leaving the dancers rather beginning to romp. This will not do, because the belles are not good enough to please in a sober way, and if liberties are taken they would be offended, or at least their male relations would be for them.   Lord Wellington was soon off, and whilst there seemed to be principally occupied with little military arrangements.   He, however, seemed pleased with the thing, and asked me as I passed, if I thought Gazan ever had a better ball?   I only said, " I am sure there never were so many gentlemen in the mayor's house before." Better dancing, however, there may have been.

Still rain, without ceasing.   I have been skipping with one of my mule ropes, instead of my walk to-day with my umbrella.   I got to the wrecked ship yesterday.   The best account seems to be that she pulled up the post to which she was fastened in Sacoa harbour, and drifted out ; the captain was on shore ; the missing are three men and a woman, and they are supposed to be lost, and it is believed that the men were in the rigging trying to make things right, when the mast broke.   The Guards were set to work as fatigue-parties at low water, and the cargo removed on shore, consisting of hay and biscuit, not much damaged by the wreck.   The hay, however, of which one truss fell to my share, was previously almost mouldy with wet, perhaps a little taste of salt may give it a relish, and any how it is as good as coarse straw and furze, and better than nothing, which is my mules' long forage at present.   The muleteer is so popular, the Portuguese give him so much drink to make him dance and amuse them, that he is very ill with it, and lying below with a blister and emetic ; and the mules therefore get no grass, as I cannot turn them out; and straw I cannot afford them.

Another ingenious trick has just been told me of the French here. They advanced towards Murillo's Spaniards,—the latter fired at them; they sent in to say they were very much surprised, for they understood they were at peace with the Spaniards now, as a treaty was signed. Murillo sent back for answer, that he knew of no peace, and that, if the Cortes or Regency had signed such a peace, still he should continue to do as the English did, and fire at the French until orders came to him to the contrary, and that regularly through the Duke of Ciudad Rodrigo. This is all as it should be, but the trick is a curious one.

Saturday, 22nd.—The weather is now more like winter than it has yet been. At St. Jean de Luz we have a raw, cold air, no sun, a damp fog. La Rhüne and all the hills round are covered with snow; nothing but a little sleet has fallen here.

Sunday, Post-day.—A fine day, but really like winter; the coldest we have had, and a north-east wind, which will, I think, before it arrived here, have frozen you all up stiff in England and in Holland. We were all yesterday surprised by the news that the French picquets were all withdrawn near Bayonne on our front on this side, and that we might proceed close in to the works round Bayonne. What this exactly means we none of us know; Lord Wellington, however, was over immediately, to have a peep into the town on that side. Careless about himself, he got so close, that I understand there were some French in a house within about forty yards of him; nor did he move until he thought a French frigate lying in the harbour seemed to be making preparations to fire at the party. I mentioned to you it was on the 10th of December, in front here, that he got quite in the midst of the broken Portuguese, where there

2 B

were cross fires on all sides, and was fearful on moving
off quickly back, even though he wanted to go and order
up fresh troops, lest the bad example might increase the
disorder, and throw the men in greater confusion; so he
went leisurely back, until out of sight, and then cantered
off to the unbroken part of the column.

We have more reports of insurrections in France, and
the French have been circulating the story, that the
preliminaries of peace (a general peace) are already signed,
and have sent the report in here. I suspect that it is all
a trick, for all shifts and schemes are now resorted to;
amongst others, Bonaparte has sent back Palafox to
Spain—it is concluded, to intrigue, for he is well known
now, and the Cortes have, I am told, refused to receive
him or take any notice of him. The promotion of
O'Donaghue as Lieutenant-general, and his quitting the
situation of War Minister in consequence, is considered
a sort of triumph on our part, for he was suspected of
being inimical to Lord Wellington and the British
interests. Of his successor, Moreno, I know nothing,
except that he has generally been of the War Council,
and in civil-military employments, and has not seen much
service.

Head-Quarters, St. Jean de Luz, January 26th, 1814.—
I have now another letter to thank you for, of the date of
the 11th instant, and papers to the same period, for
which my best thanks are also due. These arrived by
the sloop of war, with Colonel Bunbury, and are particularly acceptable, for (except Lord Wellington), no one has
letters by the packet, or papers later than the 5th.
Colonel Bunbury brought one of the 13th for Lord
Wellington. In some degree, however, all your papers
now lose their interest, for we have a sort of information
through Paris very much quicker, and though not very
much to be depended upon, and not very full or accurate,
yet it gives us, making all due allowances, a tolerable

insight into what is passing. We have thus now papers of the 17th from Paris, from which it appears the Allies have been at Besançon, Dijon, and even Langres, whilst your accounts only carry them to the frontiers of Switzerland.

The deficiency of my Spanish maps does not signify, for I merely sent them home as a sort of memorial of Vittoria. All I had were only about the tenth part of Lopez, and nearly one-half of what I had are gone to the bottom in the little Catherine, in which I sent two parcels.

General G—— was always famous here for hospitality and very large parties. The only objection to them was the too great crowd at dinner. From what I saw, however, I liked him extremely. There was a wide distance between him and Lord Wellington in material points for a Commander-in-Chief, though I believe he was more popular with those under him, and particularly with his staff.

You need n ever apologize for forwarding a letter by any officer sent out express in a ship of war, and direct to head-quarters, for that is the best of all conveyances when available. They are sure to use the greatest expedition, and to have the best sailing-vessel. An officer coming out with convoy in a transport to join his regiment is quite *une autre chose*, and to be as much avoided.

We have for the last three days had a touch of your late weather, and have had snow on the ground to the sea's edge every night fresh, and remaining all day on the ground. It is still not very cold in reality, and indeed less so than could be wished, for if colder, we should feel it less. This seems paradoxical, but the truth is, that the ground here is not hard, and the snow, when trodden upon in the streets, melts, and forms a most chilling mud, and there is a cold evaporation going on worse than a hard frost. It is here every day like the first beginning of a cold thaw.

Yesterday one of my deputies, passing through here, dined with me. He is a very gentleman-like, quiet, and most diligent character, and I only hope my mention of him, in particular to General Pakenham, the Adjutant-general, coupled with that of Colonel Royals, whose Adjutant he has been, may do him some service. He has been down at Coimbra, and elsewhere. His name is Arden, and he is a lieutenant in the 61st. He was last from St. Andero, and told me a curious story about a late flag-of-truce there.

Much of our clothing was, you may have heard, carried to Santona, near there, as a prize. Many of our men were, consequently, in absolute tatters. Lord Wellington proposed to Soult to buy it at a valuation, and let the Governor of Santona have the money to pay his garrison. Soult agreed, and gave an order, with a pass. Mr. Drake, the Commissary, was ordered to go into Santona, in consequence, with a flag to treat. Instead of one trumpeter, five persons improperly went with him. The French officer on the post came out, told him he did not understand a flag-of-truce with five persons, and the Spaniards drawn up so near, that he might suspect treachery, and must do his duty, though Soult's orders and pass might be all regular. In short, said he, "I return in, and in one minute I fire a gun at you; so make the best of your way off." Though the party offered to be taken in as prisoners, the Frenchman went in; so off they ran, and just as they turned the corner of a house, a twenty-four pounder was after them. The Governor was angry with the officer. A new flag with one person advanced: Drake was admitted, but was blinded for nearly a league; and yet the person near him and another, let in afterwards, were permitted to see all. When the mission was understood, and the party discovered to be civilians, the Governor was very polite. He gave them good wine, but bad bread and meat, which the power of fancy made

Drake think was horseflesh. He then said that the shoes, gaiters, pantaloons, and some of the caps, his men then wore, so that as to those the mission was too late ; but the jackets they were welcome to purchase, with some other things, and a bargain was soon made. The Governor then said, " I know your road home is infamous to St. Andero—you shall return in our privateer row-barge." This they did in a very short time, and the finale was a formal complaint from the Spanish authorities at St. Andero, against Drake, for having dared to let a French row-boat enter St. Andero without their leave and their pass. When in the town all the children, &c., crowded round Drake and his party to see an Englishman. This made the Governor very angry, and he had them dispersed, asking them " what there was to look at in an Englishman ?" at which they shouted under his nose—" *Viva los Ingleses ! Viva ! Viva !* " I wish the higher class of Spaniards were as staunch as the peasantry and rabble.

Saturday.—Our regular mail has not yet arrived ; so your papers up to the 11th have been in most constant request ; for, though there was one here up to the 13th, there was no regular set to the 11th. The snow has ended in torrents of cold rain again ; the roads, almost more impassable, if that be possible, than they were before, of course impede all movement, even if intended. Nothing but a rising or commotions, would tempt us out, and that must be without cannon in a great measure, and dependant for provisions principally on the country, as our transport diminishes daily in the army, from the death of mules, or desertion of muleteers.

The life of the subaltern officers just now is very arduous and unpleasant ; winter quarters they certainly have, but that is all ; four or five in a room, comforts very few, a great deal of duty with forage parties, and going to Passages for corn, bread, &c., and always in the wet, and up to the knees in mud. Matters, however, must, in my opinion, end soon.

We have French papers to the 20th, and by them find the Allies at Langres, Dijon, and Lyons; we are told that they are well received. Upon this it must very much turn at last. The news from the French camp and from Bayonne is of peace. Our mayor has had a letter from his confidential friend at Bayonne. The basis was at last agreed upon on both sides, and a congress to take place at Basle. This may be fabricated, for the purpose of keeping the country and army here quiet until the event be really so. The French must now or never get rid of Bonaparte, if they wish it. It is not very flattering to the Bourbons, that even the repeated sufferings and disasters the nation has endured from Bonaparte scarcely seem to be able to rouse up the least attachment to them; and that even the last necessity seems hardly to make the people willing to run any risks for the old royal family. Yet I am almost sure the feeling would rapidly spread, from the sort of despair now prevailing as to *la pauvre France*, if a good beginning could be but once made.

You must remember the article of capitulation as to the *Commissaire de Guerre* and his family, the brother's wife, and two daughters, &c., at St. Sebastian. They have never yet returned to France, and are now here. The exchange of the *Commissaire* could never be arranged; and the ladies, though offered to return without him, would not do so, expecting that he would every day be able to accompany them. Lord Wellington let them remain at Passages, until the matter was finally settled; and there they have been all the time in the same house with one of our Commissaries, Mr. M——. And now, when they were all to go back, the latter has declared himself the admirer professed of the youngest girl, and they are after all halted here at St. Jean de Luz until he can marry her, and then the rest of the party pass into the French lines. I met them at dinner yesterday; they are a pleasant family. The girl pleasing and rather pretty, and in the English style; the mother a clever woman; the other girl not pretty, but odd, and, I think, clever.

Our new Admiral is arrived, having left England on the 21st. All our mails are thus forestalled, as we have still only mail papers and letters to the 5th. We are told that there is no news in particular, but that all is warlike. Our story here is, however, of a still later date, and may possibly still be true. The only other news we have is from Catalonia; and that, it is to be feared, is bad. You will, however, get it before you have this, I conclude, from the *Gazette*. General Donkin told me his letters stated that we had made an attack on Moulins del Rey on the Lobregat, near Barcelona; that the Spaniards were to cross the river and turn the French : that they were too slow and too late, and so the whole plan failed; but that we suffered but little, and that the loss was nearly all Spanish, who lost two colonels killed. I do not believe that all Spain would drive Suchet or his army out, except by time, and wear and tear—never by force. The Government, however, have behaved well, I believe, as to the late French attempts through Ferdinand, and through our English hero— Palafox.

I am sorry not to be able still to admire the latter. It is mortifying to strike out the name of one of the few Spanish heroes which this five years' war has produced. I am now, however, satisfied that the Spanish insurrection, and all its good consequences, was owing to the thorough ignorance and want of calculation, and of information and judgment of the Spaniards. If they had had more common sense, and knowledge of the true state of things, even their zeal and patriotism (which I

admit were considerable) would never have induced them
to adopt a course so devoid of all prospect of a favourable
result, and which every thinking, impartial, able man
must have pronounced a desperate mad scheme. We owe
it principally, I am sure, to their excessive pride and
ignorance, their good opinion, yet want of knowledge of
themselves. And this accounts for the most able men at
first all going the wrong way.

Sunday, 30th, Post-day.—Nothing but wind and rain,
wind and rain for ever, and no more news. Some of the
deserters say that the French head-quarters are removed
to my old place, Mont de Marsan; but I should think
that this can scarcely be yet. The new Admiral dined
at head-quarters yesterday, but I understand, has brought
little news. One ship under his orders, it is feared, has
been lost already, as we have a report of a sloop of war,
The Holly, lost at Passages, and several of the crew with
it. This is certainly a terrible coast. There is now a
vessel riding in the bay here, very uneasy, and cannot
enter; and one was as nearly as possible lost yesterday
morning close to Sacoa; the surf broke over her. The
exertions of the French pilots were astonishing.

Sunday, later, 5 *o'clock,* 30th.—We have two French
officers come out here from England to seek a better fate
by a little *intrigo,* I suppose. One is a Basque of this
country on half-pay from our service, and the other,
a Monsieur La Fitte, I believe a clever man, and a La
Vendée hero.

CHAPTER XXI.

Army Supplies—Offending Villages—Symptoms of Work—Arrival of the Duke D'Angoulême—The Bridge across the Adour—Wellington and his Chief Engineer—His Activity.

Head-quarters, St. Jean de Luz,
February 2, 1814.

My dear M——

Here we remain absolutely tied by the leg by the horrible state of the roads, and weather, and without any regular news from England. Nothing but reports on the side of France which would encourage us to proceed ; and, on the sea-side, of heavy gales, and lost vessels. I am just now driven in by a furious hailstorm, and yet the weather is mild, and has been till this moment pleasant enough. We have two ships in the little bay here ; one full of hay, which has been four days nearly within three hundred yards of the shore, and in hourly danger of drifting on the beach—yet we have not been able, in spite of our distress, to get out a truss ; and the other a brig transport, empty, and driven in here by stress of weather. A frigate was also off here all yesterday, apparently labouring much, and fearful of the coast. We certainly have undertaken a bold thing in wintering in such a place, but it was a choice of difficulties.

If we had money we should do well, but that is as scarce as anything else. Plenty of supplies would come in from the right from the French, had we cash to give in return. As it is, in consequence of the little ready money we gave at first, a great quantity of cattle, food,

&c., has been obtained, but now we are reduced to Treasury Bills, and that cannot last, and the loss is very great. Even the muleteers get a past payment now in those bills, and the consequence is that a person may buy them with dollars at the rate of 7s. 4d., and, I believe, 7s. 6d. a dollar. The army is also six months, and the staff seven months in arrear of their pay.

We have, however, I believe, plenty of bread and biscuit, and meal for a month with the army and corn at Passages in abundance. The short transport from thence is almost too much for us, and the supply is by no means general to the animals, whilst long forage is quite a rarity. The destruction in the oxen is frightful in the rear. Our great depôt is as far back as Palencia, and even there, in store, the cattle die very fast, and the moment they march they fall away to nothing and die by fifties. Our Commissary-general almost despairs of getting more up, although he has made depôts of bran and straw, &c., on the road, to try and obviate the total want of food. It is now in contemplation to ship cattle from St. Andero, where there is a store; but then we have rather a scarcity of naval transports also. Cattle would come in as fast as we wished from twenty leagues to our right, could we but pay for it. As it is, I am almost inclined to think that we shall, as a choice of evils, be obliged, in spite of the roads, to move towards our right in quest of food.

Two of the villages in that direction have justly incurred Lord Wellington's displeasure by plundering and seizing our forage parties, of which we have lately lost several. One or two were taken by the peasants of those two villages, and Lord Wellington has issued a proclamation addressed to them and that country, reminding them that he told them to remain at home, and be quiet, and to take no part, and that if they did so he would protect them; but that he would not have this treachery in return. If they did not like this proposal, well and good, then let them quit their *foyers* and leave their villages, and take the consequence, and he should be prepared to meet them as enemies; but they must make this election. The curé of one of these villages was carried off as a hostage for their good behaviour in future. We have strong reports of commotions and internal dissatisfactions in France, and that Bonaparte is reduced to concentrate his army round Paris. If this be true Lord Wellington must be half mad about the roads. I find he is gone out to-day to look about him. Two ninepounders have just drawn up opposite my windows with eight horses each, and the men have left their guns under the charge of the Provost guard. I suppose they are on the march. I must inquire what this means.

February 3rd.—The artillery is said to mean nothing; but still I think if we get fine weather for a week we shall have a start. In confirmation of what I have written above, as to the loss of cattle, I will give you two instances : three hundred and sixty head of convalescent bullocks, which had been left at Vittoria to get into order, were marched for the army; sixty only have arrived thus far, all the rest have been left at stations between, or been given to the different alcaldes, and receipts taken for them —a new mode lately adopted. Five hundred of another lot of fresh bullocks, collected at Palencia, were marched all this way, three hundred only have reached Vittoria, and all the bad road and scarcity of food is yet to come. This is really quite alarming.

February 3rd, later.—I find the guns mean nothing; they are only going on to the front to replace two now there, which are to come back to refit. Still, however, if we could but get fine weather, I think we should make a stir. Bets were going on as to a peace, or our being at Bayonne and across the Adour in six weeks; and symptoms of a move shortly are perceptible. The rain, however, continues. Colonel Bunbury made one attempt to go to the right of our army the day before yesterday, but only got half way, and is unwell in consequence. He is to leave this either in Lord Wellington's carriage, or to go round by water to Passages. The sea is, however, quiet, and now only torments our anxious curiosity by throwing up parts of wrecks and bodies. A ship-cable, with the G.R., was found at Bidart, and three men and a woman. Some say that the latter had silk stockings on. One body cast up here was half eaten, and I saw a back-bone only yesterday. The bodies of the mules float in and out every tide.

As a proof of the state of forage here, and of the manner in which we are imposed upon, five shillings were yesterday demanded for a sack of chopped furze from the surrounding hills, and thus sold in the market. Straw fetches two shillings for a small handful, of which a horse would eat two or three in a day.

I have just seen a Spanish Captain who was taken prisoner little more than three months since. He has been to Maçon on the Saone since, where the Allies now are, about six hundred miles from this, having been first plundered of his great coat and pantaloons. He was about thirty-five days getting there on foot all the way, staid there forty days, and then was about thirty-six days more returning here, also on foot, having been exchanged. He says the notion is that we have the Duke d'Angoulême here, and that very many wish it to be so. This is like my finding many persuaded that we had the Duke de Berri with our army when I was a prisoner. I suspect, however, we shall in part verify this notion now, as I just hear one of the best quarters in the town is to be cleared immediately for an unknown great man, now at Passages, and just arrived from England. At first they even talked of moving the Adjutant-general, Pakenham, to make room for him. This mystery will, however, soon be cleared up. Rain, which is never pleasant, was never so disagreeable as now. The fate of France may depend upon it.

The owner of my house is a well-bred woman, who lives in a great house opposite. She lives in one corner of it, whilst General Wimpfen and his staff, and Colonel M——, his wife, and three children, occupy all the best part. She has, she told me, thirteen houses round here, five are burnt, and two coming down, and yet she seems resigned and satisfied that we have really behaved very well; that it is the fate of war, and owing to the ill fortune of having property in a frontier country near armies, and is quite inevitable. She only exclaims, " *Oh la pauvre France!*" This is a novel language to the French of late.

4th, Friday.—Still rain, rain, rain, all night. All yesterday, all the night before, and still continuing. Oh! that we had your frost instead; all things would have been very different.

The great man just arrived, and now here, turns out to be the Duke d'Angoulême, and Count Damas is come out with him, but till the plot thickens the Duke is *incog.*

Our pontoons from the Bidassoa are now passing over the St. Jean de Luz bridge. This looks like something, and we have to-day at last a dry day, or at least a half day, for I must not be too sure yet. The wind is getting round to the north a little, or north-east, and if that remains it will do, especially as it is full moon; though I have not much more faith in the moon, in respect of weather than Lord Wellington has, who says it is nonsense. In addition to all your news, we have French news of a battle at St. Dizier, near Chalons, and that the Allies have been beaten. It is to be feared that it is not all to go so smoothly as hitherto, unless a rising takes place.

All odd strangers who come to head-quarters here have

been long called tigers. Of course we now have "The Royal Tiger." This is a head-quarters' joke for you. We have had for some time here a Madame de ——, the wife of the Commandant of ——, come to make arrangements beforehand, and here she certainly has been making many little arrangements not much to the advantage of her husband, and not quite consistent with conjugal fidelity. When the Commandant arrived yesterday at last, she immediately began to blame him for his unnecessary delay, and insinuated that another lady was the cause. This is very hard upon a poor old man, but I suppose the lady thought it right to take the initiative.

The publication of the Leipsig letters, which George mentions, of Murray's, will be very curious, but I think it is not right to let these be published. Similar letters were taken in Spain more than once, and police reports. The old letters which were too late (those I mean from you) were from the Secretary of State's office, not from the Judge-Advocate's office. They were probably mislaid at the former.

Sunday, Post-day.—A bright sun and a smiling sky, with a smooth bay covered with ships, quite a Vernet. I have just returned from the church service on the beach, in a square of about two thousand five hundred guards, and all the staff here present. As I returned I picked up your letter of the 26th, and papers at the post-office. I have just got some business come in, for desertion has commenced again now that we are quiet and idle. A corporal and twelve men all went off together a few nights since, all foreigners, and I believe French. Our people at home are very careless in selecting soldiers to enlist into our corps from the prisons. What can be better for a Frenchman in a prison-ship than to receive 4*l.*, new clothes, arms, &c., and then to be sent into his own country, and put in a situation to join his comrades, with only the difficulty of watching a good occasion. In yesterday's return, however, nine men have deserted, mostly English. Your English news is all good as far as it goes, and if this weather will but hold a little, you will hear of more glory and more broken heads here. In addition to the pontoons which have passed up, scaling-ladders have gone through here. If we could but cross the mouth of the Adour below Bayonne, and get at the citadel at once by scaling and storm, there would be something like a blow, and the town would be at our mercy immediately.

We have some gentlemen here, but very few, who begin to find the work too warm for them. I have been saved two cases of this sort, very awkward ones, by resignations, and have been consulted on two others by General Cole, very suspicious ones, but not so clear as the other two who are let off thus, to save the reputation of the regiments. An officer should think a little before he engages in service, such as we have had here the last few years.

More business, so I must put an end to this quickly. I have not seen the Royal Tiger, but am to dine at head-quarters to-day, and hope he may be there. The French ladies are staunch Bonapartists. They say we shall have another Quiberon business, and that the Allies are coming into France the same old road as twenty years since, and will return by it.

I have been so pressed to change my old mare, which was in high condition, that, to oblige Major D——— of the Guards, I have done so, and taken " Mother Goose" (a pet name of General Hulse's formerly) in exchange, and fifteen guineas to boot. Mother Goose is a very good mare, but never would stand fire. She is not so large or showy as my old lady, but I like her much. She was valued at eighty-five guineas, and has always sold for that. I put mine at a hundred guineas. I gave more—

four hundred dollars; as dollars cannot be had under 7*s.*, and the exchange is still higher on the muleteer Treasury bills. These, however, I should not think it right to deal in.

Head-Quarters, St. Jean de Luz, Thursday, February 10th, 1814.—Thus far the week has passed without my having commenced my usual Journal to you; for I have had a return of business, and also several gentlemen to swear, and certificates and affidavits to make out, to enable friends to take out administration in England to deceased officers' estates. We have also again had two fine days, and I have been able to get a ride or two in consequence. On Sunday, at head-quarters, I met the Royal Tiger at dinner—the Duke d'Angoulême and Monsieur Damas.

Before dinner I got into conversation with the Duke, without knowing who he was, for they were both dressed alike in a fancy uniform, very like our navy Captain's undress, a plain blue coat, with two gold epaulettes. He seemed much pleased with his prospects, and very sanguine as to the result. The day was fine; he was sure the weather would last a month. I said that the natives told me we should have rain, and no settled weather until March was half over. He was sure I had been misinformed; the fact was, however, that it rained half that very night and the whole of the next day. Every day he expected to proceed to France, and saw all difficulties vanish. " *Les pauvres conscrits de Bayonne fondaient comme la neige; ils étoient presque tous à l'hôpital,*" and so on.

That we shall make a dash soon, unless peace prevents it, I fully believe from all I see and hear, and an embargo which has been laid on all small vessels in the river here confirms this. We have also to-day an order for twelve days' hay at Passages, for which we are to send to the ships ourselves, as Government have just now sent us out a good lot of English hay, and if we march it must be all left behind, for we have no means of carrying it with us. At least the animals will thus all start with a belly full, which is something, and to many a novelty.

I do not think much of the little Duke; his figure and manners are by no means imposing, and his talents appear not very great. He seems affable and good-tempered, and though not seemingly a being to make a kingdom for himself, he may do very well to govern one when well established. Lord Wellington was in his manner droll towards them. As they went out, we drew up on each side, and Lord Wellington put them first; they bowed and scraped right and left so oddly, and so actively, that he followed with a face much nearer a grin than a smile.

They were at church on Sunday, but I cannot learn with any effect; hitherto we cannot judge, for this small corner dare not speak out their minds, if they were in his favour. We hear of a strong disposition at Bordeaux and in Brittany. I have as yet seen only apathy and indifference, but I still expect a burst if the war should last.

I must now go to Lord Wellington about a poor old Doctor, who has been charged with having a soldier servant. I expect a jobation for what I shall state in his favour, for this is a very heinous offence in the eyes of Lord Wellington.

Same day, later.—Lord Wellington, as I supposed, insisted on the Doctor's being tried, but was good-humoured, though just going out with the hounds, when in general he does not like interruption. This particular Doctor had a right to a servant of his own regiment, but he had one of another. I suggested that he had never joined his own regiment since he was appointed, and could not, therefore, have one of that corps. "Then he should have gone without," was the answer, and as for the Doctor's good character, that went for nothing. Lord

2 c

Wellington never attends to individual hardships, but to the general good, and as many abuses go on at depôts in the rear, every time he discovers an instance he is inexorable in trying to punish, especially when he finds it out himself, as he did this in another trial of the same poor Doctor, by some of the evidence. The Doctor, foolish man, desired it might be put on the minutes that he would ask such a witness no question, as he had been his servant at the time, and was so still.

I have just heard an anecdote which shows strongly the Spanish character, and also why Lord Wellington likes Colonel Dickson as his chief artillery officer. On the 9th of November last the order was given for the troops to march to the attack at four the next morning. This was when we were at Vera. Every one had known for weeks that this was to take place the earliest moment it was possible; and that the fall of Pamplona and better weather were the only reasons of the army being in such a position as we then were, perched up on the sides of all the mountains so late in the year, with the prospect of snow daily. At nine that night General Frere, the Spanish General, who is considered to be one of their best, sent word that the Spanish army under his command was without any ammunition, and could not get any up in time. At ten o'clock Dickson was sent for, just as he was going to bed. Instead of saying nothing could be done, or making any difficulties, he proposed giving the Spaniards immediately the reserve ammunition of the nearest English division, and said that he would send out orders instantly, and undertake to get the English reserve replaced in time, and this was done.

Poor E—— got a very loud discourse all the way home from church last Sunday. The oxen of the pontoon train were all dying, and in cross roads were useless, for they could not move singly except with difficulty, much less draw a pontoon of two tons weight. It had been reported in consequence that three troops of artillery must be dismounted to draw the pontoon. Lord Wellington was vexed excessively. " Where are the pontoon horses ?" " None were ever sent out from England; never had anything but oxen, and five hundred have died since we left Frenada." This answer still did not satisfy him. He must, notwithstanding, have known it from the returns which he sees, but still he seemed, though he could not tell why, to think poor E—— blameable. The latter said that he had no orders to send to England for horses, and no one seemed to think they would be necessary, and he had never had them.

Friday, 11th.—I went last night to our third ball, in hopes of seeing the Duke d'Angoulême there, and to observe how he was received. He did not attend. All our other great men were there—Lord Wellington and all the French, as yet very few in numbers. The owner of General Cole's quarters near Ustaritz, I believe named Larrique, was there. He had come over to pay his respects to the Bourbons. He was always royally disposed, and had been once imprisoned for this inclination. I am told several others have been to the Duke to pay their respects merely, but this is all they dared do as yet. They assure him the landholders and peasantry further on only wait our advance, and the absence of the French army, to rise and declare for the Bourbons. If they do not take this line soon, and that decidedly, peace may make it too late, and frustrate all these petty plans of counter-revolution in the bud. The Duke seems quite ignorant of the people here, and of the country, and those Basques I have talked to do not seem to know much more of him. The few squires left may, however, give the tone to the rest.

I hear that we have quite ruined Bayonne market by our higher prices, &c., and things are not only dear there, but not to be had, for no one will there give the price we

do for such luxuries, as poultry, vegetables, &c., certainly
are; and therefore they are brought here.

Saturday, 12th.—The news now is, that Soult and
about three thousand infantry, and one thousand eight
hundred cavalry, are gone off to the rear, and it seems to
be believed; for it has come through so many channels
to us.   Another report is, that seven of the thirty tyrants
(senators) have gone over to the Allies, to pay their respects to the Bourbons; this is not in such credit as the
other story.   In short, we have what the military men
call " shaves " (I suppose barbers' stories) every day and
every hour.   The best fact I can tell you is, that we have
had three days' fine weather now together, and this last is
absolutely warm, I only fear too warm to last; thermometer in my room, window open, and no fire, 58° in the
sun.   I rode a league out and back yesterday almost
without a splàsh.   The mule roads across the country,
though improved, are, however, still very bad; three
more such days will, nevertheless, do wonders, and about
that time I hope we shall be ready.

All the carpenters, &c., are ordered from the Guards to
the front.   The Rocket Brigade also went up last night;
and ships are ordered round from Passages.   Dr. Macgregor, who was there yesterday, tells me that he thinks
it will be three days before they will have procured ropes
and all they require with them.   This smiling sun
makes every one cheerful, though it prognosticates many
broken heads.

The only thing, it appears to me, the Guards look blue
about, is the prospect of an aquatic expedition.   Our
sick, though nothing compared to last year, have increased
this last month.   To show you how much depends on
seasoning them, two regiments, the 84th, and, I think,
the 62nd, who came out two months since, and have
scarcely had any work, but arrived after all the bad
quarters in the mountains, and have not marched forty

miles and been generally housed, are absolutely unfit for the field. One has four hundred and more sick out of six hundred. They are obliged, in consequence, to be sent in a body, as regiments, to Vera, one of the hospital stations. They are, I believe, two battalions, and mostly young lads or elderly men, neither of which class of soldiers can stand this work at all. Some of our old regiments have scarcely a man in the hospital, except the wounded, and it is astonishing how well some of the Portuguese regiments stand it, who are more exposed than our men. The last month's rest, and the new clothes, which most regiments have now received, will revive the army amazingly; some who are still without their clothes are, to be sure, absolutely in rags, or like the king of the beggars.

Head-Quarters, St. Jean de Luz, Sunday the 13th, *Post-day,* 5 *o'clock.*—Our " shave" of to-day is a Congress. Yesterday the Allies were at Paris. I am sorry to say the sea has risen, and the wind changed, and the weather threatens again. All are hard at work, however, at the bridges, &c. It will be a ticklish thing to cross at the mouth of the Adour.

Head-Quarters, St. Jean de Luz, February 15th, 1814. —The plot now thickens a little. Lord Wellington was off at three in the morning yesterday for Hasparran, for two or three days, to superintend a movement which is to take place : first, on our right, to drive the French divisions of General Foy and Harispe across the Gave d'Oleron, and prevent their molesting our right flank, whilst the passage of the Adour is attempted on the left. The accounts this morning are, that the troops assembled for this purpose yesterday, but that no affair has hitherto taken place. General Pakenham was yesterday at Passages to see to the shipping there, and clear out the hospital; and to-day he has gone over to the right, to report to Lord Wellington and to assist there. All is in motion: two bridges are preparing, one, as I supposed, below Bayonne, and another above; the former will be accompanied by an aquatic expedition.

With regard to this grand bridge, a most provoking occurrence has taken place. An embargo was laid on about twenty-four vessels in the St. Jean de Luz river to form this bridge, and to assist in the conveyance of troops, &c. Old Ocean, however, did not approve; and as he is not under Lord Wellington's orders, and seems, like the Spaniards, to like to thwart Lord Wellington a little, he (Old Ocean) threw up the day before yesterday such a mound of shingle at the mouth of the river, that he has most effectually embargoed the whole shipping, and made a dry bank, a hundred feet wide, quite firm across the entrance, which all yesterday was used as a road backwards and forwards from Sibour to this place. From the present state of the tides there was no prospect of an opening in the natural way for a week and more, until the springs; so to-day a fatigue party of the Guards are at work digging and shovelling.

In my early walk this morning I found them at it, with a young engineer officer, doing it, it struck me, very ill. I could not help meddling; however, I had no weight, until an old Frenchman came, sent by the mayor, to whom I advised them to apply; and then, as the young engineer did not understand French, I acted as interpreter. The old man's plan and mine agreed, and so I carried my point. It is hoped we shall be able to dig a way through by this evening, and to-morrow to let the shipping out. It has never happened before since we have been here, though very often the river is nearly dry.

One brig of war has arrived and the *Gleaner* ketch, and Lieutenant Douglas is on shore here superintending the fastening together of a quantity of masts, &c., to form a boom, I believe, across the Adour—I suppose to prevent anything floating down from destroying the bridge. I heard yesterday, what one can scarcely believe, that the naval officer asked leave to survey the mouth of the Adour, but that Lord Wellington told him to go to the engineers, and they would give him plans and soundings, &c.: that he went to E—— accordingly, and found he had none at all; and Toffini's coast stops short at Passages!

It is surely very odd, now that we have been in front of Bayonne for three months, that no plans should have been sent out, without being asked for, from England. I since have heard from E—— that he did write, and has nothing in consequence but a little printed plan of Bayonne, and no soundings, &c. I trust still that Lord Wellington will poke out his way across. Our outposts' reports to-day are that the Cossacks are close to Paris, and Fontainebleau pillaged by them. I am sorry for that, as that palace escaped the Revolution almost entirely. The truth of the whole story may well be questioned.

February 16*th.*—No news from the right; no one returned yet; the reports are, that the French do not stand, but retire before us. In the mean time things are going on well here. The weather is fine again, the sea quiet, the river has quite cleared his course, and to-day the navigation is open. The fort at the mouth of the Adour sent a few shots against the *Lyra* brig when cruising yesterday to inspect; but no harm done. Every one is busy.

Poor —— does not seem to draw well with Lord Wellington. The latter received him so queerly at the last interview, that —— says he shall do all he can to execute what he is ordered, and be quiet. Lord Wellington never consulted him, and has never even told him exactly where the grand bridge which he is preparing is to be; and the consequence is, the width of the river has not been precisely ascertained at the place intended, where the engineers have instruments which would do it in a minute, if they were ordered. Without orders they cannot, as it would require a guard of three hundred or four hundred men to go near enough, and that can only be with orders. But then, were I ——, I should ask for the guard and do it, propose it first, or try and get it quietly from the Adjutant-general without troubling Lord Wellington, and let him find the thing done. —— seems to be too much of the English official school; has too much regard to forms and regular orders. All this *entre nous.* Elphinstone of the Engineers tells me he wrote for a plan of Bayonne four months since, and has only received a very miserable one, of scarcely any use.

The grand bridge is to be formed of the largest vessels now in the harbour—about fifty of them. Pontoons would never do. They are to be about 25 feet or 27 feet apart, and cable bridges between to communicate with planks, each vessel carrying its own materials to plank, &c. This is a grand plan, but rather arduous. I hope it may answer, as it will be an event in military matters, crossing a great river at the mouth below the fortified town, and that in the hands of the enemy on both sides of the river.

February 17*th, Thursday.*—Still fine weather, and no one returned, and no news from Lord Wellington. I had a report here through the emigrés, and *son Altesse Royale*, as he is now called, that the Allies are within a league of Paris. " *Quelle mauvaises nouvelles! ils m'ont dit.*" Their alarm at the reported Congress at Chatillon sur Seine, and Lord Castlereagh, has to-day of course a little subsided in consequence. A peace with Bonaparte would ruin them for ever. If Paris now declares itself, on the other hand it will spread, and the whole business, in my opinion, be at an end in their favour. If not, it is clear that their party is very small, and their interests forgotten.

The 18*th, Friday.*—Still Lord Wellington not returned; but we had some news of what has been done on the right. The French retired skirmishing, but would never stand to let us charge. They were obliged to remain longer than they wished to cover some guns which they carried off; and also, the evening before last, they intended to take up their ground for the night in a position which Lord Wellington thought it would suit him to drive them from. By doing this late in the day they were obliged to resist more than they probably otherwise would, if they had expected it, and been prepared for the retreat. We have taken about ten or twelve officers prisoners, and about two hundred men. Some say that we might have had as many thousands, could we have been two hours sooner. These things are always, however, said. Supposing that we had been two hours sooner, the French would have been just where they were; and it is forgotten that if we had moved sooner, they might probably just have done the same thing. We have ourselves sustained some loss, and that in a greater proportion of officers than men. I am told, about a hundred and twenty men. General Pringle is shot in the breast,—an awkward place, but they hope not badly, considering the situation. General Byng's aide-de-camp, Captain Clitherow, is killed, and, I believe, Lieutenant Moore, of the Artillery. Aides-de-camp and Brigade-Majors have suffered much of late; Lord Wellington's are uncommonly fortunate. I have heard also that Lieutenant-colonel Bruce is wounded, a Bevan (Major or Colonel in the Portuguese service), and some subalterns of the two brigades of General Byng and General Pringle, the only two engaged.

By the last accounts Lord Wellington's head-quarters were at Garris, near St. Palais, and the French are driven

across the Bidouge, a river that runs into the Adour
below the Gaves, and near Grammont's place, Guiche, of
which he is duke. The French have only picquets on
our side the first Gave—the Gave d'Oleron, when they
are driven across. I think Lord Wellington will return
here to-morrow to inspect the grand bridge and the operations on this side, which are the most ticklish. Elphinstone would have his bridge ready to-morrow night
if the materials get round in time from Passages, and
provided one vessel is got out from our river here, for
one could not be moved over the bar yesterday, from its
having the guns on board, which are to be dropped into
the Adour, to assist in moving the vessels of the bridge.
By taking out the guns this difficulty may be got over,
but the wind is not fair from Passages. This is the
worst part of the business, for though the elements alone
may be to blame, still Lord Wellington, if his plans are
thwarted, will be in a rage with ——. He banishes the
terms difficulty, impossibility, and responsibility from his
vocabulary.

The moment he has done on the right, he wants to be
ready here, as he knows that so long as he remains there,
the attention of the French is drawn that way, and the
same when he shall return here. We have now no
troops here. The guards have moved into Bidart, and
we have now permanently occupied Biaritz in front of
Bayonne; General Vandeleur sleeps there, and all his
horses are unsaddled. The light division have crossed
the Nive. The fifth moved a little more to their right,
to occupy part of the ground of the light near Arbonne
and Arauntz, towards Ustaritz; and the third division,
under General Picton, have gone up to St. Jean Pied de
Port, but hitherto without opposition. The Adjutant-
general, when he went himself over to the hospital stations of Fontarabia and Passages, routed out about fourteen hundred convalescents, and malingerers, and they

passed through here for their regiments yesterday, for every man is wanted now. Unluckily, no reinforcements have arrived from England; why we cannot say, for the wind is fair, and the papers say they sailed a month since, and the regiments have had notice of their intended arrival. The artillery also expect five hundred horses, which would now be an inestimable treasure, as many are going and getting weak. There are also about six thousand Portuguese ready to join in Portugal, but who remain for want of transport, as I am told: this is unlucky, as they were well-seasoned recruits.

It is curious that even latterly, ever since we left the mountains, almost all our advanced troops—the advanced line—have been Portuguese; they not only stop our deserters, but go off very much less themselves. From the terrible loss of oxen, we are all now, officers and all in this neighbourhood, living upon salt rations, sea-beef and pork. Luckily for me, however, we can now buy a little fresh meat. I am very much vexed with myself for not having desired you to send me out a good map of France, for I have only the department on this side the Adour, and the whole seat of the war is now France. I should like to have got the abridged or reduced Casini, which is used here, and liked, a map about five or six feet by four or five, and Stockdale's vicinity of Bayonne, taken from Casini's large one. These two would have been a treasure, now that we are likely to move; and I conclude Stockdale will go on publishing some more of Casini to follow us up.

We have begun to establish a recruiting-party at head-quarters, to select out of the French deserters good subjects for the *Chasseurs Britanniques*, &c. I hope it will answer, but I have my doubts. In the mean time, I shall have to play the part of a magistrate, and swear them all in. The news from Bayonne to-day is, that a courier arrived yesterday express from Paris in sixty

hours; of course he brought something very important.
The story in Bayonne is, that the negotiation and Congress is broken up already, and this is now considered
most excellent news here, excepting by a few soldiers of
fortune, and real lovers of their trade, who think it would
flourish much better after a peace with Bonaparte than
with the Bourbons. What a contrast between the *Moniteur* a year and a half since about Moscow, &c., and the
late ones about the works round Paris, and the room left
—eighteen inches—for the *piétons* only to pass, &c., and
the immense zeal and activity: *Dejà on voit les embrassures
pour quatres canons.* You will have seen all this, however, and have been as much amused, no doubt, as we
have been.

I have just seen Major D——, who is returned from
the right. He says that we have been well received in
general, and found a tolerable supply of everything in
the new country we have been in. If the inhabitants
will but stay, they will find a good market for everything;
instead of losing the produce for nothing; and stragglers,
single plunderers, dare not commit depredations on the
houses in that case. The people here are in despair at
the expected entrance of the Spaniards. We have now
shops in abundance, and a good market, and can, with
plenty of money, procure most things; and now we are
on the point of being off.

18*th February, later.*—I have just been with Elphinstone, and seen all his drawings and plans for the grand
bridge. They seem very good, and the whole will be
ready by Sunday morning, provided the naval gentleman
can carry his vessels in; but he thinks that will not do
on account of the tides before Wednesday. Six or seven
small boats are to be carried from here on carriages;
these are to be launched, and are to tow across the first
party on rafts, which are made by some platforms placed
on the pontoons. This first party I would rather not

accompany. To show you how little Lord Wellington listens to objections, and how he rather likes to cut up the routine work, I may mention that Elphinstone told him the quantity of plank necessary would take time, and make a delay. "No," says he, "there are all your platforms of your batteries which have been sent out in case of a siege. Cut them all up." "Then when we proceed with the siege what is to be done?" quoth Elphinstone. "Oh, work your guns in the sand until you can make new ones out of the pine-wood near Bayonne." So all the English battering platforms have been cut up accordingly.

At Elphinstone's I met the Admiral, who came round to-day to assist, and some small vessels have arrived with him. We have now Sacoa choked full, and quite a flotilla in the open bay, with a wind right on shore into the bay. I only hope it will not take to blowing hard in this direction whilst our operations are going on. The battering train and siege apparatus have also arrived at Passages from St. Andero. This has been done quite snug; even Elphinstone did not know of their coming until here they were.

Letters have come in from the right; all has gone on well there. The French are driven quite across the Gave de Mauleon or Soiron, as it is called in my map, a little river which is the left branch of the Gave d'Oleron, and runs into the Gave d'Oleron below Oleron town. The Adjutant-general writes, that the French have given up all that at present was wanted in that direction. Adieu!

Saturday the 19*th.*—To-day we have a French bulletin sent in to us of a victory over the forces of the Allies, the Russian army destroyed, and the French in pursuit— baggage, cannon, all taken. This is awkward when we expected daily to hear of the Allies in Paris, and it will have a bad effect on the cause in France, even if it is only a slight check to the allied armies. The French here have their proclamations printed, and *fleurs-de-lis* are being made. Lord Wellington says that they must wait until he is more advanced before they begin to circulate them. He is expected back to-day. The weather has been very cold again, and sleet or snow has just begun to fall. I have also to-day to acknowledge a letter from you of the 8th, and papers from the 2nd to the 8th inclusive.

I am just interrupted by a noise at the Provost guard opposite, and the arrival of about a hundred and eighty French prisoners escorted by a party of the 57th regiment, who might with great advantage change clothes with the French. The latter are in general very well clothed, and very fine young men, a few older soldiers amongst them in particular. The young conscripts look rather pale and sickly. Our 57th men are absolutely in rags and tatters, here and there five or six inches of bare thigh or arm are visible through the patches; some have had only linen pantaloons all winter through. They all get their new clothing to-morrow at Sacoa; the whole regiment comes down here for that purpose, and then nearly the whole will have had their clothing this year, all but one or two regiments.

Later, 4 o'clock.—Lord Wellington is just returned from the right, and so eager is he when anything is in hand, that I saw him going round by the Admiral's and Colonel Elphinstone's before he went home on horseback, after a tolerably long ride too. The Admiral he carried off with him.

20th February, Post-day.—The first thing I saw this morning in my walk on the wall was Lord Wellington looking at the sea at half-past seven. The wind was strong, right into the bay, and not a ship could stir. He soon saw the Admiral come out also to look, and carried him off home. I saw Lord Wellington about some Courts-martial just now, and expected to be rather snubbed; but he was in high good humour, and I was, of course, as short as possible. The moment is, however, ticklish. Had the gale this morning increased, none of the ships in the bay, in my opinion, could have stood it. It was right into the bay against them, and they were anchored within two hundred, three hundred, or four hundred yards of the shore. The slip of an anchor or breaking of a cable would have been destruction, and we have now a wreck on each side of the bay, which is ominous and terrific to strangers and new-comers.

Later.—Lord Wellington is already beginning to provide against the failure of his bridge plan from winds and tides, and I understand will not wait above a day or two on this account. Arrangements are in consequence being formed to make the main movement still by the right altogether, and to come round on Bayonne in case the bridge scheme will not very speedily answer.

CHAPTER XXII.

Movements of the Army—Narrow Escape of Wellington—Anecdote of
Wellington at Rodrigo—Novel Scaling Ladders—Sir Alexander Dickson
—Wellington's Vanity — Operations resumed — Spanish Officers—The
Passage of the Adour—The Road to Bayonne—Death of Captain Pitts.

Head-quarters, St. Jean de Luz,
. Tuesday, February 22, 1814.

My dear M——,

As the movements going on give me now a little
more leisure, and it is impossible to say how soon my
opportunities of writing may be arrested by a march, I
begin my weekly despatch early this week.   Lord Wellington, when he returned from driving the French across
the Gave, found his expedition here could not leave port
owing to bad wind and tide, though all was ready.   He
therefore instantly set about new arrangements, so as to
be independent in a great measure of the result of this
grand bridge.

All the divisions of the army consequently moved
towards the right yesterday, except the Guards and the
rest of the first division, which remain in our front backed
by a corps of Spaniards at Guethany and Bidart, in
advance of St. Jean de Luz, through which place, however, they did not march.   To superintend this movement Lord Wellington was off again yesterday for Garris,
near to St. Palais, with most of the head-quarters' staff,
Adjutant-general Pakenham remaining here on account
of a slight illness.

The last move left us in front of the Gave, the French

still strong in Sauveterre and on a ridge of hills and strong ground running between the two Gaves d'Oleron and Pau. The plan is now, it is concluded, to drive them across both Gaves, and then make good our way round to the other side of the Adour and the citadel of Bayonne. In the meantime, as the plan here is still expected to take effect to-morrow morning early, we are all alive; the little bay full of shipping and small ships of war, which cruise backward and forwards, or anchor there, with carpenters, sappers, soldiers, &c., on board, and all the flotilla ready in Sacoa, and the Admiral superintending.

Head-quarters are come home delighted with the country on the Gaves, and with their reception. The people in many instances come in numbers to meet our troops instead of offering resistance. The prisoners also many of them say they are ready to serve *son Altesse Royale*, but this is rather too soon to begin, it is thought, for this may be only to escape and return to their old army.

One young man, who was of the country, ran into his father's house as they were marching by, and all the family were found around him. He was separated and marched off; but the story has been told at head-quarters, and General Pakenham has sent for the man back (who was on his way to Passages), and means to send him home to his friends.

I was talking to General Pakenham yesterday about forming a French royalist corps out of the prisoners and deserters. It must be done very cautiously of course at first, but it would in my opinion have a good effect and soon increase. At present the idea that all deserters must be sent away from their own country to England deters many from deserting, who would otherwise be willing. This object would also do away with the disgraceful ideas naturally attached to desertion in a soldier's mind.

2 D

Reports say that Lord Wellington had a narrow escape with his staff, whilst reconnoitring on the right in the late move. He is said to have been going up a hill when a French cavalry regiment was coming up on the other side. The engineer officer was going round and saw the regiment; upon which he galloped back to give information, but before he could reach Lord Wellington they were just close to the top of the hill, and Colonel Gordon, who was in the advance, saw some of the French videttes close. He gave the alarm, but they all had a gallop for it, pursued by some of the dragoons.

Though the English horses were most of them well tired, they were soon out of reach of the French, and all escaped. Lord Wellington relies almost too confidently on the fleetness and excellence of his animals, when we consider what the loss would be if he were caught; he is, however, now rather more cautious.

A few days since I heard an anecdote about the siege of Rodrigo, which shows the man. Scarcely any one knew what was to be done; the great preparations were all made in Almeida, and most supposed, as I believe the French did, that everything which arrived was for the purpose of defence there, not of attack elsewhere. On a sudden the army was in front of Rodrigo. A new advanced work was discovered, which had to be taken before any progress could be made in the siege. To save men and time, an instant attack was resolved upon. Scaling-ladders were necessary; the engineers were applied to; they had none with them, for they were quite ignorant of the plans—an inconvenience which has often arisen in different departments from Lord Wellington's great secrecy, though the general result, assisted by his genius, has been so good. The scaling could not take place without ladders; Lord Wellington was informed of this. " Well," says he, " you have brought up your ammunition and stores, never mind the waggons, cut them all up directly, they will make excellent ladders —there you see, each side piece is already cut." This was done, and by the help of these novel ladders, the work was scaled forthwith.

At Badajoz, he found so little to be had in the regular way for a siege, from want of transport, and so many difficulties in consequence from the regular bred artillery generals, that he became principal engineer himself, making use of Colonel Dickson, the acting man, as his instrument. These sieges procured Dickson his majority and lieutenant-colonelcy; and though only a Captain in the Royal Regiment of Artillery, he now conducts the whole of that department here, because he makes no difficulties.

In one instance Lord Wellington is not like Frederick the Great. He is remarkably neat, and most particular in his dress, considering his situation. He is well made, knows it, and is willing to set off to the best what nature has bestowed. In short, like every great man present or past, almost without exception, he is vain. He cuts the skirts of his own coats shorter, to make them look smarter: and only a short time since, on going to him on business, I found him discussing the cut of his half-boots, and suggesting alterations to his servant. The vanity of great men shows itself in different ways, but in my opinion always exists in some shape or other.

February 22nd, 5 o'clock.—The flotilla has just got out of Sacoa Bay preparatory to the operations to-morrow. A beautiful sight! Six or seven ships of war, and fifty other vessels—everyone alive! Forty form the bridge. I hope it may succeed, but many doubt it.

P.S. Lord Wellington is moving on the Gaves with seven divisions. The cable bridge is in the boats, and the engineers on board. The affair is to begin by driving in the picquets, when five hundred men are then to be sent over on the rafts, the guns of the French battery spiked, the French corvette burnt, and then the bridge is to be thrown across !

February 24*th*, 1814.—I rose at half-past four, to go over and see the crossing of the Adour yesterday, and the formation of the bridge. At daylight I discovered that the whole flotilla had been dispersed by the gale of the night before, and no part was near the mouth of the Adour. Several officers returned in consequence, declaring that nothing could be done. Thinking otherwise myself, and that this movement would somehow take place, being connected with Lord Wellington's movement on our right on the Gaves, I went on, and found all the Spaniards on the road in front of Bayonne, but doing nothing. All was quiet for a very long time. About twelve o'clock, however, they were ordered to move on and make a feint, and an attack was made by our great guns and rockets at the same time, on the French armed corvette and gun-boats, to destroy the latter, and at the same time to draw off the attention of the French from the mouth of the river below Anglet, where we intended to cross on the rafts.

The Spaniards were not much opposed, and went on boldly enough, as far as was intended, and had a few wounded. The sharp-shooting, however, was very slack. The fifth division at the same time, made a show on their side, between the Nive and the Adour, but not with any serious intention. I then went into an empty house with Dr. Macgregor and some others, to make a fire and get some breakfast, which they had brought with them ; and adding our several stocks together, we fared very well. We then made our way through Anglet, and across the sands, and through a pine-wood, to the river's mouth. A brigade of Guards, another of the King's German Legion, the Light Battalion (most excellent men), and a Rocket Brigade, were there all ready to pass, but from the immense difficulties which had been met with in the transport of the boats and pontoons over land, only two of the light companies were over about one o'clock, when I arrived, and a temporary suspension of the passage of men had been ordered by General Hope.

The order, however, had just come again to pass over as fast as possible, and before I left the spot (about three o'clock) three rafts, formed each upon three pontoons, and carrying each about fifty or fifty-five men, were at work ferrying across on a cable, and the six small boats were also plying, so that about five hundred men were then nearly over, and they were going at the rate of two hundred, or two hundred and fifty per hour. I left the rocket men, each with one rocket ready in his hand, and three on his back in a case, with three poles on his shoulder, just going to cross.

Elphinstone had been quite in despair; the pontoon car sunk so much in the sand, that at last thirty horses would not move them, and for the last five hundred yards they were conveyed on the shoulders of the guardsmen; twenty-six men to a pontoon. At length all his difficulties were thus overcome, and the non-arrival of the bridge, of which we could see nothing, was not his fault, but that of the weather.

I helped the engineering again a little, by joining the party who were endeavouring to find the best place to which to fix cables against high-water—as I discovered the last tide-mark in the sands, and thus found a landing-place and post, clearly above high-water mark; for the springs were past, and of course every succeeding tide would rise to a less height. We then proceeded along the river towards our battery on the bank, which was firing at the corvette, &c. When we had gone a little way through the pine-wood, we found all the roads almost stopped by trees cut down by the French, and the

road we took near the bank, which was clear, carried us
opposite a smaller French corvette and three gun-boats,
which had just placed themselves in the river. At first
we thought them a part of our intended bridge, but soon
found it otherwise, and that we should be fired at, for
our small party on the other side the river had not
advanced, and all the opposite bank and village, as well
as the boats, were still in possession of the French. We
therefore turned, and at last made our way through to
the battery. There we learnt that the guns and rockets
had sunk one gun-boat, and frightened away the rest
and the corvette, which had all been hauled up close to
the bridge under Bayonne, where we saw them.

I could not understand that the rockets had done
more than cause some alarm, though twelve had been
fired at once at the shipping, and from no great distance.
Only one, or at most two, had fairly struck, and nothing
had been burnt. The heavy guns had struck the corvette,
but could not do much damage before she was off, and
just at first the corvette and battery on the French side
seem to have had the best of it. Count Damas, who
was there with the Duke d'Angoulême, looking on, told
me that the artillery had knocked off the colours of the
corvette whilst he was there, and that one of the light
Germans had jumped into the water, had fetched out the
colours, and had presented them to the commanding
artillery officer. Others say that these colours were on
the gun-boat. The French were so alarmed at the
rockets, that the vessel, when struck, was abandoned.

Close to our guns we found the other brigade of
Guards, &c., making an immense fire with the fir-trees,
which had been cut down on all sides, for the day,
though fine, was very cold. Dr. Macgregor, one or two
others, as well as myself, went up a little sand-hill near,
just to look round, when a twenty-four pound shot from
Bayonne came close to us point blank. The horses

turned right round, and the Doctor losing his hat, I thought at first that he had been struck. Of course we soon beat a retreat, and found we were in a spot where this was the usual reception, and a position of which the French were jealous.

Just as I came away, a little before five, I saw a column of French, apparently about seven hundred, going very quickly through the wood on the opposite bank from the citadel towards our men, who had passed to attack them. I knew that we had nearly a battalion across, about seven hundred men, and did not feel much alarm with regard to the event. I pitied the men more for the cold night they were likely to pass on the bare sands, without baggage, &c. This morning I have heard an attack was made just afterwards, but that some of the rocket skirmishers were put in advance with the other skirmishers on our side, and the French were so alarmed that, though much superior, they would not advance, and our men beat them off.

The flotilla was this morning collected near the mouth of the Adour, and, I suppose, before this the bridge is begun. At any rate we could have passed across as many men as we wished before this. No one has returned to-day to this moment, and as I had business, and one of my horses was a little sore in the back, I staid at home. My grey pony started before six yesterday morning, and I was not at home till past seven at night, having ridden above thirty miles.

Some of the Spanish regiments were very fine men, and well equipped in every respect, much better than some of our poor fellows; but the officers looked very bad indeed; and when the men advanced, they were led on by their officers with cloaks on, folded over their mouths, looking as miserable as possible.

The men also, like the French, always march with their great coats on over everything, so that our good new clothes were all concealed by their own old thread-bare overcoats. On the other hand, none of our men had their coats on, cold as it was, and everyone was alive and in activity. I stood next to Don Carlos d'Espagne, and heard him receive his directions and information as to what parts we occupied and what the French, &c. General Hope (though not well, and too soon, I believe) came on to take the command, of which the division were very glad.

I fear the Spaniards, though better than they were, and though only the best were in advance, will soon begin to do mischief. As I returned here I saw all their stragglers about the houses near the road, and telling every one that in Spain *Francesi roban e rompen todos todos*. They soon soil our new clothing, and go about with dirty and scowling discontented faces, like some of our good countrymen in Ireland. The industry of the French on the sand-banks had been very great in the cultivation of the vine. The south-east side of the very bank on which the sea beat on the north-west, a pure white sand, was divided with square reed enclosures, and covered with vines. The Anglet wine (which, as a very light wine, is in repute), I believe, is there pro-duced. Many of the inhabitants at Anglet and the neighbourhood, remained, and, in general, seemed glad the movement was over. One old woman, in a house that was near the river's mouth, said she was most happy to see us, as she had been for the last two months in complete misery, not being allowed to speak to any strangers by the French, nor even allowed to go to Bayonne to buy a few sous-worth of snuff. I suppose they feared the spread of information, for this was close to the spot intended for our bridge, of which I under-stand, and have no doubt, they had a very clear know-ledge. Two persons of the better class have come in here by sea from Bordeaux, round by Passages, to pay their respects, and give information to *son Altesse Royale*. Colonel La Fitte told me that they were as anxious there for Lord Wellington as the Jews were for the Messiah, so sanguine are the emigrés.

February 26*th.*—All accounts now agree that the French have from ten thousand to above eleven thousand in the town and citadel, three thousand in the latter, the rest in the town and lines. Another show was made against our people the morning after they crossed, but no attack. Considering that the French had eleven thousand men, that it was eight or nine hours before we had above five or six hundred men across, this passage of the Adour and our establishment on the right bank is most disgraceful to their troops, or to their General, and proportionally creditable to ours. In the evening of the 24th our flotilla crossed the bar and got into the Adour over a most tremendous surf. Several accidents ensued in consequence, and many lives were lost; some say as many as forty in the whole, of all nations. I believe about fifteen English sailors were lost. None but the English sailors would have dared to enter at such a time. Five boats were upset, most of them very near it, and one brig, with stores, aground, as well as one small ship of war, a gun-vessel I believe. Some of the flotilla never got in at all. The place fixed for the bridge was not so wide as was expected and prepared for, so sufficient boats are ready, and last night all but about three were moored in their berths ready, and, in my opinion, the bridge would be passable to-day.

The loss of the French in the gun-boats and corvettes was greater than we supposed, for the inhabitants inform us that a Captain of cannoniers was killed, and several men, and the Captain of the corvette lost his arm. The rockets also did mischief on shore: one man who is now in here, had both legs carried off by a rocket. I have been since told, the French lay down on their faces, and

then ran away from them.   An order has been issued in
Bayonne for all persons who have not and cannot procure
six months' provisions to quit the town, and numbers
were coming this way along the road yesterday.   I went
out that way on purpose to meet them, and talk to them.
They all agreed in the number of men, about eleven
thousand, but said that a great part were conscripts and
weakly.

This I concluded to be the case, as all those unequal
to an active campaign would be naturally left in the walls
for quiet garrison duty.   The alarm had been terrible
in the town, where an attack was expected two days
since.   Every householder was ordered to have an
immense tub filled with water, ready at his door, &c.
Count Reille has gone to the rear, some said ill, and
Thouvenot commanded again, and most said that Marshal
Soult was gone to Paris, some to Mount Marsan, and
that Count Gazan commanded.   A Frenchman, who
came yesterday, told Monsieur d'Arcangues, an inhabitant
here, that he had just passed through La Vendée, and
that that country was in arms again ; that he had himself
seen several armed parties, amounting some of them to
seven or eight hundred men.   This will at least stop the
conscription a little.

I communicated this good news to *son Altesse Royale*,
and at the same time made him a little *cadeau*, by
begging that he would permit me to send him King
Joseph's saddle-cloth, which I had picked up at Vittoria,
but had never used, as being rather too splendid (blue
with a very broad gold border).   He was very civil, and
in return lent me a paper of the 11th, which he had
just got out with his baggage from England, a second
edition of the *Courier*, containing in the corner a notice
of the arrival of the message through France from Lord
Castlereagh, a piece of news which alarmed him not a
little, though our French accounts still say that the

negotiations are broken off, and the Allies close to Paris.

General Harispe had raised about three thousand or three thousand eight hundred of his countrymen, the Basques, a fine race of people, but since our late move most of them have run home, and his corps, the maire here told me yesterday, is reduced to about five hundred. Our officers remain delighted with their reception on the right. They all say that every one talks with horror of making war in an enemy's country; but they can declare from experience that they never wish again to make war in a friendly one, if this is to be the manner of making war in an enemy's. Nothing has been done on the right of any consequence yet, merely preparations in case this bridge had failed; if so, I think we should now have Lord Wellington back here directly from Garris, where he has been, and the move will at last take place.

I have just got my mules back from Passages, with six days' hay, and am now ready, though my Guardsman tailor has carried half my new clothes with him across the Adour, and I never expect to see them more, and have a Frenchman at work. Considering your lost box and all contingencies, my last suit will probably stand me in about 35*l.* sterling!

The ride along the high road to Bayonne yesterday was interesting. The refugees from the town, several of them very pretty Basques, were all coming this way, laden with the little baggage they could carry off; our artillery all moving up the contrary way; as well as the Spanish troops; and hundreds of Basques, men and women, with great loads on their heads (like our Welsh fruit-women going to Covent-Garden), only their baskets were full of bread, biscuits, &c., and all in requisition for the Spaniards. The bât animals and baggage parties of the Spaniards are not a little amusing, and their led

chargers with their tails buckled up, and in swaddling
clothes, with dirty magnificent housings, dancing about
half-starved, with their heads in the air. Every fifty
yards a dead bullock or horse, but chiefly the former,
and every two hundred, an ox dying, and a Spanish
muleteer or straggler waiting until the bullock driver
abandoned him, to turn him up, and cut his heart out,
before he was dead, but when in a state too weak to
resist. The heart alone seemed to be worth the trouble,
as nothing else could be cut off from the bones, and bone
and all did not pay the cutting up and carriage.

The destruction and present price of cattle are tremendous, and I hear we have been obliged to give the
Spaniards some of our best Irish cattle, as we had no
other at hand. The only meat they seemed to have
with them was a number of ox cars with sides of Spanish
bacon; this, and sardines, seemed to form their supply.
The men, however, are very fine men, and in my opinion,
were they well commanded, would make excellent troops.
Nevertheless, I was by no means sorry to find that we
had still an English brigade of about twelve or fifteen
hundred men (Lord Aylmer's) between us and the eleven
thousand French at Bayonne, for I am sure five thousand
French would force their way through the fifteen thousand Spaniards if they chose to try, though we should
in the end prevent their return. At any rate we should
have early notice, and alarm from the runaways. The
French beat our men at that, for we cannot catch them,
and the Spaniards would not be easily caught by the
French.

We had a most anxious scene here two nights since.
Just as our vessels got into the Adour, a suttling brig,
Dutch-built, and very strong, to save pilotage fees, tried
to get into this river without the pilot boats. The boats
towing missed the mouth, were both swamped, and the
men in most imminent danger, as well as the vessel,

which was driven in without guidance, aground for an hour, but saved, and at last all lives were saved, or at least all but one.   When the boat was filled, another wave drove it against the ship, and three caught hold of the ship-chains and got in; the fourth was knocked about in the water between the ship, the boat, and the wall, but at last got his chin on the sinking boat, came up the harbour so, was hauled in and saved.   In my morning walk on the sea wall, I found another ship on shore, a large brig with a valuable cargo, a private speculation.   This will be the third wreck, but considering how many vessels have been here, and how they have been all exposed, and half of them absolutely at the mercy of any north or north-west squalls, we have been most fortunate.

Later.—In my ride to-day I met about thirty or forty wounded men of the Buffs and 39th, second division; but this is the consequence of the last move, I believe, as they told me they were wounded at or near Cambo.   We have reports of an affair, but here nothing is yet known. We are becoming, instead of being like head-quarters, the centre of all good information, a mere hospital station in the rear, and famous as usual for ill-founded reports, which the medical men probably invent from *ennui* on these occasions.   A large brig has arrived from Bordeaux with wine, but, in my opinion, almost too late for the speculation.

Sunday, 27th February, Post-day.—In my walk this morning I saw another boat swamped, trying to get out of the river over the bar.   It was actually worked by the surf into this position, with the stern stuck into the sand of the bar, and fairly went over, with the five men. For some time all five were visible, two swimming, and three clinging to the keel of the wreck, which was bottom uppermost.   Another boat, which had intended to follow this one out, was fortunately close at hand, just

out of the reach of the surf, and by this means the two
swimmers were saved by giving them a rope's end,
and also one of the three from the wreck, as it floated
inwards.   There was a struggle between the three, when
a wave came, and two appeared no more.   The relations
of the two men witnessed their loss, as well as myself,
for we were standing on the edge of the wall within ten
yards of the men, but unable to help them.   The distress
you may conceive.   We become in some degree hardened by seeing death so continually, and in so many
forms, as we do here.

I have also this morning met with five English seamen,
part of the crew of one of our provision ships, which
were lost some months since on this coast.   The master
and four men, being from St. Andero, and the French
having heard of the fever there at that time, they were
put under quarantine on the coast, about forty miles on
the other side of Bayonne.   Afterwards they escaped,
and lived among the inhabitants, who, they say, treated
them well, as the master had money.   At last, hearing
from the French that we had crossed the Adour, they
made through the woods this way, and fell in with our
cavalry about three leagues on the other side of Bayonne,
General Vandeleur being on that side of the Adour, with
two regiments.   They mention that they saw on the
road going to Dax a number of the wounded French from
Bayonne, and also troops retiring that way, they were
told, to the amount of fifteen thousand, but the number
must have been considerably exaggerated.

The servant of Captain Pitts, of the Engineers, came
in yesterday with an account of his master's death.
Captain Pitts was one of General Cole's staff, and a most
spirited, zealous, skilful, and promising young man.   He
was killed on the right a few days since, when our men
had driven the French over the Gave d'Oleron.   He
went down to reconnoitre, and take a sketch of the

banks, and make observations with a view to the formation of a bridge. His servant says that he had finished, and was looking round just before he came off, when a ball struck him on the head. General Cole's staff have been very unfortunate this last year, and indeed the loss of officers in his whole division has been very considerable. I used to think that it sometimes affected his spirits, though it never induced him to endeavour to diminish it, for he always was and would be foremost in danger.

Count Damas has just informed me, that Lord Wellington has now crossed both the Gaves, and is near Orthes; but we have no authentic news from him. All accounts agree that General Picton was wounded in the affair on crossing the Gave; but, it is said, not badly.

I picked up this morning a Spanish paper, and on making it out, found that it was a letter from a Spanish officer in camp, near Bayonne, telling some friend in the rear that Murillo and Mina had beat the French across the Gave, and were in pursuit along with two English divisions, having taken forty guns, &c., and adding that the inhabitants were *muy malos*, but that we treated them as well as Spaniards, and that they, the Spaniards, were ordered to do the same, but that we should see, &c.

Head-Quarters, St. Jean de Luz, February 28th, 1814. —Lieut.-Colonel C—— has now returned here, and we have at length some authentic accounts of what has passed. Lord Wellington was at Orthes, where he left him, intending to stay there a short time to arrange communications with General Hope's column, &c. Our men forded the Gave de Pau, and drove the enemy from Orthes. As they made some stand in that town, it was a little *rompé'd*, as we call it. General Picton was not wounded, and our loss has been inconsiderable upon the whole. Colonel C—— returned by my old road through Peyrehorade, Ramons, and across the Adour, at Port de Lanne, and so to Bayonne, and then across the new bridge here. He found the first division driving the French from the heights above the citadel of Bayonne, close into the town last night. This was done, but with some loss and much firing. Those hills are important, for in some measure they command the citadel. To-morrow we march to join head-quarters. I believe we shall not pass the new bridge, as a Spanish army crosses that way, and will occupy it all day, and the road also; in addition to which, we have hitherto only cavalry patroles along that road, and the French have halted a force at Dax, or Acks, or Ax (in the different maps). I understand that we are to go by Ustaritz, Hasparran, Garris, Sauveterre, and Orthes. This is a roundabout bad road, but will be a new country to me. The weather most luckily continues fine hitherto.

Our accounts from the interior are, that Toulouse and Bordeaux are both ready to hoist the white flag, and only wait for our sanction and declaration. This point of etiquette may spoil all. I think we should declare our readiness to support them the moment they declare publicly their readiness to take that part. This is a critical moment. Many are alarmed at Schwartzenburg's not having made more progress; he seems to have hung back, for his army was stronger than Blucher's, and was forwarded six weeks since, and yet we only hear of Blucher being near Paris. I must now prepare to "*romper de march*," as Jack Portugoose calls it. So adieu.

CHAPTER XXIII.

Passage of the River—Start for Orthes—Effect of the Battle—Feelings of the French —Wellington wounded — St. Sever—Church and School— Aire—Wellington on the Conduct of the Allies—Indurating effects of War.

Head-quarters, St. Sever,
March 5th, 1814.

My dear M——,

Here I am with head-quarters, and within two leagues of my old quarter, Mont de Marsan. We have had a most unpleasant, and, for the baggage animals, a most laborious journey, from the terrible state of the weather—hail-storms, rain-storms, with violent south-westerly winds almost all the time. By warm clothing and good living I have escaped with only one day's return of rheumatism, which has now gone off, and I feel in very tolerable repair.

On the 1st of March we left St. Jean de Luz, and passed the grand bridge below Bayonne, in sight of, and I really believe within gunshot of the walls. We all filed over in safety, and then along the sea-wall for half a mile, with water on both sides, to Boucaut. I was surprised that the animals were not more alarmed.

The bridge answered perfectly; it consisted of thirty-six two-masted vessels, with anchors across all the way at the head and stern of each; a strong beam across the centre of each, between the masts, to which the cables were fastened, to form the road, so that each formed a separate bridge, and the destruction of one cable only

2 E

affected one space.   The boards were then fixed on these
cables, and were interlaced all the way by small cords,
through notches in the boards ; and thus we went safely
along between the masts, in a road about twelve or
fourteen feet wide, differing, however, from a common
bridge, for the arches between the boats (from the
stretching of the cables) formed concaves instead of
convex arches, some of them descending nearly to the
water's edge.   It answered, however, perfectly, and will
continue to do so, unless the Spaniards suffer the French
to come and destroy it.   Of this I have my doubts.   The
crews were living in their vessels at the head and stern,
cooking away and going on as usual.   Five or six gun-
boats were moored about it, then came the boom and
boats ready to tow ashore any fireship.

At Boucaut we found Sir John Hope and his staff, so
we were ordered to the next village on the road.   Our
managing Quarter-Master clumsily went to a bad village
of a dozen houses, out of the road, when there was a very
good one on the right road, only a few miles further on.
Several of us had no houses, and were told we must find
them for ourselves.   After waiting for some time until
my baggage came, I determined to go on the right road
until I found a quarter vacant, trusting with full confidence to the good disposition of the inhabitants, which
is most excellent towards the English.   After looking
into five, I found a vacant one a mile and a-half off, no
officer within half a mile, and no English troops within
two miles, and none at all towards the interior of France
on that road.   The people expected some one, and a bed
was ready, and a hearty welcome I received.

In my way I went round by the picquet, within about
eight hundred yards of Bayonne citadel, where my tailor
was on fatigue-duty in the works, and I thus recovered
my clothes.   As I was just going to bed at eight o'clock,
a violent cannonading and sharp musketry commenced

sounding close by us. I did not think it prudent to go to bed until it ceased, for we were within about a mile and a-half of a garrison of eleven thousand men; but suspecting what was the case, that it was only our people driving the French out of a field-work on the hill, and hemming them in closer to the citadel, I was little alarmed.

My host and his family were great royalists in their professions, as they had for the last six months been more than usually oppressed by the French. He had a house and ten acres of land; the house probably worth about 10l. a-year in England. The rent of his land was one-half the produce of corn and maize; the taxes on his house had been already that year sixty francs, and his contributions fifteen bushels of maize and, I think, ten of corn. He said that no one could live if this continued, and that all the young men were carried off. He had one quarter to pay still, but expecting us every day, he put it off from time to time, though much threatened, and now thought himself safe.

From thence we started early for Peyrehorade, rather a large place, nearly as large as Kingston-upon-Thames. It was a market-day, and the people of the country crowded in as usual. They all stared at us, most saluted us; all were civil, and we got our quarters with much more facility, and met with ten times the civility we had ever done in Spain. I never witnessed a single quarrel, though the town was crowded as it is during an election with you, and we had only about twenty dragoons to protect all the twelve hundred animals and baggage of head-quarters.

My host was particularly civil, and gave me a very good apartment and an excellent dinner—some roast beef à l'Anglaise, a duck, and a fowl. The whole family dined with us, wife, mother, and two daughters. The eldest

2 E 2

son, who had been intended for an attorney, had been taken as a conscript, and was wounded at Leipsic—since that time they had not heard of him. I comforted them by suggesting that he must have been left at Mayence. The next son was sixteen, and at school at St. Sever; next year it became his turn to take his chance as a conscript. You may well conceive that we were considered as welcome guests; independently of the expectation of having coffee and sugar cheap for grandmamma, and English linens, muslins, &c., for the two ugly misses.

On the 3rd of March we started again for Orthes, the scene of the famous battle, of which you will have heard before you receive this letter, and of which we received several imperfect accounts as we went along. The reception all along the road, and at Orthes, was the same as at Peyrehorade. Dr. M—— and Major G—— just stopped in the stable of a château for shelter, when the owner came out and took them in, and gave them cold turkey and champaigne. At Orthes I got an excellent quarter at the house of the *Juge de Paix*, who was very hospitable as usual; and as the weather was so excessively bad, and my Portuguese almost dead with their walk of twenty miles in the rain and mud, I stopped the night there, notwithstanding the head-quarters were regularly eight miles further at Sault. I knew the latter was a miserable place, which was another inducement with me to remain.

At Orthes I found about two thousand wounded, one thousand English, and the others French and Portuguese; the latter had behaved well, as usual. I found the Adjutant-general, Pakenham, confined to his bed, ill at the inn, but, at nine at night, and this morning, very much better. The hospitals are all established, and in full activity. Lord March was shot in the chest, but the surgeon hoped he would do well, and thought so; he could not, however, find the ball, but had reason to think it had not passed the lungs. Colonel Brook's brother (a schoolfellow of George's) was shot through the lungs, and there is little hope of him.

The affair at Orthes was quite unexpected; as they had suffered our army to pass all the rivers, no one expected this desperate stand, for such I am told it was, the French having seldom fought better. They stood some time after they had ʿceased to fire, and it is therefore concluded that they had had no ammunition left; and even after our cavalry (who behaved well) was in the midst of them cutting away. At last they gave way, and then fled quickly. Their loss no one knows, as the wounded got off to the villages round; but all say that their army is actually reduced above eight thousand men, as the conscripts are all running home as fast as they can. Above twenty had come back to Peyrehorade; and one gentlemanlike young man I met at my quarter there was a convalescent conscript, and such he said he should now always remain, unless affairs took another turn again.

Our state here is most curious; all riding about singly, entering any house we please, and well received everywhere, the baggage straggling all over the country; every one declaring that one man had caused all their misery for the last three years. The Bourbons are almost forgotten; and few, even of the better sort of people, know who the Duke d'Angoulême is. All want peace, and, therefore, wish him well. The French people are just now humbled to a most astonishing degree—I could scarcely have believed it possible.

I went about talking to the people, and explaining a little who our "royal tiger" is, and why he came as he did. At Flagenan I found the *maire* and townspeople waiting to pay their respects to him in form. This was bolder than at most places; and I was sorry to mortify them by telling them he had already passed. At Peyrehorade, when the French army went by, every place was shut up; when we came, every place and all the shops were opened.

Their horror of the Spaniards is, however, very great. Still the people would take no active part; they remained quiet, hoping for peace. At Orthes Marshal Soult ordered the inhabitants to arm and assist; and the action was so close, on a formidable position on the hills above the town, that several balls fell into the houses; but instead, the inhabitants all shut themselves up, and there waited the event. He vowed vengeance, and declared that the town should be pillaged in consequence. Of course they wished us success, as you may well conceive.

In many places the French have done much injury to the inhabitants as they went off, burning mills, bridges, forage, and the suburbs of Navarens, on military accounts, but plundering also very considerably on private accounts. The people now fear that we are too weak, and begin to tremble.

It is a trying time for them. The schoolmaster here has rubbed out his *Collége Impériale.* This may be his ruin if matters change again. At Mont de Marsan, as I expected, we have found immense stores. This place, St. Sever, is larger than Orthes or Peyrehorade, and is said to have had much *émigrée* and *ancienne noblesse.* The reception, however, as to quarters, has not been quite so good as hitherto, more from alarm, probably than anything else.

Lord Wellington and General Alava were close together when struck, and both on the hip, but on different sides, and neither seriously injured, as the surgeon told me who dressed them Lord Wellington's was a bad bruise, and the skin was broken. I fear that his riding so much since has made it rather of more consequence; but hope the two days' halt here will put him in the right way again, as all our prospects here would vanish with that man.

From this vicinity the French took the road to Toulouse, and, you will observe, made another stand near Aire. The Portuguese, I am sorry to say, ran at that place; and we were at first repulsed, but General Barnes's brigade came up, and set all to rights, by driving the French on again, and taking some prisoners. Our way here has been in some degree difficult and dangerous, from the flooded rivers and broken-down bridges, which have been hitherto only slightly repaired, so as to be just passable. At the Adour, it is reported that we have here actually been delayed two days. At Port de Lanne, we passed it on two large rafts, and two ferry-boats, with some risk: my boat was nearly over, from two spirited horses being on board; and my little mule, with his panniers on, jumped into the water. This put my linen and sugar, &c., in a pretty mess, as you may suppose, and drowned the live fowls on his back. At Peyrehorade I also lost a mule, and was obliged, consequently, to overload the rest.

At this place I last night recovered my mule, and lost nothing on the road, except the drowned fowls, which can now be replaced here. The history of all the mishaps on a march is curious. I dined at the ferry-house, and did not go away till all my own nine animals were clear over. Some persons have never heard of their baggage since, and are now here without it: it will turn up soon, no doubt, at least in great part.

My old host at Mont de Marsan has sent to inquire after me. One feels now quite strange in an enemy's country, meeting deserters around on the road, gens-d'armes, the same conscripts going home, and a stout peasantry with great Irish bludgeons, all very civil and friendly; and Lord Wellington, by proclamation, ordering the *maires* to form an armed police, and protect their own districts themselves from stragglers, muleteers, &c.

I always expected that Soult would retire towards Toulouse, to fall back on Suchet, and either hang on our flank, if we should go on to Bordeaux, or draw us from the sea and our supplies if we follow him up. We can push on to Bordeaux and the river, in my opinion, and then sweep on before us towards Toulouse. Time will show Lord Wellington's plans, which no one can do more than guess at. In the end I was right as to his crossing the Gaves in force.

I have just met with the Baron de Barthe. He tells me that all prospers with the royal cause, and that the French provinces of Poitou, Guienne, Brittany, &c., are all in open insurrection, and the white flag flying. P——'s account of the state of France on his side coincides, as you must observe, almost precisely with mine, as far as I have yet seen. The people are all at market here to-day, just as if nothing were the matter, and we were not here. Hitherto there is only hatred in many of the lower classes and a few of the higher to Bonaparte; but no effort for the Bourbons, and much alarm in the purchasers of national property. The *ancienne noblesse* is beginning to talk and to stir a little, and the *nouveaux riches* are by some laughed at. Public opinion begins to dare to vent itself, and the minds of the people at large are, I think, veering fast. Many think us too weak at present. It is said that we move to-morrow to Aire, on the Toulouse road; but nothing is fixed. I went to inquire after Lord Wellington to-day; he was busy writing, and said he was better, and looked well enough. The Duke d'Angoulême has sent to Mont de Marsan as his agent a *professeur*, who was despised there, and this has given offence. The truth is that he does not know where as yet to find men of weight and talent.

St. Sever, March 6th, 1814.—The mail is to be dispatched to-day, so I add a few lines, as we halt here again to-day, and probably to-morrow, owing to the flooded state of the river, and the enemy having destroyed the bridges in their retreat to Auch, where we are told they now are. Marshal Soult, it is said, finding that the Italians also are now beginning to desert since Murat's new alliances, has ordered all Italian soldiers to be disarmed. Another story current, but not so much to be relied on, is, that Bonaparte has been badly wounded, and desired General Macdonald to put him out of his misery ; and that the latter took him at his word, and shot him.

The Duke d'Angoulême was at high mass again to-day, at which some hundreds of the new levy attended, my hosts tell me, known by their short cropped heads. Our situation here is so different from what it was in Spain, that it is quite droll. I have a general invitation from my host whilst I stay. To-day I go to Lord Wellington's.

Later on the 7th.—We stay to-day, as the bridges are not repaired and the floods have not quite subsided. I walked down to the bridge with Lord Wellington yesterday, and observed him limp a little, and he said he was in rather more pain than usual, but that it was nothing. At dinner yesterday, he said he was laughing at General Alava having had a knock, and telling him it was all nonsense, and that he was not hurt, when he received this blow, and a worse one, in the same place himself. Alava said it was to punish him for laughing at him. At dinner we had the new Swedish tiger, the Prince's aide-de-camp, who had been here a few days, covered with gold. His pantaloons are most *magnifique.* He seemed a good-tempered man, but I did not think very much of him.

Two of the Bordeaux people were also there, who are to return to-day, and General Frere's aide-de-camp from

Peyrehorade, as he is marching up that way by Orthes. The people in office at Pau sent to say that they were ready to declare for the King, and Count Damas boldly enough went over there to see the state of things. He has come back safe, and reports them ready, but that they cannot take any public step until we are in force there. Amongst other opinions and feelings here, we, the English, have our partisans. Many say they should like an English Government, and Lord Wellington told me, laughing, he believed we had almost as many friends and partisans as the Bourbons. Peace certainly is by far the most popular project of all. I am excessively hurried with business to-day, and must prepare to see Lord Wellington.

Head-Quarters, Aire, March 11th, 1814.—By a sudden order we moved from St. Sever to this place yesterday, so far on our road to Toulouse, and the scene of the battle a few days since, when the Algarve brigade (all Portuguese) took to their heels, and the English brigade of General Barnes behaved so well.

We are now playing a bolder game than usual. The French, as I suspected, took the Toulouse road from St. Sever, and have a column in our front on the road to Auch, I believe, and another near or towards Tarbes. This leaves Bordeaux open. To take advantage of this, we have also divided two divisions under Marshal Beresford; the seventh and the fourth are gone to Bordeaux, and must be by this time close to the town, which is said to be ripe to join us, and declare for the King. The Duke d'Angoulême is gone that way.

In front here we have Sir Rowland Hill's corps, the second and sixth divisions, and also the third and light divisions; and General Frere's Spanish army of twelve thousand men, to be fed by us, is on its road up, and to be, it is understood, at St. Sever to-day; and to support this main movement against Soult, who is said to be near Auch. In the meantime, General Hope remains with the first division, including all the Guards and German Legion (the choice men and in high order, and undiminished by service nearly), together with the fifth division and General Don Carlos d'Espagne's Spanish brigade, and, it is believed, also Lord Aylmer's British one, to blockade and take Bayonne. It is most unfortunate that so large a force should be required for that object; but we dare not trust, I conclude, the bridge and our communications to the Spaniards' keeping.

Great preparations are making against Bayonne, and the garrison have been driven in very close to the citadel; but no steps have been hitherto taken for the actual siege by regular approaches or batteries. Our army is thus very much divided just now, and the communications would be difficult, except that the country is with us. All the French posting establishment has remained, and nearly everything goes on as usual. The people quietly suffer us to take our own measures, and offer no opposition, though not openly declaring or helping us. It is remarkable that we go about as if in England, and yet no mischief has been done either to officers, men, or baggage. If the country people had been like the Spaniards, and against us, what we are now doing would have been out of the question. Half our army, by straggling about, would have been knocked on the head. We have, fortunately, just now plenty of money, and pay for everything; and the English are in the highest repute.

In general, also, we have behaved well. There are, however, many instances to the contrary; and many more, I am sorry to say, amongst the Portuguese. When the Spaniards come, I am afraid things will be much worse. The mischief done by, and injury arising from, the passing through a country of the very best disciplined army is considerable. The people feel that, and are ready in general to submit to much, especially as the French army has been so much worse than ours, and does not pay for anything, whilst, on the other hand, we enable many to make almost little fortunes against quiet times; and Lord Wellington begins upon a plan, which I hope he will have funds to continue, of paying for all damage done when fairly stated. Some most exaggerated and unreasonable demands have been made to him in consequence. Guineas are already spread all over this province, and pass most readily.

I am at an apothecary's here, who was, I am sorry to say, robbed by our men just after the attack. Lord Hill offered to send him the money, nearly 15*l*. and a watch; but he declined taking it.

Lord Wellington has a cold, but rode here yesterday in his white cloak, in a terribly cold day, with the snow directly in his face; for we have now got another little winter here, which is unusual.

At the latter place there was a large church which was built by the English. In general, it is exactly in the style we call Saxon, or Old English, circular arches and Saxon ornaments. I suspect, however, it must have been built just as the Gothic style was coming into fashion, as the side aisle arches and part of the body of the church were Pointed or Gothic; and this did not appear to have been, like some of ours, a subsequent alteration. A handsome small old Corinthian façade was inserted within the large Saxon heavy arch, which formed the original entrance of the front of the church. In the town was a very good school, called *Le Collége Impérial*. About ninety-two boys were then in the school, who all remained, and were very civil to our officers whenever we went there. The boys seemed to wish us well; and they do not usually conceal their real opinions. The establishment was in an old Benedictine abbey, and was exceedingly good. The lower cloisters and the great church, gutted at the Revolution, formed excellent play-places; and all the great corridors above were half enclosed by small wooden rooms for the boys, each having one to himself about eight feet by five, holding his bed, his chair, table, and box; and, by being all open at the top to the gallery, they were airy and yet retired and private. The expense of this school is about 400 francs, or 20*l.* a-year. For this, Latin, writing, French, geography, music, dancing, and a little mathematics were taught. Some boys could read Livy, Tacitus, and Cicero. The dinner and other arrangements are cleanly and good. Napoleon gave them the building. The funds were all private, no foundation, lands, or allowances from Government.

The road from St. Sever here was through a rich flat bottom near the Adour, with a high bank all the way on the south side, with several chateaux. We crossed the Adour to come here at Sever, over our newly-made bridge; came along the great road on the north bank, and recrossed again at a ferry at this place, this for the fourth time since we left St. Jean de Luz. The country seems well cultivated, and not unlike parts of the Bath road, in Berkshire—a flat corn country, with wooded, rising grounds and villas at some distance, which formed the valley. We passed Grenade, rather a large village, about eight miles from St. Sever, and a large chateau about six miles off, belonging to the Marquis de St. Maurice, the chateau deriving its name from him. We also passed a small village, about four miles further on, called Cageres; and four miles more brought us here. The bridge at Barcelonne is about a mile and a half higher up, over the Adour, and has not been destroyed by the French; they only broke one arch of wood, which we have repaired. We were to have crossed there to get hither, but I came almost the first, found a ferry just re-established, and came over ; most followed the same way.

Aire is not so large a town as St. Sever or Orthes ; it is about the size of Epsom. It is close to the river, is old and dirty, and half deserted. Several good houses gutted, or, at least, without furniture ; and the ruins of a very large modern-built bishop's palace, destroyed during the Revolution, when this place suffered much. At Upper Aire, which stands well on a hill half a mile above this, is a celebrated school or college, or rather two united. It was first formed about sixty or eighty years since, a handsome building erected for the purpose, and well contrived—in plan much like that at St. Sever. It was in great repute before the Revolution, but was then destroyed, and almost completely gutted. Within the last ten years, the professors and clergy have by degrees, by charities, charity sermons, and great exertions, nearly restored the whole again without Government assistance ; and, before this late attack, above two hundred boys were there. In one building there are above a hundred boys, all destined for the church ; in another, above a hundred for lay employments. An old church built by the English, but much altered, and in a much later style than that at St. Sever, stands between the schools, is used by them as a church, and unites the two esta- blishments. The whole has a good broad play-terrace on the brow of the hill above the river. Education here is cheaper than at St. Sever, though there are no Govern- ment funds at either. The yearly cost is about three hundred or three hundred and fifty francs. I rather think clothing was, however, included in the estimate at St. Sever, and that would make the two much alike. The studies are the same. It puts me in mind of Maynooth College, near Dublin, and seemed what our colleges were three or four centuries ago.

My patron or host at St. Sever is a sort of small landholder and noble, with his house in town and villa two miles off, which dated, as he took care to tell me, 130 years, as the builder's mark and his ancestor's name proved, and therefore, " *C'est clair, mais ce n'est rien pour moi, c'est bien vrai maintenant, que ma famille est supérieure à celle de M. le Maire de notre ville,*" &c. M. le Maire had made most of his money by dabbling with national property during the Revolution, and succeeded better than many others here. " But," continued my host, " as I have always been considered one of the noblesse, I have suffered accordingly ; *mais n'importe*—I am grown a philosopher. I never can see such times as Robespierre's again ; so I see English, Spanish, Portuguese, and all with indifference, and remain quiet. At the same time I am now English (he always said *nous autres,* which often puzzled me), and I wish the cause well, and would contribute much to its success." He seemed surprised that this contribution of maize for our horses was all paid for instantly, and that in gold, and at a fair good price, even though M. le Maire, who managed it (no one knew for what), detained eleven sous out of every eighty from all to whom he made payments. M. La Borde de Menos was my host's name. He was very civil, and I dined with his family—his wife, two daughters, and a son—whenever I was not engaged, which happened only twice, at Lord Wellington's. He also gave my men wine, &c. ; in short, I believe he rejoiced much at the change he had experienced in having me instead of a whole company of officers, men and all, which he had one day when we first came.

In return for his treatment, I bought toys for the lad ; gave some tea to Madame in case of sickness, and a pretty cadeau to Mademoiselle. In a word, we parted excellent friends. The many stories he told me of what had passed in Robespierre's time were curious. M. La Borde

was obliged to act with the Representant, and attend all
meetings, to be only pillaged and abused by every one,
and to bow and say, "Thank you all," with his hat in
his hand; and this was to prevent their having an excuse
for guillotining him, as thirty of the principal people
were put to death in the small town of St. Sever. The
living alone and staying away was of itself a heinous
offence, and every requisition of a cart for a day's use was
called for *sous peine de mort*. That was the form of all
demands. A ball was given by the Representant.
Every one was obliged to go or be suspected. Madame
went. She had a valuable gold watch-chain; but not
daring to show it, she went with a cut steel one. The
Representant said, "*Mais où est donc votre chaine d'or?
Le publique en a besoin.*" She was obliged to swear it
had been stolen, and to hide it ever afterwards. The
Representant seemed incredulous, and the risk of this
fraud was great, but it answered. Monsieur was not so
lucky; he had a valuable ring, and attended one of the
meetings with it on. The Representant said, "*Tu
F—— Noble, donnez moi ta bague, ce n'est pas pour des
gens comme toi; le publique en a besoin.*" He took it off
and gave it up, and some months after saw it on the
finger of one of the Representant's relations.

I have now a will to draw up in case of accident,
for Sir N. P——, bart., to secure 10,000*l.* to each of his
younger children. He is here with his regiment; so
adieu.

Lord Wellington abuses the Allies for having been
beaten when they had the game in their hands; and
says, one ran his head against the Marne, and the other
against the Seine, and the whole was ill-managed. We
have the further news of a French column having made
its way from Lyons to near Geneva again; but a report
still later, that the Allies, under Blucher, got into Bona-

parte's rear. These checks are, even if they end in nothing, of the greatest use to him. They deter people from declaring their opinions; may make every difference in that way here and at Bordeaux; and I should not be surprised if they encouraged Marshal Soult to make another stand near here, on this side the Garonne, which I do not think he would otherwise have done.

I am told that he is in a position at present from Tarbes to Plaisance, on a ridge of hills, and that the country is full of positions. My news is from M. D——, the husband of my young Spanish Bilboa lady, who came to me to-day. They have left Bayonne from fear, and are waiting the events of the war at Pau, whence he came over here—and like a true placeman, thinking matters were about to change, he insinuated to me that he should like an appointment under the new order of things—under the direction of the Bourbons or the English.

He also wanted a passport for his little wife's brother to go back to Bilboa, from General Alava. This I have obtained for him; but on condition that the civil authorities are written to, and the brother examined on his arrival, as to his conduct, &c. M. D—— was Colonel F——'s friend and not mine; and to confess the truth, I had no great opinion of him, but thought he was only attentive to Colonel F—— to serve his own purposes, and seemed to be rather an intriguing gentleman. It is, however, quite my principle that every one should be allowed to go home, and go about his business; and I am sure that Spain will profit by the residence of any one who has lived at all with the French, and acquired some notions of what mankind are capable of, and of human exertion.

In my walks to-day, I met a poor gentleman who told me we had taken all his forage, and that his oxen were

2 F

starving, and that he must sell them ; he was going to a
contractor for that purpose. I advised him to go to our
Commissary Haines, to whom I took him, for I thought
each would gain by a bargain direct. His oxen are to
be inspected to-morrow. During our conversation, he
told me that he was the brother-in-law of Dulau, the
French bookseller in Soho Square, and that the latter had
no nearer relation, but that he could never hear of him,
or write to him. I undertook to send his letter. If such
a letter is enclosed to you, therefore, you will know all
about it, and my poor man may get a legacy or something by it, from the great Mr. Dulau, for such he
must be.

Saturday, March 12*th*.—We remain here to-day, and
shall do so probably for a few days, unless the French
move off. We seem to be moving up. A brigade of
artillery and some troops were yesterday taking the
direction to Pau, to secure that town, I conclude, as we
have now only artillery there, and also, perhaps, to turn
the left of the French position at Tarbes. Lord Wellington is better ; his hounds go out to-day, and I should
not be surprised at his being out with them. As a proof
how savage war makes every one, even an English soldier, I may tell you that poor H——'s body was stript
by the English soldiers of his own division, to which he
was acting as Adjutant-general, and almost before his
body was cold. I believe two or three men have been
flogged for this. By degrees we all get hardened to anything.

I find the same sort of custom here as to letting land,
as is to be found near Bayonne. The landlord puts a
peasant into a little farm, furnishes it, pays the taxes, and
finds the necessary cattle, beasts, and horses, for the cultivation of the land ; in return, he receives the full half
of the clear produce as rent, but in kind, and very little

money is seen. Before we came, bread was three sous the pound, which would be about sixpence three-farthings the quartern loaf. A goose has been five francs of late, but that is dear. Fowls are now only half-a-crown or three shillings each, and very good even to the English. If we remain long in a place, we soon cause the prices to rise.

CHAPTER XXIV.

Reports from the Seat of War—The Duke d'Angoulême—The German Cavalry—Misconduct of the Spaniards—Attacks on our Grazing Parties —Movement of Head-Quarters—Death of Colonel Sturgeon—Visit to the Hospital—New Quarters—Skirmishes—Wellington and the Mayor.

Head-quarters, Aire,
March 16, 1814.

My dear M——,

HERE we remain still, and probably shall do so for a few days, for the French Marshal not only keeps his position near Conchez, across our road to Tarbes and Toulouse, but does not seem disposed to go beyond demonstrations, and cannot muster courage to attack us, and we, I believe, are not quite prepared to attack him. The glorious reception Marshal Beresford met with at Bordeaux, and the spirited and decided conduct of the *maire*, &c., there, you will have heard by the last mail, for the news came after my letter, but before Lord Wellington's bag was dispatched. We have all sorts of reports from the vicinity of Paris, about the battle at Meaux, of a large French corps having gone over to Bernadotte. There are reports from Bordeaux, but all uncertain; I think, however, that the *maire* must have had some good intelligence to induce him to take the line he has done, which must be his ruin, and that of all his friends, if we make peace at last with Bonaparte.

The Duke d'Angoulême, at first, it is said, declined a burgher guard, and preferred an English one. This will

not do: he must show confidence and spirit, and rely
upon his French friends, and give no offence by par-
tialities for the English. This was bad advice in some
one about him, for I understand he personally has always
wished to take a decided line, and risk his personal safety
for the cause.

We hear the Royalist party are beginning *à la lanterne*
again, but I hope this is not true. The inhabitants of
Bordeaux must arm and protect themselves. We shall
leave but a small force there. The river and their own
people must be their chief reliance. Lord Wellington
has sent for the fourth division from Marshal Beresford
to help here. Canning went off at four o'clock on the
14th, with these orders (as I understand); he was sent
from Gartin by Lord Wellington, eleven miles from this
in front, and was here in an hour. Whilst he was dressing and getting a fresh horse, I got him his money from
the Paymaster, and he was off, remounted for Roquefort,
twenty miles; and thence he was was to post the other
seventy miles all night to Bordeaux. He was heard of
at Langon, about three or four in the morning, so that by
nine o'clock on the 15th he would be in Bordeaux; and
as the fourth division, which was at Langon, would
march that day, in about two days more they will be
here. All our 18-pounders and some other reinforcements will arrive, and then Soult must be off, or I hope
get another beating.

The heavy German Cavalry (for by its name they wish
to be known, for it carries credit with it), went through
here two days since in admirable order, the horses in particular, but the latter are altogether too slight for the
men, who are all large, bony, heavy men, of a certain age,
and experienced heroes. It will not be easy by a royal
order, and light jacket and caps, to transform these gentlemen into light Germans, nor do the corps like it at all.
Ponsonby's heavy brigade is also close by, fresh from

Spain, like the Germans, and in the same excellent condition. Nearly ten thousand Spaniards, very fine-looking men, and in good discipline, are also two miles from this, at or near Barcelona. Hitherto they have behaved in general much better than was expected on the march; but we feed them, as they have no transport. If they will but fight a little in return, and take their share of loss, we should do famously.

Murillo's Spaniards, I am sorry to say, have begun very ill in our front. The day before yesterday, Soult made an advance against them; when they were ordered to fall back a little to a rivulet, and there defend themselves. Once with their backs turned, however, away they went, and never stopped until the Buffs were ordered up to stop the French, who, the moment they saw the red coats coming on, were off home again very quickly, but not quite so rapidly as the Spaniards had run from them.

The Portuguese cavalry had a little affair, and behaved well. The 14th Dragoons had also an affair the day before yesterday. Half a squadron under Captain Babington were ordered by Colonel Harvey to drive off a French half squadron, and then halt until he came up. They upset the French, saw another whole squadron beyond, were tempted to go on by their first success, and succeeded in a great measure again, but Captain Babington was taken. The wounded French dragoons of the 5th regiment, brought in here prisoners, are all very fine men, and the whole regiment are said to be the same sort of men. They came in much cut about the head and hands.

The forage animals of head-quarters were yesterday very nearly getting into a terrible scrape—about two hundred and fifty animals, and two of mine in the number. They foolishly went in front of our picquets, or nearly so, though regularly under commissariat directions.

Whilst they were loading at a farm, one peasant slipped away, and it is concluded told some French dragoons near what was going on, whilst the other in the house gave some of the party wine. There were four artillery-men unarmed in the house, and about six Portuguese, one of whom was mine, when a French officer of cavalry, with his sword drawn, came to the window, told them all to come out, and that they were prisoners. When they came out, seeing that he was alone and his party three or four hundred yards off, they mounted their mules, and nearly all got off, with the loss of, it is said, only one man and two or three mules. Some fellows galloped all the way here without their loads or cords, and at first spread an alarm that all were taken. They arrived home in the course of the day, and my Portu-guese brought home a load of good hay and two de-serted ropes in triumph. It is thought that the party should have brought off the officer prisoner, but most are satisfied with having got their own property back again. He cut one of the artillerymen on the finger, who put up his arm to save himself.

Another party of muleteers with stores from Mont de Marsan to Bordeaux, with supplies for the seventh division, to which they belonged, were attacked three days since on their road near Roquefort, quite in our rear and on our communications, by some French par-tizans, a sort of guerillas called *La Bande*. These now, it is said, are employed by Soult: they were formerly a set of *douaniers*, or smuggler catchers. Several mules were killed and wounded, and, I believe, some muleteers killed, and some of the money taken. It is to be feared that the Spanish muleteers will begin to be alarmed at this. We have cavalry, however, on the road, and they will now be more on the look out in future.

This place is now much crowded. Three new Ge-nerals came in yesterday and to-day,—Sir Stapleton

Cotton to-day, with about a hundred animals belonging to himself and his staff. I was turned out of my stable in consequence, though but a very bad one, and my animals are now in a back kitchen turned into a stable. At Barcelona the Spaniards turned out the cavalry with much less ceremony. It is said that a company, with a Captain at their head, gallantly charged Captain S——'s horses and bâtmen (General C——'s aide-de-camp), and were very successful. One little blood-horse kicked about, broke loose, and made a good defence, without injuring himself; but another horse, not so quick in his retreat, received two slight bayonet wounds, and a slight cut with a sabre, and the Spaniards carried the day, behaving like heroes!

Our people are all moved in consequence, and I hope that these *valorosos* and blood-thirsty gentlemen will soon be allowed to contend with a more glorious enemy, and will behave with equal spirit when the opportunity shall arrive.

The Swedish (Bernadotte's) aide-de-camp is, it seems, to campaign with us; he is buying horses, &c., and preparing for the field. He is a great talker, and, I understand, of this country. From his conversation he seems to have served against us under Massena in Portugal, but how he is what he is I do not exactly understand.

The weather is still very cold. Lord Wellington would not even condescend to-day to go and look at the French. He only sent Colonel Gordon to go on to Gartin, and report.

Head-Quarters, 17th March, Aire.—About three o'clock yesterday we learnt that the French were off, and filed through Conchez, apparently on the way to Tarbes. I think they will not venture to go too near the mountains, but must make for Toulouse. If not, our fourth division, which, it is said, will be here to-night, will make us strong enough, I hope, to push a column through Auch straight to Toulouse, while the rest follow Soult, and we should then be at Toulouse first. I conclude he will turn that way from Tarbes. General Hill moved a little after the French yesterday to keep them in sight. The rest of the army will, in my opinion, get in motion to-day or to-morrow, and head-quarters move on very soon afterwards. About fifty prisoners were sent in here last night, mostly dragoons.

We are all alive again with regard to the Allies, and the stories from Bordeaux are most animating. In addition to this, we move after Soult to-morrow. Head-quarters to be at Viella, nearly three leagues in advance, towards Auch. I fear we shall, as part of head-quarters, see neither Toulouse nor Bordeaux; for if my general-ship correspond with Lord Wellington's, Soult will in my opinion cross the Garonne, and our right will go to Toulouse, and we, as part of head-quarters, shall pass the river by some bridge to be laid down below near Agen,—more towards the centre of our movements. The scene at Bordeaux I much regret to have lost. We already hear of disturbances at Toulouse, and even reports of Louis XVIII. being proclaimed at Paris. From the want of a popular Bourbon cry at Bordeaux, I hear they have set up "Henri IV.," and "Gode sav de King." The weather to-day is delightful: I only hope it will last. We are told that Suchet has offered to withdraw all his garrisons from Spain into France, and give up the towns in their present state; this has been referred, it is said, to Lord Wellington, and by him refused, as only releasing so many men for present use, who must sooner or later, if we persevere, be prisoners. This is quite right no doubt for the common cause.

Viella, 18*th*.—I have just time to add a few lines at this place, which is about nine miles from Aire, on

the road to Tarbes, and our head-quarters to-day. It
is a small scattered village, so much so that I am at a
farm at least two miles or more from the main village,
and nearly by myself at the last house in the commune.
I have, however, a doctor and a commissary within a
quarter of a mile, and as we are fortunately well received, and welcomed everywhere, it does not signify. I
feel quite at ease.

We had a tiresome march here, for the third division,
the sixth, and the heavy Germans with the baggage
of all three, the whole of the pontoon train, the artillery
of the two divisions, head-quarter's baggage, and eight
thousand Spaniards all went the same road, over our
newly-made bridge across the Leis, a small stream which
falls into the Adour, near Barcelonne. The French, in
destroying this bridge, had not blown up or burnt the
main centre pier, so that about twenty-five elm trees,
about twenty-five feet long, and bundles of fascines,
about twelve feet long, placed crosswise, and then
covered with dirt, in two days' time made us a famous
bridge.

Some time hence, when the fascines get rotten, some
luckless car or horseman will no doubt go through into
the water, which is deep, and about twenty feet below.
The high roads are excellent, and the country, though
not a rich soil, very pretty and loveable. Almost every
drain under the road, or a small arch for streams to pass
under, had been broken down; some left so from neglect
of late, some I believe just made on purpose to delay us:
faggots, and a little mould, with a few small trees at
bottom, soon made a passage, but created delays.

19*th*, 7 *o'clock.*—To-day we move to Maubourguet,
nearly in the Tarbes road. This looks as if Soult was
making for Tarbes, and not Toulouse. I can scarcely
believe this. If he places his rear on the mountains,
he gives up Toulouse, and the richest country; and if

beaten when up there, will, in my opinion, escape with difficulty. He may expect some reinforcements from Suchet that way, but still must go to Toulouse.

We, however, have now a chance of seeing the latter, whereas I thought we should have crossed nearer Agen, lower down the river.

My patron here is very friendly. The French plundered him terribly, and all his neighbours. They call them brigands, and dread them more than our army. My man let five Portuguese dragoons through his premises, and, he says, saved them. He is of a class of men that existed in former days in England; the owner and cultivator of eighty acres of land, partly corn, partly wood, partly vineyards, and partly meadow—thus he has all within himself. He has a wife and four children, two women servants, two pair of oxen, of which he has been obliged to sell one pair to pay the French contributions. He has two labourers, both deserters, for keeping whom he knows he is liable to a fine of from five hundred to three thousand francs, and to be confined five years, but he can get no other servants, and of course these are faithful.

His land, he says, is worth about 50s. an acre. It requires much labour, but when left alone he says is good enough to make them very happy. In spite of all that he has suffered, and his earnest desire for peace, he is certainly no friend to the Bourbons. He curses Bonaparte for his ambition, has a tolerably just notion of all his losses in the North, and in Spain, from the soldiers; but still, would rather, in my opinion, have Bonaparte and peace than the Bourbons. I can never get him to say a word, good or bad, as to the latter. At the same time, like all the rest of the French, he would just now submit to anything for peace. All have the highest respect for Lord Wellington, which they say they learn from the French army, high and low.

Maubourguet, 5 *o'clock.*—We left Viella at nine, and after a tiresome ride through baggage the whole way, arrived here about four o'clock, though it is only about fifteen miles. The bridges were all broken down, and nearly every gutter across the road, but this only caused delays, and was quite ineffectual. The troops and artillery waggons all found some way round or through. When about twelve miles on our road, we found the last three miles quite choked with all the baggage of head-quarters and the troops. At first I conceived the delay arose in a broken bridge being repaired, and was patient; but a sharp firing and cannonade soon commenced in front of Maubourguet, near Vic, and then, guessing that it was an intentional halt, I made my way through it here, and found every one in front, and a sharp firing about four miles in advance, near Vic Bigorre.

I met also a party of the fine German cavalry wounded going to the rear; they had had an affair the day before yesterday in advance of Madiran, half way between that place and this, and with two squadrons instantly upset four squadrons of French chasseurs, took many horses, and cut up many men, but the French ran too fast to leave any prisoners. This tempted the Germans to attack yesterday a very superior force, it is said three times their number—three French regiments; and I hear they suffered much.

In the first affair they had about four killed and eighteen wounded. We were at first without orders as to staying here and unpacking, but a report soon reached us that the French would not stand, and were off. So we all unpacked quietly before the firing ceased, and prepared for dinner in this town, where five hundred French cavalry had passed the night, and had only departed about eight in the morning, with the curses of the inhabitants. Our Portuguese were principally engaged, it is said, yesterday, and without much loss. The sixth division entered Vic last night.

Maubourguet, 7 o'clock, 20th, Sunday.—No orders last night. Lord Wellington very late home; but I have just learned that we are to move to-day to Tarbes, taking it for granted that the French will be out to make room for us. This is very strange, and so is the confidence of our men. When we halted yesterday the bâtmen were saying, when within three miles of this place, the head-quarters, "We must only wait a little till the troops have cleared our quarters for us and made room."

I now cannot understand Soult's plans. He seems to be making for the mountains, and to have suffered us in some measure to cut him off from Toulouse. Colonel Canning arrived last night from Bordeaux with an account of a grand defeat of Bonaparte, and that he had fallen back on Orleans. This I expected if he were not killed, as I concluded he would try and unite with the Lyons army and Soult's, and make one more stand in the heart of the kingdom. If this be true, Lord Wellington must be careful as to passing the Garonne; Soult's junction, nevertheless, will at any rate be doubtful. Our men are in the highest spirits, and driving all before them; weather fine.

Tournay, March 21st.—At nine left Maubourguet; about four miles further I stopped at Vic Bigorre, to see poor Colonel Sturgeon's body. He was a very clever man and officer, and particularly skilful as a bridge engineer, and in all languages. He went too close to the skirmishers, to reconnoitre, and was shot in the head just under the eye. I also went over the hospital, to assist Dr. M'Gregor in giving directions to the French as to arrangements, to talk to and satisfy some wounded French officers, and to get bedding, straw, and help from the *maire* by requisition instantly. We had about two hundred wounded there of all nations, many Portuguese, one of whom was undergoing the operation of amputation of his leg and thigh, very high up, and seemed in great agony. The French surgeon thought that Dr. M'Gregor was finding fault, and stopped, and turned to us to explain. I understand he was doing it in a clumsy way, but Dr. M'Gregor begged me to praise him highly, or he would be alarmed and do it still worse. Close to Vic, by the road-side, were about a dozen bodies of men killed by cannon-shot, and terribly mauled.

Having loaded a mule with oats from a French store at Vic, I proceeded towards Tournay. The road was crammed, and some sharp skirmishing going on about three miles beyond the town, which had commenced on the Vic side. The French only left the town about nine o'clock, and tried to blow up the bridge, but were stopped by two or three gun-shots. They stood their ground tolerably, on a very strong ridge of hills, until night, and remained *en bivouac* on them last night. At three this morning they were off; and here we are after them again, about nine miles on the road to Toulouse, at this place, Tournay, which was last night Marshal Soult's head-quarters.

Tarbes is a good town and contains a number of good houses. From the houses being large, and having yards and gardens, and from there being one or two large open spaces or squares, it covers a good deal of ground, but does not count, I understand, above ten or eleven thousand inhabitants. The people received us in general very well, but were quite passive, taking no part in any way. They had been kept quite in ignorance of all that was going on in the north, and at Bordeaux in particular—at least a great part of them. I explained, and harangued all I could in order to set them right. My own patron was, it struck me, a strong Bonapartist, and I took some pains to plague him a little accordingly. We have had no sort of interruption to-day, except from the multitudes passing, which form a continued stream, from five in the morning, along a wide road, until about four or five in the day. The fine weather has unfortunately turned to rain, but I hope will return to us again.

You will see by the map that Soult has taken to the Toulouse road at last. He is at Mont St. Jean to-day, it is said; and that, as usual, when inclined to run, the French beat our people in marching, and we cannot cut him off. He has run some risks by going this roundabout road; and had we been strong enough to have pushed along the Auch road also, we should have puzzled him a little. We shall now, most probably, drive him gradually to the Garonne. It is likely, in my opinion, that he will make another stand. I have been turned out of my stable, and had much trouble with the *maire*, so have only time to seal up.

P.S. The country, from Maubourguet to Vic, Tarbes, and part of the way here, was all a flat, of rich country, like the country between Bridgewater and across into Somersetshire; except that half the meadows at least were vineyards and orchards in one, and interlaced very prettily; the fruit-trees kept small, about ten feet high, and the vines trained off at about six, and all intertwined and furled together with withy-bands. This was famous cover, as no musquet-ball could pass far through the trees; a few common shot had destroyed the quincunx regularity in many places. The water meadows were very beautiful, and the system seemed to be understood and well managed; the streams beautifully clear. The background of this large flat was all the way to the Haute Pyrenees covered with snow; but the higher Pic du Midi was never visible, always in the clouds; the lower one was. The Alps are far superior, as far as I can judge. Adieu.

Nine o'clock at night, Isle en Dodon, March 24th, 1814.—Our post and movements are now so uncertain and sudden, that I know not when or how to write to you, and fear that my last was sent too late, and may probably be sent with this, by which means all the zest of late news from the army will be lost. I have just heard, by accident, that a mail will go to-night, and have only time to scribble a few hasty lines immediately after dinner. My last finished at Tournay; thence we proceeded the next day to Galan, a poor village, and rather a wild mountain road, the short cut to Toulouse. Our second division and cavalry followed the enemy along the high road by Lannernezon, Mont St. Jean, and St. Gaudens. One corps of their army went also through Galan. The *maire* of the latter was a fine old man of eighty-two, and a good friend.

I was at a miserable half-furnished house, and my baggage being stopped by the Spanish troops, it did not arrive until seven o'clock; luckily it came in time for me to dress, in order to dine with Lord Wellington, a mile off, in the rain. The *maire* had been an hour in the room with Lord Wellington before he found him out, talking by the fire in his quarter, until at last Lord Wellington, having let him go on some time, asked him to dinner. This staggered him, and led to an explanation. The *maire* said, that the night before he had had Generals Clausel and Harispe, and that they only ordered a dinner to be prepared, and did not ask him to eat part of his own, or thank him, or take the least notice of him. He could not, therefore, believe that Lord Wellington was the enemy's General, after having been so treated, as he said, "like a dog," by his friends.

My own patron was a half-starved apothecary without

medicines or drugs. He offered to dress a fowl for me, but was very willing instead to sell me one for twice its value, for dinner the next day.

23rd.—We moved again to Boulognes, about sixteen miles, rather a long march, and in part bad road, though in general the roads all over this part of France are very much superior to ours in England; compared with our best roads, they are very superior to any in the distant counties, and to many of our main and best roads, even in the neighbourhood of London. The light, third, fourth, and sixth divisions of cavalry, and about eight thousand Spaniards, all move with this column, and we reach of course by mid-day, when all is in motion, with the artillery and baggage, about ten miles. The second division and cavalry follow the French. At St. Gaudens the 13th Dragoons came up with the French rear cavalry, formed just outside the town, charged, broke them, drove them pell-mell through the town on their reverse beyond it. There they re-formed; the 13th charged again; then the French ran, with the 13th after them, for two miles. The result is said to be a hundred and twenty prisoners and horses, besides killed.

From Boulognes we to-day marched to this place— Isle en Dodon. The majority of the people here seem to be friends of Bonaparte, and the assistant *maire* in particular, with whom I had much conversation; for he gave Doctor Hume and me a joint billet at the empty house where he gave out the billets, and no stable at all. As I was obliged to have him in the room so long, I determined to work him a little for treating us so ill.

The *maire* of Boulognes ran away at first. At night he came back and went to Lord Wellington, who showed him his proclamations and regulations, &c. The *maire* said he had taken the oath to Bonaparte, and would not act. " Very well," said Lord Wellington, " then the people must choose another; but now you have taken your line, I must take mine, and send you over the Garonne into the French lines." He gave orders accordingly, to Colonel S——. The *maire* ran away, and could not be found. Colonel S—— took up the father, to march him off until the son appeared. This brought him out; he remonstrated with Lord Wellington, said he was one of the first men of the country, and should be ruined by this. Lord Wellington said, "He should have thought of that sooner, and he must go;" and to this place he came to-day a prisoner.

We have just received orders to march to Samatan to-morrow. All here have a notion that Suchet's forces join Soult near here; that is, have done so, or are to do so; but we are a little in the dark, and the ignorance of the French about everything is astonishing: they seem quite stupified. But Bonaparte has many friends still, and the reports in the French papers, though upon the whole good, are not decisive. The armistice seems to have gone off from the arrangements about Italy. We are living, like the rest of the armies and the French, by requisitions; but we hitherto pay in money, which others do not. We consume everything, however, like locusts.

Lord Wellington popped between Colonel G—— and me as we were discussing the allied battles this morning, and suddenly took a part, to my great astonishment, in our conversation.

On leaving Tarbes a party of civilians went round by Bagnières to see the baths, the rooms, &c., a sort of Spa, about twelve miles round, and where no troops had been; not an Englishman there, but they were told they would be well received, and so they were indeed. The *maire* addressed them; the people were in crowds, so that it required force to enable them to pass. The National Guard turned out and presented arms to them: it was like Lord Wellington's entry into Zamora, they say, such an outcry! such a display! A ball was proposed, but as there was a French garrison about six miles off, and no allied troops near, the party declined staying, and went off highly pleased with their excursion. This is very odd, for on the road we go, all is stupefaction and indifference. I should have enjoyed this, but am obliged to be very prudent now, after my late escape. Adieu again.

The schoolmaster, or *prêtre,* at Boulognes had written a long poem entitled " *Mon Rêve,*" a prophecy nearly of everything which has taken place, and containing much in honour of Lord Wellington. He said he had long had it concealed, and volunteered spouting it out to us, to his own great satisfaction, and it really was not bad.

CHAPTER XXV.

Difficulties of the March—Failure of the Bridge of Boats—The Garonne—
Excesses of Murillo's Corps — Bad News — Exchange of Prisoners —
Arrival before Toulouse—A Prisoner of War—Anecdote of Wellington.

Head-quarters, Samatan,
March 25, 1814.

My dear M——,

At eight this morning, we left L'Isle en Dodon
for this place, about eight miles nearer to Toulouse, from
which we (the head-quarters) are now only distant about
twenty-six miles.   Our troops at St. Lys, and St. Foy,
and that vicinity, are within eleven miles; our right is
still a little more in the rear on the St. Gaudens' road,
near Martres, under General Hill.

I have just met with a corn-factor who left Toulouse
this morning.   He says that Marshal Soult arrived
there with about eight thousand men last night.   The
same number were expected to-day, and a force of twelve
thousand men from Suchet's army was expected to join,
or rather, the twelve thousand men were to be principally
a reinforcement of conscripts, collected by the Imperial
Commissioner Caffarelli.   A small bridge, called St.
Antoine, near St. Martin, about a mile from Toulouse,
was destroyed on the road from Isle Jourdain to Toulouse, and some works were being formed, and an appearance of defence was being made near to St. Martin,
at a place where three roads branch off, a mile from
Toulouse, and called La Pate d'Ore.   The narrator,

though no judge, thought the works could not be completed in time, and that if we pressed on we should pass them without much difficulty. The bridge, he said also, was mined; it is a very noble bridge, but it was reported that there was a ford passable so near, that it was thought the mine would not be made use of.

The news from Paris had ceased for some days, and this gave rise to many stories of Paris having been taken, &c. I am lodged here with some very civil good people, and who, in my opinion, really wish us well, and are very different from the *maire adjoint* at the last place, who seemed a good Bonapartist, as are many of the people at L'Isle en Dodon. About six miles from that place, and ten from this, we passed through a very good old-fashioned town, larger than this, called Lombez, where the people, in spite of having had a division of troops quartered in their houses and in the church, seemed to wish us very well.

The country in this neighbourhood is a wide flat near the river, with a gently rising boundary of hill and good corn land, the soil heavy, and the roads very deep in consequence. I always expected my horses' shoes to be sucked off every ten minutes by the strong clay.

The *maire* of Boulognes continues his route with us, looking very forlorn, and with three staff corps men round him, our gens-d'armes. He began to repent to-day, and offered to act as *maire*, but Lord Wellington said it was too late. He then wrote to his wife, saying, " He was a martyr to his principles," &c., when his offer had been refused. So much for the principles of this good friend of Napoleon ! Had his offer been accepted, he would have gone on as *maire*. His friend Bonaparte was, however, I really and truly think, never greater than he has been in his adversity during the last three months. The manner in which he has fought against all his difficulties is very astonishing, and it would not surprise me now if he succeeded in fighting himself into a tolerable peace. His boldness in finding fault with his generals, &c., and having them disgraced and tried at this moment, is very striking. In short, I am almost inclined to believe that his own spirit, the bad conduct of the Cossacks, and the wavering policy of some of our Allies, will enable him to keep his place amongst the list of sovereigns, though never to triumph over them all, as he intended, and very nearly managed to do.

There are several good chateaux near here I am told : one of these is occupied by Major M——, in our service, who was a prisoner of war, and thought it the best way to pass his captivity in double chains, or rather to cast off one chain by taking another, and by marrying an heiress, enjoy himself whilst here. I understand that he has served as *maire* of the place; General Pakenham and Colonel Campbell know him.

The army is now almost entirely fed on the country, and the rations paid for in bills or ready money. Our transports, such as they were, are quite outrun by our continual marches and distance from the depôts. We do not even resort to our grand prize-magazine at Mont de Marsan. We are also boldly isolated in the country, with scarcely five hundred men the whole way between this and Bayonne; and between this and Tarbes I believe none at all. Were not the general disposition of the people so good, at least so submissive, the stragglers and parties joining the army would be all destroyed; as it is, we have had few accidents. An affair is expected in a day or two near Toulouse, but this is doubtful. In the meantime King Ferdinand must be in Spain, as he long since passed through Toulouse on his way there.

9 o'clock at night.—Later accounts from the front say that the French are leaving Toulouse, but I think they will make a show of resistance at least. Lord Wellington said at dinner to-day he feared that they would blow up the bridge, but that he had his pontoons with him, and by showing the enemy that he could pass either above or below the bridge, he would try to save it. To-morrow will determine much, as head-quarters move four leagues to St. Lys, within about three leagues of Toulouse, and the troops are to move down into the plain in which the town stands. This is hard work for the men and baggage-animals, as the roads are excessively deep, and it is said will be worse to-morrow than to-day. We pass through St. Foy. We cannot learn where Marshal Suchet is; Lord Wellington does not know. He received despatches by a courier from Catalonia after dinner to-day, dated the 16th of March. It was not known there for certain that he had quitted Catalonia; several here say positively that he is gone towards Lyons. The post goes to-morrow early. You probably get two or three of my letters together, for we have now no regular post-day, and I am often quartered at a distance. I do not know when the mail leaves head-quarters, and by wishing to send you the last news, I may miss the post altogether.

Head-Quarters, St. Lys, March 27th, 1814.—To-day, Sunday, we make a halt here, which most of the army is very much in need of. This is in order to enable Lord Wellington to make arrangements and reconnoitre, &c. Four divisions are in our front, and General Hill on our right. Nothing has been done to-day but the driving in of some French picquets on this side of a little stream about two leagues from hence, and half-way to Toulouse, and we are now placed on that stream. There seemed to be but little firing. I saw it from the top of the tower of the church here, but it was soon over. From the same place the view all around was very extensive and magnificent; Toulouse was plainly visible, and much of the country beyond, together with a number of villages, chateaux, &c., in the large plain through which the Garonne takes its circular course from the Pyrenees. The snowy summits of the latter closed the prospect with their heads in the clouds.

Having had some trouble to mount to this gallery round the church, by means of the bells and their scaffolding, for there was no ladder, I was up there for two hours with my glass, in a tolerably clear and fine day. Of the importance of the latter you have no idea. Yesterday was entirely rainy, and our road was, perhaps, as bad as any we have ever passed with artillery, and that is saying much. The troops were splashed up to their caps, and hundreds were walking barefoot in the clay up to the calves of their legs for about five miles, whilst the best of the road was that like to Hounslow in the worst season after a thaw. Lord Wellington said, the French, after consultation, had determined that this road was not passable for their artillery, but by means of lighter carriages and better horses, five brigades of our guns have got over this difficulty.

To give you a notion of it, I may mention that Lord Wellington's barouche was three hours stuck fast in it at one place; one hind wheel up to the axle, the other in the air. No one was in it except General Alava, who was unwell. I left them endeavouring to move it by means of four artillery horses, in addition to his own six mules, but in vain; six oxen in addition at last got it clear. Lord Wellington is gone to-day round by Plaisance to the right, to General Hill on the St. Gaudens' road, as that division is now approaching near us. I am always afraid of some accident in these parties in an enemy's country, for there is generally no escort—only a few officers and two or three orderlies at the most.

In a Toulouse paper of the 22nd, which I saw yesterday, I was amused with observing, among other articles—" Bourdeaux, 12th March. By accounts from this place troops without number are pouring through to join the grand army under the Duke of Dalmatia. The disposition of the people is excellent." Then again, " March 15th. The prefect is taking measures for a number of improvements in the different communes." These lies and frauds are curious. We also notice, that in publishing Soult's proclamations in the Paris papers, in which he calls Lord Wellington the commander of brigands, the introductory part relating to the battle of Orthes is omitted altogether. It does not appear that any battle has taken place at all. We hope the silence as to Schwartzenburg means as much, and that the truth will be a set-off to any check given to St. Priest.

Bonaparte's movements to Rheims and Chalons we cannot here comprehend. Many of the people here talk such bad French that I am often taken for a Frenchman, and my patron here told me that I need not be afraid to own it, for he was a Royalist, and always had been so. His simplicity yesterday provoked me excessively. I gave him some of my old silver spoons to take care of. Thinking all soldiers and followers of an army virtuous and honest, he left the spoons, with a loaf, in his kitchen, and left his door open, to let every one in who chose. On my return, his loaf and my spoons were gone. This vexed me excessively, but redress was in vain.

Seisses, 28th March.—At daybreak this morning head-quarters moved to this place, most of us, in my opinion, fully expecting to be in Toulouse before night. We arrived here, within a league of the Garonne, by eight o'clock, when, to our great mortification, the part of the second division which had left this village at ten last night was just returning here again after daylight, owing to the bridge of boats having been too short, and the troops therefore unable to pass the river.

This is most vexatious, for the immediate passage of the Garonne without a halt, and triumphant entry into Toulouse would have been an exploit worthy of our General. With five more pontoons the whole would have been effected, and, most probably, with little loss. In front of Toulouse the enemy had been left quiet, and pressed but little; the grand movement was to have been on the right to the banks of the river near Portet. Just below where the Arrige and the Garonne unite, a league above Toulouse, the bridge was to have been laid in the night, and half the army over or ready to pass by daylight. The width of the river was supposed to be about one hundred and forty yards, or four hundred and fifty feet, the stream strong; for this we were prepared. The boats were in the river, the cables, I believe, fixed, and every precaution taken for secresy, when the discovery was made that five more pontoons would be necessary, as the river was twenty yards, or about eighty feet wider. The boats were all withdrawn, and the troops all in their way to head-quarters again before daylight; but it was a *grand coup manqué*. Apparently there must have been great inadvertence somewhere, though it may have been that no measurement was allowed, or even close observations, for fear of exciting suspicion.

I think it will be a triumph to E——, though I am sure he will not feel it as such. He told Lord Wellington at St. Jean de Luz that, in consequence of some order of his, the pontoon train would be rendered imperfect, and that if the army met with a wide river it would be stopped. Thus it has happened, and Lord Wellington, though in general so much a gainer by his decision and resources in getting rid of difficulties, has for once suffered for not attending to the counsel of his more steady and regularly-bred scientific advisers.

As the troops were not yet ordered out of the town, and were in possession of the houses, we remained for some hours with our baggage standing loaded, until our billets were settled. Most part of this time I spent in surveying the immense plain covered with farms, villas, villages, towns, and chateaux, in the neighbourhood of Toulouse, as well as the town itself. The number of apparently splendid mansions was considerable, some belonging to merchants of Toulouse; some to the old nobles who had not emigrated; some to the *nouveaux riches* of the Revolution and Bonaparte. The latter were much abused, the *fournisseurs* of the army, the intendents or tax-gatherers, &c. I believe there was much fraud in the management of the collection of contributions; and of late, particularly, much more was collected under the pretence of the necessities of the army, and to provision Bayonne, than ever reached its destination; and being but ill paid regularly, the managers took the liberty of paying themselves well irregularly.

Murillo's corps has plundered again of late, and was guilty of some excesses last night. One man was caught in the fact, stealing wine, and brought forward. Lord Wellington had him shot in the most impressive manner this morning, before all the corps, after a solemn admonition, and much parade. The man, it is said, appeared absolutely dead from fear before a musquet was fired. He was unluckily one of the least culpable, for he had only taken away a bottle of wine by force; but he was caught in the fact, and suffered for the sake of example —as the least guilty in reality often do, from the most guilty being also the most knowing.

Lord Wellington has not yet returned; he must now exert his wits, to cure this mishap, which will not, in my opinion, put him in the best of humours.

The Pyrenees were to-day perfectly clear, and very striking. An immense snowy barrier almost entirely white, with scarcely any bare rock visible. They are not by any means so picturesque as the Alps. They

form a large mass, without much variety of form and
character; and have not that contrast of pointed, craggy,
fancifully-shaped rocks, rounded lower hills covered
with verdure, and fine forest scenery, which is seen in
Switzerland.

Two of the medical officers and one of the 42nd of the
sixth division, taken at Hagenau, have escaped and come
into us, but plundered of everything. The French
marched them seven or eight leagues a-day, nearly thirty
miles; and the one I spoke to had been concealed four
days after his escape with scarcely anything to eat, until
he had an opportunity of joining our corps under General
Hill.

Head-Quarters, Seisses, March 31*st*, 1814.—Our disappointment in crossing the river on the 28th has kept us
here ever since: and the halt has given me employment,
which has prevented my writing to you. As soon as we
become quiet, I am set to work in order to prevent all
arrears, and to let punishment follow the offence as fast
as possible.

Our General has spent his mornings in riding all over
the country to reconnoitre; and he dispatches all his
other multitude of business at odd hours and times.
The new plan was at last resolved upon, and last night
the execution of it commenced. The divisions on this
side Toulouse are pushed in close to the suburbs of St.
Cyprien, near which the French have been for some days
most busily at work, fortifying themselves to defend the
bridge. Finding the river so wide below the junction
with the Arrige at Portet, General Hill (with great difficulty owing to the rapidity of the Garonne, caused by
the last two days' continual rain) succeeded at last, in
pursuance of his orders, in fixing his pontoons across that
river above the junction with the Arrige; and having
been nearly all night at work, began to cross about four
o'clock this morning, and has sent word that he is over.

A ridge of high land forms a sort of tongue between the two rivers. This he is to take post upon immediately, and march off a corps as rapidly as possible, about three leagues, to a bridge over the Arrige, which he is to surprise and preserve if possible, and defend, thus fixing himself securely between the two rivers, preparatory to further movements of the rest of the army. The Spaniards under Murillo crossed with General Hill. General Frere's Spaniards move into the ground which General Hill leaves.

I was upon the church-tower early this morning, and saw the Spanish column moving all along the plain, headed by some of our heavy dragoons; the fog on the river prevented my seeing more. On descending, I found Lord Wellington and all his suite, just about to be off, when the arrival of an English mail to the 16th, stopped him. By this we have your very bad news from Holland, and many private letters accounting for the failure. All here are open-mouthed at the reported consequences; namely, that the reinforcements intended for Lord Wellington are going to Holland. This is worse than the defeat. Very little was ever expected here from that army from various causes; it was always considered as so many men quite thrown away, as regards the main cause. I thought them, latterly, worse than inefficient, after they had once given the Dutch an opportunity of arming, by clearing their country, for they have the effect of preventing exertion on the part of the Dutch. The moment they had cleared Holland they should, in my opinion, have been sent to us, and thus by a sense of pressing danger, ought to have roused the sleepy heavy Dutchmen to do something for themselves when once well in the scrape, getting only arms and artillery and stores from England.

By the exchange of prisoners, the officers so much wanted by the French, whom Lord Wellington has taken here, will get back again by these losses in Holland, another way in which that army has done more harm than good. It would have been better to leave our people prisoners than to release French regular officers at this moment, for their value in the newly-raised corps is immense, and considerably beyond that of ours to England. Besides the numbers in the town would have hastened its surrender, or compelled the governor to send them out without exchange.

This is, however, reasoning upon general principles, and not upon personal feelings as to the officers taken : I do think, however, that this exchange was permitting humanity to have more weight than policy. There seem to have been much blundering and confusion in the execution of our attack, and from what I can hear the plan was allowed to fail just when the difficulties were nearly all over. It is always to be regretted when our people are ordered to run their heads against stone walls and heavy guns, and that even here, for I think the French seem to understand that work best, and we lose more in one of these affairs than we do in gaining a great battle in the fair field, where the French cannot be brought now to stand against us. On this ground, I feel a little anxious, even as to Toulouse, supposing the French to remain firm, which is doubtful, and still more as to Bayonne.

Mr. C——— and a commissariat officer arrived here yesterday from Bordeaux : the accounts they bring are bad enough. The National Guard are disarmed; no arming of any consequence going on; no efficient English naval force has arrived; and the people, though they shout for the King at the opera, &c., are all in a terrible fright lest the French should return, since we have so small a force there; and, according to report, many repent of what they have done.

The Duke d'Angoulême does not appear to me to be

made of stuff to gain a kingdom, though he would have kept one and been popular, from his amiable qualities. He has committed many blunders, I am told, and the white cockade gentry, like the *emigrés* of old, amuse themselves with inventing lies concerning Bonaparte and his armies, which the *maire* of Bordeaux publishes in a bulletin, which Bonaparte's bulletins, lying as they are, effectually and satisfactorily contradict the next day.

The *maire* is becoming daily more unpopular. We have an account of Augereau having been defeated— which I hope rests upon better foundations; as well as private accounts from Paris of the great reduction of Bonaparte's forces by his various rapid marches, continual fighting, and desertion. Almost the only town in this country, excepting Bordeaux, which has been active in the Royal cause is Bagnières, which has proclaimed the king; no troops of either army have passed that way.

The rest of the population in our rear are in general quietly waiting the event, and are now with a very few exceptions only on our side, because they think they see an end to the war quicker that way. But I am sure, from personal observation, that let Bonaparte be successful a little, and Lord Wellington be compelled to retreat, and let them only see the same prospect of peace by Bonaparte's means, and three-fourths of the population would all be against us again.

The sulky *maires*, and other public functionaries, now all submission, would then become active enemies, and all the *pensionnaires* and *douaniers* and national landholders who are now really frightened to death, would be roused into activity. This is a picture, however, which I hope never to see realized; and if Toulouse and Lyons can be induced to enter into a common cause with Bordeaux, the events will, it is to be hoped, be far different. Had I the Duke d'Angoulême's stake to play for, I should somehow have raised a force before this at Bordeaux, and should certainly have been over here post to enter Toulouse, and have paraded through Pau, Tarbes, &c., in the way, and tried to do something.

The only great hit he has hitherto made is to get the new prefect of the department des Landes to publish and circulate his proclamations, and sign them: this certainly is a beginning, and it is said that some have found their way into Toulouse. The *maire* of Galan, who was really in my opinion a Royalist, pointing to his head, asked me, speaking of the Duke d'Angoulême, whether " *il y voit quelque chose là?* " of which he seemed to have doubts. The lower, and older population in the villages certainly, though knowing nothing of the Bourbons, have a sort of vague wish for old times again, and therefore were friendly. The middling classes are not by any means so favourably disposed.

You have no conception of my obligation to you for sending the newspapers so regularly, and getting them forwarded in Lord Wellington's bag. On the march in our present state, by this means I have my letters and papers sometimes almost a week before any one else; for the public bag has been lately obliged to come up, for want of transport, in a bullock-car, with one weak soldier of the guides as a guard. When we are stationary I sometimes suffer by this plan, for single papers are got a-day or two later than my letter, but now I am a great gainer, and my newspapers are in the greatest request.

Head-Quarters, Seisses, April 1st, 1814.—Here we are still in front of " the great big town where the French are," as the Irishmen call Toulouse. The French yesterday moved about four divisions out of Toulouse after General Hill's movement, and in the evening went back again into the town. This I believe made Lord Wellington suspect that Soult intended to try an attack upon the columns of the British who remained in front of the town on this side, and he would have wished, in my opinion, for nothing better, as we had a rising ground commanding the roads where they must make their debouches, and cannon ready placed to give them a warm reception instantly. In consequence of this expectation, Lord Wellington and his staff were off early to the front; about eleven o'clock, finding all quiet, they returned, and we remained *in statu quo* for the day.

I never expected that anything would be done if it depended on the French, for their game seems to be merely to endeavour to keep us on this side of the river, and to leave us to get over the difficulties as we can, and not to run any hazards by molesting us, or giving us even a fair chance by an attack on their posts. It is said that after all it is found that General Hill's road would lead us so much round, and that the roads round that way to Toulouse would be so bad, that the plan mentioned in my letter under date of the 31st is abandoned; that in consequence General Hill will be ordered to return across the river to-night, and that the pontoons will be taken up afterwards, and an attempt made to place them lower down the river at last, and below Toulouse, which, if it succeeds, will place us at once upon the main good road to Bordeaux. Time will show whether this information of mine is correct. If this plan be practicable, it will be far better than the other. In truth the Garonne is a formidable barrier just now, when there are no fords.

The disappointment of not having Graham's army here is very great, much worse so if the reinforcements intended for us should go that way. So much did Lord Dalhousie with his weak divisions at Bordeaux expect General Graham's army, that I am told he has twice sent to the coast in expectation of their arrival, together with a naval expedition, on a report of some distant sails being seen. This last *Gazette* is a woeful contrast!

2 H

The importance of that ten thousand men at Bordeaux is immense, and all agree that the country northwards would be ready to come forward and join us if we were stronger and dared advance. The weak state of our force at Bordeaux alarms them all, and keeps everything back; a naval force to co-operate and to assist against the castle of Blaye, was also expected to be ready the moment the news of our arrival at Bordeaux was received, as it must have been such a probable event. As it is Lord Dalhousie was about to make some attempt, I understand, to take a position across the Garonne, between the Dordogne and the Garonne.

I have just been told another piece of news—unpleasant if it be true. It is said that the Duke d'Angoulême's new *Préfet des Landes* ordered the *maire* of St. Sever to proclaim Louis XVIII., and that the old maire, a prudent sly fellow, who has made much money in the Revolution, declined to do so unless by Lord Wellington's orders, and wrote to Lord Wellington to know if he was obliged to do what he was desired. It is said that Lord Wellington replied " No," and suspended the new préfet for giving the order. This is a most awkward state of things; each town, each *maire*, is allowed thus to take this strong step if they please, but there is to be no influence used, so that all prudent people naturally enough will remain quiet and do nothing, and the desperately zealous alone will act; yet so long as the conferences remain in existence, this cannot be otherwise.

Some more Spaniards are ordered up whom we are to feed also; how far they will come I know not. The siege of Bayonne is, it is understood, at last determined upon in earnest; as yet only preparation of fascines, &c., have been made. I am told now, that the horses of the brigades of artillery of General Hope's column, are sent down to Renteria to bring up the heavy battery train and siege stores. The Guards begin to talk of more " bloody work," but I sincerely hope not another Bergen-op-Zoom! That left column once released, would set us quite at ease here. Just now, our necessarily-divided army cannot be so efficient as from its numbers compared with the French it might be presumed to be.

For fear of being too late for the post, I shall now seal up my three letters in one packet and send it off.

In appearance, the size of Toulouse is very considerable, particularly its length. It seems much larger than Bristol; whether really so or not we have not just now conveniently the means of ascertaining.

All who come from Bordeaux are in ecstacies with the place and the life there. It seems everything a bachelor officer with a little money could wish for—everything to be had, and everything (except maps now) very cheap.

Head-Quarters, Grenade, April 5th, 1814.—In pursuance of the change of plans as to the passage of this formidable river, the Garonne, in the face of thirty thousand men, under the command of Marshal Soult, we very suddenly moved on Sunday morning, the 3rd, to Colomiers, a poor dirty village on the high road from Auch to Toulouse. The pontoons had been previously moved in the night from the neighbourhood of Carbonne, where they had been previously fixed, and where General Hill had passed over to the vicinity of Grenade. On the night of the 4th, about eight or nine o'clock, the whole army, excepting General Hill's columns, were put in motion towards Grenade, the pontoons were launched in the river, the bridge successfully formed during the night, and about ten thousand men passed over without resistance by daybreak. It rained furiously almost all the night, and a failure was in consequence much apprehended by many, from the increased rapidity and breadth of the current of the river. Hitherto all has gone on well. General Hill's corps remained in front of the suburbs and bridge of St. Cyprien near Toulouse.

2 H 2

Lord Wellington and his staff were all off about two or three o'clock in the morning, or rather night, for the river side near the bridge, and passed over early in the morning. Lord Wellington reconnoitred yesterday on the right bank to within about five or six miles of Toulouse, and did not return here until after dark. Civil departments and baggage were ordered to move across the country to Corn Barieu, a poor dirty place on the cross-road to Grenade, at daylight, and there to remain loaded till further orders. It was only four miles of bad road, and we were there about half-past six. I conclude we were kept at that point so that we might be secure, and away from the high road out of Toulouse, in case of accidents, and at the same time ready to go into Toulouse, in case the French should abandon the town and bridge on hearing of our passage of the river; whilst, on the other hand, if they remained fast, we were ready to come on here.

The poor mules remained loaded until near two o'clock before they were ordered on, and afterwards fell in with such columns of baggage, cavalry, and troops, particularly Spaniards, all converging to the bridge, that they did not arrive here until about seven or eight o'clock at night, having had to pass a deep cross country, by a clayey un-formed road, in places sinking up to the middle, for the night's rain and quantity of animals passing had quite cut it up. I left the printing-press and Mr. S——'s carriage fast in the mud, and many a load upset; at last I believe all arrived safe.

Whilst we were waiting in suspense, as I dare not again go much to the front, Dr. M'Gregor and several other civilians and I passed our time pleasantly enough. There was a chateau on a hill close to us, which com-manded all the country, and particularly Toulouse. To that we bent our steps, and finding a young lad, son of the owner, in the house, we got our horses into the stable, bought corn for them, and from the Doctor's canteen made a good breakfast, and then posted ourselves with our glasses to see what was going on. Had there been any fight we should have commanded the whole scene beautifully. As it was, we only traced our columns of baggage, Spaniards, and cavalry across the country, in two lines of about six or seven miles' length, all moving gradually to the bridge. We also saw some large fires in Toulouse, but have not yet learnt whether they were anything in particular. About half-past one we set out again, and fought our way through mud and clay and baggage and Spaniards for about ten miles ; and I am now again in a civilized home, but with rather a forward tradesman, who gave me a roast fowl for supper, but took his place and had his full share with me. It is odd enough that a man of his description, in a large good house, stables, and three or four horses, should boast, as he does, that he can talk French, and that his daughter of eight years old has learnt to talk French, and can speak and understand it a little when she chooses. Their patois I can scarcely make out, certainly, not so well as Spanish or Portuguese.

The country is all very rich and populous, and covered with villages and chateaux. The former are generally in evident decay ; the latter are large and showy on the outside, but for the most part old, dirty, out of repair, and nearly unfurnished inside, with none of the comforts even of a cit's villa, and still less of a 'great man's house in England. At the same time one cannot but feel how much of what we in England think necessaries are mere superfluity. One cause of their present appearance in part may be, that the owners generally live from seven to ten months in the year in the great towns, Toulouse in particular, and only spend September and October in their chateaux to see to the harvests, so that they, somewhat like the Portuguese lords, when they do come, bring nearly all their furniture and comforts with them. By this means, luckily, we have not done these chateaux much damage. The young man whom we found in the chateau near Corn Barieu, had been sent out just before we arrived, to see what was going on, and to protect the place. He had not been able to hold any communication with his friends in Toulouse since, and I dare say, as I told him, they were in a terrible fright, and thought the Spaniards had roasted and eaten him up.

It unfortunately rained again all last night. This has swelled the river, and alarmed us a little, for there are at times such floods here that our bridge would not stand them, and we are now half on each side. This was also very unlucky for the troops, many of whom must have bivouacked without their tents and baggage. I have hitherto heard of no ill consequences, and it is thought that the French must either come out and fight us imme-diately, or be off and leave us at our ease for a short time to try and refit and get shoes for our poor barefooted soldiers. In the meantime we are here with no other orders than to be ready packed to march at ten o'clock, but not loaded. It is now half-past ten, and I have been quietly writing this, and four letters on business, since breakfast.

When last at Seysses I met at Lord Wellington's Major M——, of the 53rd, the *ci-devant* prisoner and French squire, whom I mentioned before in my letters. He was at Toulouse when we came by his former house, and he took the opportunity of our pontoon bridge at Carbonne to come over to us, for to go out he was com-pelled.

I do not quite understand his own story, so as to make his conduct correct. He was always on a sort of parole in Languedoc and Gascony. On our coming near Tou-louse he was told that he must retire towards Montpelier. He asked delay on the plea of health, got a day, and was then ordered to move post by Carcassonne. He went two stages, then turned to the right, came over to us, and now rides about, a strange figure, in a new handsome 53rd uniform, and a great French cocked hat, with his English loop and button. He is, moreover, a round broken-backed country-squire volunteer sort of gentleman, on a high white tumble-down French nag. He was of course full of information and conversation, but I rather doubted the accuracy of the former.

He told us that Bonaparte was making for Metz, giving up Paris; and that he intended to relieve his garrisons in that direction even as far as Wesel, and then to try and bring the war to the frontier again. This would be giving up nearly all France, and putting himself between the Crown Prince at Liege and the Allies near Paris; whereas, if compelled to leave Paris, his line, in my opinion, must be to fall back towards Lyons, and to endeavour to unite in that direction with Augereau, and even with Soult, who will very likely fall back that way also. If Bonaparte were to go to Metz, Lord Wellington said he thought then the Allies, on entering Paris, would probably let the King he proclaimed, and that he should not then despair of seeing Bonaparte a grand Guerilla chief on a large scale, fighting about for his existence, which he had never expected to happen in his life-time. Major M——— also said that Soult's plan was, if obliged to give up Toulouse, to go towards the Black Mountains, and retreat by way of Carcassonne, making his stand there in a country where our superior cavalry could not act. If he does this, I think half his men will desert, and the remainder be in jeopardy, unless Suchet brings him more assistance than is thought possible. Suchet is said to be withdrawing everything, and to be mustering all he can. Oh that we had your English reinforcements, and General Graham's army! for our own real English army dwindles away very fast in this active service, and

ten thousand men may make all the difference in regard
to the event.   The 53rd regiment and the eighteen-
pounders are, I hear, hutted at Tarbes, to try to reduce a
small garrison at Lourdes.   The Householders are also
arrived, I believe, as far as Tarbes.

On the 23rd of March, Caffarelli sent his orders to all
the communes round Toulouse, for a considerable distance
(about fifty communes), to send men to work at the fortifications in front of Toulouse.   The numbers to be sent
by requisition were very considerable ; but we have rather
disturbed the march of the larger half.   He also called
upon all the inhabitants to arm, and to make the town a
second Saragoza.

Major M—— says he was told that there was not the
same motive.   I understand they have been obliged to
arm by compulsion, but it is supposed will do nothing.
Some old French officers also came to Soult to offer to
raise Guerillas corps in our rear.   Major M—— said that
their offers were to be accepted ; but, except a few for
plunder, I do not think, as yet, they will find many followers.   Lord Wellington makes the *maires* responsible
for any disturbances in the rear, and threatens garrisons,
as on the French plan, *garnissaires*, in case of a breach of
order.   To execute this duty the *maires* are allowed to
arm guards in their communes.   All the communes
around here were to have *garnissaires*, in case the workmen did not arrive—that is, soldiers to keep in their
houses gratis.

One o'clock, same day.—Here we are still ; and I hope
shall not move to-day, unless to go into Toulouse, for
there is a report that the French are moving off now, and
that we have taken two cars of money.   This I will not
vouch for.   What is more certain is, that our pontoon
bridge is on its legs again by land, and moving towards
Toulouse, to be laid down nearer the town, to make our
communications shorter between the two parts of our

army, on the right and left bank. This, it is to be feared, may draw head-quarters into some little dirty village near the bridge; and I should like to enjoy the tolerable clean brick room which I have to myself, and a little stable with some hay for my horses, for one day, if it suits our plans.

At first I was surprised at Major M——'s boldness, and, as it appeared to me, folly, in going about in his uniform, in a way to do no good to anybody, and possible harm to himself. I have now heard that he has been divorced from his lady, and of course by the French law from his *château* and *terre* also, and that now he has nothing whatever to lose. He may as well make a merit of his love of England and the Bourbons. His daughter, about sixteen, is married, and the property goes with her. A party of five dragoons took yesterday a messenger from Montauban to Soult. It was known by eleven o'clock at Montauban that we had cut off the communications on the main road. The messenger was sent round a bye-road but was caught. His despatches were, it is reported, principally complaints that the people would not arm for the fight, and were not very material. I pitied the man. He was a respectable man of business in Montauban; but being told that unless he became a civic soldier he must be a regular, he put on his sword "by compulsion," was sent to carry these letters, and thus fell into our hands. He says that it will be his ruin to send him to England as a prisoner; and I hope, though he is threatened with this, that Lord Wellington will soon release him. This is to be hoped, for I believe his story to be true, for the Préfet of Montauban is reported to be a most furious Bonapartist, and that he compels the people to take up arms in the cause, and even threatens their lives if they do not. All here profess great friendship for us, and I believe, at present, are sincere.

Six o'clock.—About two o'clock I saw Lord Wellington come in, and the real news was, that all was quiet on both sides the river, but that the floods had carried away or sunk one pontoon, and that the bridge was impassable. It was just on the point of being moved higher when this happened. Just now, it is not safe to place it anywhere. We have only three divisions and three brigades of artillery across, and two or three, it is believed, of cavalry. The Spaniards are not over, as I supposed, but were to have gone over this morning. Unless Soult is an arrant coward, he must now attack these men, and it is to be feared that we shall have sharp work. A position, however, may be taken near the river, so as to enable our artillery on this side to assist. The river has fallen above a foot since morning, as it has hitherto been fine to-day, but I am sorry to say it has now begun to rain again, and it looks very much like another bad night. Rain upon the present river would be tremendous. A quarter of an hour after Lord Wellington came home from Toulouse, I met him going off again to cross the river; it is to be concluded, therefore, that something important had happened.

6th of April, 9 *o'clock at night. Head-Quarters at Grenade.*—My principal occupation to-day, when not engaged by business, has been to watch the river. It continued to fall many hours after the last rain had ceased, and began to rise at ten to-day, about fifteen hours after the last rain commenced, and five after it ceased; at this rate it will continue to rise until six or eight to-night, and then fall again; and if the weather relent a little, to-morrow, probably, our bridge will be restored.

Marshal Soult has left our three divisions quite quiet on the other side. If he knows their numbers this is playing the game of a coward. At present he seems to think of nothing but fortifying Toulouse with ditches and works, and his men are hard at work. This makes the delay very unfortunate for us. It has, indeed, been so on every account, for we have to-day received accounts which appear to be believed, that twelve hundred French cavalry, cuirassiers, from Suchet's army, joined yesterday; and that he is endeavouring to gain time; and the elements seem to favour his obtaining it.

The only two events here to-day have been, first, the arrival of the pontoon which was lost and floated away. Lieutenant Reid, of the Engineers, galloped to Verdan, two leagues down the river, offered a reward of *cent francs*, or five pounds, to any inhabitants who would get boats and stop the pontoon and bring it ashore: the deserter was thus secured, and to-day brought back in triumph by a party of soldiers. The other arrival astonished us all. A troop of the Royal Horse Guards Blue arrived with drawn swords and a Captain's guard escorting a carriage. Some said that it was the Duke d'Angoulême, some one great person, some another. One officer asked the Captain if it was King Ferdinand? This was a hoax. At last it was discovered to be a *maire* of a small commune near Tarbes, and his wife. The *maire* is supposed to have been endeavouring to favour a guerilla system, and exciting the people to arm. He was in consequence ordered to be sent to head-quarters. The Blues were in high condition; and Lord Wellington, when he was told of the French cuirassiers, said, " Well, then, we must have the Householders for these gentlemen, and see what they can make of them."

I must tell you two little anecdotes about the pontoon bridge. The French were very jealous of any attempt of the kind, and had cavalry videttes, &c., all along their banks of the river. The engineer wished to measure the breadth of the river at the spot intended; and for this purpose got into conversation with the French vidette a long time, but had no opportunity. At last he pretended that the calls of nature were imperative. The French-man, out of decency, withdrew. The engineer popped out his sextant, took the angle, &c., and was off.

Lord Wellington himself, with two other officers went to the spot also to reconnoitre with his own eyes. Con-cealing his General's hat with an oil-skin, he got into conversation with the French vidette, dismounted, got down to the water-side, looked all about him, saw all he wished, and came away. This was, in my opinion, risk-ing too much; but no French soldier would have any idea of the commander of the Allied Forces going about thus with two attendants. Lord Wellington was yes-terday over alone on foot, and went on upon a horse of General Cole's, as horses could not pass. Even General P—— was a little uneasy, and sent about eight o'clock to know if he had come back safe. He returned about seven o'clock, when it was dusk. To-day he has a great dinner in honour of Badajos.

7th April, Grenade.—We have at last a fine clear day, and warm. The river is falling rapidly. By this even-ing probably our bridge may be re-established, and to-morrow I conclude that we shall pass more troops and advance against Toulouse and the French marshal, who is digging and working away as usual. The French made several attempts to destroy our bridge before the floods did the business for them. They sent us down all their dead horses, several trees, &c., and a large old boat, which struck a pontoon, and went down itself instead of the pontoon. They sent down also a sort of armed log stuck round with swords, and rolling round and round in the stream as it went along, like a great fish, in hopes that the swords would strike and cut the cable which holds the boats.

Major M—— has just told me that he has had news from the interior of another defeat of Bonaparte at Arcis-sur Aube, and of his having lost one hundred guns, &c.,

and being then manœuvring in the rear of the Allies. This seems probable. He has also an account of the departments in the west of France having all sent in to the Duke d'Angoulême at Bordeaux for orders; this is also probable, and that the Royalists gain ground fast. His accounts add in the postscript,—" The Allies entered Paris April 1st." This ought to be, I think, from former accounts, and I hope it is so. The last *Moniteur* we have of the 30th talks of Bonaparte's return to Paris to cover the city. How he could then get there seems the difficulty. Lord Wellington also had yesterday a private letter from the interior, in which it is said, " *un événement bien imprévu est arrivé à Paris,*" and no comment. He guesses it to be the flight of the Empress. You see what confused accounts we get of all late events!

7th (6 *o'clock.*)—In addition to the above we have now news that the Bourbons have been proclaimed at Paris, and that in the name of the Emperor of Austria the house of Napoleon has been declared to cease to reign. I must now seal up, for Lord Wellington has written his English letters to-day, Thursday, although Saturday is the usual day. In addition to this, I think, from many symptoms, that we shall move to-morrow.

P.S.—The *maire* brought in with such a magnificent escort, is now quietly walking about here with his wife and no guard. The bridge is to be fixed nearly in the same place again to-night.

CHAPTER XXVI.

Uncertain Intelligence—Capture of Toulouse—Wellington at the Theatre
—The "Liberator"—Ball at the Prefecture—The Feelings of the French
—Soult and Suchet—Ball at the Capitole.

Head-quarters, Grenade,
April 10, 1814, 1 o'clock.

My DEAR M——,

HERE we are still, away from all that is going on,
but expecting every moment an order to enter Toulouse.
The day before yesterday the bridge was re-established
(the 8th), and by one o'clock the Spaniards had all passed
over. The order then came for a brigade of Portuguese
artillery to do the same. They were passing when I
went there, soon after one o'clock ; and just as a gun was
quitting the last boat to ascend the bank, down went the
boat ; the gun, however, run off safe, but two of the
Portuguese pontoon-train sailors got a ducking, which
was all the mischief except a delay of about two hours to
fish up the pontoon, drag it on shore, turn it upside
down, to clear out the water, and then launch it again,
and refit the board.

By four o'clock I left the remainder of the guns going
over. The head-quarters of Lord Wellington remained
at St. Jouy that night, and last night Lord Wellington
has only pushed the troops on a little, to reconnoitre, and
in the evening the 18th Hussars, under Colonel Vivian,
had a brilliant affair. They charged the French cavalry
on the high-road, broke them, sabred several, and took

about seventy prisoners, with the loss of a few officers wounded, and, it is believed, only about six or eight men. Unluckily, Colonel Vivian received a ball in the arm, which, it is feared, will render amputation necessary. Yesterday (the 9th), the bridge was taken up very early, and ordered to be immediately fixed about four miles nearer the town of Toulouse, at a little place called Assaic. The light divisions were close to that point, on this side of the river, as a security in case of any attack on the second division, near St. Cyprien and the bridge of Toulouse. They were ordered to cross the river as soon as our pontoons were ready, and a movement was intended, and ordered yesterday.

From some difficulties, or bad management, the bridge of boats was not ready until nearly three o'clock, when it was thought too late. Lord Wellington was more vexed, and in a greater state of anger, than he usually is when things go wrong, even without any good cause. He said that his whole plans for the day were frustrated and nothing could be done; and the light divisions were counter-ordered to remain where they were on this side the river, and head-quarters remained at St. Jouy.

The French, it appeared, while still keeping a force to defend the bridge of Toulouse, had before this taken a strong position on the hills beyond the town, and had made there some strong works, upon which they were constantly busy. The last two days and nights their main body rested on the hills, bivouacking in this position, and in an uncomfortable state, hourly expecting an attack. This morning about seven it commenced: the firing was heavy for about two hours, until nine, and has continued partially since. As I dare not cross the river and go to the front, I went with my glass to the highest look-out here, and saw the French redoubt very plainly, firing away briskly: since that all has been silent here, and free from smoke. The stories of the people here are that, with the loss of six thousand men, we have taken the redoubt and thirty-six pieces of ordnance.

The former, from the direction of the fire, it is certain, is a lie, and perhaps the latter. As, however, we have now some sort of official news that the Allies are in Paris, and the Imperial Court at Orleans, and as there is no account of Bonaparte, the French here will probably not fight much; and if beaten, it is certain that many, nay thousands, will run home, and the army be much diminished. I suspect that Bonaparte will try to unite his corps and all the remains of corps near Paris, and Augereau's from Lyons, and Marshal Soult's and Suchet's from Provence, towards Montpelier; but it is to be hoped that even regiments, and perhaps Marshals, will begin to desert, when it is found that Paris is taken, and the royal party proclaimed and gaining ground.

We certainly are in a very odd state just now in France. Our military chest, Paymaster, Doctors, Commissaries, &c., and nearly all our money, are in this place, which is altogether without troops; only about a dozen staff corps men, and about ten of the paymaster's ordinary marching guard. The whole army is nearly four leagues in front, and our only protection is the good-will of the people, and the river. Yet we are told that there are French troops at Montauban, about four leagues off, and nothing between us except the river. All feel, notwithstanding, quite secure, and have no anxiety but to enter Toulouse.

In the mean time Lord Dalhousie with a part of the seventh division has crossed, not only the Gironde, but the Dordogne, and we are told, is to take Fort. Blaze by storm: I suppose his whole force is not above three thousand five hundred men. Bayonne has not yet been seriously attacked, nor do we hear of any very great distress in the town, which is surprising, considering the length of the blockade.

In the attack to-day, it is said that the third and sixth divisions were to form the right of the attack on the river, the fourth the centre, and the light and large body of Spaniards to make the flank movement on the left, to get on the hills and turn the French position, whilst the cavalry advance also in that direction, to be ready to take advantage of the enemy's retreat.

Five o'clock, same day.—No one returned, and no news: and yet no firing heard, and no orders. I fear that the resistance has been greater than was expected, and begin to be fidgety and uneasy. The reports are now, that eight thousand English wounded, and fighting in the streets now going on. If such complete ignorance of the truth exists within ten miles of what is passing, you may judge how false reports circulate : we receive contradictory rumours every hour. All we know for certain is, that two hours ago Lord Wellington's baggage remained at St. Jouy without orders ; I despair, therefore, of seeing Toulouse to-day.

Grenade, April 11th, 8 o'clock, morning.—The firing continued all day yesterday, and until past eight at night, and began again at four this morning, and has continued to this time, but has now lessened. Several of our civilians returned home here last night. I understand our loss is very considerable. We drove the enemy from all the heights, but with difficulty. The Spaniards failed in the attack of a redoubt, were put to the rout completely, and, it is reported, would have lost their guns, which the French were within two or three hundred yards of, had not the Portuguese stepped in to their support, and enabled them to rally again.

This is really too bad—my friend says the ground was covered with dead Spaniards, and that he saw but few French ; this is generally the result of alarm and flight. The redoubt was taken, but not by the Spaniards, it is said ; the fire close to Lord Wellington was most severe.

Near the town the French fought very hard in the houses, particularly at some houses near the lock of the canal close to the river. We each occupied some of the houses, and fired continually; the French houses were loop-holed, and they had the best. We were obliged to bring guns, &c.; and, unfortunately, the most successful shell fell into one of our own houses, and burnt out our own people. Among the killed, &c., I hear, is Colonel Coghlan of the 61st, an excellent officer, Lieutenant-colonel Forbes, Captain Gordon, 10th Hussars. Colonel Fitzclarence is wounded in the thigh: he charged with his troops two French squadrons, he says, up a hill, beat them, but on the top was received by infantry: the first shot carried away part of his sword, the second hit him on the thigh, and they fell back. We were close to the town and to the bridge last night on all sides, and had moved our bridge up within two miles of the town. The French have barricaded the houses and streets, fixed swivels on the tops, lined the roofs with men, &c., and seem determined to defend the town with desperation. An officer deserted yesterday, and says he will serve no longer under a man who acts like a madman, as Soult now does, in defending a town like Toulouse in such a manner.—It is madness.

Four Spanish officers came in here yesterday, who had escaped from Italy through Switzerland, and had walked here. They seemed in great distress. We had no Commissary here: I therefore gave them eight pounds of bread and a dozen eggs, got them a quarter for the night, and advised them to stay here until this mornimg, and then proceed to head-quarters. One had served in Colonel Roche's corps in Catalonia, and spoke English tolerably. Our delay here, and in taking the town, has alarmed the people very much. All who have relations and friends in Toulouse are terribly frightened. The officer who deserted says that many will do the same as

soon as the business is over, and occasions arise.   Captain
O. K——, the French-English officer from Toulouse,
who came over to the Duke d'Angoulême at St. Jean de
Luz, arrived here yesterday from Bordeaux.   He says,
that things are going on well, especially since the news
from Paris ; that the Duke has now eighteen hundred
men formed; and that French officers come in every
day with fleur-de-lys embroidered on their Napoleon
uniforms, and thus tender their services.   O. K—— was
here on his road to Aurillac, to Auvergne, &c., where, he
says, a party is formed and ready to rise.   He must take
care of his head, for he goes about talking very im-
prudently.

Head-Quarters, Toulouse, April 13*th*, 1814, *Section* 3,
No. 676.—To give you any notion of what we have all
felt from the changes which the last thirty-six hours have
produced, you must go back to my first sheet, and you
will feel more as I did, by reading in succession what has
occurred than by anything I can now write.   I was
about to destroy the first sheet, as much of it is now not
worth the trouble of reading ; but thought it would give
you a better idea of the feelings, from day to day, of the
army.

An order came for civil departments to march, to cross
the pontoons, and to proceed on the high road to Toulouse to a church only three miles from the town, and
there halt and wait for orders.   We were off in ecstasies,
expecting all to dine in Toulouse, and that the French
were off, and our men after them.   Judge of our vexation, when, on arriving at the church, we were all turned
back off the road, to a miserable village of about ten
houses, called St. Albains ; and were there to find
quarters for the night, in places just quitted by the plundering Spaniards, and left nearly in the state in which
the French left the houses in Spain as they passed.

When we arrived, we found many of the Spaniards

still in possession, and four of us disarmed and seized three of them in the act of plundering. The people were screaming in every direction, the houses abandoned, and the inhabitants just beginning to return to witness the mischief done. Everything had been ransacked—all the closets, &c., broken open; the rags and remnants on the floor, mixed with hundreds of egg-shells, and the feathers of the plundered fowls, &c. Much linen was carried off, the sheets and heavy articles in the yard; the tables were covered with broken dishes, bottles, bones, and twine; and the cellars with the wine-casks running. In about two hours we got possession of the quarters, and got the inhabitants in to clean them, and by five o'clock had divided the places among us. My whole baggage lost its road, and did not arrive at all—five mules and a horse loaded.

You may conceive the disappointment and the vexation we experienced. Dr. M'Gregor said that our loss was terrible! He was just returned from collecting all the wounded in villages, and, by Lord Wellington's desire, was hurrying every one possible instantly to the rear. They were passing all night in cars. The Spaniards were moaning and crying most desperately, and were to reach Fenoullet that night, Sole Jourdain the next, and then to be sent on further if necessary. The accommodations were very bad. The accounts from the town were that the French were continuing to barricade every house and loophole, and arming to defend themselves to the last.

The army was said to be now much weakened; the Spaniards could not be depended upon; the reinforcements were not come up from England, and a story was going about and believed by many who ought to have known better, that we were out of ammunition, and could not use our artillery. You may conceive that I went (without my baggage and comforts), with this news, sorrowfully to bed, ordering my servant to be off at five in the morning in search of my stragglers.

On the 12th, at 6 o'clock, I was up and wandering about alone, listening to an occasional heavy gun, seeing wounded men pass, and waiting for the return of my man. About eight I saw Henry returning alone, and was expecting more bad news, when he told me that the French were off, that we were to march for Toulouse directly, and that my baggage was all safe at a house a league off on the road; and that, therefore, he had ordered them to pack and be off with the rest. Think of our sensations on hearing of this welcome change! The last twenty-four hours had been among the most critical of the war, and now all was safe and right again. I found out the clergyman, Mr. B——, got a razor and a cup of tea, whilst my horse was getting ready, and was then off, to go round by head-quarters and to enter Toulouse with Lord Wellington. About eleven I arrived at the fortified entrance, and found, instead of the enemy behind the new works, the *maire* of the town, almost all the officers of the *garde urbaine*, a considerable number of national guard officers, deserters, &c., and about two hundred smart but awkward men of the city guard, and a band of music, all with the white cockade, and a great crowd of citizens besides, all waiting with anxiety to receive Lord Wellington, and carry him in form to the mayoralty. Unluckily, from some mismanagement and mistake, he went in at another entrance, and passed on, almost unknown. Hearing this, I went to the mayoralty with General Packington's aide-de-camp, and found it was so; and, therefore, we went back to inform the mayor officially, and to beg he would return to the *maison commune*. He did so, though an immense crowd entered the mayoralty in form, and an introduction then took place, and Lord Wellington showed himself at the window, amidst the shouts and waving handkerchiefs and hats of every one.

The procession then went with Lord Wellington to his quarters, the Prefêt's palace, amidst the applause of the inhabitants all the way. Nothing could be more gratifying than his reception, and that, indeed, of all the English ; the most respectable inhabitants, many of them, not only anxiously showing us the way to our billets, but offering their homes without any billets, or receiving us with a sincere welcome as soon as the paper was delivered. Lord Wellington announced a ball in the evening at the Prefecture, and left Marshal Beresford with three divisions and cavalry to follow Marshal Soult for the day.

We thought nothing could make us happier, when at five o'clock in came Colonel Ponsonby from Bordeaux with the Paris news, which you know. He told us that the official accounts would arrive in an hour or two. Ponsonby came through Montauban : the French officer commanding there taking his word, and letting him pass. I had been, at Colonel Campbell's request, examining General St. Hilaire and his servant. St. Hilaire was found, under suspicious circumstances, in the town, and was just put under arrest, and Campbell luckily asked me to dine with Lord Wellington, which I should have been very sorry to have missed.

Just as we were sitting down to dinner, about forty of us, General Frere, and several Spaniards, General Picton, and Baron Alten, the principal French, &c., in came Cooke with the despatches. The whole was out directly, champagne went round, and after dinner Lord Wellington gave "Louis XVIII.," which was very cordially received with three times three, and white cockades were ordered for us to wear at the theatre in the evening. In the interim, however, General Alava got up, and with great warmth gave Lord Wellington's health, as the *Liberador del'Espagna !* Every one jumped up, and there was a

sort of general exclamation from all the foreigners—
French, Spanish, Portuguese, Germans, and all—*El
Liberador d'Espagna*! *Liberador de Portugal*! *Le
Liberateur de la France*! *Le Liberateur de l'Europe*!
And this was followed, not by a regular three times
three, but a cheering all in confusion for nearly ten
minutes! Lord Wellington bowed, confused, and immediately called for coffee. He must have been not a little
gratified with what had passed.

We then all went to the play. The public were quite
in the dark as to what had just arrived, but Lord Wellington was received in the stage-box (where he sat,
supported by Generals Picton, Frere, and Alava, &c., and
also the *maire*) with no little applause, I assure you. At
the door the people would scarcely take the money from
us ; and in the opposite stage-box the French left the box
themselves, and made room for us. We had the white
cockades on the breast. The English officers in the house
stared, and did not know what to make of it. Some
thought it a foolish, giddy trick. In about ten minutes
Lord Wellington turned his hat outwards to the front of
the box : it was seen, and a shout ensued immediately.
The play was "*Richard, oh mon Roi*," which was fixed
upon really before the news came. The "*Henri IV.*"
was played, and then the new French constitution was
read aloud from one of the boxes. The people most
anxious, and in general pleased ; in some things not. I
think most of it very good, if the French can enjoy anything so like our own constitution, for such it is, under
other names ; but this is doubtful. The article worst
received was that leaving all the sales of emigrant lands
to stand good; and it does appear to me that, when, by
means of paper, an estate had been bought for the price
of a team of horses, an equitable arrangement would have
been better, to be settled by Government Commissioners.
This was followed by " God save the King," which was
received with great applause.

When the play was over, we adjourned to the ball at Lord Wellington's. The only drawback was our meeting on the way the cars of the wounded in the streets, now moving to the excellent hospitals here. This on consideration was also a satisfaction, for many lives will be saved by the wounded being brought here, instead of being sent to rear. You will now guess what we felt, and what a species of trance we were in.

Here we are halted, whilst the news is sent on to Soult, with whom Marshal Beresford could not come up. The arrival of the news was at the moment we should have selected, except for the loss of life. For Lord Wellington's character, however, even that was good, and eight hours sooner it would have been said that the late battle was no victory on our part, and that we should never have entered Toulouse, nor would the real sentiments of the town have been known.

On inquiry, I find that the French loss has been great. General Taupin, one of my friends on La Rhüne, killed; General D'Armagnac, who took me, wounded; Harispe wounded, and here a prisoner; two other Generals wounded, &c. Our loss fell principally, you will see, on the sixth division, and the Scotch Brigade in particular, and on the Spaniards. With regard to the latter, it is said that, upon the whole, the men for a long time behaved well, and that if General Frere had been as skilful as brave, and the officers better, they probably would have succeeded in their object, which certainly happened to be the most arduous duty of the day. They arrived on a sort of smooth glacis below the French works, under a fire admitted to be more severe than almost any since Albuera. Decision and skill and rapidity were then required. The men were kept too long in this fire—they broke—and then ran like sheep. One French regiment, it is said, drove more than four thousand of them, and in such a manner that they almost upset a Caçadore Portuguese regiment by main force.

Three companies of the latter stood firm, beat back the Spaniards with their firelocks, laughed at them, enjoyed it, and completely checked the French. The redoubt was afterwards taken by our men, with great loss, as you will see. General Frere was in despair; he exerted himself to the utmost to rally his men; at last, by his exertions, assisted by Lord Wellington in person, one or two Spanish companies were formed, and became steady. Upon this the rest soon followed, and formed up also. The Spaniards had then a less arduous post assigned them; all went on well again, and I believe they behaved fairly enough. Their loss is considerable.

This morning the whole conversation of the officers turns upon half-pay and starvation. With some, want of preferment; with others, promotion; and with those who have promotion, a determination to enjoy themselves now that all is over, and their dangers and sufferings past. As to my own prospects, they are so completely in the air, that my being never much of an architect for building in that element, I go quietly on with my work, and trust to the future.

I shall defer any account of this place, &c., for fear of being too late for the despatches, and now say adieu.

Pray forward the enclosed two letters, which are from Madame de Baudré, my hostess at Mont de Marsan, who desired me to take care of them, and enclosed them in a letter of great professions of kindness for me, only exceeded by the most romantic ones for the Bourbons, and stating the great losses her family and connexions have lately sustained.

Head-Quarters, Toulouse, April 15th, 1814.—Here we are quietly waiting the result of the communication of the late news to Marshal Soult, &c. Cooke has come back from his head-quarters. The Marshal hesitates a little at present. He objects that he has no authentic documents from Bonaparte or the authorities whom he represents, and seems to have some doubts of the extent of the late news—or pretends to have. In short, as yet he takes no decided line, but it is said has applied for an armistice, probably wishing to gain time, to consult Suchet, &c., and learn more of the state of things.

Colonel Gordon was sent to him yesterday by Lord Wellington with a flag-of-truce ; and it is understood that a positive answer and determination was required, and the armistice refused. Lord Wellington and all the officers yesterday attended Colonel Coghlan's funeral in the morning, at the Temple, and went from thence in procession to the Protestant burial-ground out of the town.

In the evening Lord Wellington gave another more magnificent ball at the Prefecture. It was too crowded to dance much, or well, but went off with great glee and general satisfaction. The ladies were very prettily dressed, in general, with the exception of a few of the high ugly bonnets, and there were several very pleasing-looking girls, and good dancers ; but I do not think that in general the women are handsome here. I met with one very good-humoured chatty lady, about eighteen probably, who said she had only left her " Maman," with whom she had always lived near Carcassonne, one month, and that, in that time she had witnessed many strange things :—the ravages of the French army, the passage of our army over the Garonne, a great battle (which was all visible quite plainly from the churches here, and even from the houses), the preparations for a siege, the retreat of the French, our triumphal entry, the change of the national government, and her own marriage.

Captain Tovey, of the 20th, taken at Orthes, has escaped, and came in here yesterday. He would not give his parole, and made several attempts to be off. In consequence he was hardly treated, but is now safe. He met with every assistance from the French inhabitants ;

and at the last house he was in, the owner made him leave his peasant's dress, and equipped him in a new suit, boots and all, French cut, to pass our lines, and go to head-quarters in. The villages through which he passed were proclaiming the King; and he was told that Soult's house, near Carcassonne, had been destroyed by the mob.

The French here discover the same volatile character as ever. *Vive le Roi!* is shouted as vigorously as *Vive l'Empereur!* was, I am told, a few years since, when Bonaparte made his then really popular entry, and gave his fêtes here, of which the most fulsome *procès verbal* still exists, signed by a maire-adjoint of the same name as the one who now signs the King's proclamation, and I believe he is the same man—Lameluc.

The inhabitants are all at work as usual, and very active. Fleurs-de-lys are now upon the skirts of the coats instead of eagles, and last night on the theatre drop-scene. The busts of Bonaparte are smashed. The Capitolium ornaments are all undergoing a change. All the N.'s and B.'s, &c., are effaced; and the workmen are now busily employed working round the cornice of the great staircase at the Capitol, changing all the alternate ornaments of a handsome cornice, every other one having been a *bee*. The English are everything, and in general estimation. To return the compliment of our wearing their white cockade on our black one, they now wear a black one on their white. The Spaniards are considered much as the Cossacks. The Capitolium is a very fine building, and as the splendid velvet and gold canopy, and the throne of Bonaparte at one end, had no decided emblems except that of authority generally, it has, after some doubts, been allowed to remain, and is not destroyed. We are to have a grand ball there, it is said, given on Sunday, by the inhabitants, if approved of, and we stay.

The theatre is about the size of the Haymarket Theatre ; in width rather larger, but much deeper, and something in the improved shape of Covent Garden. The actors are tolerable. It is, however, inferior to the Bordeaux Theatre, and certainly to that of Lyons.

The stone bridge over the Garonne, of seven arches, is very solid and substantial, wide, and upon the whole a splendid work, but not very graceful in its architecture. It is like Kew bridge in general shape, but in much heavier and substantial proportions.

Several improvements have been some time since commenced in the city, but most of them are now at a stand, and have been so for some time. The cathedral of St. Etienne is an unfinished Gothic building, the great aisle being wanting to the new building. Instead of this, a large sort of Westminster Hall, of more ancient date, joins the cathedral on one side. This was originally intended to be pulled down or altered.

There is some good tapestry and fine painted glass, which have escaped here, as in several other churches, the revolutionary destruction.

The streets here are like the old parts of Paris, in general narrow, with a gutter in the middle ; and the houses very good, but high shops below, and three stories of good rooms above. Several handsome hotels, with their great gates and small gardens. I am in a dirty place, but tolerably well off. The people are civil ; I have good stabling, and one comfortable room, now it is cleaned.

C—— gives rather a strange account of our Allies, but seems to think from their numbers, and the general feeling, that the business has at last been well-blundered through. There is a good story told of an incident which happened at the interview with Soult the other day. The substance of the news somehow got wind, and the army, whilst the Marshal was closeted with C——, gave a loud shout. The aide-de-camp went to inquire the cause, and returned saying, " *Ce n'est qu'un lièvre, Monseigneur.*" You ought to know that nothing causes a louder shout amongst troops than a hare crossing them. General M—— said the aide-de-camp should have been asked whether it was a Leipzig hare? If Soult does not declare himself, his army will, I think, desert him. I have now only just received a letter from you, of the 22nd March, and papers.

The French works at the entrance of the town, by the bridge (*tête de pont*), were very strong, and cost much in labour and materials, for no use. They were formed by close piles of timber like the caissons for the foundation of a bridge, filled up with earth, and the tops lined by barrels of earth, with a ditch and guns, &c., placed, and the walls of the buildings round all loop-holed.

I rode all over the positions of the battle yesterday, on the hills, and examined all the forts and the monuments of French industry and British courage. They were most formidable places to approach, for the hills formed a regular smooth glacis from the works at the top to the valley below, and half way down were long low heaps of sod, or turf, made up to protect the advanced sharp-shooters, who were lyng safe on the ground, protected behind them, though the barrier was not above two feet high. A church and a house loop-holed, formed the sort of citadel to two of the forts or redoubts for musquetry, with the guns around the outside. The ditches were not so deep, nor the works so complete as those near Vera, where the French had more time, nor were the roads or mountains so difficult to ascend ; but there was less shelter to approach, from the greater smoothness of the ground. Almost the only chance of safety was following some hollow roads, and a ride or two on the hills.

16*th* (4 *o'clock*).—I have just heard that the mail goes in half an hour. There is, therefore, little time to add to

this. Colonel G—— is come back: Soult very civil, but
high and proud in his manner, not yet satisfied, and so
circumstanced, does not yet join the royal cause; the
consequence is, I hear, that the troops move to-morrow
morning, and I fear we shall do the same then or soon
after. This is very provoking, for the general result
seems clear, and all bloodshed now useless. I suspect
the truth of the hare story, as it is said that Soult's army
is still ignorant of what has happened, at least, nearly so.
Pains are now being taken to circulate the proclamations,
news, &c., in all directions round him, that the troops
may learn the real state of things. I have to-day
received the parcel from you, letter to 29th, and newspapers. Many thanks.

The museum here contains but a bad second-rate set
of pictures. About a hundred have been carried away
during the month of March, no one knows where; but I
presume they were the best of those which were portable from their size.

There has been some difference of opinion, and confusion, we hear, at Montauban about royalty. Bayonne, it
is to be feared, will abide by Soult, and do nothing yet.

Head-Quarters, Toulouse, April 18*th*, 1814, 5 *o'clock.*—
The troops moved as I told you yesterday, and the order
was actually out for head-quarters to move to-day, when
Count Gazan came in yesterday, about mid-day, to an-
nounce Marshal Soult's submission, I believe, to the new
order of things, and to arrange cantonments, &c., for the
two armies. He was closeted with General Murray a
long time, and arrangements were made. He returned
this morning to have the articles ratified, and to-night
Lord G. Lennox has orders to be in readiness to go to
England through Paris with the news. This last fact
you will, perhaps, have heard, and probably before you
get this.

We had yesterday a grand *Te Deum,* a most strange

noisy military and religious ceremony attended with all the drums and military band; French civic soldiers, with their hats on, hallooing, shouting, singing, organs, &c., an immense crowd, and great cordiality. Unluckily, Gazan passed the door as the crowd was coming out; he was hooted, and saluted with " *A bas Soult !*" &c. This was a pity, but these changeable gentlemen are all in extremes. The troops are all going into cantonments immediately, and we shall for some time, I conclude, be quiet.

The bad news from Bayonne is very unlucky. General Hope is, I hear, not dangerously wounded ; and his aide-de-camp is gone to Bayonne to comfort him in his confinement, which I trust will now be soon over. The affair seems to have been a surprise in a great measure, and the chief loss was in regaining the church, &c., of St. Etienne, which had been easily lost at first. Lord Dalhousie, on the other hand, seems to have gone on well alone, across the Dordogne.

The arsenal is here on a very large scale, and would have been a very great acquisition, were the war to have gone on. The French carried away almost everything but materials, of which there is abundance of wheel carriages, &c., and all the forges, &c., in order.

Head-Quarters, Toulouse, April 23rd, 1814.—Our life has now fallen into the old routine way again, and not only without daily events and little incidents to excite the mind, as has hitherto been the case, but also with the additional flatness and indifference, which cannot but be felt so immediately after a succession of such occurrences as have taken place within the last month. You will now have only the tittle-tattle of a country town (a French town certainly, and therefore somewhat novel), with which you must be satisfied. When Count Gazan came over here, to settle the terms of the armistice and line of demarcation, &c., with Generals Murray and

Wimpfen, he was so much engaged that I could not see him, as I wished to do, and he went very suddenly back again. The terms you will see in the papers.

When all the Spanish garrisons are collected in France, this southern French army will again be respectable. Our troops are all moving into their cantonments along the Garonne on the left bank, except a few on this right bank, within the department of the Haute Garonne, which remains nearly all ours for the present. We have had a variety of strangers—the two Sir Charles Stewarts the first place. The Lisbon minister only stopped here one day on his way to Holland; the other Sir Charles, from Paris, came, as it is whispered here, to signify a wish on the part of the Allies that Lord Wellington would be the English commissioner at the general Congress. If so, and this seems very probable, I think he does well to refuse, for he cannot stand higher than he does. Were he to go, the other diplomatists would be surprised at his method of getting through business. We should certainly have a general peace many weeks sooner, if not months, than we are likely to have otherwise.

I was walking with C—— in Lord Wellington's garden about eight o'clock in the morning, three days since, when we saw a queer-looking figure approach, of whom we could make out nothing from the complete mixture of undress and magnificence—a pair of not clean overalls on, a common short pelisse, and a foraging cap, but the whole breast covered with stars and little crosses, and swords and orders of all sorts.

I was not a little surprised at being introduced to Sir Charles Stewart. He had arrived at two in the morning and had gone to bed, without sending word to Lord Wellington, depending upon finding him at home at eight o'clock, when to his mortification he found that Lord Wellington had been since five in the morning out hunting ; and when Sir Charles asked where he could go to meet him, the best information he could get was, that it was in a forest somewhere about eighteen miles distant, but no one knew exactly where, for the only persons who knew, about four in number, were out with him. Patience, therefore, was his only remedy ; and instead of being off again in two hours as he said he had intended, he was obliged to stay long enough to give us a few anecdotes from the Allies. Two of Marshal Suchet's aides-de-camp, and two or three French colonels from his army and that of Soult, have also been here.

With one of Suchet's aides-de-camp I had much conversation. He is a gentleman-like young man. He told me that Suchet was at Perpignan when he heard of Soult's affair here ; but that he then thought it prudent to hasten to Narbonne, and there he was when the news from Paris arrived. Had the war gone on, therefore, we should evidently have had a dance, as I expected, to the Mediterranean, on the road to Montpelier, after these united marshals, and should have required your utmost exertions and reinforcements from England ; as it is, all is well. Suchet's aide-de-camp said that he found very different feelings towards Soult in this country from what there were towards his master in the districts where he had commanded, and that he feared Soult had conducted himself very badly. The two marshals are, I understand, very jealous of each other. I asked him if Suchet had the least notion or expectation previously of what has happened. He said, " No : who could expect such a change in the minds of every one, and such a revolution in seven days' time ?" Then he laughed, and said, " At present we were *à la mode* ;" and as I met him at the grand ball at the Capitole here again, he said, " There, you have nothing to do now but to make the most of your advantages, and amuse yourselves : all the beauties have now declared for you."

2 K

I rather pitied him, when at that meeting a number of pert apprentices, with immense white cockades on, and some still with Napoleon buttons and smart civic uniforms, were continually coming up to him, and reaching about up to his chin, asking him, pertly, " Oh! are you Soult's aide-de-camp, or Suchet's? Well, how do you like what is going on?" fellows, that a month ago would have almost cleaned his shoes had they been asked. Some of them even thought he was English, and in bad patois French, complimented him on the progress he had made in the French language. His military pride was much put to the trial, and he could hardly smother his feelings. He then asked me to show him his new King, of whom there was an old picture hung up, as he said it was now time to make acquaintance with his new sovereign, as well as with this new state of society.

The grand ball given by the town at the Capitole on Thursday went off well, except that it was just such a crowd as an Easter Monday ball at the Mansion House. The rooms were very handsome, and the five hundred English, Spanish, and Portuguese officers added not a little to the effect of the scene. Nearly the whole were generals, aide-de-camps, staff-officers, or at least field-officers, and every order and ornament of every nation was worn. Lord Wellington was most splendid. The amusement commenced by leading him into the Salle de Trone ci-devant Bonaparte, where, over the vacant chair in the centre, was the picture of King Louis XVIII., and on each side that of the Duke d'Angoulême, and one of Lord Wellington himself—the latter a hasty caricature likeness taken by a painter here at the play from memory. He was then entertained with a short concert, principally consisting of La Chasse d'Henri IV., and " God save the King," sung by the public singers from a gallery, amidst the clouds—goddesses and cupids painted above them.

I had got Mr. K——, the famous English officer

singer, to go with me to the leader of the band, and to give him the catch-club harmony of " God save the King," and we wrote them down full instructions, and all the words for the song, solo, trio, chorus, &c., the words spelt also according to the French pronunciation, while the musician caught by the ear and scribbled down all the parts, one by one, from K——'s singing. It was an interesting scene. They had a rehearsal, and Mr. K—— gave the *prima donna* a few private lessons, and the whole in consequence went off really surprisingly well. The supper-tables were filled by about four sets successively, the English having the preference, sentinels letting us in, and keeping out the French until the last. This went on until there was not even bread and water remaining.

The press, now, is at work here, printing Cevallo's old history of the conduct of the French in Spain, and a variety of things, which to the natives are news. There seems to be a disposition to buy the books and read; nothing, however, will make the French what Cobbett calls us, " a thinking people." They seem to be as frivolous as ever. The next thing wished for here, and at Bordeaux, is to get rid of this new constitution, and have the Bourbons as before; at least the party is strong for this line, and, unless something decisive is done soon, and the old military dispersed about, and gens-d'armes, I think they will even yet have a squabble about several things among themselves, which makes me wish that we should be off as soon as possible, and have nothing to do with them. As soon as all the foreign garrisons are withdrawn, and the line of the French empire settled, the faster we withdraw from within it the better. I always expected the royal cause would gain ground as it has, when once fairly tried. It was the only source of peace, and that was what all wanted, on any terms. Of course the acceptance of the Bourbons made it all easy; but I believe all the southern departments would gladly have been English, to secure peace, and get sugar, sell their wines, and get rid of conscriptions and acquisitions.

Lord Wellington gives another grand ball at the *ci-devant* Prefecture, now Palais Royale, on Monday next. On Tuesday, he resigns his place there to the Duke d'Angoulême, and as there is an ` old adage about two kings of Brentford, I suspect he will soon afterwards take a trip somewhere else, at least for a time. I doubt, however, his leaving the armies altogether, while they remain in force, and the French marshals likewise.

Bordeaux must be very proud of the example they have given to France. They must take especial care to conceal their subsequent alarms, and half-repentance of what they have done.

CHAPTER XXVII.

Toulouse—Its Churches—Protestant Service—Libraries—Reception of the
Duke d'Angoulême —The French Generals—Popularity of Wellington.

Head-quarters, Toulouse,
April 27, 1814.

My dear M——,

Though I have nothing now to amuse you with,
but the result of my morning walks and inquiries in this
town, I shall proceed as usual, more with a wish to
preserve my own crude observations, than hoping to
interest you much by the perusal.

My last was finished on Saturday. On Sunday, about
half-past eleven, I attended the service at the Protestant
chapel, established under the sanction and patronage of
Bonaparte, as a sort of church-wardenish gold-lettered
record informed me. The service began with a prayer by
the clerk; he then gave out a psalm, more noisy than
musical, and without the accompaniment of the organ. I
was astonished that such a small congregation could
make so much noise and discord. One greasy-headed,
methodistical-looking man, near me, continued in an
unceasing roar, bearing much more resemblance to a
well-known noise with which our mules so frequently
indulge us, than any known harmony. A short prayer,
and a long chapter from the New Testament, with the
Commentary, as printed in the book, was then delivered
from the pulpit or reading-desk (for there was but one)

by a clergyman, who then entered. Another psalm ensued. The organ then played to introduce a young preacher, who took the reader's place, and gave us a prayer and the Ten Commandments, and another psalm, partly to the organ; but before half a stave was finished, the organist found that his notes and the vocal ones were so different, that he ceased playing, and though he made two or three attempts at a single note afterwards, he found it would not do, and gave it up.

The young preacher then read a text from the Bible, and gave us a very good extempore discourse about half-an-hour long. The subject was the vanity of this world, and the danger of temptation and evil communication. The language and delivery were clear and distinct; there was no rant, but much propriety of manner. A psalm followed, and the organ was not so much distanced; then the Lord's Prayer and Belief, and a prayer for all descriptions of persons and denominations, like that of our own Church praying for dignitaries, &c. And then another psalm, at last, in tolerable harmony, but very noisy. A blessing concluded the whole.

At first there were only about forty-five persons; some half-dozen old gentlemen were in the seats near the altar. These had backs. About twenty-five women were in the right-hand seats; and about fifteen men in the left. The side-seats were chairs placed in rows, and all fastened to each other. In the course of the service, the numbers increased to about sixty or seventy. The congregation appeared to be nearly all of the middling class of tradesmen; only about three of our poor men took their allotted seats, quite at the back. As no one ever knelt down, there was no occasion for either room or cushions for that purpose. The men sat with their hats occasionally on and off, and legs crossed, at their ease, in the style of the House of Commons; but were attentive to the sermon. The three poor men all fell asleep, snoring so loud that a sort of beadle was obliged to awaken them. I was not much surprised on the whole, comparing this scene with that in the Roman Catholic churches, that the proselytes amongst the highest and lowest classes were not not numerous. This service suits neither. It is most adapted to an independent tradesman, who thinks a little for himself, and can see the errors of the Catholics, and likes the economy of the chapel. It might be accident, but I saw scarcely any white cockades,—only one or two of the elder, and I suppose richer, members of the community wear them in their hats.

On Monday I looked into nearly all the churches, present and *ci-devant*, of Toulouse. The cathedral of St. Etienne I have already mentioned. The next in size and consequence is St. Saturnin, or more commonly called St. Surnin. This is a curious building, in the dark heavy Saxon style (reminding one of the early attempts at Grecian revival, and the introduction of the Gothic), all circular except the angular main pillars of the centre of the cross, which were heavy octagons; the roof circular, and upper windows double circles. Except the pillars, nearly the whole is made of the flat tile or brick, which is curious. It was built in the present form about the year 1160 to 1190. There are monuments of the Earls of Toulouse, &c., of founders, and in a dark vaulted chapel under the grand altar are relics innumerable—of the thorns in the crown placed on the head of Christ; the heads of Barnabas, of Simon, and of Jude; parts of their bodies also; parts of Peter; besides bishops, &c.; the body and figure of Thomas Aquinas; and an English saint, a king, whose name I could not make out. We heard much of the riches with which all these relics were formerly surrounded. It is said that the revolutionists carried off four hundredweight of gold, besides silver. All the most valuable part, however, as the good Catholics are bound to think, were fortunately spared, and still remain in excellent preservation, and tolerably fine with gilding.

The general effect of the building is gloomy and superstitious, and a strange unpleasant smell, which some say proceeds from large vaults underneath, which are filled with bodies which do not corrupt, makes one glad to get out of the building as soon as curiosity is satisfied. They do not bury their dead in the church now, and the vaults I mentioned are walled up. In the remaining churches now in use there is little worthy of notice, but there are two very large *ci-divant* convent churches. That of the Jacobins is worthy of notice; one long building only, like King's College Chapel (not a cross), and with one lofty row of circular pillars all down the centre. This forms as it were two equal main aisles, and no side aisles. On the sides are rows of chapels and a large cloister. Almost the whole is in brick, except the centre pillars. It is now regularly fitted up as cavalry barrack stables; and they are excellent, easily containing in the whole, I should think, about seven hundred horses. There is an octagon building adjoining, with a slender pillar, fitted up the same. Near this is another large, long, similar building, formerly a chapel, but without the centre pillars, and the scale of course somewhat smaller. This is the forage store for the cavalry barrack. We have them now both in use, as the French had. I must now go in my best to meet the Duke d'Angoulême.

Friday, the 26th.—About two o'clock on Wednesday the most interesting scene commenced since that of the first day of our entrance, and a more splendid one still. Lord Wellington, surrounded by about three hundred horsemen, composed of general officers, aides-de-camp, and staff officers of all descriptions, and of the four nations, Spanish, English, French and Portuguese, went out to meet the Duke d'Angoulême, all in their best uniforms, on their best chargers, and covered with white cockades. The only French general of the opposing army who came in time for this was Clausel, and he was for some time side by side with Lord Wellington. When we had gone about six miles, and arrived at a sort of triumphal arch on a hill, the Duke appeared, escorted by a guard of our heavy dragoons and a double French guard of honour from Bordeaux and Toulouse. We drew up on each side, after the interview with Lord Wellington, to let them pass, and then all joined in the procession to the town.

The sides of the road were crowded with carriages and people, and the enthusiasm of the lower classes, and of the women in particular, was excessive. The Duke and Lord Wellington, after being joined by more guards of honour and more suite, as we approached the town, entered the street over the grand bridge, amidst the shouts and acclamations of a multitude crowding every window. The scene reminded me of the London streets at Lord Nelson's funeral. From the *tête de pont*, which still in part exists, over the bridge, up to the cathedral through all the principal streets, was a double line of English troops, between which the procession passed. Several of the regiments had got their clothing, and they looked admirably, especially the Scotch 91st.

A sort of moveable *garde urbaine de l'infanterie* on each side kept also with us all the way. White flags, exhibiting French ingenuity to the utmost, were hanging from every window. Sheets, table-cloths, towels, &c., covered with green paper fleurs-de-lys formed excellent standards, and paper flags were innumerable. The women, and some of the old men, were quite mad with joy, and screamed, *Vive le Roi et vivent les Anglois!* till they were stopped by absolute exhaustion, or some by tears of joy. Every house was hung with laurel mixed with the white, and the lower story covered entirely with old tapestry, old carpets, or sheets, and paper fleurs-de-lys. In the morning this made the streets look something like Brokers'-alley certainly, but the effect, when mixed with the rest of the scene, was not bad.

After passing under another triumphal arch of table-cloths, laurel, fleurs-de-lys, &c., we reached the cathedral, and a *Te Deum* succeeded. This was much like the last, only rather more in order, and the public bodies were more numerous and in their costume. The ten Judges and the President, in their red robes, like our aldermen, with small black-and-gold caps. The Judges de Premier Instance, in black Master-of-Arts gowns, with sky-blue sashes; the Avocats in black gowns alone; the professors of sciences and arts in their crimson-coloured Master-of-Arts gowns, and those of belles-lettres in orange; the Archbishop and clergy in full costume. The music was not very striking, but many of the old people cried with joy.

About six o'clock the Duke dined with Lord Wellington, and went to the play in the evening, where the acclamations were renewed with fresh vigour; the women in the streets caught hold of his coat to kiss it. Yesterday the Duke had a *grande messe*, and then a full-dress drawing-room—this in the morning. In the evening the great rooms of the Capitolium were opened again for music and dancing. The Duke came in there too soon, when scarcely five hundred people were arrived, but in another hour the crowd was immense. The dresses of the women were very splendid, and the variety of orders and uni-forms made the scene very gay. General Vilette was there, as well as Clausel, and a number of French officers. The Duke was just the same as at St. Jean de Luz, and remembered all his old acquaintance there, myself among the rest.

He not only gave me a gracious nod during the first

procession, but surprised me by coming round behind the chairs of the ladies, where I was standing, in the music-room, and gave me his hand, and reminded me of King Joseph's saddle-cloth, which I had given the Duke, and which was on his horse, as I observed, when he entered the town. His affability and good-nature are striking; but he must acquire more dignity and self-possession, as his figure is against him in appearance, and he seems shy; in short he must learn the trade of kingcraft, like any other, and a quiet rational man is just now the best king the French can have. The great rock to avoid is the probability of being misled by indiscreet emigrants.

I was, it must be confessed, rather at a loss what to say to the Duke, but when he talked of the saddle-cloth, I replied, that " Its only merit, which was as a trophy, now was at an end, as the family of the Bonapartes had ceased to be objects to triumph over." This, and a lame congratulation on what had happened, completed my speech; as, however, it was as new to me to address royalty as it was to him to act it, I hope if occasion offers I may improve by practice as well as his Highness. One circumstance amused me much in all this scene: the good city of Toulouse covered its streets with sand, and made the air resound with cries, and every house had two paper lanterns in every window at night; and they were, in general, I am convinced, sincere in this, although one might have been induced to think otherwise from the acts of the authorities and public offices. A set of *garde urbaine* officers (the new gens-d'armes) ran all the way at the head of the procession, prompting the cries, and setting them going all the way we went; and the illuminations were, by special order of the mayor, from the Bureau d'Illuminations, as usual in the time of Bonaparte's system. My intended observation is this—the city loyalty vented itself in cries, in *Te Deums*, in music, and in farthing candles, and dancing, shouting, draperies, &c.,

but the Royal Duke was placed in the Palais Royale (*ci-devant* Prefecture), and no provision made for his table or for his establishment or Bordeaux guard of honour, and our head-quarters' Commissary was called upon to feed the animals, &c., of the guard and followers, and Lord Wellington to entertain the Prince and invite the principal citizens to meet him.

The old notion of the sign of the Four Alls—"John Bull pays for all," seems to be as well known here as elsewhere in the world. There seems no principle now-a-days more generally diffused or adopted more readily in every quarter. Our rations are all procured, you must be aware, by requisitions, through the mayors of the country, &c., to be provided by the districts, and you would naturally think the same authority could provide for all French deserters, and for the Royal troops of guards and establishment; but then who would pay for all these requisitions? All we have is paid for; and it is *bien plus commode* to come to our store ready collected than to form one for these purposes.

An odd incident occurred to me just before the procession on Wednesday. I was at Lord Wellington's new hotel, the great inn, the Hotel de France, endeavouring to find his room, to leave a Court-martial, when I stumbled on my friend the Dutch aide-de-camp of General Clausel, who told me he was looking for one of our Marshal's aides-de-camp in waiting to introduce his General, who was behind him, and who, on my turning round, recognized me, as he and his division took me prisoner. To their great surprise, I told them that there was no chance of finding an aide-de-camp, but perhaps we might find a serjeant, and I was on the search. It so happened that there was no one but an ignorant sentinel. In trying a door or two, we all blundered upon Lord Wellington, who came himself to the door; so I introduced the astonished Clausel, and walked off.

My Dutch friend told me that Soult and Suchet would have had about six aides-de-camp, &c., in the first room, and a general officer in waiting in the second. I own that I think our great man goes to the opposite extreme; but he does not like being watched and plagued. Just after the state *levée* yesterday, I saw him cross the crowded square in his blue coat and round hat, almost unnoticed and unknown even to the very people who half an hour before had been cheering him. In one angle of Lord Wellington's hotel lives Madam C——, a Spanish beauty, married into a French family of rank, who are the proprietors of the hotel, but who have been obliged to let nearly the whole, reserving this angle. I do not mean to be scandalous; but this, perhaps, may have decided the choice of the house.

Lord Wellington to-day had intelligence that Marshal Suchet was on his way here, and has been with his staff about a dozen miles to meet him in form. The French Marshal, from some confusion, did not appear, and Lord Wellington would wait no longer, but returned alone. In our grand procession to meet the royal Duke on Wednesday a ridiculous accident happened. A French post carriage with three horses abreast ran away, and came full drive down upon us, the Frenchmen all bawling, the horses pulling all ways, and clearing all before them. Our three hundred warriors were all broken in an instant, and dispersed over the ditches, and in all directions, until at last one unfortunate horseman ran foul of the French horses, and the whole came down together. Fortunately nobody was materially hurt.

Saturday, Post-day.—As I returned home last night by the Palais Royal from dinner, I found every one going, without regular invitation, into the Palais Royal to the Prince, who held a *soirée*; so I entered likewise, and found him surrounded by dancing as usual, and by Marshals and Generals only to be outdone at Paris. Suchet had arrived with his staff. Colonel Canning, who was left behind for him, brought him in about two hours after Lord Wellington returned. General Lamarque and several other officers came with him, two Generals, as aides-de-camp, besides Colonels, &c. The Marshal himself was a strange figure. His head and cheeks and chin all overgrown with hair, like a wild man of the woods: and his dress more splendid than the drum-major of one of our Guards' bands on a birth-day.

The contrast had a singular effect. The uniform was blue, but almost concealed, and could have stood alone with gold embroidery. Every seam, edge, and button, before and behind, above and below, was *galloné* with a sort of oak-leaf pattern about three inches wide, and on his breast were two gold and silver stars, as large as our Garter star, and several small orders of different kinds. He would have been rather a good-looking man if dressed in a more moderate style. Lord Wellington and several of his Generals, being in their plain uniforms, made the French General's extravagance the more striking.

Soult's aide-de-camp also came in, and a guard was ready, and an hotel for him, but he did not appear. Generals Lamarque, Clausel, Villette, and three or four more, and a number of embroidered *Payeurs* and *Commissaires Généraux, Préfêts*, &c., increased the general glitter; but nothing looked better than our scarlet. The Prince and Suchet had much conversation, and seemed more easy and gay than I had seen the former before with any of his new friends.

Scarcely any Frenchman has worn the Spanish or Portuguese cockade; and amidst all the cries you never hear a *viva* for either Spaniards or Portuguese. They are in consequence very angry and sulky, and I think a little jealous of us. This you may well imagine, when you learn that they all along consider that *they* have accomplished all that has happened, and that we have assisted a little certainly, but that they could have done without us. Except those about Lord Wellington, who do it more out of compliment to him, the Spaniards in general, and a great number of the Portuguese, will not in consequence wear the white cockade.

I see no harm in this, for as we fought a whole century to prevent the two kingdoms of France and Spain from being both under the Bourbons, it is quite as well now that it happens to be our interest to fight for the contrary doctrine, that there should be as little cordiality between them as possible. A Spanish soldier was told the other day in the street to cry " *Vive le Roi! Vivent les Bourbons!*" He made no answer. The request was repeated, and he was asked why he made a difficulty. He was still silent at first, but then rapped out a favourite Spanish oath, then " *Viva Fernando VII.! Viva Lord Wellington!* Los Espanoles care for nothing more;" and nothing more would he say.

It is remarkable enough, but the fact is that Lord Wellington is very popular with the common Spanish soldiers, I am told, and with the country people; but with the generality of officers, regimental in particular, and with the highest classes in Spain, it is rather the reverse.

It is curious now to see Lord Wellington play the second fiddle, having been so long established leader. It will serve to break him in by degrees for England and peace. He carries it off very well. Most of our Lieutenant-generals are gone to Paris, or going, and many other officers. I suppose it will be best for me to remain with the army to the last, or at least as long as Lord Wellington remains, and then go straight to London and report my arrival.

At the Capitolium on Thursday, young B——, with whom I was talking, as we were very hot and tired, persuaded me to sit down with him on the bottom step of the vacant throne. The Prince and all the grandees were then in another room, but we were soon routed up by the *garde urbaine* sentinel, to the mortification and vexation of my young honourable companion at not being allowed at Toulouse what he was entitled to in the House of Lords in England. He is well; and dancing away cotillions, waltzes, &c.

Later.—We have just had an arrival, and Lord Wellington quits this place for Paris immediately : I hope, however, that he will return shortly, as he now intends to do. We all here said that matters would never be well arranged at Paris without him, and that he would go at last.

Head-Quarters, Toulouse, May 2nd, 1814.—Having thanked you for your letter of the 12th of April, and papers to the same date, I must proceed on my old subject, Toulouse, and its sights and curiosities, regretting on your account, as well as my own, that they are not more interesting.

The great cannon-foundry here was formerly one of the most prominent, but it has now ceased to work for nearly three or four years. How or why this could happen, when military works and manufactures seemed alone to flourish in France during that period, I cannot say. The fact is, everything remains in a state as if the workmen were only all gone away to dinner, but in silent desolation, like a scene in Herculaneum, or Southey's town under water. Unfinished moulds, guns, &c., and tools are lying about in all directions. To show how much the whole has been neglected, even *Egalité* has been suffered to remain on one entrance pillar, *Liberté* on the other, and the word *Impérial* in the middle. The fleur-de-lys will, I suppose, find its way there soon by some accident.

Suchet now commands both armies here. He told the Duke d'Angouleme that he had sixteen thousand men of his own army at his service. This hero, to whom the day of the month, yesterday (May-day), reminded me of a much nearer resemblance than the drum-major, has left us, and is off to his troops.

There are two public libraries here, in which I have spent the better part of a morning each, one containing about thirty thousand volumes, the other about twenty-five thousand. The former has too large a proportion of ecclesiastical learning; but they both contain some good editions of classics and good historians, annals, &c., particularly the smaller library. They are old episcopal and private foundations, and have neither gained nor lost much by the Revolution, which is rather extraordinary. There seems to have been no very valuable early editions or manuscripts—nothing very much worth plundering; and they say they were too conscientious to take advantage of the times, and enrich themselves by plunder. The arrangement of the books is not bad. Firstly, good polyglot and other Bibles of all kinds; then commentaries on sacred history, &c.; then history in general; then laws of nations, &c; then laws in general, essays, &c.; then French voyages, arts, sciences, classics, and belles lettres. There is an atlas of the Grand Canal and its vicinity on an immense scale, which might have been important had we proceeded, though I think no other stand would have been made until after we had gone beyond the limits of the canal, and after a junction of Soult with Suchet at Narbonne. Amongst the books pointed out as of the most interest, were Racine's Greek editions of Euripides and Æschylus, containing his name and several notes in his own handwriting,—a remarkably neat hand. The editions were Stephens' and Stanley's. The notes were either short free translations of passages and sentiments, or memoranda to call attention to particular passages for future use and application, or they were short remarks of approbation or disapprobation of

2 L

scenes, passages, &c. I copied out nearly the whole, not being very long, and I now enclose them. Will you oblige me by putting them into my Euripides or somewhere, to be preserved.

Several of the private houses here of the merchants and nobles are on a very large scale, and contain very spacious suites of rooms round the court-yard. The architecture is, in general, very moderate. Most of the mansions have only the merit of extent ; and one or two which have an attempt at more are in bad taste. The one most remarkable is particularly so. It has an immense heavy stone cornice, out of all proportion, and the capitals of all the pillars are a species of false Corinthian, or rather, Composite, with the upper ornaments, spread eagles, in most barbarous taste, and in the place of the most beautiful part of the true pillars of the Composite order.

Toulouse appears to have been for a very considerable time nearly stationary in size. There is not, as in some of our country towns, and in some of those in France, the new town as well as the old. The old brick walls, with occasional towers, remain entire almost all round, and still form nearly the city boundary, for there is scarcely any suburbs without the walls. At several of the entrances within there seems to have been some vacant spaces, and in two or three places an ornamental sort of crescent or square has been commenced,—one lately, but the others before the Revolution. They are all unfinished. In general, however, all within the city walls is covered with building of some sort or another.

The splendid façade of the Capitolium was raised before the Revolution. Henry IV. commenced the work, it is said, and his statue remains there. A very small beginning has been made towards stone façades on one of the other sides of the Grande Place of the Capital, but in general the old shabby buildings still remain, and seem likely to do so, for some time to come.

May 3rd.—Our Prince is gone to review his new army under Suchet, and leaves us quiet. Every day carries off some of our higher officers, and we all expect to move the instant Lord Wellington returns, if not before. To-morrow, if possible, I go with a party and passport to see the great basin de Feriol, the main feeder of the Grand Canal. It is the sight of this country, and therefore, though expecting to be disappointed, I have agreed to join Dr. Macgregor and a party to-morrow, and return the next day. It is near Revel, about thirty-two miles off.

I yesterday attended the Court of Appeal here for the four departments around—Aude, Tarn, Lot and Garonne, and Arriège. There were ten judges present : there exist, and may be present, as many as sixteen, and a quorum of seven is necessary to form a Court. There were, besides the *Procureur-Général* and *Advocat-Général*, about twenty-five barristers in gowns, nearly like ours, but with bonnets instead of wigs. They were dirty, and mostly old, and looked precisely like a set of provincial barristers in England. The same habits make the manners and appearance so similar in nations nearly equally civilized, that, until the language betrayed the difference, I could have fancied myself in England again.

The subject in dispute was half an acre of vineyard, and it turned on the construction of a confused legacy in a will of an old gentleman. The eagerness with which the contest was maintained reminded me of a Court of Quarter Sessions in England,—all talking at once, and with abundance of noise and action, especially just as the ten judges, like our juries, had laid their heads together to consider, and whilst *le Procureur-Général* was summing up the law and argument previously to the Court. Either the lawyers and judges must be starving, or the judicial establishment must be very expensive in France now.

There are, besides this Court, others of *Première In stance* in each department, and in four departments you have more judges than in England. Unless some changes are made, the French, in my opinion, will find their whole government, which is calculated for a larger empire, in every way much too expensive. This will prevent any great reduction of ordinary taxation. The King and his court to be paid; the senate; all the marshals and grand dignitaries, the prefêts, &c. Each department now has a salary to pay its prefêt nearly as large as that of an intendant of a whole province before the Revolution. The King will find abundance of patronage, if this goes on; but a great part of the national income will be consumed in the management and support of the different species of rulers. One advantage in this, it is to be hoped, will be to keep France more quiet in future, as I have otherwise little faith in the present temper of this changeable race.

May 7, 1814. *Post-day.*—At five o'clock on Wednesday morning I went to Dr. Macgregor's to breakfast, preparatory to our expedition to St. Feriol, having obtained our leave and a passport for that purpose. Our party consisted of Dr. H——, Colonel G——, and P——, General H——, and Mr. J——, and Mrs. J——. On account of the latter, who was in an interesting condition, we set out on the canal road towards Castelnaudary, that she might go in the boat. We rode along the towing-path very pleasantly for about twenty miles. Finding that Castlenaudary would be so much out of the way, we then left the canal and rode across through Villefranche and St. Felix to Revel, about twenty-two miles further. This water scheme delayed us much, so that we did not reach Revel until seven or eight at night, and it also lengthened our ride considerably.

The ordinary dinner at twelve, at the lock-house, was however, entertaining, and partly made up for this; but, in truth, ladies should learn on these occasions, when in such a state, to stay at home. We expected a *malheur* every hour, she was so fatigued.

On Thursday morning, after breakfast, we went three miles to Sorège, to see the great college or school establishment there, which is about three miles from Revel. It was formerly attached to a convent, and a sort of Government military establishment. At the Revolution the buildings were sold, and the present director and his brother, who was one of the professors of the old establishment, bought the whole, and undertook to continue, and, as they say, to improve the plan as a private specuation. There are now about three hundred boys, from eight to nineteen, or even twenty-one years old. On the present arrangement, four hundred and forty is the limit. The number, it is said, once amounted to nearly six or seven hundred. There are now about thirty Protestant boys. The rest are Catholics. Most of the Spanish boys, once very numerous, left the school during the late war. This peace, it is supposed, will bring them back, even in greater numbers. English boys are also expected to come again, as formerly.

The building is very spacious, and is prettily situated, under the side of a mountainous tract of country, at the head of a valley. The accommodation is very ample, and the order and arrangement very great; though, in my opinion, it is less cleanly than the college at Aire. The studies are more varied; and the whole is complete in itself; for there is a priest, a doctor, an Italian professor of mineralogy, anatomy, a riding-master, and teachers of all kinds. The regular studies for all the boys are French, Latin, a little Greek, mathematics to some extent, dancing, swimming, drawing from models and casts, perspective, drawing from anatomical study, fortification, &c.; and for the upper boys, riding—for which purpose about sixteen horses are at the disposal of the riding-master. In addition to this, every boy has his own bedstead of iron; and all the two upper classes of the three into which the whole school is divided have separate places to sleep in. Every boy, at a certain time, either follows in his studies the choice of his parents, or his own inclination, and may learn Italian, German, English, Spanish, or any musical instrument; even the pianoforte. The drawing-school is hung round with the approved productions of the boys, and is spacious, and so is the riding-school. There is also a theatre, regularly fitted up, in which the boys recite, and act plays and perform concerts; asking the neighbours to come and form an audience. The establishment also contains a small botanical garden, a tolerable collection of mineralogy, and a piece of water for the purpose of swimming. The boys were all in uniform, and looked healthy and well. As they come from all quarters, it is usual to leave them there all the year round, and this is rather expected and desired. They come clothed at first, but afterwards everything is found them, and the parents have nothing to do but to pay *mille francs*, about 45*l.* or 50*l.*, annually, and no bills or extras of any kind are ever sent or charged, whatever may be learnt by the boys: this is rather dearer than at Aire or St. Sever, I believe, but not much, when all circumstances are considered.

We found the schoolmasters consequential and prosy, as they usually are with us. The Italian, who was more particularly so, was formerly the professor who managed the Grand Duke of Tuscany's collection. This education would, I think, suit many an orphan or natural son destined for the English army, and with small means. He would join his regiment at eighteen, with much more useful knowledge than could be obtained for the same money in England, as to languages, &c., and much information useful to a military man. He would also come away, with at least one or two accomplishments probably, by which he might amuse himself in country-quarters, and be kept out of mischief. It might also answer for mercantile men, merchants, clerks, &c., though, perhaps, some of these pursuits would only make them idle. Most of the boys are destined for merchants or soldiers, I understood. For other professions, probably, we have as good, or better, and as cheap an education in York-shire, and other places in England. This sort of educa-tion accounts for the general distribution of a certain extent of acquirement which we see amongst the French officers, and for the advantages they possess as to the power of self-amusement. When prisoners of war, they have a smattering of drawing, dancing, singing, music, acting, &c.

We then went to the basin of St. Feriol. On our way I rode up a valley to see some foundries of copper, which were much talked of; only one of a number was at work, as times were so bad. I found the copper was Swedish, and only worked there on account of the facilities of wood and water to work the bellows and anvil. The work in which the men were then engaged, was making saucepans and pots, and stewing-pans for the Toulouse ships, and on a very small scale. I always like to ascer-tain that there is nothing to see when a sight is talked of. We went then over the hill to the basin.

The extent of this basin rather surprised me; but though it was almost exactly what I expected to find it, I was very glad to have seen it. The shape of the ground, and course of the stream, were particularly fortu-nate and well adapted to the plan, and the great dam or dyke, which pens back the water, so as to form a small lake, in depth, near the wall, from fifty to sixty feet, is a noble work. It consists of three main walls, well ter-rassed or puddled between each, and with two large arched vaults, one quite at the bottom, covering the natural bed of the river; the other higher up, and leading to the robinets or great cocks, which let out the water as required. The river coming down the valley fills the basin, not being able to find its vent, and therefore spreading over the ground, and filling all the hollows up to the dam wall, which is about sixty feet high. The banks, except the natural dam, are the natural shape of the ground, and there is no excavation at all. When full, the water as required is let out by a hatch, and so runs by into the stream, which conducts it, after about ten miles' circuit, to the highest point of the canal, whence the locks descend both ways to Toulouse, and to the Mediterranean. It then supplies both. When the basin is low, the next opening is a sort of hatch or floodgate, lower down in the wall; when lower still, the water is let off by three great *robinets* or cocks at the end of the *voute*, about thirty feet or so below the surface. When these are opened, the rushing of the water makes a tremendous noise, at a distance like that of thunder. When it is required to empty or clean the basin, the river is turned off, and the contents of the basin empty themselves in the original bed of the stream : the contents of the basin are, in my opinion, six millions of tons of water. There is another smaller basin, about ten miles higher up, in the mountains, and another near the canal, whence the stream enters it.

The whole seems well managed. The canal itself is kept in great order, like our New River, the bands trimmed, &c. ; and in width it exceeds even our Royal Canal in Ireland, probably by several yards.

With much delay and difficulty, we got Mrs. J—— through these sights, after much unnecessary alarm and fright in the vaults. We returned about five to dinner at Revel, where we slept again yesterday. We had a hot ride home through Caraman and Lentar, about thirty-two miles. The country round the canal and in the bottoms is rich and fertile, but it contains little wood. It is like some of our Somersetshire and Dorsetshire valleys, but more covered with villas and chateaux, and villages. The road back, by Caraman, is through a much poorer country, but also like the higher bad parts of Somersetshire, and that neighbourhood—such as near Chard and the hills round Bath.

The villages seem in a state of decay, and the inhabitants poor, but the country upon the whole is in much better condition, in point of cultivation and appearance, than one could suppose after what has passed in the last twenty years. In one or two out-of-the-way places we were stared at, and followed like monsters or sights, but were everywhere well received by the people. At Sorège some French cavalry was quartered; but they were nearly all gone to the grand review before the Duke d'Angoulême. I should like to have been there also; but we understood it would not be liked, and that the Duke was to go without English altogether: this was quite right. I am told that the review went off well, and that Soult himself set a good example.

It is strange to think of our carrying off Bonaparte in a frigate; and his conversation with Augereau is curious after the address of the latter to his men. King Joseph is gone off and escaped; but no one need be much afraid of him now.

The style of nearly all the French chateaux is similar; all front and appearance.

On my return yesterday I dined with Mr. B—— and his French hosts, for I scarcely know whose dinner it was; I believe a joint effort. The wines were the patron's, and very good. He is a man of fortune, a Monsieur de T——, and speaks English tolerably. The wife is a pleasing woman, and rather good-looking and young. They were very civil, and she sang and played in the evening very fairly. At least she had much execution and dash, if not feeling, in her playing. Like most of our young female players, she left out all the andantes and slow passages.

The furniture of the two or three rooms in which she lived was very splendid. Handsome carpets were alone wanting to make her own room in particular an elegant fine lady's drawing-room in England. In some respects, particularly as to the gilding, there was both more show and taste than generally are seen with us. The piano-forte was particularly handsome; it was by Erard of Paris, and, though only a small one, cost a hundred louis d'or. The whole content of her room cost, it is said, a thousand louis d'or.

In the variety and materials of the ladies' dresses here, there seems to be also a very considerable degree of luxury—more perhaps than with us.

We are now very dull, and as the Prince is still absent, do not even hear the " *Vive le Roi!* " or " *Vivent les Bourbons!* " &c., as usual. I was much amused yesterday at seeing pasted up at a country inn, a halfpenny print of the royal Duke d'Angoulême in his best, on horseback, and surrounded by a copy of most loyal verses singing his praises and those of the Bourbons, and the English, in the measure, and going to the music of the famous Marseillais hymn; in short, a sort of parody of that song, beginning " *Allons enfans de la Garonne,* " &c. What changes!

CHAPTER XXVIII.

Toulouse—Mr. Macarthy's Library—The Marquess of Buckingham—
General Hope—Wellington's Dukedom—The Theatre—A Romantic
Story—Feeling towards the English—The Duke on the Russian Cavalry.

Head-Quarters, Toulouse,
May 11, 1814.

My dear M——.

The very small number of sights which this town
affords being exhausted, and Lord Wellington being still
absent, we are in truth more dull than we should be in a
country town in England. The only interesting subject
of conversation now is, who goes to America, and who
does not? Some of the regiments move to-day towards
Bordeaux from hence for the purpose of embarking upon
this new expedition, which I should think would all end
in a mere demonstration. Lord Wellington is expected
here to-morrow, and we shall then know what is to
happen; and head-quarters will, I conclude, move immediately.

I have heard nothing since my last, and seen but one
thing worth mentioning, and that is, Mr. Macarthy's
library, which the old father and grandfather have been
sixty years collecting, and which is now to be sold on the
father's death for the benefit of the widow and nine
children. This is the library for which the Duke of
Devonshire offered 25,000*l.* sterling as it stands; but the
bargain was never closed, as he wished the whole to be
embarked at the risk of the owner, and they wanted to

have the money for it as it stands here, to be moved by the purchaser. The owner now talks of sending it to Paris, and having a public sale there by auction, thinking that emperors and kings will then bid against the Duke of Devonshire, Earl Spencer, and others of our book-loving nobles.

It contains a considerable number of fine copies of " Principes editiones," filling one side of a large room all upon vellum. There is also Cardinal Ximenes' polyglot edition of the Bible; his own copy—the only one on vellum; and a number of valuable books and some fine MSS. Amongst the rest is the first printed edition of the Psalms in 1457, of which we are told the only other perfect copy is in our king's (George the Third's) library; that Lord Spencer had only an imperfect copy, and that twelve thousand francs had been already offered for this one volume! So the world goes! This sum would fur-nish a handsome set of all the best French authors, and amusement for life; but many, you find, prefer a single black-letter volume, which one must go to school again to learn to read, and which, indeed, looks like a child's great black-letter spelling book, or the books among the giant friends of Gulliver. A single page as a specimen would be as good to me as the whole, and thus five hundred curiosos would be gratified for a few guineas a-head; or a lottery would be still better—fifty pages for the highest prize, and a few lines for every one; no blanks! There would be another advantage in this, that it would be employ-ment for some worthy collector for half his life to re-assemble all the parts and put the book together again.

The Marquess of Buckingham has been here, and is now going to Tarbes and Barege, and then returns to see our great man. We hear the latter was at the review at Paris in his blue coat and round hat. This is quite like him, and upon a good principle; the marshals, the public functionaries, the kings and the emperors, would have outdone anything he could have put on except this.

I am sorry not to have returned from Revel through Castelnaudry. Some of the officers did so, and by that means fell in with a division of the French army. The French officers were very civil, but told the same story—" If the Emperor had not deserted us, we never would have deserted him; and the men are of the same opinion; but as it was, there was nothing else to be done." Colonels B—— and C—— went over to the second review at Montauban, where the Duke d'Angoulême reviewed Count Reille's corps—two divisions. If I had known this had been permitted, I should have been very curious to be of the party. The men, it is said, were well equipped and in high order. The officers in general looked very shabby and unlike gentlemen.

Souchet was smiling and in high good humour, and very fine as he was here. Soult was only to be distinguished by a most enormous hat, and by a surly look, which is described as unpleasantly penetrating, and more bespeaking talent than amiability. He took little notice of the English officers, but the aides-de-camp and staff officers, both belonging to Soult and to the other Generals, did so when they learnt who they were, and appeared very earnest in their attentions and civilities. They went there in a carriage, but were splendidly mounted immediately; Colonel —— on Count Erlar's led and caparisoned charger.

Thursday, 12th.—Lord Wellington not having yet returned, and of course nothing positive being known as to our destination, we have only those passing reports which the military men call " shaves."

General Hope is, I fear, likely to suffer long from his wounds. He has astonished the Generals at Bayonne by making three of them presents each of an English horse out of his stud. It is an odd circumstance, but I believe true, that the sort of notice we had of an intended sortie by the enemy at Bayonne, which was given by a deserter just before it took place, only did us mischief. The out-picquets were doubled, and as no picquets could stand the rush of four or five thousand men, we only lost so many more prisoners by this. The men were alarmed with the expectation of such an attack. The only fault spoken of in this business was the abandonment of the church of St. Etienne, which might and ought to have been main-tained. The fifth division were but just on duty there, and scarcely knew their posts. General Hay met the men running back from it, and was stopping and leading them on again, telling them he would show them how to defend the church, when he was killed. Some of the muskets of our men were found there, broken by the French, and thrown away unfired. An English officer, with about twenty men, maintained himself in a house near the church the whole time, though it was much less defensible than the church.

Our position there, close under the works, it is said, was liable to such a sortie every night, and some well-informed persons wonder it did not take place sooner. General Hope's eager courage led him into a situation where, I am told, no one could under ordinary circum-stances remain the shortest time without almost a certainty of destruction. Even as it was, it is said that a party of Guards ought to have carried him off, as at first only four Frenchmen were near him when his horse fell, and the Guards then were close by. The French had made the outworks of the citadel very strong; they must have been stormed first, which would have cost us about twelve or fifteen thousand men. It would then have taken sixteen days to establish batteries on the crest of the glacis, the only possible way of breaching the citadel. The garrison, who are now excessively bold, and who have demanded rations for nineteen thousand two hundred men, say they should have even then stood a storming twice—in the citadel, and again in the town at last.

Making all due allowance for this gasconading, it is quite as well to have been saved the necessity of taking Bayonne. It would have taken all our transports about sixteen days to bring up materials for four days' open trenches from Passages by land, and we must then, for the remainder of the time, have trusted to the uncertainty of the water communication. The object of the French sortie was supposed to be the destruction of our three stores of fascines and gabions, &c., which we had been six weeks and more cutting, collecting, and forming, and for which purpose we had stripped the environs for near five miles round the town. In that respect we were quite prepared for the whole siege, and it is remarkable enough that we remained nearly all that time sufficiently near the French works to form the first parallel, and that without making works to protect ourselves, because doing so would only have drawn down a fire which no works could have enabled us to live under, and there was nothing to be done but to remain as quiet as possible until the siege began. Had we withdrawn at all, the French having seen the importance of the ground, which we got as it were almost by accident, would have made it necessary to begin the siege by the storming of the works they would soon have made there. Thus we were obliged to keep what we had got, unless resolved to turn the whole into blockade. The French engineers admire our bridge very much, and say it will figure in military history; but their officers in general in Bayonne have hitherto been very sulky, and we are yet by no means friends. Very little accommodation is afforded us in any way.

We are infinitely obliged to Bonaparte for having lost his head, and blundered as he did latterly, and

suffered the Allies to enter Paris, and put an end to the
war. Had he succeeded at Paris, or had Soult and
Suchet united succeeded against us here, near the shores
of the Mediterranean, where our next conflict would have
been, you would have found, when a retreat became
necessary, and that the French saw that way out of their
difficulties, instead of a return to royalty, that we should
have had the other party, and that a strong one, uppermost, and a cry the other way, with parties in our rear.
Thinking, as we do, the French army, and a great part
of the French nation, quite as much responsible and to
blame as Bonaparte, for a considerable portion of the
misery caused by France (for to effect this they were his
willing agents so long as it was out of France, and only
deserted him when he was in distress, and because his
good fortune had left him, and by no means from principle)—thinking this, their excess of loyalty only disgusts
us. Of course we are glad to promote it, but must
despise the majority of the Bourbon shouters—a few
honourable individuals, and a small party, of course,
excepted.

Friday, 13*th May*.—Lord Wellington not yet returned, and the late very warm weather turned to a
steady rain. The Paris papers of the 8th, received this
morning, make Lord Wellington ambassador in France,
and a Duke.

I was last night at the play to see *La Reine de Gol-
conde*, an opera, with some pretty music. I mention this
merely on account of a curious circumstance attending it.
A French General, according to the story, fights for the
deposed Queen and restores her. The troops of this
French General and liberator were a part of the grenadier
company of our Scotch *sans culottes* here in their own
costume ; and as they marched past, commanded and
headed by the French General in the full costume of a
general officer of Bonaparte's army, the house imme-

diately applauded the English heroes. The sensations of the French officers present must have been strange, and not very agreeable. These Scotchmen are considered by all the inhabitants (particularly of the town) as having had the principal share in their defeats in sight of the town. The mutes, bearers, and others in the procession were all English soldiers.

We have had no disturbances or quarrels here, and our officers seem all to have behaved with considerable propriety; in short, the inhabitants dread our departure, and the return of their own people. They say that all order ceases, and all security, the moment our side of the line of demarcation is passed. One furious old gentleman at the *café* this morning said publicly, that he thought the only regret was, that the war had not lasted three months longer, to destroy the remainder of the French brigands; and that as for Soult, he should have been sent in here, that the women might cut pieces out of his flesh with their scissors, and that he might afterwards have been executed publicly for his conduct to this city.

Saturday, Post-day.—Lord Wellington returned in the middle of the night, and, having had a cold, that and the effects of his journey make him look rather thin. He has been so taken up with business that I only saw him for a moment. Report says that he leaves us again in a day or two. I shall, if possible, ask leave, on our arrival at Bordeaux, to be independent, and find my own way home : yet I believe it would be best to go home with the army.

Head-Quarters, Toulouse, May 21, 1814.—Immediately after my last, Lord Wellington left us for Madrid. Nearly every one has quitted the army ; I mean the great men, generals, &c. We are reduced to a few quiet parties and have no events to observe upon, and see no strangers to write about ; everything is tame and stupid, and the weather growing hot makes us languid and idle.

2 M

Lord Wellington, on his return here, was absolutely overwhelmed with business, and every department was at work in a sort of confusion and hurry that has never happened before.

On Sunday, the Duke gave a splendid ball and supper at the Prefêt's or Palais Royal, where everything went off much as usual. The ladies dressed well, and danced admirably; and the supper was not a matter of mere form with them. Their early dinners, and their greater exertion in dancing, make them certainly more voracious than our fair ones.

On Monday, the Marquess of Buckingham returned, and was introduced to his new cousin of Wellington. The latter seemed, I understand, not a little surprised at being embraced and saluted on the cheek by his new relative. He had not been in the habit of receiving those embraces *à la mode Française*, and, I take it, prefers very much the kind attentions of the fair ones here, with whom he is an universal favourite.

On Monday the Marquess of Buckingham dined with him, as well as a large party of French and English. I was of the number, and we all went to a concert of very moderate music in the evening at the Capitolium. The Duke at eight the next morning was off for Madrid. He intends to rejoin us at Bordeaux, and then to return through Paris, and to be in London about the 10th of June. This is a great deal too much, and I think almost impossible. These exertions make him look thin and rather worn; but he was very gay, and in excellent spirits whilst here.

The American party was all settled by him finally, and is all on the road to Bordeaux, or now there. It will be of about nine or ten thousand men, I should think, and strong in artillery. Our faithful six 18-pounders, which have marched all the way from Lisbon since this day twelvemonth! on roads which never have, I think, or

will see such animals again, were embarked yesterday on
the Garonne, for Bordeaux, to be of the party ; and their
little grand-children, the mountain guns, go also. At
first the expedition was by no means popular, but is now
tolerably so, and the staff appointments have been of
course much in request. Lord Fitzroy Somerset, who is
the great manager of all this, and prime minister, has
been very busy, and we have all the intrigues of a little
court in miniature. Those who have been long here on
the staff, and with high brevet rank, will feel much a
return to their regimental duty and rank, and still more
if their fate be half-pay ? I hear of nothing except all
this, and the schemes to get provided for. The regimental officers are those who like this new expedition the
least.

On seeing the Duke of Wellington the last time, I
said, I concluded he would wish me to go down to Bordeaux with the army. He answered, " Oh, yes, you had
better." We are already almost without Generals. We
shall remain here, it is said, some days yet. The orders,
however, are all given for our movement as soon after we
receive official news of the garrison of Figueras having
marched for France as possible. In the mean time all
wounded, &c., are moving now. The cavalry also are to
set out on their way overland to England as soon as the
French Government have finally agreed to that arrangement. I should not at all dislike to march with this
party. The Portuguese troops remain with the British
until the Commissaries can part entirely with the mule
transport. They then separate, taking all the mules and
muleteers with them attached to different regiments for
rations, &c., and set out through Spain for Portugal, a
good three months' trip, the weather growing warmer and
warmer all the way, to the great enjoyment, I conclude,
of the natives. At Almeida the muleteers have been
promised to be paid all their arrears.

The British from hence are to encamp near Bordeaux, ready to be off as transports arrive. The Spaniards move out of France the first of all, at the signal of Figueras, to the joy of all parties. The Guards and troops at Bayonne are likely to be the last, for they are to remain until all stores, wounded, &c., are clear out of the Adour and St. Jean de Luz, &c. The people here will be very sorry to lose us, partly from the loss of the money spent here, and partly from their dread of those who will succeed us— their own countrymen.

I understand General Clausel was the only one of the French here who admitted the truth that they were fairly beaten into taking their King. The others feel it, but will not own it, and are very sulky in consequence; and in general not civil to our officers. Some of the French gens-d'armes are expected on Monday in this town to do duty, I believe, to levy taxes, &c. It is to be hoped that this will not lead to quarrels with our men.

The continuance of the *Droits réunis* is very unpopular, and, in my opinion, the effervescence of loyalty is somewhat subsiding already. We all expect disturbances also in Spain. I hope the Duke will resign his command, and have nothing to do with either party. It is said even the armies are divided, and ours here (Frere's) is for the Cortes. What with Spain, Ireland, Norway, America, and perhaps the interior of France, the world will after all, it is feared, not be in that state of profound peace which was generally expected.

Yesterday and to-day I have received letters from you of the 3rd and 10th of May, and papers to the latter date, which contain precisely the same news as those from London through Paris. There seems to be nothing very important either way.

I have just got the papers relating to a most extraordinary story of a murder at Lisbon. It is a most complete novel, and would be incredibly romantic as such. A Commissary named R—— had an English girl (a lady) who lived with him. Another Commissary named S——, his friend, had long been living in the same house with him. After a time Mr. R—— conceived that Mr. S—— was undermining the affections of the lady. He taxes her with it, she confesses, and says she has promised to live with S——, but swears nothing improper had ever passed. Mr. R—— persuades her to give up this scheme, stating how dishonourably S—— had betrayed him, his friend. He then tells this friend his discovery, and upbraids him. S—— says that the lady has been faithless to R——; and is the betrayer. R——, in despair, is going to quit the house, the lady, and the whole connexion; but he previously repeats to her what Mr. S—— told him. She solemnly denies it, and then goes out with S——. I should have mentioned that the three had just before this conversation ridden out together without speaking, and sat together at dinner without speaking or eating. The explanation between R—— and the lady then took place, immediately after which S—— and the lady went out of the house. Three pistol-shots are heard. R—— goes into the garden, finds his mistress shot dead. S—— ran by him into the house apparently wounded, his handkerchief to his head. He forced his way to a table-drawer, took out a razor, and cut his throat quite across. He still survived both wounds when the account came away, and deliberately confesses in writing that by the lady's desire, by their joint consent and agreement, he was to kill both; her first, and then himself. This he endeavoured to accomplish, but in vain as to himself. Mr. R—— declines telling who the lady is, except in a court of justice, in order to prevent unnecessary pain to her friends in England.

I have been asked, "What is to be done?" and whether, if the delinquent is mad, I thought that he must be tried for the murder? It surely was very unfortunate that the poor man had not been left in the hands of the Portuguese surgeons and doctors, who pronounced him a dead man, and his wounds incurable. The skill of an English surgeon has unluckily enabled this unhappy being to stand the chance of either being hung or confined for life as a madman for the rest of his days.

The 22nd, Post-day.—I send you, being dull myself, a part of a *Gazette de France*, which paper I take in regularly. Some part of the *Franc parleur* is well done. The same feelings exist here in the army. Were I a French officer I should feel in the same way.

We have now rain, and the weather cooler again: hitherto it has not been ever very unpleasantly hot, though at times above our summer heat, and with rain and without sun at 69°.

You ask me in your last letter about religion and manners here? The former seems again much what it was before the Revolution. The churches are in general well attended, but principally (as the case is all over the world, I believe,) by your sex in particular of all ages, by the very old of both sexes, who go there to make their peace; and the very young who are taken there by their older friends and relations. With regard to manners, the old French memoirs would still, I think, apply very tolerably to the description of their present state, except that the same things are done and said with rather more coarseness perhaps now than in old times.

Our cavalry have not moved yet, as the approval of the French Government has not arrived. They are intended to move in two columns, one up the Paris road, nearly through Cahors, &c.; the other more to the left, through Angoulême, Poictiers, and to unite at a town on the Seine.

Head-Quarters, Toulouse, May 27th, 1814.—My new friends and acquaintance fall off daily around me, and our party at head-quarters is continually on the decline.

I am not a little amused with the Toulouse paper of yesterday. We, the English, have been for these last six weeks praised to the skies, and treated as, and called the deliverers of Toulouse city and its inhabitants. Soult's troops are now expected in here in a few days, and the gens-d'armes have actually arrived. The Toulouse *Gazette*, therefore, exhorts the inhabitants to receive with open arms and to feast, and entertain those brave troops, whose courage and noble conduct they witnessed on the hills, above this city, when fighting for the defence of the inhabitants. They also assure the public, that the statement in an early number of the *Gazette*, that Marshal Soult owed the safety of his retreat to the clemency of Lord Wellington, under whose guns the French troops filed off, was all an error and mistake (as it certainly was), and that the retreat was in fact as secure as the defence of the heights was noble and courageous. Had we had but about five thousand more men up, to cross the canal at once, this might have been another story. The *Gazette* should have waited until we were off.

I dined yesterday with a Monsieur Castellan, a gentleman of very good fortune, and who, I understand, has a good house, pictures, library, &c., at Paris, and lands in Normandy and elsewhere. He was formerly, at the commencement of the Revolution, Attorney-general to the Parliament of Toulouse, and on that account desired to be introduced to me, and gave us an excellent dinner. In 1781, he was a man who figured much here, and also in the English papers, on account of his early resistance to the orders of the Court, and being imprisoned in consequence. He was followed by all the inhabitants to his prison, and released in a short time by the triumph of his own party. He seems to be a good constitutionalist.

He mentioned several curious facts of Bonaparte's tyranny, such as his putting persons to death without trial, and without inquiry. Two of these persons he knew in particular. They were chiefs of La Vendée. When all the hopes of that party were gone, terms were offered to these two men. One came in to sign them, when he was instantly shot. The other, in consequence, remained concealed three years in Normandy. At last he was told privately, that if he would retire from the country quietly, a passport should be given to him. He agreed, received his pass, and made for the coast; but when he arrived near the sea-side two gens-d'armes shot him.

This made a noise; the Juge de Paix began a *procès verbal*, and the Préfet was active in endeavouring to apprehend the soldiers. The Judge and Préfet were not in the secret. Suddenly a senator came from Paris. The Préfet was suspended from his office, and the Juge de Paix enjoined at his peril not to stir a step in the business. Monsieur Castellan's servant acted as clerk in the *procès verbal* which had commenced, and the murder took place close to his estate in Normandy. He therefore, he said, knew the facts.

Another story, for the truth of which he vouched, and which from the circumstances appeared to be true, shows a little the state of Napoleon's court and their morals. A young cousin of Monsieur de Castellan was the Emperor's page—a very good-looking boy. At the carnival he was dressed as a girl at the play, and one of the grand chamberlains fell in love with him. The page continued the disguise and the joke every night during the carnival, and was courted and fêted with presents by the lover. At last the discovery was made, and the mortified chamberlain stopped the boy's promotion in consequence, under the pretence that the page was ordered not to go to the play.

I wished very much to have had time during my visit to Monsieur Castellan to look over a very curious collection of original letters which he had in portfolios, and of

which I looked at one or two only. The most valuable
were of the Valois family, and were numerous and confidential, coming to M. Castellan through a great-uncle,
and derived from an ambassador of the family in Spain.
There were several from Catherine de Medicis, mostly
about the marriage of her daughters with the Spanish
royal family, and which (as she had good occasion to do)
she always finished by desiring might be burnt as soon
as read.

The eldest daughter was first sent, being intended for
the son, Don Carlos, but Philip the Second took a fancy
to her, and though the son was in love, married her. An
intrigue was suspected with the son, as the daughter was
also in love with Don Carlos; the finale was, as history
records and romance writers have improved upon, that
Don Carlos and the lady suffered death. After this, and
knowing, as she must have done, the cause, or at least the
reports of all suspected, Catherine writes, saying that she
must forget the mother in the Queen, and proposes to
make up a match between King Philip and her youngest
daughter. The writer desires the person addressed to get
at the King's mistress and his confessor, and to secure
them both as friends to her plans. The remaining letters
were those of eminent men, some from Rousseau, Voltaire, &c., and appeared to contain nothing particularly
interesting.

A few days since I think I half made a convert of a fat
silversmith's lady here, of whom I was purchasing some
articles. She asked me if we had a religion in England
at all like theirs. I said, " Yes; very like." " But,"
said she (and that weighed very much with her), " you do
not use these great silver cups, &c., in your country?"
To this I replied, " Indeed we do, and want them much
larger than you do in France, for with us we let every
one taste that pleases of the wine, and you only let the

priests." This rather staggered her, when the sale of the cups and sacramental plate came into her head.

May 28th, Saturday, Post-day.—Our cavalry have at last got leave to pass through France, and will commence their route on the 1st of June. It is probable that we shall move soon after. I have this moment received a packet from you, with papers and enclosures to the 16th, and having your letter now before me, will go through it in answer. The alarms you mention about the quarrels between the Allies, and the French, and the army, and the National Guards, seem to have been principally of English invention. We have heard little of this matter here, though I have no doubt that the French officers and soldiers are vexed and mortified, and as the Irish say sometimes, they would easily " pick a quarrel " just now, when they meet with any occasion. There is the same feeling here, only hitherto scarcely any officers of the army have arrived.

I witnessed last Sunday a quarrel between a gend'arme and a garde-urbaine, about cutting off some acacia blossoms in the public walk. The latter was disarmed at last, after a scuffle and fight, in which, from the noise and confusion, you would have supposed several limbs and lives would have been lost (as would have been the case in half the time in England), but in which in reality no one seemed to come out the worse. The gend'arme, however, was very neatly beaten at last, as two of the garde-urbaine overtook him again, and whilst one tried to wrest the conquered sword back again, the other cut the belt of the gend'arme, by which his own sword fell, and in recovering that he lost the trophy, with which the two lads made off in triumph.

An officer of the French regular army who was here by accident a few days since, saw the caricature of Bonaparte in a window, the face made up of " *victimes,*" with the cobwebs, &c., introduced, which I conclude you have seen. He entered the shop in a rage, and desired the shopman to take it from the window, threatening to cut him down if he refused. It has not appeared in the window since, and the man when now asked for the print by an Englishman or Royalist, says, "They are all sold."

The Duke of Wellington's misfortune from the Cossack charge I have not heard of here. He came back most highly admiring and praising the Russian cavalry as in appearance the best in Europe, and saying there was scarcely a private horse in the regiment he saw for which a short time ago we should not willingly have given a hundred and fifty or two hundred guineas in Spain. The draught and artillery horses, also, though very small, and unlike those of the cavalry, he thought had great appearance of hardiness and activity. Some of your other stories concerning us here are really, in my opinion, mere inventions.

By-the-by, what inventions and scandal we shall have now to fill the newspapers and afford conversation for all our idlers! As soon as peace is signed, they will have little else but that to live upon; whilst the politician must pore over all the debates of the multiplied popular assemblies in modern Europe, which will all be aping our House of Commons.

Our clergy here were ten days ago praying for rain, and they have not sued in vain, for we have had it for this week in showers only, and in the English fashion, not like our mountain and St. Jean de Luz rain. We have also had tremendous storms of wind, which were not prayed for ; and more than that, a bit of an earthquake, felt principally at Pau and in that vicinity, but, it is said, by some perceived here. It is not surprising that old Mother Earth should just at first shake a little at all that has passed lately ; but I hope she will take it quietly, and be as peaceably inclined as her inhabitants now are. The recovery of the balance of Europe will be a fine subject for an essay. This superiority over the ancient associated states of Greece, which when once upset never could right themselves again, is a matter of considerable triumph for the moderns, and promises to check for some time another age of barbarism. I should say that one great cause of this has been the more general diffusion of knowledge amongst the middling classes. Public opinion and more fixed principles of the advantages of independence, have got the better at last of a system of universal tyranny of the most ingenious and complicated nature, and extending to every individual, and every hole and corner within its clutches. I must now seal up for the post.

CHAPTER XXIX.

Preparations for Departure—Bordeaux—Imposition on the English—
Greetings from the Women—Mausoleum of Louis XVI.

Wednesday, June 1, 1814.
Toulouse.

MY DEAR M——,

HERE we are still, but on the point of moving.
The orders are actually out, and our route fixed. We
start on Saturday, the 4th of June, I suspect on purpose
to avoid festivities on that day. On the 10th we hope
to be at Bordeaux: 4th, Isle en Jordain; 5th, Auch;
6th, Condom; 7th, halt; 8th, Castel Jelous; 9th,
Langon; 10th, Bordeaux. This will be sharp work for
loaded mules, and warm for us all, for the weather is now
clearing up, and promises to be hot again.

I am tired of Toulouse, and not sorry to leave it,
though the inhabitants continue to be civil and friendly.
So indeed they ought to be, as they have made no little
money out of us, and have been continually entertained
by balls, &c. Since the Duke has been away we have
had three balls given by the Adjutant-general, General
Byng, and by the aides-de-camp. At last I was, by accident, introduced to a Madame de Vaudreuil. She was
it turns out, wife to the son of the old admiral, our
emigré Marquis in England, and your cousin. I was
then introduced to the husband, and we had some conversation on family matters. He mentioned his nephew,
the aide-de-camp in Ireland, and inquired much after the

Hochepieds, &c. To-morrow I am to breakfast with them, and you shall hear more. He is a little man, but high, and in repute here.

No events of any consequence have occurred. The only thing at all worth mentioning which I can recollect is a trait of the conduct of the French lower officers of Soult's army. Two of the officers of the 43rd British rode towards Montauban a few days since, out of their own limits, without a passport. This, though foolish just now, was a venial offence, and committed by many French, who come in here within our line of demarcation. On a bridge near the town our two gentlemen were met by about eight or ten, not gentlemen, but officers of the French garrison there. The latter immediately attacked the two British officers rudely, told them that they ought to know better their own limits, and added at last that if they intended to come again, they advised them to come with their coats off, sleeves turned up, and swords drawn. One man actually went so far as to come behind one of our officers to knock his hat off, that he might get out the white cockade; in short, the two Englishmen were obliged to yield and return back.

An apology was, it is said, sent in to our General, from the commanding officer at Montauban, stating that he was sorry for what had happened, and hoping we would consider it as the act of some *mauvais sujets* in the lower commissioned ranks of the army, and not the act of, or sanctioned by, the garrison in general. I believe, however, that it is intended still to make some remonstrance on the subject.

Dr. Macgregor has returned here, delighted with his trip to Montpelier, Avignon, Nismes, Valence, &c. He was received most cordially everywhere, and at some places quite enthusiastically. Almost at every place, he fell in with fêtes and entertainments in consequence of the late changes, and the whole country was covered with conscripts and deserters going home : he thinks he must have seen from ten to fifteen thousand. Everywhere, he found much jealousy between the military, the national guards, and the civilians, as is the case here. There were several quarrels in consequence. At the playhouse at Montpelier the applause was so violent at a new popular piece called " The Conscript," that a French General, who was there with his suite, conceived it a marked insult to himself, and rose to leave the house, but was persuaded to remain.

The Society of Medicine at Montpelier made the Doctor a member, with such fine speeches, that even though he only half understood them, they raised his blushes.

Friday, June 3rd.—In the midst of the bustle and confusion of my preparations for the march of to-morrow, I received this day your letter and papers to the 24th of May. I had just been reading in to-day's French paper London news of the same date, so that, even this late mail, of only nine or ten days from London, brought us nothing new politically from England. The details, however, and private news are always interesting. I shall have more occasion for them as I am going the road on this (the Toulouse) side of the Garonne, instead of our military route, and shall be nearly, if not quite, alone, for almost every other person who goes this way intends to travel post, or ride faster than would suit me this warm weather. This road is said to be by far the most picturesque, rich, and amusing ; and, having a passport ready, I mean to start at five to-morrow. My route is through Grisolles, Castel Sarazin, Monteil, Moissac, Agen, Port St. Marie (where I shall try and see our *emigré* friend, the Baron de Trenqueléon), Tomeirs, Reolle ; then, if necessary, cross the river to Langon, but if not, keep the right bank, opposite Bordeaux. I have sent my baggage and Henry on in the line of march, and only take a Portuguese *ci-devant* servant to the Prince of Orange, and now mine, on a pony, with a small valise, and intend to trust to the inns for everything. Thus I shall avoid troops, and nearly all places through which they have passed.

The last detachment of cavalry will leave this to-morrow, to start to Grisolles and Montauban on Sunday. The Hussars in advance leave Montauban to-day. The last infantry will move from hence on Sunday; and the whole infantry from hence will be assembled at Bordeaux (excepting what may be embarked) by the 17th of June. The last Portuguese will pass Bayonne about the 23rd; and then the Guards and troops there will be at liberty to move—not before. The Spaniards are nearly all out of the country already!

Sir W. W. Wynne has been here these last five or six days, to succeed the Marquess of Buckingham; they are specimens of what are considered our greatest peers and commoners. The people here stare at them, and look strange. The inhabitants are seriously sorry for our departure, I really believe. We had a sort of farewell party at the Duke's house yesterday, given by Colonel C. Campbell, of all the great men here: we dined, then went to the play, and then to the ball. Some of our Generals are so pleased that they talk seriously of returning here after peace is signed, and they have laid by their laurels in England. Having so many things to do, I must now end this, and leave it to go by the post, for I shall be away from head-quarters, and the regular post, perhaps, next mail. Do not be surprised if you do not hear again very soon. On my arrival at Bordeaux I shall endeavour to write immediately, and let you know my plans.

Head-Quarters, Bordeaux, June 13*th,* 1814.—On Saturday (11th), I sent you a few hasty lines, I will now try and fill up the interval from Toulouse here, with an account of my proceedings during that time.

After a tremendous thunder-storm, at six in the morning of the 4th of June, I started along the rich plain in which Toulouse stands, and proceeded through Grisolles, and a number of small places, to Castle Sarazin ; but not liking the appearance of the latter, I went on to Moissac, which is just across the Tarn, at which place the plain ceases, and the road becomes hilly.

The distance was about forty-five miles to Moissac; the country all rich and fertile, but much too bare of wood, and the road is tiresome from its uniformly level character. The river ran the whole way, about half a mile from the road, and the opposite bank being high, bounded the view on that side, and formed a picturesque object, though not the most profitable, for the soil seemed less rich. The flat lands must be subject to great losses and damage from floods, as there is no fall for the sudden torrents which descend. The corn in many places had suffered much this year.

At Grisolles, I passed the last of the cavalry (the Blues) on their way home. The Life Guards entered Montauban with laurels. The Préfet immediately told the commanding officer, that he understood his men were come into the town in a triumphant manner, and seemed much vexed, until reminded that it was the 4th of June, when he became civil, and admitted the validity of the reason. On stopping at the village of Fignan, to give my horses some corn, I was very glad to find the inhabitants regretting the departure of the Portuguese regiment which had been quartered there, as they had behaved so well. They told me the people cried when they crossed the water, and the next day so many soldiers came back to take another farewell of their new friends, that the officers were compelled to place a guard to prevent it.

The Tarn at Moissac was wide, and the current very strong. The passage by the ferry, a troublesome one, backwards and forwards, through the remains of the ruined buttresses of an old bridge. On landing I asked

2 N

for the Commandant or French General. There had been unpleasant altercations of late near that place and neighbourhood. The officer of whom I inquired pointed to General Rey, the late governor of St. Sebastian, who happened to be near. I announced myself to him, and was received civilly by him, and then immediately went to the inn.

The only sights noticeable in the town are a great water-mill in the river, with about twenty-four pair of mill-stones, and a number of establishments for purifying wheat and preparing flour. These last were on a large scale, but without machinery of any ingenuity, and one steam-engine would have saved them nearly all their labour, which was great. The country round is famous as a corn country, and Moissac was once a great place of export for flour and wheat by the canal, &c., of Toulouse, to Montpelier, and by the Tarn and Garonne to Bordeaux, and thence to the French islands and foreign settlements. The inhabitants wished much to begin dealing with the English; but I told them that our Parliament was about to prevent that taking place.

There is a curious old church at Moissac with many carved grotesque figures at the entrance. The style is nearly the old English, but in some places, the early Gothic. The accommodation at the inns is very good; but the joke of Milord Anglois has commenced, and is increasing fast. We were all *mon Commandant* and *mon Général*; and paid accordingly.

The next day, on leaving Moissac, I ascended a long hill, and continued on rich high ground above the river, in a country of cultivated, undulating scenery, with more wood, somewhat resembling Devonshire or Somersetshire, with the exception of the want of hedges. This continued about seven miles, when I came down again, having a fine view of the river, and continued my way along the banks over a rich flat through several villages and small

towns to Agen, about thirty-four miles from Moissac.
The valley was here much narrower and varied than that
at Toulouse, bounded on both sides by gentle hills, cultivated and rich, as well as apparently populous, along the
whole way. The French troops were in cantonments in
every village, and in general looked very sulky. A few
touched their caps to me, as I was in my scarlet uniform;
but most looked sulky and took no notice. I was, however, never insulted. The cries of the children all the
way, and often of the country-women, and sometimes of
the men, of *vivent les Anglois!* certainly did not contribute
to put their soldiers and officers in better humour. If so
disposed, I could easily, as the Irish say, "have picked a
quarrel."

At Agen all was gaiety and bustle. It was the
Sunday before their great fair ; and all was preparing for
that, as well as for the service which was to take place in
the great church the next day for Louis XVI., the
Queen, &c. I immediately went to the Commandant of
the town. He was civil, but the numerous officers looked
very much disposed to be impertinent, if occasion should
offer. The eager curiosity of the towns-people to see the
English, and to be civil, was very pleasing ; every one
seemed anxious to show some attention. Here I fell in
with Dr. M—— and Mr. and Mrs. J——, and after
dining together, we went to the play.

It was a little narrow theatre, but almost new, and
very clean and neat. The performances were not despicable. There was a good-looking singer, with no bad
voice, from Bordeaux. In the character she acted much
happened to be said of her innocence and inexperience.
From the constant joking this gave rise to in the
audience, and from some very prominent feature in her
person, I conclude that she had lately been under the
necessity of retiring from Bordeaux, from some little

faux pas. And this, I was told afterwards, was the case.

Agen is an old and rather shabby town of about ten or eleven thousand inhabitants; but the walks and country around it are picturesque. The next morning I staid until after the ceremony had commenced in the church, and peeped in, to see what was going on, and whether the military attended. Many of the latter did so, with crape round their arms. I was immediately admitted without a ticket; and the old priests, several of whom had been *emigrés*, and spoke a little English, were very civil to me. About twenty milliners had made really a very elegant linen and crape mausoleum for the occasion, nearly twenty feet high. Four fluted pillars, one at each corner, were made of fine white linen, the festoons round the base were of black and white crape, urns on the pillars, and other ornaments of the same. About a hundred and fifty wax candles were arranged up the steps on every side of the tomb, and above it were lilies springing fresh from the centre, and the crown, in elegant crape, suspended above the whole.

About ten o'clock I started again to find out the Baron de Trenqueléon at Port St. Marie, which was about twelve miles from Agen. On inquiry at the inn, I found a friend of his son's who had left him only a few hours before. I, therefore, determined to cross the river again, in order to pay him a visit, and to stay there the night. Trenqueléon Chateau is about five miles from Port St. Marie, on the road thence to Nerac, on the side of the hills which enclose the valley in which the Garonne descends. It is old-fashioned, in the style of the Tuileries, and apparently large. In reality, it does not contain much room, but is a comfortable place.

Except two higher wings, it is, in fact, only a ground-floor house. The rooms are lofty, spacious, and decently furnished for a French house in the country. There is a great square garden in front, like a wilderness full of weeds, with a square plantation and straight walks. The roads run about two hundred yards from it on one side, and a small river navigable for boats on the other, which runs into the Garonne about four miles below. This would be convenient to export the produce, if there were a market, which of late had been the case.

I found the old Baron feeble, without the use of his limbs, in a great chair penned in like a child. He was surrounded by a large party—his wife, his son, and his son's wife, daughter to the *maire* of Agen; an old lady, whom I took for the Baron's sister; and five young ladies, who called him "Papa." One of these was in weeds, and one about twenty-five or thirty; the rest young. One was a fresh, ruddy, English-looking girl. All were most attentive and civil. The old Baron made me repeatedly kiss him, and cried several times as he conversed with me. He remembered all our friends in England during his emigration. He was very anxious to know all I could tell him of my brothers. He asked much after your sister and brother, and the T—— family. His table was bad, but there was quantity, and a hearty welcome. I was put into his uncle's room, our old friend the Bishop of Montpelier. His family seemed attentive to him, and, except at meal times, seemed to live around him, some at work, some reading the papers to him, and some sitting ready to talk, and with no other occupation. The poor girls must lead a very dull life in the Chateau de Trenqueléon, for from the state of the Baron's health they do not go out to balls or amusements even at Agen.

On the following morning I left Trenqueléon about twelve o'clock, and crossed the river again at a ferry near Aiguillon, which is a pretty town, small, but well situated. I got on to Tomeins that night. The country continues to be the same rich valley the whole way, and is very populous. Tomeins is a small ill-built town of perhaps about five thousand inhabitants. There is nothing of interest in it, except a fine sort of Richmond-terrace view from the public walk overhanging the river. The women struck us as very pretty, and they were peculiarly eager about "*les Anglois*," one or two calling out in English, as we passed near the windows where they were, "How you do? how you do?" &c., and then running away to hide themselves. And this came from well-dressed girls in good houses.

On the 8th I proceeded through Marmande de la Reolle, to breakfast; and then crossing the river again near Langon, I intended to stop at the pretty village of Barsac, about five miles on this side Langon, where the good wine of that name comes from. Finding all this part full of our sixth division, just arrived, I was obliged to push on to Ceron, a mere post stage and a poor inn.

On the 9th I proceeded to this place (Bordeaux), and arrived by one o'clock, when my order to proceed to Tarragona (for the trial of Sir J. Murray) was put into my hands. I found every one in the same hurry and confusion as when the Duke paid us his last visit at Toulouse.

The country continued nearly the same until we got some way beyond Barsac; we then began to skirt the Landes, and had only sand and firs, a sort of Bagshot Heath, but still broken by frequent villages and chateaux, which are very numerous around Bordeaux.

During my journey I always stopped at some small inn for a feed of corn in the course of the way, and also during rain, which was frequent and heavy. I gave the chance passengers their wine to make them talk. A drunken Frenchman seemed much like an English one, and was sometimes very entertaining; but the feeling of the soldiers was the most curious. At one place I found two discharged soldiers going home on leave; they said that they had been betrayed by their Generals, &c., and that the game was up, so they had applied for their discharges, for they would not fight for the King. They had served seven or eight years, and now intended to be quiet, though their wounds would not have prevented their fighting for the Emperor. One had lost a finger only, the other had received a knock in the leg, which rather made him halt a little; they had both above sixteen months' pay due to them, but said that they concluded, of course, the King would never pay the Emperor's debts, and they were satisfied to be discharged without pensions. They said that nine-tenths of the soldiers of the army would have remained firm to the Emperor if their Generals had been faithful, and had agreed in opinion with them; " *mais n'importe—c'est fini.*"

The Trenqueléon party told me, they were for some time in great uneasiness, for we had no troops near them on the left bank of the river, and on the right bank only came down to the river Lot. Thus Agen was the centre of the formation of partisan corps who were to cross the river near them, and scour the country to annoy us.

In three or four instances they succeeded in this; and the Commissioner was issuing most violent orders to compel all persons to form their corps immediately (these if caught by us would be hung), and to teach the women also, to entice our soldiers into their houses by wine, &c., to make them prisoners and kill them, and even to instruct their children to cut the back sinews of the horses in the stables at night, saying they must do as the Spaniards did by them in Spain.

The Baron's family said they had different feelings, but would have been compelled to do much of this had matters gone on. They also talked with much horror of the state of terror in which they had been kept by Bonaparte's agents. One deputy Préfet some time since

alarmed them by quietly telling some of their neighbours
(who told them again) that they were in a terrible scrape,
and had been detected corresponding with the English.
They went instantly to the Préfet to know what this
meant, and found it was one of my father's letters about
the Bishop of Montpelier's affairs, which had been stopped
by the police.   My father was the Bishop's executor in
England.   The Préfet afterwards told him to be easy—
"*ce n'étoit rien.*"   The Baron seems to have been a
popular character in the neighbourhood.

12*th, later.*—A mail goes to-day, and I have a pile of
papers a foot high to arrange by to-morrow.   The Duke
goes away and leaves the army the day after, Wednesday
the 14th, consequently all is a bustle of business, balls,
dinners, operas, plays, all proceeding at once.   My next
will give you an account of this handsome town.   I am
in quarters at Monsieur Emerigon's, a barrister now at
Paris, but daily expected to return.   The Duke has
written strongly home to put off this intended Court-
martial at Tarragona ; all here detest it, and grumble.
The worst is, that we are to remain here in suspense
until an answer arrives.

I am writing without my coat, and so are all the
Duke's Secretaries, &c., on account of the heat.   The
thermometer shut up in my writing-desk is at 76°.   The
un most ardent when out.

CHAPTER XXX.

The Opera-house—The Cathedral—The Synagogue—A Jewish Wedding—
Strange Show-house—Wellington and King Ferdinand.

Head-quarters, Bordeaux,
June 16, 1814.

MY DEAR M——,

As I have no news to communicate, you must be satisfied with the best account of Bordeaux which the excessive heat permits me to give you. The Duke is gone for good, and we are left here in a state of dull, and almost feverish uncertainty. Time slips away fast, however, and my fate will soon be decided.

Before breakfast I take an hour's ride to look about the town and suburbs, and make my observations. The restaurateurs are so hot that I prefer my own society and a mutton-chop with abundance of vegetables and fruit, and my bottle of claret or Sauterne, to the incessant dinners going on in public. My wine I get from the housekeeper of my landlord, Monsieur Emerigon, the counsellor, as she in his absence sells his produce for him —his wine, namely Sauterne Emerigon, which is really very good, his pigeons, his ortolans, his poultry, his cherries, his vegetables, &c. As he has not yet returned from Paris, I have also taken possession of his *salle à manger*, and drawing-room, in addition to my bed-room. I only now want to get into his library. He is a royalist, and one of the commissioners sent from Bordeaux to Paris.

Bordeaux is a very handsome town, and very superior to Toulouse—as a city indeed there is no comparison; still in my opinion there was more *ton* and fashion at Toulouse. The prosperity of the place was arrested by the Revolution, when it was in a state of splendid commercial prosperity, rapidly increasing in magnificence. Toulouse, on the contrary, I take it, was even then on the decline. Another advantage Bordeaux has, in addition to its having been laid out, like Bath, with modern improvement as to the width of the streets, namely, the convenience of stone quarries close at hand, instead of bricks to form the buildings, and this with water carriage. It has besides a stone somewhat similar to Portland stone, a complete Bath stone cut by the saw and adze like that at Bath; and of course these advantages have not been neglected by Frenchmen.

The Garonne is a noble river, not very much wider than the Thames at London Bridge, but it appears deeper, and of more importance; the tide occasionally reaches up as high as the neighbourhood of Langon. The quays probably extend nearly two miles, and in general are well-built and handsome, and the river just now full of shipping. The quays are inferior to those at Lyons, and the few half-rotten ships on the stocks in the spacious yard, show strongly the urgent necessity of what the people did on the late occasion.

The Grand Theatre is a very handsome building, with a colonnade of twelve pillars in front. The whole height of the building, with its connexions of taverns, Exeter Change, &c., runs back to the river. In its front is a square, with two handsome streets branching off right and left. One has the double row of trees, in the foreign fashion, in the centre, with paved carriage-roads outside, and is spacious, ornamental, and useful. At the end of this is the other Theatre, de la Gaieté, and that leads into a sort of wide avenue street planted all the way, and nearly a mile long. On one side again of this is the *ci-devant* Champ de Mars, or Jardin Publique, a spacious public planted walk. The town contains several other planted wide streets, and a handsome Palais-Royal, *ci-devant* Du Préfet. There is not any one very handsome square, and upon the whole Brussels is to be preferred; and it is a town probably nearly of the same size.

The Opera House is handsome in the inside, but dirty, and not well contrived so as to hold the greatest numbers. It consists of twelve large Corinthian pillars, which occupy much of the room; and all the upper boxes are like baskets projecting between them, and only two deep. The shape of the house is a flat horse-shoe, and well proportioned. The singing tolerably good; and the dancing by no means despicable. Except perhaps one or two of our best, it is better than at our London theatres. The dresses are rich and expensive. The reception of our Duke was very gracious; and it was not a little curious to hear " God save the King " sung constantly with " *Vive Henri IV. !*" *A l'Anglois, à l'Anglois!* was also a popular cry, and produced a hornpipe tune, always attended with great acclamation, but what the connexion was I cannot say. Some impudent sailors always called out for " Rule Britannia," but French *politesse* could not go so far. Two Americans would not pull off their hats one night to " God save the King," and were shouldered out of the house in consequence.

The upper boxes are entirely filled with very smartly dressed ladies of a certain class, whose wardrobes have improved during the last two months, I have no doubt, as much as that of the similar class of ladies at Toulouse, —and the last was very visible. The Theatre de la Gaieté is a sort of Sadler's Wells, neither more elegant, nor more chaste. The rope dancing is decidedly good. There is also a Musée here, as well as at Toulouse, but much inferior. There are not half a dozen original pictures of any tolerable master. The antique inscriptions are very uninteresting, to me at least, and there were no antiques affording pleasure to an artist or amateur. The collection of birds, serpents, butterflies, minerals, &c., are tolerable, but only of the second order. The library also appeared smaller and inferior to that at Toulouse, but there were many more readers, which surprised me.

There is also a deaf and dumb establishment here similar to that at Paris, and a very civil and apparently very intelligent master. I stayed there two hours, to have a regular lesson of the principles of the education illustrated by the female pupils, who were the most forward. There were about seventy scholars, mainly supported by the Government. The pupils were not quite so skilful as those at Paris, but it is always an interesting exhibition. To find out what we were, the teacher ingeniously made a pupil ask us what nation we were of, and of what profession, and as all the deaf and dumb pupils rejoiced in the answer, and seemed much pleased, I determined to keep up our good character, and gave the damsels a Napoleon, for which I got much dumb-show thanks in return.

The cathedral, or principal church, of St. André, is a good Gothic building of about the second class, built by " *vos Messieurs les Anglais,*" as we are instantly told. It is in one respect unfinished; for both the north and south fronts are intended to have each two light Gothic spires on the towers, whereas only one pair is built—the other has been but just commenced. The pair that exist were some little time since out of repair, and a part had fallen down. Bonaparte saw this, and graciously said they must be put in order directly. The Bourdelois were grateful, thinking he intended to have it done, but he only ordered it, and a tax on the commune at the same time, to pay for it. In the same way, as he came from

Lyons to Bordeaux, he found the road bad, and much out of repair : this he also ordered to be repaired immediately; but an *impôt* all along the communes on the road, beyond the expense of the repairs, followed likewise as immediately. The Préfet's palace he also ordered to be put in complete order, and it was just finished in time to receive the Duke d'Angoulême, which was not quite according to the wishes and intentions of the said Bonaparte.

The Exchange at Bordeaux is a well-contrived handsome building, and the square in the centre, roofed in with sky-lights, to form a convenient place for the different walks. The cloisters round are full of shops, jewellery, maps, &c.

June 28th.—I have just returned from the synagogue, where I have been these two hours. There are nearly two thousand Jews at Bordeaux. " It is no wonder the Christians are well fleeced," as my French companion observed, " when there are two thousand persons in the town who impose it upon themselves as a duty, and cheat for religion's sake." The chapel is a new building, the style of architecture not good, being a sort of imitation of Saxon, or rather of no particular order, but the shape of the temple is excellent, the proportions good, and the whole imposing. A colonnade formed by pillars runs all round, with a gallery above for the women, who are separated from the men. The altar at the end, with the ark of the covenant and the books of Moses, &c. The branch in the centre; round this the reading-desks, with the rows of lights for the priests, &c. The upper gallery is arched over like Covent Garden, with a circular roof.

The Jews were very civil. The singing was tolerably good ; the singing boys, about twenty in number, in white surplices and sky-blue silk sashes and scarfs, and bonnets, had a good effect, mixed with the old priests in

their hoods. The ceremony of producing the books of
Moses and returning them to the ark was the most
imposing in point of solemnity, and was attended by
music; but what to me was the most striking, was when
at a certain period in the service called the Benediction,
every parent found immediately his son or grandson, or
the children their parents. In short, after a few moments' bustle, you saw every one, whatever his age,
imposing his hooded head and hands on his own off-
spring, and every generation thus at the same instant
receiving the benediction from his own parent respectively. This was really an imposing scene.

The most truly Jewish part followed, for by solemn
proclamation every sacred office, namely, the opening of
the ark, the drawing the curtains, carrying the books,
putting on the ornaments, reading out of them when
produced, the right of assisting in every part of the cere-
monies, was regularly put up to auction, and sold to the
highest bidder. The biddings were from one franc to
three and five, and even at times up to forty and fifty.
As I was informed, these profits were given to the poor.
There was a little spoilt Jew child, about six years old,
for whom its papa had, I conclude, bought the privilege
of placing the silver ornaments on the tops of the
wooden rollers of the vellum Pentateuch, and the little
creature seemed much pleased and excessively proud
of his office. On Wednesday next there is to be a
wedding, and if not engaged, it is my intention to be
present.

The coffee-houses here, before we came, were very good,
and are not very dear. They are now so hot and
crowded, and in such confusion that I prefer my dinner
solo. Being in a great measure fixed by *la carte* as to
prices, I believe we are less imposed upon at the restaurateurs than anywhere else.

I rode out one day about four miles on the old

Bayonne road, to see a house and garden much talked of
here, belonging to a Mons. R——, the Portuguese Consul,
a queer old man, who goes about in a scarlet uniform
like that of our former English Generals, and with a
white-feathered General's hat. The grounds and gardens
are large, and in the first style of a Paddington tea-
garden, with a mixture of Hawkstone nonsense and
Walsh Porter's sham villages, &c. The house is nothing
remarkable, consisting of a number of rooms by no means
good;¹ not a single good picture, only some bad indecent
ones and very free prints. The most ludicrous part was
a regular inscription of " Library " over a door which led
to a little closet with one small set of book-shelves, containing a dozen or two of great almanacs, and a few odd
volumes of all sorts of books, the whole in number about
a hundred.

On the landing-place on the stairs is a negro, carved in
wood, holding a bottle and glass. The flower-garden—
which is in the old style, is tolerable. There are no good
statues, but plenty of cut trees in all shapes, temples,
&c., the whole being an endeavour to make poor Nature
as little likely to know herself as possible. There were
trees with the stems in frames and the tops pointed. In
the cut promenades in the woods were tombs and
wooden painted figures, of all sorts and descriptions.
There were dogs in their houses, the prodigal son feeding
swine, a mad lady half naked in a cage, &c. In another
part of the garden was a labyrinth, and a windmill with
a wooden man looking out of one window and a woman
out of the other, and below these a wooden cow and
some sheep, goats, deer of the same material, grazing.

Strangers are admitted to survey this place on any day.
The doors were opened to about a dozen of us, and we
were turned loose, without any showman, into the house
and grounds, and ranged about where we pleased. On
Sunday every one is admitted, and it is said there is much

company. The walks are cool, and it is not surprising
that they are frequented. The whole is one mode out of
many of obtaining notoriety. An ingenious way for pre-
serving the flowers is by an inscription insinuating that
every flower is a transformed female. This would not, I
fear, succeed in England. The poor ladies would have
many a pinch and squeeze, and lose many a limb, if
Kensington Gardens were full of such flowers, and had
no other protector.

Sunday, 19th.—The embarkation of the troops is now
going on with more spirit. The fourth division are, I
believe, all on board, if not sailed, and everything is by
degrees moving down towards the camp at Blanquefort,
and the place of embarkation, Rouillac, about thirty-five
miles below this. From the state of uncertainty in
which I remain I shall be one of the last, if I go at all,
that is, whether our Tarragona Court-martial is put an
end to. All accounts which have reached me agree with
P——'s. I have thought all along that, with the help
and assistance of Bonaparte himself, who was our best
ally, almost the whole of what has happened has arisen,
as it were, from the peculiar state of the nations of Europe, and from a natural course of events directed by
Providence, and with which the Allies had nothing
to do, except not to prevent it by their blunders or
quarrels.

We have various letters from Toulouse, to officers of
the army, full of regret for the loss of their English
friends, and by no means satisfied with the exchange for
their own countrymen. The army is vexed at this, and
matters are worse, as they do nothing but grumble and
quarrel in consequence. The reception of the [French
troops when they entered, it is said, was very flat and
provoking. D'Armagnac, who was supposed to have
saved the town by advising Soult to be off, was sent in
first, with two thousand five hundred men, and he and

his officers bowed and were very anxious to court a cordial greeting ; but the dull silence was scarcely broken, and the French officers could not contain their vexation and abuse in consequence.   There was, I believe, more sincerity in the professions of the Toulousians towards us, as far as the majority was concerned, than is usual with Frenchmen, or than we could reasonably have expected from them.

On the other hand, the accounts from the cavalry, of their treatment in their march through France, is very different from ours at Toulouse :—in this they all agree. The officers, trusting to French hospitality, have left their own beds behind, and having had to bivouack almost as much as in Spain, they have had a bad time of it.   Several letters have come from Mr. H——, who went with the column through Angoulême and Poictiers.   He has written from both these places.   He says, "The inhabitants profess openly that, as we chose to march through France, they will try and make us repent of it.   They scarcely give any quarters, send the men leagues about out of the road, and only let the Commissary buy his provisions on the road.   At Angoulême, a town which might quarter ten thousand men without inconvenience for a short time, they would only suffer a few officers and the General in the town, and most of those were quartered at inns.   The General and one servant got a billet at a private house, but he was to pay if he took more in with him.   The incivility is general; the doors were all shut against us.   The playhouse at Angoulême was empty the night it was known that our officers would be there. Nothing to be had without paying."   This is the same spirit of vexation as that in the army—a conviction that they have been beaten, and that this march is a sort of proof and token of it.

Head-Quarters, Bordeaux, June 26th, 1814.—My life has been every day the same — a ride early, at work

2 o

at home all the middle of the day, a dinner generally solo, and another walk or ride in the evening, or, as the weather has become cooler again, sometimes the play.

I have spoken to Colonel M—— about your friends who think of a removal to the south of France, he having many connexions at Toulouse. He is decidedly of opinion that that should be the place of abode, for a family of ladies especially; I am rather disposed to be of the same opinion. Pau, however, which I have not seen, is much recommended. Supposing they fix on Toulouse, Colonel M—— says, of course, that the house which they will require for comfort must be large, giving them four rooms with *lits de maître*, and four beds for *filles de chambres*, and about four other servants, and three good sitting rooms, &c. He thinks such a house may be had for about eighteen hundred francs a-year, that is, about 75*l.* a-year. I can assure them, that in point of economy, all must depend upon their arrangements being made by some French friends, and not by an English one. In house-rent, in wine, in everything, an inhabitant will get articles at one-third of the price demanded of the English. The French have no ideas of honesty or moderation towards the English, and not much towards any one in matters of trade. The extortion, and even the downright frauds committed, especially on travellers, are quite disgraceful, and every tradesman assists his neighbour in getting a job, and fleecing the *milords*. I believe they are like the Jews, and have, from continual practice, arrived at the same conclusion as the others from religion, namely, that they are performing a duty when they cheat an Englishman.

There are two Protestant chapels here, and one excellent preacher, in the style of a London chapel preacher, only extempore; I heard one very eloquent French sermon delivered by him, with great propriety. The service, the singing, and other parts of the duty, are but moderately performed.

The courts of justice are much the same as at Toulouse, and about nine or ten judges generally attend. I was unfortunately obliged to leave Toulouse before their criminal sessions with a jury commenced, and on my arrival here they were over. This takes place only once in three months, unless something extraordinary or a great press of business occurs. I attended a case of misdemeanor, a bad assault, in the criminal court, but that was an appeal only, and being of the class of *petits delits*, there never is a jury—but a president and five judges. The same number presides when there is a jury, in more penal trials; and in certain cases when the jury are divided, as for instance seven against five, then the judges are called in to vote as jurymen, and the proportion of votes required by law calculated on the whole numbers. There was much unnecessary delay and argument in the case I heard. It was like one of our worst-managed cases of motions for a new trial on account of deficiency of evidence, which are always of the most tiresome class.

Post-day, June 27th.—I have been to the Jew's wedding. The ceremony consists principally of singing and drinking, and blessings in Hebrew. There must be something Jewish, however, as usual, and that is concerning the ring, which, as soon as it is produced, is shown round to all the rabbies near, and some elders, &c., and to the sponsors, to be sure it is really gold, or otherwise the marriage is void, and the true old clothesman-like way in which they all spied at the ring was very amusing. Nearly the last ceremony is the bridegroom's smashing a wine-glass in a plate on the floor, with an idea that he and his spouse are then as difficult to separate as it would be to reunite the glass. The gentleman showed gallantry by exerting all his force, and looking most fiercely as he broke the glass.

2 o 2

I understand that the Duke of Wellington came back from Madrid with a much better impression of King Ferdinand than when he went, thinking that he showed talent, firmness, and character. The manner in which he received the Duke may have somewhat disposed him to this favourable judgment. I understand the King immediately treated the Duke as a grandee of Spain, by shaking hands with him, and putting his hat on, and that the king declared almost the only two acts of the Cortes, which he approved of *in toto*, were those which made the Duke commander of all the Spanish armies, and gave him the estate in the South.

We have had news from our cavalry from the vicinity of Paris, from Chartres; all the officers have deserted their regiments to see Paris—that present wonder of wonders! They have occasionally lately been better treated, that is, whenever they met with a Royalist patron at their quarters. H—— says there seems to be two parties everywhere, and it is a sort of lottery which they fall into the hands of; that, when he wrote last from Chartres he had been " stuffed to death," made to eat three or four meals a-day, and to attend a party given on purpose for him every evening: this, I conclude, was all a *douce* violence.

Still no news as to our Tarragona plan. My patron, Monsieur Emerigon, says, that at Paris the Emperor of Russia individually was the most popular, except perhaps the English and our Duke; that the Russian troops were not in such favour; the King of Prussia so-so. Blucher and his troops better, but the Emperor of Austria the worst of all; and every one must have observed the marked difference of his reception from that of the other sovereigns.

I am to-day turned out of my room, which is the dining-room, as my patron gives a dinner, to which he has asked me. I must not therefore complain.

We have been paid up a good deal of money at this place, where the quantity of gold and silver we have circulated is quite incredible. Every one talks of it, and the piles and piles of empty money-boxes of all sorts, and from all quarters, fully prove it. At present we have immense quantities of French money, Napoleons and Louis, gold and silver, from Paris, whilst, on the other hand, I am told that the French are here buying up our guineas and Portuguese gold, to turn them into Louis, as they have begun a new coinage both here and at Paris.

CHAPTER XXXI.

Country Fêtes — Brawls with the French — The Duke d'Angoulême —
Mademoiselle Georges—The Actress and the Emperor—French Acting
and French Audiences—Presentation of a Sword to Lord Dalhousie—
Georges' Benefit—Departure.

Head-quarters, Bordeaux, July 4, 1814,
Post-day.

My dear M——,

WE have still had no instruction how to proceed,
and are waiting the determination in England.   In
the mean time I am being gradually stewed, for the heat
has again commenced, and is in full operation.   My life
is quite retired and monotonous, and affords no incidents.
The only variety that has arisen is, that yesterday I
dined at three o'clock with my patron's sister, a West
Indian elderly single lady, and a female party.   I was
the only beau, the brother was engaged ; and in the
evening I rode over about three miles to Briges, a village,
where they were keeping an annual fête.

The crowd of country-people dancing and singing was
very considerable, and the road was covered with the
lower class, going and returning.   The difference between
this and our country fêtes seems to be, that there was
nothing to buy or sell, and but little eating and drinking going on, the principal occupation being dancing and
talking, laughing, and parading about.   It seems impossible to make such a people as the French very unhappy
in any way, however bad their government, except by
the conscription.

Those who are satisfied with salads, sour wine, dancing, and other amusements entirely depending upon themselves and the meeting of the two sexes, can only be disappointed and deprived of their happiness by the removal of one sex altogether. Leave them alone, and they have nearly all they wish. John Bull, on the contrary, wants many things more to put him into the same state of joy and satisfaction.

Several of Marshal Soult's officers have got into Bordeaux of late; disputes and quarrels have been the consequence, but hitherto they have been of no great moment. Every opportunity of seeking a row was eagerly laid hold of by the French—a jostle on the stairs at the theatre was sufficient. Lord Dalhousie, who is in command here now, has been obliged to forbid any officer going to the Theatre de la Gaieté where this was most likely to arise, and to order off every officer not on duty here to camp. We have here now only the Guards and staff officers. The inhabitants are all with us, particularly a set of very fine-looking young men, but a little hot-headed, who compose the Duke d'Angoulême's guard of honour. They have been also insulted, and a few days since paraded with bludgeons to see if this would be repeated either against themselves or the English, and they determined to resist either on the spot. No great harm has yet happened. As far as I can learn, there have been about three fights, but none fatal.

A young Tyrolean, in the pay-office department. having been insulted, watched and followed the offender home. He then went for his sword, which we never wear (but the French always do), returned, and insisted upon instant satisfaction. Upon this the Frenchman's zeal began to cool, but it was too late; the Tyrolean insisted upon his going out into a backyard and fighting directly. He cut him across the face, and was just about running his sword into his body, when a friend interfered, and stopped him, saying that "he had done enough."

Another Frenchman has been horsewhipped by an English officer, who, when insulted, returned with his sword and whip, and offered the Frenchman his choice, and as the latter persisted in asking for time, he chose for him and gave him the whip. All this makes Lord Dalhousie anxious to get the troops off, and as I hear Lord Keith has promised plenty of transports, in answer to his pressing letters on the subject, we expect to be all away in ten days' time, and some immediately. There are nearly eighteen thousand men still in France, including the fifth division at Bayonne, where, by-the-by, the disposition on the part of the French to be uncivil, sulky, and quarrelsome has been much greater. On the contrary, the generals and superior officers are very civil, particularly Marshal Suchet, to the few English officers remaining at Toulouse, and General Villette, who is here, is also very civil.

Later.—A ship is just arrived in sixty-four hours from Plymouth, telling us that fifteen sail of the line, and as many frigates are close at hand, but no news of our destination.

Head-Quarters, Bordeaux, July 10th, 1814.—I have now received two letters and packets of papers from you by the last mail, including those up to the 28th June. The same mail brought orders for all the members of the Court-martial appointed for Tarragona to proceed direct for England, and there report themselves to the Adjutant-general. Upon this I asked Lord Dalhousie (our present chief) what I was to do? and was by him desired to remain here to the last and move with the head-quarters, who remain here till the troops move. This must, I think, take place in about a week or ten days, unless you cease to send shipping from England. We shall in three days' time have only a brigade of Guards remaining for the city duty. The rest who will not be already embarked will be at Poulliac in readiness.

We have now got our small share of Royalty also at Bordeaux, as the Duke d'Angoulême has arrived again, and means to stay a few days before he goes to join Madame la Duchesse at the Baths at Vichy. He looks worn, and less calculated than ever for public show, but still apparently as amiable as before. The Duc de G——, though still, I believe, in our 10th Hussars, came in with him, as his aide-de-camp. The Duc de G—— is come back much disgusted with Paris, and even almost with France and Frenchmen. He says that Paris is a dirty place, without society and manners, and that he has met with no one to whose word or whose honour he would fairly trust: that all seemed to be a system of deception and falsehood, and that unless things mend, and alter considerably, he should feel almost disposed, in case of any unfortunate quarrel with England, to renounce France, rejoin his regiment, and become an Englishman. This, I conclude, is the depression of first feelings, which, in the case of emigrants, must be very strong just now. Matters have not quite proceeded to their tastes, and they must every hour meet with that which must inevitably disgust them.

We have now also at Bordeaux the celebrated Mademoiselle Georges, the actress from Paris, and Mons. Joami, also from the metropolis. In spite of the heat, I have been three times to hear them in Voltaire's plays, *Merope*, *Phedre*, and *l'Orphelin de la Chine*. The man has neither much figure nor countenance, and I should place him only as a second-rate performer, though still very superior to the ordinary set here in that line. In fact there are no tragic performers here at all; and the inferiority, beneath mediocrity, with which every other part is sustained, takes off the interest with which these tragedies would be otherwise attended.

Mdlle. Georges herself is also in many parts deficient, both in good taste and in 'true nature. She is of a large figure, but now fallen to pieces; and I am rather surprised that the *ci-devant* Emperor should have fancied her anywhere except during his Moscow campaign. The story, however, goes here, that at one of their interviews, Bonaparte was taken ill, and in her confusion and ignorance Mdlle. Georges rang the Empress's bell instead of that for the attendants, and that on the arrival of Maria Louise there was of course a scene.

Mdlle. Georges' voice is good, and her countenance would by many be considered fine. In some parts of her acting I think she is strikingly great, but generally forced and extravagant. She runs into extremes from crying to laughing, and from low ghost-like intonations to loud vulgar screams. Upon the whole, one comes away fatigued from one of these representations, and not much pleased or affected. And what convinces me that it really is inferiority in the drama or in the actress, and not merely the difference of style and manner, or national feeling as to composition and taste, which causes this, is, that the French part of the audience never seem affected like an English audience under the influence of really fine acting. You never hear the generally suppressed sobs, or see the eyes full of tears all round the house as with us at an English tragedy, when, for example, Mrs. Siddons plays, and every one goes away with a serious impression. In the French auditors you only hear bursts of "*Très beau, très beau! superbe! magnifique!*" &c., always applied to some extravagant and sudden change of tone or manner; and now, at this present moment, if there happens to be a royal sentiment which can be applied, it is encored like a song. No one seems carried away by feelings which he cannot command; but the applause is given as it would be to a mountebank for a clever trick. The distressed heroine or empress spits in her pocket-handkerchief, or on the stage in the true French style, and certainly not in a manner to excite admiration or interest, or to impress the spectators very strongly with ideas of her dignity and elegance.

The first night the Duke d'Angoulême was at the play (on his arrival here this time), we had verses and songs in his honour, and " Vive Henry IV.!" without end. At last came for once, " God save the King," which was received very differently from what it was even when I first came here; coolly and civilly enough, except by a few ; and I believe we have a few sincere friends here.

As Paris gave a sword to General Sacken, Bordeaux is to give one to Lord Dalhousie; and I really think the town has (as they certainly ought to have) some feelings of gratitude towards him for his attention to everything which can be of service to the city, and in successful efforts to preserve order, and prevent any mischief being done to the inhabitants. This sword will be a curious heir-loom in the Dalhousie family, given to their ancestor by the French civil authorities of Bordeaux.

As a trait of the natural French feelings of vanity, I may tell you, that my loyal patron Mons. Emerigon said, not only should we have been all originally prevented from entering France, had the people been of one mind with the Emperor and the army, but that all along a single word of complaint from Louis XVIII. of the conduct of the allied troops would have been a signal for their entire destruction at any period since.

I am now told that the fifth division, from Bayonne are also on their march hither to embark. This will probably cause some little more delay; but I think in ten days we must be on board ship.

Head-Quarters, Bordeaux, July 15th, 1814.—Our final departure from hence appears, at last, to be gradually approaching. The numbers of the English diminish daily; and though we have for this month past been talking of the "next week," I begin to think that another week will really and truly see us off, and the French army again in possession of Bordeaux.

The tradesmen of the town will miss us greatly. They have made a famous time of it these last three months, for the army has in that time received six months' pay, and most of it has found its way into the pockets of the keepers of the restaurateurs, the hotels, &c. Bordeaux has had its full share of the spoils of the *milords*. Nor have the inhabitants suffered anything by the army, except the little inconvenience of giving up a room or two in general as quarters for the officers, who partly made up even for this by giving their hosts tickets for the play, taking boxes for the ladies, &c., and making them presents every now and then. The only persons who have suffered by us at all in the neighbourhood, are those who have small gardens near the camp. They certainly have had their vegetables and fruit gathered gratis, and have generally not even had their share. This evil is, however, exaggerated, and much of it which really exists, has been done by the French peasantry and country servants, who, if a soldier takes six cabbages, immediately take a dozen more themselves, sell them in the camp, and swear to the owners that the soldiers are the culprits.

Those who have vineyards as well as gardens, have also their full revenge in the price of their wines, which were immediately doubled, by the arrival of the troops, and the latter in fact pay dearly for their vegetables, though they get a good part for nothing. It is fortunate for the inhabitants that we shall be off before the grapes begin to ripen, and for our own soldiers likewise. Surrounded by vineyards, the temptations would be irresistible, and the means of offence almost boundless; so that the loss to the cultivators of their principal harvest, and the injury to the soldiers, would be very considerable.

I have bought a violoncello to amuse myself this warm weather, and as my host, M. Emerigon, plays the violin in very excellent style, we have frequently music of an evening before he goes to his consultations.

We most of us, nevertheless, begin to find Bordeaux dull,—I do in particular. My occupation has nearly ceased, except as to swearing the paymasters, &c., to their accounts, and now and then a Court-martial,—not enough to give me full employment. The constant expectation of moving, the uncertainty when I may be wanted, and the natural indolence arising from the heat, prevent me from voluntarily engaging in any regular study or pursuit, and even prevent my making any excursions beyond a league or two on my pony. Shut up in this town, which, though airy, as to the general breadth of the streets and openings, is still in fact hot and low, and built in a country like that round Woolwich or Deptford, I get thin and languid, and shall be glad to be braced by the sea-air and the cooler climate of England.

Saturday, 1st.—As yet we have had no packets this week, and being beyond the usual time, this makes us believe the reports which have been some days in circulation, that you mean to send no more packets from England. I have still hopes.

I must tell you a trait completely French, of one of the noble guard of honour of the Duke d'Angoulême at Bordeaux. I had met him twice in the family with whom I live : on one of these occasions, at dinner. He dined here yesterday, and whilst the rest of the party were taking their coffee, I went to my room to dress, as I dined at Lord Dalhousie's. This guardsman slipped up stairs after me. He came bowing into my room, whilst I was in my shirt, and without any excuse or apology, immediately began to tell me he had a little favour to ask, and hoped that I would oblige him, and say nothing of it in the family, for he would not ask them, and was anxious they should not know anything about it; and at last said, " Could I just let him have five guineas or so, for which he would give me a bit of paper." In short, he added that he was rather deficient in cash, and I should oblige him infinitely by the loan, which should be paid when he could. As I fully expected an application to ask some favour of Lord Dalhousie or the Duke of Wellington, or something very disagreeable, I felt rather relieved by the explanation in full. As he was quite a young man, had just got a commission in the new regiment to be raised in Martinique, and was, I concluded, of good character, from his connexion with M. Emerigon and his family, who are held in great esteem, I counted him out his five guineas (all the time in my shirt), and he went away very happy, saying that he would go below and leave me a bit of paper, though I told him there was pen and ink in my room. The paper said that he would send Mr. —— six guineas to England (a guinea more than I had given him) as soon as he could. It was signed— *P. de V. De R*——, *De La Martinique*, leaving my name a blank, and not inquiring where he should send, so as to reserve, I presume, enough to satisfy his conscience in not repaying the money, that he should never know where to send it. His bit of paper only confirmed me in my notion that I was doing an act of charity, and not turning Jew or money-lender.

The guard of honour are to-day dismissed, by order of the higher powers from Paris. In truth, there are quite troops enough in France, without adding the expense of these gentlemen, with their white feathers a yard long, who would be of no use except to quarrel with the regular troops. Only four years since Bonaparte, when at Bordeaux, was attended everywhere by a guard of honour of the same description. Volunteers were his only body-guard.

The Prefêt of Bordeaux last night gave a fête to the Duke d'Angoulême. I went with M. Emerigon. The Duke came a few minutes after eight o'clock in his carriage and six, dressed, I believe, in the uniform of a Field-Marshal, with the *cordon-bleu*, &c. He was received by the Prefêt, attended by Generals Villette, Blagnac, Clement de la Ronciere, &c., &c., and a number of old and new nobility, all in their best; and having been, as it were, proclaimed to the company by the Prefêt, the Duke went about most graciously, talking to every one as usual.

About ten supper was announced, for the Duke has very early habits; and in about half an hour afterwards he came to the window to see very pretty fireworks, which were let off in the main street, surrounded by thousands of people below, and at all the windows. It was a gay and attractive scene. Soon after eleven the Duke went home, for he rises at five, and works hard at business, on petitions, &c., and at four o'clock to-morrow morning is to start for Bayonne. He had been at two reviews in the course of yesterday, and had both times been in tolerably severe storms. I fancy he must now and then wish himself quiet again, as he has been for the last twenty years. I am almost sure I should. The new barons and nobility seem to make very good courtiers. Indeed, the duties are all the same; it is only a change in the cry and the idol, the same worship exists as before. The Prefêt, Monsieur le Baron de V——, while the fireworks were going on, observed to all around him (loud enough on purpose for the Duke to hear)—how fortunate he was to have thought of the fireworks; that the idea had come into his head, as he observed that every one would see Monseigneur so well at the window, whilst the fireworks were going off; and then how plainly we can read the inscriptions—O yes, observe *Vive le Duc d'Angoulême! Vivent les Bourbons!*

and the fleurs-de-lys—how well they look in the midst of
the fire! He felt quite happy that he had thought of
all this to gratify the people, as it necessarily must do.—
Now the inscriptions were close to us, and in letters
a foot long. And note besides, that this Baron was one
of the functionaries who ran away from Bordeaux, when
the Duke came here on the 12th of March, and who
would probably not now hold his situation, if my patron
and some others had not persuaded him to return in
good time, and continue in his office to wait the result.
The Duke must see through this, and be disgusted.

The women here are not as well dressed as at Toulouse
—not so stylish. They do not show so much blood and
fashion. I believe, however, among the higher orders,
that there is much more morality, and that there is a
greater difference in reality, as well as in outward appearance, between the ladies in the dress-boxes, and those in
the tier above, than there was at Toulouse.

Shortly after eleven o'clock the few English who were
present at the fête, had nearly all gone home, being chiefly
Generals and their aides-de-camp. I came away, leaving
the company waltzing and dancing away with less spirit
and skill than at Toulouse.

I met with some very liberal Catholics here; for
instance, a gentleman said yesterday, before me, that if
all the pieces of the true Cross were collected, they
would, when put together, make a cross half a mile long.
A lady in company said to a friend (also before me), that
she did not much trouble the father confessor, and indeed
that it was what she liked the least of any part of her
duty. She added that their religion depended on faith,
hope, and charity, and that she understood (addressing
me), ours did so too, but that theirs required a good deal
of hope. Madame Emerigon, with whom I live, has
returned home highly delighted with Paris, but abuses
the inhabitants, who, she says, think only of making

money, taking in strangers, provincials and foreigners, and amusing themselves day and night.

She is a French creole from one of the islands. A little mulatto girl, about fourteen, always stands behind her chair, laughing at all her mistress says. The hair-dresser is genernlly seated in one corner of the room, half the dinner-time, joining in the conversation, and sometimes adorning Madame, whilst we are taking our wine, and during this time an idle Paris lad, of the girl's age, whom Madame seems to have fancied because he speaks such good French, and not the Patois, is running about, bustling, but in reality doing little or nothing from morning till night. Three other female servants, and a nephew of the family, complete the party on this side of the house, or rather wing.

In an opposite wing, are, first in the upper part, two respectable old ladies, and their servants; below them *au-premier*, is an old West Indian gentleman and his two sons, both *ci-devant* of the Imperial guard of honour, from Bordeaux, and his two daughters, with servants, &c. None of these are very elegant, nor, as far as I can judge from one visit, very well bred. They amused me the whole time with talking of the superiority of the French troops, and how the Imperial guards in particular could beat all the Allies if not more than two to one, as they always had done, to which I only said that I believed the Imperial Guards had been all withdrawn from the army of Spain, at least I supposed so, and that I had had, therefore, no opportunity of judging. One Miss also asked what the English lived upon? as she understood we ate no bread. Upon which a French visitor, to save me the trouble of explanation, informed her that we principally lived upon *des potates* (which is now the word here for potatoes) and *betraves*, with which accurate information she seemed quite satisfied. This sort of conversation, and a few songs quite in the French

2 P

style, which I do not at all admire, though one of the demoiselles had a good voice, have not tempted me to pay another visit.

The other night I went to the benefit of Madame Georges. She acted Semiramis, in Voltaire's play, and with considerable success, particularly when she let Nature have its way. She also acted in the sentimental farce of *La Belle Fermière,* and really well, if she had but omitted a miserable song, accompanied by an old violin or two behind the scenes, all out of tune. The orchestra, as well as every part of the house, was full— almost every passage crammed near the openings to the boxes. The play began at seven o'clock, and the company were all ready by four, and I saw many well-dressed women going to the play at two and three o'clock, as a box cannot be engaged without paying almost double price. The Duke was very well received, and as there was luckily no band, we escaped about five-and-twenty *Vive Henry IV.!* which we should otherwise have had.

Mr. Wilberforce should exert himself in getting little essays written in French, on the Slave Trade, circulated in France, in some degree at least to enlighten the people. At present, even the more intelligent and better sort of men seem only to consider the English as playing the part of Don Quixote in this business, and consider the whole as a sort of romantic affectation of humanity ; whilst many others insinuate motives not quite so honourable, by stating that, having well supplied our own islands with slaves, we wish to give up all the other colonies, with a diminished black population, and in bad condition, and then to prevent their ever recovering themselves. This is to be done by the abolition of the Slave Trade ; whilst our own islands, in full prosperity, will be ready to reap the benefit of the distress of their rivals.

July 18*th.*—I have now only time to seal up and to tell you that the returns of embarkations are just arrived from Pouillac, by which it appears that all the troops are now actually on board, except the two brigades of Guards, one of which entered Pouillac to-day to be prepared, and the other is still here. At present no more shipping is ready, though more are expected; some say we shall be moving about to-morrow week, some this day fortnight; but I believe no one knows anything of the matter.

From the following entry in the Diary kept by Mrs. Larpent, it appears that Mr. F. S. Larpent arrived at his father's house, at East Sheen, on the 8th August, 1814.

8th August, 1814.—" In the evening came Seymour, looking younger than when he went away, and in excellent health, after having been absent two years, all but a fortnight. We thanked God sincerely for this great mercy and happiness."

APPENDIX.

[Although the annexed letter does not come chronologically within the scope of Mr. Larpent's Journal, as there is an anticipatory notice, towards the close of the second volume, of Sir John Murray's trial, it may not inappropriately be inserted here.]

Paris, January 19th, 1815.

MY DEAR SIR,

IN regard to Sir John Murray's trial, I intended to prove the charges framed by my directions against him, in consequence of the orders of Government, by the production of my Instructions and his Reports, all of which are in the Government Offices.

Sir John Murray contends that one paragraph of my Instructions directed him not to risk an action. I think he has mistaken my meaning in that paragraph; but whether he has or not, that paragraph did not recall the other Instructions for his conduct.

The object of that paragraph was to prevent the Spanish Generals Elio and the Duque del Parque, from taking advantage of Sir John

Murray's absence, and the temporary command which they had of the cavalry belonging to Sir John Murray's and Whittingham's corps, to attack the French. There existed a prevailing opinion among the Spanish officers that their failures were to be attributed to the want of good cavalry; and this paragraph of the Instructions was drawn with the view of preventing those officers from attempting to fight a general action when circumstances should have placed a small body of good cavalry at their disposal, more particularly as all the manœuvres ordered by the Instructions had in view to prevent the necessity of a general action.

I have not by me the Instructions, but, as well as I recollect, this meaning of the paragraph is obvious; and it will be particularly observed that it comes in after the directions for the formation of the Corps Romain in Bohemia with the Duque del Parque and General Elio. I think, as I before stated, that this paragraph has nothing to say to the question of Sir John Murray's guilt or innocence of the two charges, though it has to that brought against him by the Admiral.

The Court has, of course, a right to judge of my meaning by the words in which it is conveyed, in whatever manner I may now explain it or you may explain it for me, as the obvious meaning of those words was to be the guide of Sir John Murray's conduct. I must add also, that whatever care I may have taken, it is not improbable that in drawing an Instruction for the operations of so many corps, all with separate Commanders-in-Chief, I may not in every instance have made use of the language which should convey the meaning I had in my mind.

There is nothing else that occurs to me; but I shall be glad to hear from you occasionally during the trial, and receive a copy of the evidence when it can be got.

Believe me,

Ever yours, most faithfully,

WELLINGTON.

To F. S. Larpent, Esq.
&c.   &c.

LONDON: W. CLOWES AND SONS, STAMFORD STREET AND CHARING CROSS.

Also published in facsimile in *The Spellmount Library of Military History* and available from all good bookshops. In case of difficulty, please contact Spellmount Publishers (01580 893730).

HAMILTON'S CAMPAIGN WITH MOORE AND WELLINGTON DURING THE PENINSULAR WAR by Sergeant Anthony Hamilton
Introduction by James Colquhoun
Anthony Hamilton served as a Sergeant in the 43rd Regiment of Foot, later the Oxford and Buckinghamshire Light Infantry. He fought at Vimiero and took part in the retreat to Corunna, vividly describing the appalling conditions and the breakdown of the morale of the British Army. He subsequently fought at Talavera, Busaco, the Coa, Sabugal, Fuentes de Oñoro, Salamanca and Vitoria. He also volunteered to take part in the storming parties of the sieges of Ciudad Rodrigo and Badajoz. During these actions, he was wounded three times. Published privately in New York in 1847, this rare and fascinating account has never before been published in the United Kingdom.

RANDOM SHOTS FROM A RIFLEMAN by Captain John Kincaid
Introduction by Ian Fletcher
Originally published in 1835, this was the author's follow-up to *Adventures in the Rifle Brigade* – and is a collection of highly amusing, entertaining and informative anecdotes set against the background of the Peninsular War and Waterloo campaign.

RECOLLECTIONS OF THE PENINSULA by Moyle Sherer
Introduction by Philip Haythornthwaite
Reissued more than 170 years after its first publication, this is one of the acknowledged classic accounts of the Peninsular War. Moyle Sherer, described by a comrade as 'a gentleman, a scholar, an author and a most zealous soldier', had a keen eye for observation and an ability to describe both the battles – Busaco, Albuera, Arroyo dos Molinos, Vitoria and the Pyrenees – and the emotions he felt at the time with uncommon clarity.

ROUGH NOTES OF SEVEN CAMPAIGNS: in Portugal, Spain, France and America during the Years 1809 –1815 by John Spencer Cooper
Introduction by Ian Fletcher
Originally published in 1869, this is one of the most sought-after volumes of Peninsular War reminiscences. A vivid account of the greatest battles and sieges of the war including Talavera, Busaco, Albuera, Ciudad Rodrigo, Badajoz, Vitoria, the Pyrenees, Orthes and Toulouse and the New Orleans campaign of 1815.

ADVENTURES IN THE RIFLE BRIGADE IN THE PENINSULA, FRANCE, AND THE NETHERLANDS FROM 1809–1815 by Captain John Kincaid

Introduction by Ian Fletcher

This is probably the most well-known and most popular of the many memoirs written by the men who served under Wellington in the Peninsular and Waterloo campaigns. The author, Captain John Kincaid, served in the 95th Rifles, the most famous of Wellington's regiments, a regiment which 'was first in the field and last out'. Kincaid fought in most of the great campaigns in the Peninsula between 1809 and 1814 and at Waterloo, in 1815, where he served as adjutant to the 1st Battalion of the Regiment.

THE MILITARY ADVENTURES OF CHARLES O'NEIL by Charles O'Neil

Introduction by Bernard Cornwell

First published in 1851, these are the memoirs of an Irish soldier who served with Wellington's Army during the Peninsular War and the continental campaigns from 1811 to 1815. Almost unknown in the UK, as the author emigrated to America straight after, it includes his eye-witness accounts of the bloody battle of Barossa, the memorable siege of Badajoz – and a graphic description of the battle of Waterloo where he was badly wounded.

MEMOIRS OF THE LATE MAJOR-GENERAL LE MARCHANT by Denis Le Marchant

Introduction by Nicholas Leadbetter   Foreword by Dr David Chandler

Only 93 copies of the memoirs of the founder of what is now the RMA Sandhurst were published by his son Denis in 1812. His death at Salamanca in 1841 meant that Britain was robbed of its most forward-thinking officer. This facsimile edition is enhanced with additional watercolour pictures by Le Marchant himself.

THE JOURNAL OF AN ARMY SURGEON DURING THE PENINSULAR WAR by Charles Boutflower

Introduction by Dr Christopher Ticehurst

A facsimile edition of a rare journal written by an army surgeon who joined the 40th Regiment in Malta in 1801 and subsequently served with it in the West Indies, South America and the Peninsular War. Described by his family 'as a man of great activity and a general favourite with all his acquaintances', he saw action from 1810 to 1813 including Busaco, Ciudad Rodrigo, Badajoz and Salamanca – gaining a well-deserved promotion to Surgeon to the staff of Sir Rowland Hill's Brigade in 1812.

THE DIARY OF A CAVALRY OFFICER 1809-1815 by Lieut-Col William Tomkinson

Introduction by the Marquess of Anglesey

The importance of *The Diary of a Cavalry Officer* for students of the Peninsular War of 1808-14 and of the Waterloo campaign of 1815, as well as its capacity to interest and inform the nonspecialist, is attested to by its scarcity in secondhand bookshops. It is eagerly sought after by both types of reader. There is hardly a serious account of the Peninsular 'running sore' (to use Napoleon's own words), which was a chief reason for his downfall, or of Waterloo, that does not rely in some degree on Tomkinson.

In Spain and Portugal he served with distinction for nearly five gruelling years in the 16th Light Dragoons, later 16th Lancers, one of the best cavalry regiments in the Peninsula.

Some of the important and patently accurate details of many actions in which he took part appear in no other accounts but it is chiefly for the penetrating comments on both esoteric and homely, mainly non-military, situations that the general reader will welcome this reprint.

As a temporary staff officer Tomkinson was at times close to Wellington and his detailed account of the Iron Duke's working day when not actually in the field is unique.

RECOLLECTIONS OF THE EVENTFUL LIFE OF A SOLDIER by Joseph Donaldson

Introduction by Ian Fletcher

When 16 year-old Joseph Donaldson announced to his parents in 1809 that he had 'gone for a soldier', they were understandably horrified, given the bleak and uncertain prospects facing their beloved son, of whom they had such high hopes. Donaldson returned safe and sound at the end of the Napoleonic Wars and the end result of Donaldson's writings was this wonderfully graphic, gripping and often poignant memoir, reproduced here in facsimile for the first time since 1852, along with his two other works, *The War in the Peninsula* and *Scenes and Sketches in Ireland*. In them, Donaldson writes with great skill of his experiences in Portugal, Spain and the south of France, serving with Wellington's army as it fought its way through the Peninsula. His account includes such episodes as Massena's retreat from Portugal, the storming of Ciudad Rodrigo, the storming and sacking of the fortress of Badajoz (a really gripping piece), the battles of Salamanca, Vitoria, the Pyrenees, the invasion of France and the battles of Orthes and Toulouse, all of which Donaldson witnessed as a soldier in the ranks of Sir Thomas Picton's 'Fighting' 3rd Division, the toughest division in Wellington's army.

This is a classic book which ranks amongst the most graphic and enjoyable of the many memoirs of the Peninsular War.

For a free catalogue, telephone

Spellmount Publishers on

01580 893730

or write to

The Old Rectory

Staplehurst

Kent TN12 0AZ

United Kingdom

(Facsimile 01580 893731)

(e-mail enquiries@spellmount.com)

(Website www.spellmount.com)